THE HISTORY OF BRAZIL, 1500-1627

*Brazil at the Dawn of the Eighteenth Century*André João Antonil
Preface by Stuart Schwartz
Translated & Edited by Timothy Coates

Essays on Some Maladies of Angola
José Pinto de Azeredo,
Edited by Timothy D. Walker with Adelino Cardoso,
António Braz de Oliveira, and Manuel Silvério Marques
Translated by Stewart Lloyd-Jones

*Dialog of a Veteran Soldier Discussing the Frauds and
Realities of Portuguese India*
Diogo do Couto
Foreword by M. N. Pearson
Translated by Timothy J. Coates

THE HISTORY OF BRAZIL, 1500–1627

Frei Vicente do Salvador

Translated and edited by Timothy J. Coates

Foreword by Alida C. Metcalf

TAGUS PRESS
University of Massachusetts Dartmouth
Dartmouth, MA

Tagus Press is the publishing arm of the Center for Portuguese Studies and Culture at the University of Massachusetts Dartmouth.

Classic Histories from the Portuguese-Speaking World in Translation 4

Executive Editor: Mario Pereira
Copy edited by Sharon Brinkman
Cover design by Frank Gutbrod
Cover art by Theodor de Bry *Religious dance of Native Americans of Brazil,* 1592. ©John Carter Brown Library.
Cover design by Frank Gutb
Designed and typeset by Jen Jackowitz Design

For all inquiries, please contact:
Tagus Press
Center for Portuguese Studies and Culture
University of Massachusetts Dartmouth
285 Old Westport Road
North Dartmouth, MA 02747–2300
(508) 999-8255, fax (508) 999-9272
https://www.umassd.edu/portuguese-studies-center/

ISBN: 978-1-951470-17-3
Library of Congress control number: 2023930313

CONTENTS

Foreword by Alida C. Metcalf   *xvii*

Introduction by Timothy J. Coates   *xxxi*

Bibliography   *xxxv*

Vocabulary of Foreign and Archaic English Terms   *xxxvi*

Tables   *xxxviii*

Maps and Illustrations   *xliii*

THE HISTORY OF BRAZIL BY FREI VICENTE DO SALVADOR

....

BOOK 1

*The Discovery of Brazil, the Customs of Its Natives, Its Birds,
Fish, Animals, etc. All of Brazil*   *1*

CHAPTER 1

How This State Was Discovered   *1*

CHAPTER 2

The Name of Brazil   *2*

CHAPTER 3

Mapping Brazil's Coast and Land Boundaries with Peru and the Spanish Indies   *4*

CHAPTER 4

The Weather and Climate of Brazil   *9*

CHAPTER 5

The Mines of Metal and Precious Stones in Brazil   *10*

CHAPTER 6

The Native Trees of Brazil   *11*

CHAPTER 7

Medicinal Uses for Trees and Herbs and Their Other Hidden Qualities   *17*

CHAPTER 8

Staple Crops Grown in Brazil   *18*

CHAPTER 9
Brazil's Animals and Insects   20

CHAPTER 10
The Birds   23

CHAPTER 11
The Other Things on the Sea and Land of Brazil   26

CHAPTER 12
The Origin of the Peoples of Brazil and the Diversity of Their Languages   28

CHAPTER 13
Native Villages   30

CHAPTER 14
Native Marriages and Raising Children   32

CHAPTER 15
How the Natives Cure Their Sick and Bury Their Dead   34

CHAPTER 16
How the Natives of Brazil Conduct War   36

CHAPTER 17
War Prisoners   38

....

BOOK 2
The History of Brazil at the Time of Its Discovery   41

CHAPTER 1
How the Discovery of Brazil Continued and Orders Were Issued for Its Settlement   41

CHAPTER 2
*The Captaincies and Lands That the King Awarded to the Brothers
Pero Lopes and Martim Afonso de Sousa   43*

CHAPTER 3
The Lands and Captaincy That the King Awarded to Pedro de Góis   45

CHAPTER 4
*The Lands and Captaincy of Espírito Santo That the King Awarded to
Vasco Fernandes Coutinho   46*

CHAPTER 5
The Captaincy of Porto Seguro   48

Contents   vii

CHAPTER 6

The Captaincy of Ilhéus 49

CHAPTER 7

The Captaincy of Bahia 50

CHAPTER 8

The Captaincy of Pernambuco, Which the King Awarded to Duarte Coelho 53

CHAPTER 9

How Duarte Coelho Sailed the Coastline of His Captaincy, Conducted War against the French,
Made Peace with the Natives, and Returned to Portugal 56

CHAPTER 10

How Jerónimo de Albuquerque Governed the Captaincy of Pernambuco in the
Absence of Duarte Coelho; What Occurred Then 58

CHAPTER 11

The Captaincy of Itamaracá 61

CHAPTER 12

What Happened in the Captaincy of Itamaracá after the Departure of
Donatary Pero Lopes de Sousa 64

CHAPTER 13

The Lands and Captaincy That King D. João III Awarded to João de Barros 66

CHAPTER 14

The Lands and Captaincy of Maranhão That King D. João III Awarded to
Luís de Melo da Silva 68

....

BOOK 3

The History of Brazil from the Time Tomé de Sousa Governed to the Arrival of
Manuel Teles Barreto (1549–80) 71

CHAPTER 1

How the King Again Ordered the Colonization of Bahia by Tomé de Sousa, the
First Governor General of Brazil 71

CHAPTER 2

The Other Two Fleets That the King Sent to Bahia with People and Provisions 74

CHAPTER 3

The Second Governor-General the King Sent to Brazil 75

CHAPTER 4

*Regarding a Ship Bound for India, Forced to Dock in Bahia during the Rule of
Governor D. Duarte da Costa   76*

CHAPTER 5

Another Ship Bound for India That Cast Anchor in Bahia   78

CHAPTER 6

Mem de Sá, the Third Governor of Brazil   80

CHAPTER 7

*How the Governor Sent His Son Fernão de Sá to Assist Vasco Fernandes Coutinho and
How He Was Killed There by Natives   81*

CHAPTER 8

The Arrival of the French in Rio de Janeiro and the War Waged by the Governor   82

CHAPTER 9

*How the Governor Returned to Bahia from Rio de Janeiro and the Fortune of a
Ship Bound for India That Provisioned There   84*

CHAPTER 10

*How the Tamoios of Rio de Janeiro Afflicted the People of the Captaincy of São Vicente and
How the Governor Ordered a Second War against Them   86*

CHAPTER 11

What Occurred on Jorge de Albuquerque's Journey from Pernambuco to Portugal   90

CHAPTER 12

*How Governor Mem de Sá Returned to Rio de Janeiro and Founded the City of Saint Sebastian de
Rio de Janeiro and the Other Things He Did There until Returning to Bahia   94*

CHAPTER 13

How the Governor Returned to Bahia and a Ship Bound for India Sheltered There   97

CHAPTER 14

*After the Governor Left, How the Tamoios and the French Went from
Cabo Frio to Rio de Janeiro to Capture a Village and What Followed   98*

CHAPTER 15

The Wars in Pernambuco at That Time   99

CHAPTER 16

*How D. Luís Fernandes de Vasconcelos Was Killed by Pirates on
His Journey to Become the Governor of Brazil   103*

CHAPTER 17

The Death of Governor Mem de Sá   104

CHAPTER 18

*How King D. Sebastião Appointed Cristóvão de Barros as Captain-Major
to Govern Rio de Janeiro* 107

CHAPTER 19

The Fourth Governor of Brazil, Luís de Brito de Almeida, and His Journey to the Real River 108

CHAPTER 20

The Expeditions into the Interior at That Time 109

CHAPTER 21

*The Differences between the Governor and the Bishop regarding a
Prisoner Sheltering in a Church* 113

CHAPTER 22

The Beginning of the Rebellion and Wars with the Natives of Paraíba 114

CHAPTER 23

*How the King Divided the Government of Brazil, Sending Doctor António de Selema to Govern
Rio de Janeiro and Porto Seguro and the Other Southern Captaincies, and Governor Luís de Brito
to Govern Bahia and the Other Northern Captaincies and How He Conquered Paraíba* 117

CHAPTER 24

*How Governor Luís de Brito Ordered the Superior Court Magistrate Fernão da Silva
to Lead the Conquest of Paraíba and How He Later Went in Person but Could
Not Reach It because of Contrary Winds* 118

CHAPTER 25

An Excursion from Pernambuco into the Interior 119

CHAPTER 26

The Death of Governor Lourenço da Veiga 123

....

BOOK 4

*The History of Brazil When It Was Governed by Manuel Teles Barreto (1584–88)
until the Arrival of Governor Gaspar de Sousa (1613)* 127

CHAPTER 1

*How Governor Manuel Teles Barreto Came to Rule Brazil and What Happened to
Some French and English Ships in Rio de Janeiro and São Vicente* 127

CHAPTER 2

*The Fleet Sent by His Majesty to the Straits of Magellan Led by
General Diogo Flores de Valdez and Its Success* 128

CHAPTER 3

On the Assistance Requested by Paraíba from Governor Manuel Teles
and the Resolution regarding It 131

CHAPTER 4

How Doctor Martim Leitão, Superior Court Magistrate, Was Sent by the Governor with General
Diogo Flores de Valdez to Conquer Paraíba and Build a Fort at the River's Mouth 133

CHAPTER 5

The Assistance Sent to Paraíba because of the Efforts of the Head Justice 135

CHAPTER 6

How the Superior Court Magistrate Martim Leitão Went to Paraíba the First Time,
How the Trip Was Organized, and the First Siege 138

CHAPTER 7

How Peace Was Attempted with Braço de Peixe and When He Declined,
How They Conducted War 141

CHAPTER 8

How General Martim Leitão Arrived at the Fort and Ordered Captain João Pais
to the Bay of Traição and Afterward Departed for Pernambuco 144

CHAPTER 9

How Captain Castejon Fled the Fort and the Superior Court Magistrate
Apprehended Him and Provided for the Soldiers 146

CHAPTER 10

How Braço de Peixe Asked for Peace and Assistance against the Potiguarás
and the Superior Court Magistrate Returned to Paraíba to Establish a Town 148

CHAPTER 11

How the Magistrate Went to the Bay of Traição 151

CHAPTER 12

How They Left the Bay of Traição for Tujucupapo and Returned to Pernambuco 153

CHAPTER 13

The Arrival of Captain Morales from Portugal and the Return of the
Superior Court Magistrate to Paraíba 155

CHAPTER 14

How the Superior Court Magistrate Left Paraíba for Copaoba 157

CHAPTER 15

Once Copaoba Was Destroyed, How They Searched for Tujucupapo 160

CHAPTER 16

*After Disbanding the People, How the Superior Court Magistrate
Constructed the Fort of São Sebastião* 162

CHAPTER 17

*The Great Treachery of the Natives of Sergipe toward the Men of Bahia and the
War Conducted by the Governor against the Aimorés* 163

CHAPTER 18

*The Death of Governor Manuel Teles de Barreto and How Bishop D. António Barreiros,
the Head Superintendent Cristóvão de Barros, and the Superior Court
Magistrate Governed in His Place* 165

CHAPTER 19

Regarding Three English Ships That Came to Bahia at That Time 166

CHAPTER 20

The War Conducted by Cristóvão de Barros against the Natives of Sergipe 167

CHAPTER 21

*An Expedition into the Interior Seeking Natives Who Fled from the Wars in
Sergipe and Other Natives* 170

CHAPTER 22

*On the Continued Wars in Paraíba against the Potiguarás,
Who Were Assisted by the French* 173

CHAPTER 23

*How Francisco Giraldes was Appointed Governor of Brazil but Never Arrived, He Returned to
Portugal and Died; D. Francisco de Sousa Came as the Seventh Governor* 175

CHAPTER 24

*On the Journey Gabriel Soares de Sousa Made to the Mines in the Interior,
Which Was Halted by His Death* 177

CHAPTER 25

How Feliciano Coelho de Carvalho Came to Govern Paraíba and Continue the Wars There 179

CHAPTER 30 180

CHAPTER 31

*How Manuel Mascarenhas Homem Built the Fort of Rio Grande and the Assistance
Sent to Him by Feliciano Coelho de Carvalho* 181

CHAPTER 32

*Once the Fort at the Rio Grande Was Completed, It Was Turned Over to Captain Jerónimo
de Albuquerque. The Captains from Pernambuco and Paraíba Returned Home;
Their Battles with the Potiguarás along the Way* 185

CHAPTER 33

*How Jerónimo de Albuquerque Made Peace with the Potiguarás and
Began to Colonize the Rio Grande   187*

CHAPTER 34

*How the Governor-General Went to the Mines in São Vicente and Álvaro de Carvalho
Continued Governing Bahia and the Dutch Who Came There   190*

CHAPTER 35

*The War with the Native Aimorés and How Captain-Major Álvaro de Carvalho
Made Peace with Them   192*

CHAPTER 36

What the Governor Did in the Mines   193

CHAPTER 37

*The Eighth Governor of Brazil and the First Who Came via Pernambuco, Diogo Botelho; How He
Brought Those Shipwrecked from a Nau from India on the Island of Fernando da Noronha   195*

CHAPTER 38

*The Expedition of Pero Coelho de Sousa to Paraíba and the Mountains of Boapaba,
Done with the Governor's Permission   197*

CHAPTER 39

The Passion Shown by Governor Diogo Botelho in Converting Natives Using Priests   200

CHAPTER 40

*How the Governor Went from Pernambuco to Bahia and Sent Zorobabé to Paraíba with His
Potiguarás to Paraíba to Follow the Escaped Negros from Guinea at Palmares on the Itapucuru
River; How Whaling Began   202*

CHAPTER 41

*How Zorobabé Arrived in Paraíba and Was Suspected of Rebellion, Imprisoned,
and Sent to Portugal   205*

CHAPTER 42

*What Happened to a Flemish Nau on Business in the Captaincy of Espírito
Santo Loading Brazilwood   207*

CHAPTER 43

Pero Coelho de Sousa's Disastrous Second Expedition to the Boapabé Mountains   210

CHAPTER 44

*The Mission and Expedition by Two Jesuits Ordered by Governor Diogo Botelho to the
Same Boapaba Mountains; How Different Orders Pray   212*

CHAPTER 45

How Governor D. Diogo de Menezes Came to Rule Bahia and Preside over the High Court   213

CHAPTER 46

*How D. Francisco de Sousa Came to Brazil to Govern the Southern Captaincies
and regarding His Death* 215

CHAPTER 47

On the New Invention of the Sugar Mill 216

Additional Section 1: From the *Santuário Mariano* 219

Additional Section 2: From the *Santuário Mariano* 221

....

BOOK 5

*The History of Brazil from the Time of Governor Gaspar de Sousa (1613–17) until
the Arrival of Governor Diogo Luís de Oliveira (1627)* 223

CHAPTER 1

*The Arrival of the Tenth Governor of Brazil, Gaspar de Sousa, and How He Came
via Pernambuco to Organize the Conquest of Maranhão* 223

CHAPTER 2

How the Governor Ordered Jerónimo de Albuquerque to Conquer Maranhão 224

CHAPTER 3

The War in Maranhão and the Victory That Was Achieved 226

CHAPTER 4

The Truce Made between Our Forces and the French in Maranhão 228

CHAPTER 5

*Regarding Francisco Caldeira de Castelo Branco Who Was Sent to Maranhão
by Governor Gaspar de Sousa to Provide Assistance* 231

CHAPTER 6

*How Captain Baltasar de Aragão Left Bahia with a Fleet to Fight the
French and How He Lost* 233

CHAPTER 7

Governor Gaspar de Sousa's Journey from Pernambuco to Bahia and What He Did There 235

CHAPTER 8

How the Governor Returned to Pernambuco and Sent Alexandre de Moura to Maranhão 236

CHAPTER 9

*Regarding a Dutch Fleet Passing by Rio de Janeiro for the Straits of Magellan and a
French Fleet Loading Brazilwood at Cape Frio* 238

CHAPTER 18

*How Henrique Correia da Silva Was Appointed Governor of Brazil but Did Not Arrive, Why
This Occurred, and How Diogo Mendonça Furtado Came in His Place* 239

CHAPTER 19

*The Arrival of Governor Diogo de Mendonça in Bahia and the Departure for P
ortugal of His Predecessor D. Luís de Sousa*   *240*

CHAPTER 20

*How António Barreiros, the Son of the Head of the Treasury, Was Appointed to Govern Maranhão
by Governor-General Diogo de Mendonça Furtado and Bento Maciel to Rule Grão-Pará; Captain
Luís Aranha Was Sent to Explore North of the Cape by Order of His Majesty*   *241*

CHAPTER 21

*The Fortifications and Other Good Works Completed in Bahia by Governor Diogo de Mendonça
Furtado and the Questions Existing among the Governor, the Bishop, and Others*   *245*

CHAPTER 22

How the Dutch Captured Bahia   *247*

CHAPTER 23

*How Governor Diogo de Mendonça Was Captured by the Dutch and Their Colonel Jan Van Dorth
Governed the City*   *250*

CHAPTER 24

*How the Bishop Was Elected by the People to Be the Captain-Major and Matias de Albuquerque in
Pernambuco Was Made Governor-General*   *252*

CHAPTER 25

*How the Dutch Colonel Jan Van Dorth Was Killed and Was Succeeded by Albert
Schouten and the Bishop Planned an Assault from His Encampment*   *254*

CHAPTER 26

The Assaults Undertaken When the Bishop Governed   *256*

CHAPTER 27

Other Attacks against the Dutch along the Coast   *258*

CHAPTER 28

The Ships and People the Dutch Captured in the Harbor of Salvador   *261*

CHAPTER 29

*After He Received the Appointment as Governor, Matias de Albuquerque Turned to
Assisting Bahia and Fortifying Pernambuco; Francisco Coelho de Carvalho, the
Governor of Maranhão, Remained in Pernambuco*   *263*

CHAPTER 30

*In Pernambuco, How Governor-General Matias de Albuquerque Appointed Francisco Nunes
Marinho as Captain General of Bahia and the Death of the Bishop*   *265*

CHAPTER 31

*The Encounters with the Dutch While Captain-Major Francisco Nunes Marinho
Governed Our Camp   266*

CHAPTER 32

*How D. Francisco de Moura Was Ordered by His Majesty to Come Aid Bahia and
Govern the Camp   268*

CHAPTER 33

*The Death of Colonel Albert Schouten and the Succession of His Brother,
Willem Schouten, and the Continuation of the Raids   271*

CHAPTER 34

The Fleet Sent by His Majesty to Recover Bahia and the Portuguese Nobles Who Joined It   273

CHAPTER 35

The Financial Contributions of the King's Portuguese Vassals for This Fleet   277

CHAPTER 36

*How the Portuguese Fleet Awaited the Spanish Ships in Cape Verde and
Sailed Together to Bahia   278*

CHAPTER 37

*How Salvador Correia from Rio de Janeiro and Jerónimo Cavalcanti from Pernambuco Came to
the Aid of Bahia and What Occurred with the Dutch on the Way   280*

CHAPTER 38

*How Those on the Armada Disembarked and the Dutch Attacked Them at São Bento,
Where the First Battery Was Located[1]   283*

CHAPTER 39

*About the Second Battery at the Monastery of Carmo with General Dom Fadrique
de Toledo and Two Other Batteries Created from It   285*

CHAPTER 40

*Regarding the Other Trenches Dug near São Bento and How the French and the
Dutch Were Divided   288*

CHAPTER 41

*How the Dutch Soldiers Rebelled against Their Colonel Willem Schouten, Removed
Him from Office, and Elected His Replacement   289*

CHAPTER 42

How the Dutch Agreed to Surrender   290

CHAPTER 43

*How the City Was Reoccupied; the Thanks Given to God for the
Victory and the News Sent to Spain* 292

CHAPTER 44

*The War Governor Matias de Albuquerque Ordered against the Natives of the
Copaoba Mountains Who Rebelled While the Dutch Were Here* 296

CHAPTER 45

*On the Fleet That Came from Holland to Aid the Dutch and What Else
Occurred until Our Fleet Departed* 298

CHAPTER 46

The Return of Our Fleet to Portugal and the Dutch to Their Land 301

CHAPTER 47

*How Governor Matias de Albuquerque Ordered a Party to Locate the Cargo of a
Nau from India Shipwrecked on Santa Helena Island* 305

CHAPTER 48

*Regarding the Dutch Who Sailed along the Coast of Bahia to Paraíba in the Year 1626
and the Departure of Governor Francisco Coelho de Carvalho for Maranhão* 307

CHAPTER 49

*How Diogo Luís de Oliveira Arrived to Govern Brazil and His Predecessor M
atias de Albuquerque Departed for Portugal* 310

Additional Section 1: From the *Santuário Mariano* 312
Additional Section 2: From the *Santuário Mariano* 312
Additional Section 3: From the *Santuário Mariano* 315

Notes 319

Index 335

FOREWORD

Alida C. Metcalf

When the Franciscan friar known as Frei Vicente do Salvador finished his *History of Brazil* (*História do Brasil*) in 1630, he was sixty-three years old.[1] Born in Brazil in 1566 or 1567 and baptized as Vicente Rodrigues Palha, the future Franciscan was the son of Portuguese colonists—João Rodrigues Paes and Mécia de Lemos—who met and married in the 1550s. Frei Vicente's father came from a modest background "with little to live on," as Frei Vicente puts it, and left Portugal on an expedition to Maranhão, a region in northern Brazil. The expedition met a disastrous end, but Frei Vicente's father survived and made his way to Bahia, the Portuguese settlement in the Bay of All Saints, where he met and married Mécia, the daughter of a Portuguese nobleman. Even though Frei Vicente's father arrived penniless, he would have been an attractive suitor for Mécia given his Portuguese birth. The couple had seven children, a house in the city, and a farm on a sugar plantation in one of the rural parishes outside of the capital city, known as Salvador da Bahia.

Educated by the first Jesuits in Brazil, Frei Vicente learned Latin and Greek and studied the advanced curriculum for arts and theology, which included logic, mathematics, philosophy, and a deep reading of the writings of St. Thomas Aquinas. He continued his education in Portugal at the University of Coimbra, where he most likely received his doctorate in law. Returning to Brazil, he entered the Franciscan order in 1599. Unlike Mexico, where the Franciscans were the primary missionaries for the indigenous population, in Brazil that role had been taken on by the Jesuits, who arrived with the first royal governor in 1549. The Franciscan mission to Brazil arrived a generation later, in the 1580s, and its early mission was directed to the Tabajara and Potiguar indigenous peoples in Paraíba, a region to the north of Bahia. Frei Vicente rose rapidly, becoming the custodian of the order in Brazil in 1614. A few years later, Frei Vicente wrote his first book, *A Crónica da Custódia do Brasil* (1618), a history of the Franciscans in Brazil.

In 1624, sailing into the Bay of All Saints, Frei Vicente was captured, along with ten Jesuits, four Benedictines, and his Franciscan companion, by Dutch seamen. Just weeks earlier, a Dutch fleet had attacked Salvador. At this time, Atlantic rivalries were at an all-time high. Under the Iberian Union (1580–1640), the Hapsburg kings of Spain ruled over Portugal, even though much of the administration of Brazil remained in Portuguese hands. Yet under Spanish rules of mercantilism, Brazil's rich sugar trade was closed to Dutch merchants. The Dutch, part of the seventeen provinces that Spain claimed in Northern Europe—today the Netherlands, Belgium, Luxembourg, and parts of France—had declared their independence in 1581. As the Dutch West India Company (WIC) sought to monopolize the profitable transatlantic slave and sugar trades, the WIC attached Spanish and Portuguese ships, forts, and colonies, one of which was Salvador.

Frei Vicente writes the history of Brazil from 1500 to 1630, emphasizing the fifty years from 1570 to 1630 that corresponded to his own lifetime. His narrative voice is complex. He was an educated Franciscan, he was born and raised in Brazil, he crossed the Atlantic several times, he served as a missionary to indigenous groups, and he lived through many of the political events he describes. Each of these perspectives can be seen in his history. Frei Vicente's classical education, as well as his belief in the value and importance of writing history, is immediately visible in the dedication of *História do Brasil* to the canon of the cathedral in Evora, Portugal. Citing Cicero, Frei Vicente notes that "history books are lights of truth; they give life to memory and are masters of life."

Frei Vicente's voice as a Franciscan emerges in the first paragraphs of book 1, where he writes about the accidental discovery of Brazil in 1500 by Pedro Álvares Cabral and the history of the new land's name. The Franciscans who sailed with Cabral, Frei Vicente suggests, missed a unique opportunity, for it was Franciscans who made the first contact with indigenous peoples and it was positive. After celebrating the first Mass in Brazil, the Franciscans in Cabral's armada wanted to remain and begin evangelism, but Cabral required them to continue on to India, which he deemed more important. Here, as with his description of how the name of the newly discovered place changed from "Land of the Holy Cross" to "Brazil," Frei Vicente laments a road not taken. Had the Franciscans remained, evangelism would have progressed differently, he seems to believe, and the overarching greed of merchants and colonists might have been contained. This lost opportunity is symbolized in the new name—Brazil—which came from a "tree with the shiny orange and yellow wood used to dye cloth." This is what merchants valued, not God. In this name change, Frei Vicente sees the hand of the devil.

Frei Vicente's intimate knowledge of Brazil emerges in his accounts of the climate and peoples. Breaking with the classical authorities who had claimed the tropical zones of Earth unsuitable for humans, Frei Vicente (as had others before him with direct experience with the New World) states that "the tropics are habitable and that in some of its regions men can live with greater health than in all the temperate zone." For Frei Vicente, Brazil is not a hot, hell-like place. On the contrary, wild animals roam vast forests, blossoms burst from trees, all kinds of crops can be harvested from fertile soils, cattle and other domestic animals thrive in rich pastures, oceans jump with fish, and lagoons and swamps harbor shrimp, octopi, crabs, and lobsters. Brazil has everything, Frei Vicente writes, and is completely self-sustaining. A passage in book 1 takes the form of a rhetorical dialogue, as if he were posing and answering his own questions:

I ask, does wheat come from Portugal?
Wheat from here is sufficient.
Wine?
The wine from sugar is very smooth, and for those who want it
    strong, cooking it for two days will make it as strong as wine from
    grapes.
Olive oil?
It can be substituted by that from coconuts from palm trees.
Cloth?
It is made from cotton here with less effort than linen and wool are
    made in Portugal because the cotton plant allows the spinner to
    collect and spin. Nor does Brazil lack dyes to use.
Salt?
Here there is both natural and man-made sources, as stated earlier.
Iron?
There are many iron mines, and in São Vicente there is a mill where
    they make excellent ironworks.
Spices?

There are many types of pepper and ginger.
Almonds?
These can be substituted with cashews, and so on.

Frei Vicente's account of the history of the native peoples of Brazil before contact is short and to the point: "These people came from somewhere else, but we do not know where." His descriptions of their customs, however, is extensive and informed by what he had seen and by what had been written by others, such as the Jesuits. Frei Vicente understands the logic to the lifeways of indigenous groups even as he sees them as "savage." Like the Jesuits who wrote lengthy descriptions of native peoples, Frei Vicente admires the sophistication of the common language spoken along the coast and the oratory practiced by chiefs. His descriptions of village life are rich with comments on the leadership of chiefs, the roles of women, childrearing, marriage, warfare, and the cannibalism ceremony. Even when recounting the rituals used in the cannibalism ceremony, Frei Vicente's tone is matter-of-fact and not overly judgmental. Perhaps his training as a Franciscan had been influenced by the great Franciscan of sixteenth-century Mexico, Bernardino de Sahagún. For Sahagún, it was essential for Franciscans to understand the culture of the Aztecs they intended to convert to Christianity. Without a detailed, anthropological comprehension, no full conversion could be achieved.

In book 2, Frei Vicente's historian voice emerges, and the reader is given a chronological account of the early colonization of Brazil. Beginning in the south, he covers the large grants given by the king to prominent men and the successes and failures of their captaincies. For Frei Vicente, each captaincy has its own distinctive history, influenced by the character of its original donatary, its geography, and especially the resident indigenous groups. Where native peoples resisted, the colonies had little success.

The historian's voice continues in book 3, which begins in 1549 when the Portuguese king sent the first royal official to Brazil with authority over all of Brazil (limiting the powers given to the donataries) and carefully crafted instructions to establish the capital at Salvador in the Bay of All Saints. With Captain General Tomé de Souza arrived the first Jesuits, who had the responsibility for evangelizing the native population. Soldiers and prisoners, who were known as *degredados* and whose sentences were commuted in return for serving as colonists, also accompanied the governor and first Jesuits. For Frei Vicente, this is an auspicious time. He tells the story of Diogo Álvares Caramuru, a Portuguese shipwrecked sailor, or possibly *degredado*, who lived among the native peoples and was married to a native woman who had been baptized in France as a Christian. Frei Vicente is not the first to tell the story of Diogo Álvares, known by his Indian name "Caramuru," who, with his devoted Christian wife, facilitated the survival of Tomé de Sousa's new capital city. Frei Vicente tells his readers that he recounts the story "out of respect" for Caramuru and his "very honorable widow" because "it was he [Caramuru] who held on to this land for all those years and through his efforts that Governor Tomé de Sousa was able to make peace with the natives and have them serve the whites."

This statement is key to how Frei Vicente saw the successful transformation of Brazil from a land inhabited by native peoples who "have no faith, nor do they worship a god" to a promised land within Christendom ruled by the Portuguese king. In this favored colony, the Portuguese king's special vision for Brazil would flourish. Indians would serve the Portuguese, who under Tomé de Sousa's skilled leadership and aided by Caramuru's influence, would build a new capital for the new land. Frei Vicente's enthusiasm for the enterprise is visible when he writes that "everyone [who came with the governor] delighted in his work, and each one practiced the skills he possessed. Some worked at agriculture while others raised cattle, and they practiced all manner of skills, even those that were new to them." King João had undertaken a wonderous project, and the result was a place that could harbor the Portuguese crown should it "be forced to flee." Should the necessity arise, Frei Vicente writes, Brazil is "so large" and "located at such a safe distance" from the enemies of Portugal that it "would become a great kingdom."

This utopic time would be short-lived. A new royal governor arrived, and a bishop, and conflict soon broke out. Frei Vicente blames the devil— "he who disturbs peace"—for stirring up differences between church leaders and the crown officials. The bishop "had to leave for Portugal" Frei Vicente writes, but along the way, before the ship had even left the shores of Brazil, it sank, and the survivors were attacked and captured by the Caeté, an indigenous group living along the coast. Nearly all were subjected to the cannibalism ceremony. "I do not know," writes Frei Vicente, "whether this incident encouraged more discord later between the governors and the bishops. . . . I can only tell you . . . that the spot [where the bishop was killed] was never again covered with vegetation, unlike the surrounding lands. It is as if his blood calls to God against those who spilled it. God heard this, because afterward the people of Bahia went to war against those natives and extracted their revenge."

And revenge, as well as bloody wars of conquest up and down the coast of Brazil, follow in Frei Vicente's narrative. Indigenous groups resisted the colonial settlements on the coast, and eventually these conflicts spread inland. Frei Vicente's idealistic vision of how a go-between such as Caramuru would smooth the way for peaceful colonization is increasingly replaced by an uneasy coexistence with constant atrocities on each side. As a missionary, Frei Vicente was committed to a peaceful conversion of the indigenous population to Christianity. Yet, as the Portuguese became ever more committed to colonizing Brazil, interactions with indigenous peoples seemed only to encourage more violence.

Frei Vicente's optimism for Brazil returns as he discusses the governorship of Mem de Sá, who brought peace to Bahia, expelled the French from Rio de Janeiro, and clamped down on the illegal enslavement of Indians by colonists. Still, the picture is grim as Frei Vicente must recount how Mem de Sá's son lost his life fighting against the Aimoré in Espíritu Santo and how the fight over the Guanabara Bay required several campaigns against the French and their Tamoio allies, which took the life of his nephew. Small and large events are interspersed into the narrative, as Frei Vicente struggles not to leave out anything. He describes the arrival in Bahia of ships headed to India, famous shipwrecks, political events in Europe, such as the death of the Spanish king Charles V, and key events in India. Frei Vicente's choice to include these asides illustrates how his historical perspective was shaped by the broader Atlantic and Indian Ocean worlds. During his lifetime, he was acquainted with many for whom transatlantic travel, as terrifying as it could be, was the norm, as was the dangerous voyage around the Cape of Good Hope and across the Indian Ocean to India. The Brazil he knew was a fluid and diverse place connected not only to Lisbon but also to the Caribbean, Rio de la Plata, Angola, Congo, Mozambique, and India.

Frei Vicente narrates the beginnings of the internal slave trade that supplied coastal colonies with Indian slave labor. He describes expeditions into the interior, some of which were sanctioned as just wars against indigenous groups who had attacked the Portuguese colonies. A just war in Brazil, as Frei Vicente explains later in his history, is not only one where "those captured could be enslaved" but those enslaved served as "the spoils of war" (and even as the salaries for the soldiers). Jesuits fought bitterly against the flagrant misuse of the concept of the just war in Brazil. Increasingly, in the 1570s, expeditions, known as *entradas,* left Bahia and Pernambuco for the interior in order to bring indigenous groups to the coast. These native peoples were often referred to, as Frei Vicente occasionally does, as "negros," meaning slaves. In this internal trade, mixed-race mamelucos (sons of Indian women and Portuguese men) used their familiarity with indigenous languages and customs to convince entire villages to follow them to the coast. With "deceptions and with a few gifts of clothes and tools," Frei Vicente writes, mamelucos "persuaded entire villages. Once they reached sight of the ocean, children were separated from their parents, brothers were separated from each other, and sometimes wives removed from their husbands."

What did Frei Vicente think of these slaving expeditions? Frei Vicente echoes, although not as forcefully, the Jesuit criticism of the colonists. He writes that preachers, who we can be certain were Jesuits, "wore out their pulpits speaking against this, but it was like preaching to an empty desert." In another account, Frei Vicente seems resigned. He writes about an expedition that left the coastal settlement of Olinda, Pernambuco, headed for the interior. There, a powerful Tabajara chief helped the colonists descend with a large number of Indians to the coast. When this chief learned that his own people were to suffer the same fate, he planned their escape. He and another chief attacked the colonists when they least expected it. "That was how it was," Frei Vicente states matter-of-factly. "They [the Indians] killed all of them [the colonists]. They freed the captive natives, and all celebrated their liberty by eating the flesh of their masters."

Book 4, which begins in 1580, takes Frei Vicente deep into the violent history of the immediate frontiers surrounding the established colonial settlements in Bahia and Pernambuco. Excursions into Sergipe and Paraíba, which lay to the north of Bahia and Pernambuco, respectively, resulted in attacks on indigenous groups who fought any attempts to establish forts, create new towns, or take slaves. In both Paraíba and Sergipe, the French continued to trade for brazilwood and maintain excellent alliances with the Potiguar. In Ilhéus, which lay to the south of Bahia, the Aimoré prevented the Portuguese from expanding much beyond their coastal enclaves. For Frei Vicente, this is a critical time in Brazil, for the success of the colony rested on strong coastal settlements ruled by Portuguese officials surrounded by a peaceful frontier inhabited by indigenous peoples living in newly organized mission villages run by missionaries, such as the Jesuits.

Frei Vicente recognizes this decade of the 1580s as a vulnerable time for the colonial enterprise within Brazil, as well as a time when Portugal itself was also weak. Cardinal Henrique, who assumed the Portuguese throne after the unexpected, early death of King Sebastião in Morocco in 1578, died in 1580 with no heir, and multiple claimants emerged. Philip II of Spain would impose his claim to the Portuguese throne (which came through his mother) through an intervention led by the feared Duke of Alba. Once Philip joined the two crowns into the Iberian Union, Brazil found itself drawn into intense conflicts between Spain and the Dutch merchants who despised their former Spanish overlords and the English pirates authorized by Queen Elizabeth to attack Spanish interests. Dutch and English ships began to lurk off the Brazilian coast, and Sir Francis Drake boldly sailed along the coast of Brazil and through the Straits of Magellan in 1579.

The long battle for Paraíba, the frontier to the north of Pernambuco, takes up much of book 4. Events are described in such detail that Frei Vicente must have known of them from close hand. Multiple expeditions to Paraíba make clear the intense competition for land and influence. Frei Vicente describes one expedition as a full-fledged military campaign, complete with a general, squadrons, cavalry, drums, and interpreters, which set forth from Pernambuco in 1585. "This army," he writes, "was the most beautiful thing Pernambuco ever witnessed and for all I know will ever see." But the army soon returned to Pernambuco having accomplished little except burning villages. Indigenous chiefs remained powerful, and even when the Portuguese managed to construct forts, they were difficult to staff and provision. For Frei Vicente, although peace agreements came and went, they were still the best way forward. One important peace treaty was agreed on in 1599, in Rio Grande do Norte, the region just to the north of Paraíba, where the Portuguese had built a fort the year before. Frei Vicente describes the roles played by the Jesuits and Franciscans who found the way forward through a third party, in this case a chief held by the Portuguese captain of the fort. Released and "sending him to speak with his relatives," Frei Vicente attributed the peace agreement to this chief's persuasive speech. Villages were summoned, and when they arrived, Frei Vicente quotes the chief as saying:

All of you, brothers, children, my relatives, you all know me and who I am and how you relied on me in peacetime and during war. This is what now drives me to come from the white people and tell you all that if you want to have a quiet life in your homes and on your lands with your women and children, then you need to come with me. There will be no more discussion; we will go to the fort of the white men . . . and make peace with them. This will be a lasting peace. . . . Those who join the church are not enslaved but rather are instructed in the faith and defended. The French never did this, nor will they now. Their way is blocked by the fort where they cannot enter without being killed, and the Portuguese sink their ships with artillery.

Subsequently, the peace was "cast in solemn legal terms," according to Frei Vicente, at a meeting attended by important royal officials, such as the governor of Paraíba and the captain-major of Pernambuco and a Franciscan interpreter "very skilled in the local language" and "well-respected by the native Potiguarás and Tabajaras." The indigenous groups abandoned their alliance with the French, and Portuguese colonists began to move to Rio Grande. For Frei Vicente, the peace enabled what he saw as the potential for Brazil. A town could be founded near the fort, two sugar mills were built, and cattle ranches were opened. "We could say," Frei Vicente concludes, that "they are the worst lands in Brazil; in spite of this, if men are focused and want to work, these lands can make them rich."

Frei Vicente's voice as a storyteller emerges in the last book when he recounts the tale of the Dutch attack on Salvador in 1624. Frei Vicente witnessed most of the Dutch occupation, the arrival of the Spanish and Portuguese fleet that retook the city, and the aftermath. Although he missed the initial Dutch attack by only a few weeks and was confined to a ship in the Bay of All Saints, he had a view of the occupied city, and later he was allowed to go ashore. Not surprisingly, Frei Vicente sees the Portuguese resistance to the Dutch as heroic, and the battle to retake the city as proof of God's grace. He proudly lists all the noblemen from Portugal who arrived on the armada sent to take back Salvador, and he saw their victory as proof that the Protestant Dutch were true heretics. Frei Vicente is optimistic that the promise of Brazil will be fulfilled.

Frei Vicente's history of Brazil is not easy for modern readers. One is taken back to formative moments in Brazilian history, many of which were violent and streaked with greed, revenge, and suffering. One moment, read metaphorically, offers the modern reader a poetic under-standing of what was gained and what was lost. It is Frei Vicente's account of the beginning of whale hunting, which he places toward the end of book 4. Frei Vicente writes with a trace of sadness, even though he sees the harvesting of whale oil as a blessing for Brazil. A Basque colonist, who arrived in Brazil from Spain shortly after 1600, together with others from his homeland, introduced whaling and taught others the technique. It is "something to watch," Frei Vicente begins, "better than any jousting or games." In June, Frei Vicente continues, whales arrive in the Bay of All Saints to give birth, each to one calf the size of a horse. In August the whales begin to leave the bay. At that time Mass is celebrated, and the priest blesses all of the boats that will soon depart in pursuit. The calf is easy to catch, for it is jumping around in the water like a dolphin, the mother never far away. Pulling the calf in, the mother is harpooned and tries to swim away, the fishermen in pursuit. But then Frei Vicente writes, "The mother then knows they have come for her. . . . She is exhausted, and all men on the pinnaces [boats] throw spears with sharp points like half-moons. She is then injured to the point that she gives out loud cries of pain. When she dies, she exhales great quantities of blood through her vent, so much that it covers the sun and makes a red cloud turning the sea red. This is the signal that it is over, and she is dead." From this haunting image, Frei Vicente returns to his matter-of-fact voice stating, "They bind the whale and bring it alongside the pinnace. All three boats then form a line and row to Itaparica Island, which is three leagues [twelve miles] distant from this city. They go to a port called Cruz where they slaughter the whale and extract its oil." He then explains how much the men are paid for their work, how much oil is extracted, how much it costs, and how whale flesh is salted and dried. The whaling season is over in two months, but the reader has learned that it will begin again the next year. It has become a repeating pattern of life in Brazil. This description of whaling offers modern readers insights into change and continuity in the early history of Brazil. Frei Vicente had written about how a new place has come into being where the actions of men—from governors, captains, and chiefs to ordinary people such as whalers—have changed the old ways. Brazil will never revert to what was, and even if there is violence, injustice, and greed, there is great potential for men and women to make it into something noble and great. This, Frei Vicente suggests, comes at great cost, but it is the meaning of the history of Brazil.

THE HISTORY OF BRAZIL, 1500-1627

INTRODUCTION

Timothy J. Coates

This history by Frei Vicente was written around 1629 and remained unpublished until 1888. Although it is incomplete in parts, it is a comprehensive work about the first five generations of contact between the Portuguese and the native peoples of Brazil. In many parts, the reader will be forgiven for thinking Frei Vicente was living in more recent times because his perspective on the native peoples and their customs is refreshingly modern and largely nonjudgmental. This was in spite of his religious training. Here the reader will find ample evidence of how the Portuguese established themselves in a land new to them and how they were eventually able to overcome native resistance and their own internal divisions.

Frei Vicente divided his work into five parts, which he calls "books." The first of these is natural history, discussing the land and its plants and animals, and part social history, where he describes the native peoples, their customs, villages, and the differences among the various groups. In the second, third, and fourth books, he turns to political and administrative history, reviewing the administration of each of the various governors-general and the donataries of the early captaincies, giving additional insight into why most failed economically. And if all of this were not sufficient, this is also a military history since much of the text deals with Portuguese- native warfare and the various alliances each side made to combat the other. In his last and fifth book, Frei Vicente turns to the struggle with the Dutch. He was an eyewitness to the Dutch occupation of Salvador in the 1620s, and he offers an unmatched level of detail on this struggle. In short, this is a very comprehensive history of the early colonial period in Brazil to the late 1620s.

The original text is incomplete in parts, missing several chapters and sections of others. The reader will note that additional sections from Brother Agostinho de Santa Maria's *Santuário Mariano* are included here at the end of Books 4 and 5. He was familiar with this *History* by Frei Vicente do Salvador and he used much of it in his own work, sometimes citing it and other times not. These may be parts of the missing sections of Frei Vicente's work and are included in the Universidade de São Paulo edition (see below).

Most works about the colonial era in Brazil have surprisingly little to say about its native peoples and their interactions with the Portuguese, a central topic in this work. This is one of the major reasons I believe this work will appeal to a wide audience, especially now that it has been translated into English.

Frei Vicente do Salvador or Vicente Rodrigues Palha was born in Bahia around 1564 and died there between 1636 and 1639. His parents had moved from Portugal to Brazil to establish a sugar mill in the area of Bahia. He studied theology and law at the University of Coimbra, graduated, and returned to Brazil. He joined the Franciscan order in 1599 and adopted his new name. He served as a missionary in Pernambuco and lived in monasteries in Rio de Janeiro and Salvador. He was the head or custodian of the order in Brazil. In 1624, he was taken prisoner by the Dutch when they occupied Salvador. This work was written in the period from 1624 to 1627. As a result, he speaks from personal experience in this text when he discusses the missionary efforts of the Church, the customs of the natives, the sugar mill owners, and the Dutch. This work is one of a handful of fundamental texts for understanding the formative years of the Brazilian colony.

One aspect that will impress the reader will be the level of detail Frei Vicente includes in his narratives. It is clear that he must have had multiple sources and reports from those on the ground in order to recount such details, such as numbers of troops, use of the cavalry, attack formations, and the like. Since he was the head of the Franciscan order in Brazil, it is quite possible that he drew on letters and reports from his Franciscan brothers in the field as well as others close to the events he describes. Another striking aspect of this history is how globally connected Brazil was by 1627. Frei Vicente mentions numerous ships coming and going on their way to or from Portugal, India, and Africa. Both the Azores and the West Indies were well connected to Brazil; Brazilian ships called on these islands with frequency.

When we at Tagus Press first began this project, we had hoped to use the most recent and complete edition of this work, a beautifully crafted version edited by Professor Maria Lêda Oliveira, that was published in several volumes in 2008. When I first contacted Dr. Oliveira to ensure that the work had never before been translated, she seemed pleased with the news that we were about to begin the first English translation of this work. Unfortunately, in a later message, she pointed out that her work is not in the public domain (something that I had not considered). All of our subsequent requests to her and to the publisher to use the 2008 text as the basis for an English translation went unanswered. As a result, we turned to the edition completed by Capistrano de Abreu and published in 1888. We used a digital copy in the public domain that was offered by the Biblioteca Nacional de Rio de Janeiro. In addition, we were pleased to receive the copyright authority to use a more recent copy published in 1982 by the Universidade de São Paulo/Editora Itatiaia, seventh edition, the USP text mentioned above. I consulted both editions of the work in crafting this translation.

Translating a work written in Portuguese in the 1620s into modern English presents a variety of challenges. The vocabulary for the day-to-day items people used, the names of the types of firearms and ships, and the official titles are all challenging to render into modern English. Frei Vicente's style of writing frequently made translating more difficult. He often switches subjects in the middle of a sentence with no overt indication or will leave the reader hanging with unclear references to pronouns, such as "the Potiguarás fought our men and they ran off." Only a very careful reading and some guesswork will reveal which side ran off. I am sure this was clear to him at the time, but it can be confusing reading it now. I have no doubt that a future translation will be able to correct any and all errors I may have made in this work.

The reader will note that many of the people listed in this text have the initial "D." in front of their first names. This stands for *Dom* (for a man) or *Dona* (for a woman), which denotes that the individual is a member of the nobility. Frei Vicente used the term *corsairs* when referring to the French at sea, but I have used the term *pirate* here. Another confusing point is that the author uses the term *negro* (black) to mean either native Brazilians or Africans. At some points, he is clearly referring to Africans; on other occasions, he is discussing natives. He uses the same term to describe either group.

Special thanks to the John Carter Brown Library (JCB) for allowing us to use many of the illustrations which accompany the text.

I presented a draft of this work in two of my classes at the College of Charleston. My students read and commented on these; I trust that by incorporating their feedback and comments, the text will be clearer. I am grateful to all of them for their help. The following students provided especially helpful and complete feedback for the sections they read: Calder Jose, Carol Fishman, Mills Pennebaker, and Grace Weidemann. Special thanks to Brad Blankemeyer for translating the Latin passages. As always, I owe a special debt to Arthur Brooks for reading the entire text and making suggested edits.

BIBLIOGRAPHY

Alden, Dauril, ed. *Colonial Roots of Modern Brazil.* Berkeley: University of California Press, 1973.

Avellar, Helio de Alcantara, and Alfredo D'Escragnolle Tauney. *História Administrativa do Brasil.* 3 vols. Rio de Janeiro: Presidência da República, Departamento Administrativo do Serviço Público, 1956.

Boxer, C. R. *The Dutch in Brazil, 1624–1654.* Oxford: Clarendon Press, 1957.

Tavares, Luís Henrique Dias. *O Primeiro Século do Brasil.* Salvador: EDUFBA, 1999.

VOCABULARY OF FOREIGN AND ARCHAIC
ENGLISH TERMS USED MORE THAN ONCE

TYPES OF SHIPS

caravel: A Mediterranean-designed ship used in exploration and trade, originally with two masts, later with three. They were smaller ships, usually seventy-five to eighty feet long.

galleass: Translation of *galeota*, a small galley.

galley: Fighting vessel powered by oars.

large caravel: Translation of *caravelão*.

lifeboat: Translation of *batel*, a small boat used to load and unload ships.

nau: Generic name for a large, ocean-going ship used for trade and defense, the exact size and description of which changed over time. As a result, I have retained the original term here.

pinnace: Translation of *patacho*, a small boat with six to eight oars.

sloop: Translation of *lanch*, a vessel with two masts.

urca: A large merchant ship of northern European design, similar to a *nau*, that could range from two hundred to nine hundred tons. In this text, Frei Vicente often uses *nau* and *urca* interchangeably.

zabra: A sort of fishing boat used in Biscay, one hundred to two hundred tons.

WEAPONS

falconet: Translation of *falcão*, a small cannon, about four feet long with the diameter of three fingers.

halberd: A pike with a battle axe on the end.

harquebus: A short rifle fired with a wick.

minion: Translation of *berço*, a small cannon.

pike: A long pole with a sharp point on the end.

pistol: Translation of *espingarda*.

rock-firing cannon: Translation of *roqueira,* a cannon designed to fire rocks.

wick: A piece of cord soaked in saltpeter (potassium nitrate) that ignited the gunpowder in a harquebus.

MONEY

cruzado: Four hundred *réis.*

dízimo: Tax of one-tenth, normally paid to the Church.

pataca: Six hundred *réis.*

réis: Money of account.

tostão: One hundred *réis.*

vintém (plural *vinténs*): Twenty *réis.*

MEASUREMENT

alqueire: Bushel, 36 liters.

arroba: Thirty-two pounds.

braça: Fathom, about seven feet. I have retained the original *braça* when referring to measurement on land.

canada: Three English pints or four *quartilhos,* 1.4 liters.

league: Distance of 3.5 to 4 miles between 5,555 and 6,600 meters.

moio: Sixty *alqueires* of 13 liters each or 780 liters (206 gallons).

pipa: Pipe used for liquid measurements, more or less 111 gallons, 420 liters, or two hogsheads.

quartilho: One-fourth of a *canada.*

quarto: One-fourth of a cask or half a pipe.

quintal (plural *quintais*): Four *arrobas* or 128 pounds.

span: Length of a hand or approximately 8.5 inches (*palmo*).

OTHER TERMS

mameluco: Person of native Brazilian and European ancestry.

Misericórdia: Charitable brotherhood with chapters in every large city in the Portuguese world.

TABLES

LIST OF GOVERNORS AND GOVERNORS-GENERAL
OF BAHIA, 1549–1635[1]

Governors

Tomé de Sousa, 1549–53

Duarte de Costa, 1553–58

Mem de Sá, 1558–72

Luís de Brito de Almeida, 1572–78

Governors-General

Lourenço de Veiga, 1578–82

council, 1582–84

Manuel Teles Barreto, 1584–88

council, 1588–91

Francisco de Sousa, 1591–1602

Diogo Botelho, 1602–8

Diogo de Meneses e Siqueira, 1608–12

Gaspar de Sousa, 1613–17

Luís de Sousa, 1618–21

Matias de Albuquerque, 1624–27

Diogo Luís de Oliveira, 1627–35

Captains-Major of Ceará, 1612–31

Martim Soares Moreno, 1612–13, 1619–31

Estêvão de Campos, 1613–14

Manuel de Brito Freire, 1614–17

Captains-Major of Espírto Santo, 1536–1627

Vasco Fernandes Coutinho, 1535–60, 1564–89

Belchior de Azeredo, 1560–64
Luisa Grinalda, 1589–93
Miguel de Azeredo, 1593–1605
Francisco de Aguiar Coutinho, 1605–27

CAPTAINS-MAJOR AND GOVERNORS OF MARANHÃO, 1616–36

Captains-Major
Jerónimo de Albuquerque, 1616–18
António de Albuquerque, 1618–19
Diogo de Costa Machado, 1619–26

Governor
Francisco de Albuquerque Coelho de Carvalho, 1626–36

CAPTAINS-MAJOR OF PARÁ, 1615–29

Francisco Caldeira Castelo Branco, 1615–18
Baltasar Rodrigues de Melo, 1618–19
Jerónimo Fragoso de Albuquerque, 1619
Matias de Albuquerque, 1619
Pedro Teixeira, 1620–21
Bento Maciel Parente, 1621–26
Manuel de Sousa d'Eça, 1626–29

CAPTAINS-MAJOR OF PARAÍBA, 1582–1633

Frutoso Barbosa, 1582 and 1587
João Tavares, 1586
Feliciano Coelho de Sousa Pereira, 1595–96
Francisco Nunes Marinho de Sá, 1603–7
André de Albuquerque Maranhão, 1607–8
Francisco de Albuquerque Coelho de Carvalho, 1608–12
João Rebelo de Lima, 1612–16

João de Brito Correia, 1616–18

Afonso de França, 1618–25

António de Albuquerque Maranhão, 1628–33

DONATARIES AND CAPTAINS-MAJOR OF
PERNAMBUCO, 1534–1635

Resident Donataries

Duarte Coelho, 1534–54

Dona Brites, 1554–60

Duarte Coelho de Albuquerque, 1560–72

Jorge de Albuquerque Coelho, 1572–76

Captains-Major

Jerónimo de Albuquerque, 1576–80

Filipe de Moura, 1584–95

Pedro Homen de Castro, 1596

Manuel Mascarenhas Homen, 1598–1603

Alexandre de Moura, 1605–17

Martim de Sousa Sampaio, 1619

Matias de Albuquerque, 1620–26, 1629–35

André Dias de França, 1626–29

GOVERNORS OF RIO DE JANEIRO, 1565–1632

Estácio de Sá, 1565–67

Salvador Correia de Sá, 1567–71, 1578–98

Cristóvão de Barros, 1571–73

António de Salema, 1574–78

Francisco de Mendonça e Vasconcelos, 1598–1602

Martim de Sá, 1602–1608, 1623–32

Afonso de Albuquerque, 1608–14

Constantino de Menelau, 1614–17

Rui Vaz Pinto, 1617–20

Francisco de Fajardo, 1620–23

CAPTAINS-MAJOR OF RIO GRANDE (DO NORTE), 1598–1631

Jerónimo de Albuquerque, 1598, 1603–10

João Rodrigues Colaço, 1599–1603

Lourenço Peixoto Cirne, 1610–13

Francisco Caldeira de Castelo Branco, 1613–15

Estêvão Soares de Albergaria, 1615–17

Ambósio Machado de Carvalho, 1617–21

André Pereira Temudo, 1621–24

Francisco Gomes de Melo, 1624

Bernado da Mota

Domingos da Veiga Cabral, –1631

CAPTAINS-MAJOR OF SÃO VICENTE, 1533–1632

Gonçalo Monteiro, 1533–38

António de Oliveira, 1538–42, 1549–52

Cristóvão de Aguiar Altero, 1542–45

Brás Cubas, 1545–49, 1552–54

Gonçalo Afonso, 1554–56

Jorge Ferreira, 1556–57

António Rodrigues de Almeida, 1557–59, 1569–71

Francisco de Morais Barreto, 1559–63

Pedro Ferraz Barreto, 1563–67

Pedro Colaço Villela, 1571–73

Jerónimo Leitão, 1573–80, 1583–92

António de Proença, 1580–83

Jorge Correia, 1592–95

João Pereira de Sousa, 1595–98

Roque Barreto, 1598, 1602–5, 1613

Diogo Arias Aguirre, 1598–1602

Pedro Vaz de Barros, 1602, 1605

Pedro Cubas, 1605–7

António Pedroso de Barros, 1607–8

Gaspar Coqueiro, 1608–12

Luís de Freitas Matoso, 12

Nuno Pereira Freire, 1612–13

Francisco de Sá Souto-Maior, 1613–14

Domingos Pereira Jácome, 1614

Paulo da Rocha e Sequeira, 1614–15

Baltasar de Seixas Rabêlo, 1615–17, 1619–20

Gonçalo Correia de Sá, 1617–18, 1626–32

Matrim Correia de Sá, 1618–19

Manuel Rodrigues de Morais, 1620–22

João de Moura Fogaça, 1622, 1626

Fernão Vieira Tavares, 1622–24

Álvaro Luís de Vale, 1624–26

CAPTAINS-MAJOR OF SERGIPE, 1590–1630

Cristóvão de Barros, 1590–91

Tomé da Rocha, 1591–95, 1603–6

Diogo de Quadros, 1595–1600

Manuel Miranda Barbosa, 1600–1602

Cosme Barbosa, 1602–3

Nicolão Faleiro de Vasconcelos, 1606–

António Pinheiro de Carvalho, –1611

João Mendes, 1611–14, 1621–23

Amaro da Cruz Portocarreiro, 1614–, 1626–30

THE HISTORY OF BRAZIL, 1500-1627

To the scholar Manuel Severim de Faria,
canon of the Holy Cathedral of Évora[2]

The motivation that Aristotle had to turn from his natural gifts and interests, that is, his logic, physics, and metaphysics, and instead write historical and moral works on his ethics, politics, and history of animals (in addition to the fact that the great Alexander requested him to do so and paid for his expenses) was that he greatly admired the work of Homer on the heroic deeds of Achilles and other valiant warriors. He liked it so much that (as Plutarch says in his *Lives of Alexander*) he normally carried a copy with him.[3] When it was not in his hands, it was locked in a desk decorated with gold and precious stones. This was a prized possession, more valued than any treasures plundered from Darius. He kept the key in his hand and trusted no one else with it. This was with very good reason since (as stated in title 2 of *Oratore*) history books are lights of truth; they give life to memory and are masters of life. Diodorus Siculus says in *Proemio sui operis* that these equalize the prudence of young men with the old because what the old achieve with a long life and many conversations, the young obtain in a couple of hours of study in their homes.[4]

This is the reason Alexander the Great so admired the work of Homer. If today there were many Alexanders there would also be many Homers, as Ovid says:

Scribentem juvat ipse favor, minuitque laborem:
Cumque suo crescens pectore fervet opus.[5]

That is, favor helps the writer, makes his work light, gives him strength, and improves his work. However, what we see now is everyone wanting to be esteemed and praised by writers; there are few that do so, fewer than those who pay their expenses. There is only Your Excellency in Portugal, who esteems and favors them as can be seen in your library, which is almost exclusively history books. Chiefly, you honor three Portuguese historians: Luís de Camões, João de Barros, and Diogo do Couto—a favor so great for a historian that you can say that even though they are deceased, you give their memories new life.[6] Since that time when they were alive, time has stimulated and given strength and fervor, shining a light on their writings; each one composes and recounts his history. This was my motivation for writing this work on Brazil as well as Your Excellency's offer to publish it at your expense, thus acting like Alexander.

Another motive was for Your Excellency to ask me and thus tell me to do this, since the requests of lords have the force of predetermination: glos il et L. 1a ff. quod jussu, which is where the following verse can be found:

> Est rogare ducum species violenta jubendi.[7]

It was thus such energy, not just on my part, that motivated a friend to suggest the work be written in verse. It would be similar to what Saint Augustine said to Saint Bishop Simpliciano of Milan when he asked the bishop to write a short text on certain problems.[8] The bishop offered two entire books and further excused himself by saying there was so much text that it might be tiresome but that he had not provided what was asked of him and would respond to the wishes of the requester. It was Saint Augustine's words that follow:

> Vereor ne ista quae, sunt a me dicta, et non satisfecerint expectationi et taedio fuerint tuae, quandoquidem et tu ex omnibus quae interrogasti unum a me libellum mitti velles, ego duos libros, eosdemque longissimos misi, et fortasse quaestionibus nequaquam expedite diligenter respondi.[9]

In the same way, Your Excellency has asked me for a work about Brazil, and I have offered two, reading that could be tiring if the manner of writing did not change and was not diverse to stimulate interest. Even with this, I fear I have not satisfied Your Excellency's hunger, but I know you will appreciate this delicate dish. This also motivated me to dedicate this work to Your Excellency and not to someone else, remembering that when Jacob was picked by his father Isaac, he obtained the blessing that his mother declared when she said:

> And now, my son, follow my counsel: Go now to the flock, and fetch me from thence two young sheep so that I may prepare from them savory food for thy father, such as he loves; and when thou hast brought in, that he may eat and bless thee.[10]

The elder Saint Isaac had discovered, even though he was blind, that Jacob had tricked him because he recognized his voice: "Truly it is the voice of Jacob." But carried away by the desire to enjoy the delicious meal, which he loved, after heavenly inspiration, he gave Jacob his blessing. This is what I ask of Your Excellency, and with that I will not have to fear any who disparage this work.

We hope that Our Lord may preserve and augment the life, health, and station of Your Excellency as well as those around you.

Bahia, December 20, 1627
Your Excellency's Servant
Frei Vicente do Salvador

BOOK 1

The Discovery of Brazil, the Customs of Its Natives, Its Birds, Fish, Animals, etc. All of Brazil

CHAPTER 1

How This State Was Discovered

The land of Brazil, which is in America, one of the four continents of the globe, was not discovered by design, with this being the main intention, but rather by chance.[1] Pedro Álvares Cabral was sent to India by King D. Manuel in the year 1500 as the commander of a fleet of eleven *naus*. Hugging the coast of West Africa, which was already known at that time as the eastern edge of the ocean, he found an unknown coastline at its western edge. He was on this coast for a few days in a storm until he arrived at a secure harbor, and the land around it was called by this same name: safe port or Porto Seguro.

This commander left his nau with his soldiers armed and prepared for fighting. Previously, he had sent a lifeboat to find a landing spot, and the men said that many natives had approached them. However, firearms were not needed because as soon as the natives saw men wearing clothes and shoes, white men with beards (which all the natives lacked), they took them for gods, something more than human, and called them *caraíbas*, which in their language means *something divine*. The natives approached our people in a peaceful manner.

The natives of New Spain did the same thing when the Spanish disembarked, calling them *viracoches*, which means *sea foam* since it seemed to them that the sea threw them out like foam. They were always known by that name afterward. In the same way, we are still called *caraíbas* and held in a loftier regard than other men. However, their respect grew much more after seeing the eight Franciscan monks who traveled with Pedro

Álvares Cabral, led by Father Henrique, who was later appointed bishop of Ceuta. He gave a Mass there and preached. When he raised the host and chalice, the natives kneeled and beat their chests as Christians do.[2] By their doing this, Christ our Lord dominated these heathens through these sacraments. This is what the faithful sing in church at the *invitatorium* for the morning prayer:[3] "Christum regem dominantem gentibus, qui se manducantibus dat spiritus pinguedinem, venite adoremus."[4]

The ancient heathens said that God the Father dominated the world and was Lord of the Universe, and they spoke the truth if they meant this Holy Host. For sure, it is He who rules all. There is hardly any place on Earth where He is not worshiped nor are there any peoples so wild that they do not venerate and adore Him just as these wild Brazilian natives did.

Our brothers wanted to remain there because of the natives' positive reception of our Catholic faith. They wanted to instruct and baptize them, but the commander wanted to take the brothers somewhere else, just as important. He left a few days later for India and took them with him. They left a raised cross and two Portuguese convicts to learn the native language.[5] The commander sent a ship to Portugal, captained by Gaspar de Lemos, with the news for King D. Manuel. The king received it with the contentment that such a great and unexpected event merited.

CHAPTER 2
The Name of Brazil

The day that Captain-Major Pedro Álvares Cabral raised the cross mentioned in the last chapter was May 3, the day celebrated as the Discovery of the Holy Cross on which Christ Our Redeemer died for us.[1] Because of this, the name of this newly discovered land was called *Land of the Holy Cross.* It was known by this name for many years. However, since the Devil lost his hold on mankind because of the sign of the cross, he feared he would lose the many souls here in this land as well. He toiled for people to forget this first name and the name *Brazil* to remain, named for the tree with the shiny orange and yellow wood used to dye cloth. There are many such trees in this land. As if the name of a tree timber used to dye cloth has greater importance than the Holy Cross that gave color and virtue to all the sacraments of the Church! On these sacraments, the Church was built and became firmly established, as we all are aware. Because of this, the name of *Brazil* was connected to *state* and called *State of Brazil*, giving it a stronger foundation. It has not even been one hundred years as I write this that it was first colonized, yet some places have been abandoned. This land is so vast and fertile, as we will discuss later, but in spite of this, the population is not growing but rather decreasing.

Some blame the kings of Portugal for this; others blame the colonizers themselves. The kings are blamed because of the little regard in which they hold this large state; they do not even claim it in their titles.[2] They call themselves *Lords of Guinea* because a little caravel comes and goes there, as the king of the Congo tells us. Yet *Brazil* is not in their titles. Even after the death of King D. João III, who ordered that Brazil be colonized and who held Brazil in esteem, there was another king who was satisfied to simply draw revenue and collect taxes from it. In the same vein, the colonizers are to blame. Those who are most firmly rooted in the land where they live and as wealthy as they have become plan to take everything back to Portugal. If their plantations and belongings could speak, they would teach them to say the same things the parrots do, which is "royal parrot bound for Portugal." They want to take everything there, not just those who came from there but also those born here. Both occupy the land, not to use it as owners, but to extract its wealth and leave it barren.

It follows that no one in this land is public-spirited or has any zeal or interest in the common good, just in what is good for himself. I did not see this as clearly as did a bishop from Tucuman of the Dominican order who passed through these lands on his way to court. He was an excellent theologian, had a good understanding of people, and was a prudent man. These things gave him great wealth. He saw how things were when he wanted to purchase a large chicken, four eggs, and a fish to have something to eat. Yet, no one could bring him anything from the market or the butcher's shop. When he ordered these, and many other things as well, from private homes, they sent them. As a result, this bishop said, "Really, in this land things are reversed. This is not a society but a collection of private houses."

In this way, the homes of the wealthy have all the provisions they require (even when they come at a high price since many are in debt) because they have slaves, fishermen, and hunters who bring them meat, fish, containers of wine and olive oil. They buy all these things in bulk, but many times in the towns none of these goods can be found for sale. What fountains, bridges, roads, and other public works that exist are pitiful because everyone only pays attention to himself. No one attends to these things even though they drink unclean water, get wet when crossing rivers, or water from potholes splashes them on the roads. This all stems from not paying attention to what will remain here but rather focusing on what they can take with them to Portugal.

These are the reasons why some say that Brazil will not endure and grow. To these, we can add what we said previously about calling it *State of Brazil* taking away the title *Land of the Holy Cross*, which would have made it secure and more firmly established.

CHAPTER 3
Mapping Brazil's Coast and Land Boundaries
with Peru and the Spanish Indies

There began to be great differences of opinion and doubts regarding the conquered lands in the New World. There would have been more daily had the Catholic kings of Castile, King D. Fernando and his wife Queen D. Isabel, and the king of Portugal, D. João II, who were about to conquer these lands, not made an agreement between them with the blessing of the pope. The agreement was that a line of longitude 370 leagues[1] to the west of the island of Santo Antão in Cape Verde would demarcate all lands to its east as belonging to the king of Portugal and all lands to its west to the crown of Castile.[2]

In accordance with this, Pedro Nunes, the famed cosmographer, says that Brazilian territory belonging to the crown of Portugal begins on the other side of the Amazon River at the Port of Vicente Pinson. This is at two degrees north latitude and runs in the interior to beyond the Bay of São Matias at forty-four degrees south latitude, more or less.[3] By these measurements (this same cosmographer says) Brazil has fifteen hundred leagues of coastline. However, that is the theory. In reality, Brazil only extends to the Rio de la Plata, which is at thirty-five degrees south latitude. As a result, the coast is still more than one thousand leagues. In some places, the coast runs from north to south, which means that coastline is only seventeen and a half leagues long between each degree. The majority of the coast, which is from Cape Santo Agostinho to the Rio de la Plata, runs from northeast to southwest for twenty-five leagues.[4] In the north from Cape Branco to the Amazon River the coastline runs almost directly east to west. When the angle changes, the number of leagues is greater. So when the angle is north-south there are not many leagues of coastline, but at thirty-five degrees there are many.

The shape of Brazil is like a harp, with the upper part larger in the north and running from east to west; on the side the interior runs from north to south and the remaining coastline from northeast to southwest. They come together at the Rio de la Plata in a point, like a harp, as can be seen on the following map.

I will not mention the distance that Brazil extends into the interior because, until now, no one has explored this region due to the negligence of the Portuguese. They are great conquerors of lands but fail to take advantage of them and are content to stick to the seashore like crabs.

After the above-mentioned treaty was negotiated, there were additional doubts about the borders of this land. A Portuguese named Fernand Magellan, a very skilled and seasoned navigator, left the court of King D. Manuel to serve Emperor Carlos V. He did this because King D. Manuel offended him by refusing to increase his stipend by one *tostão* to equal what his ancestors had received. Magellan offered the emperor better opportunities in India than what the Portuguese had by way of a shorter, cheaper, and safer route. This was by way of a strait that he would discover on the coast of Brazil, and he believed the Molucca Islands were in the territory of Castile.[5] The emperor did not just give Magellan his ear but hired him for his service. The king gave him the men and equipment needed to make the journey to the Moluccas. All of these ships were lost except for one. After enduring many hardships and five months of terrible hunger, whereby twenty-one people died on that ship, those who survived arrived in the Cape Verde Islands in great need.[6] The Portuguese there did not know anything about their journey and gave them all the provisions they required. The Spanish told them they were coming from the West Indies. However, when the Portuguese learned the truth, they secretly decided to detain the lifeboat until they could send notice about it to Portugal. The Castilians figured out what the Portuguese were planning and set sail with such haste that they left one of their little boats behind. The people of Cape Verde grabbed the boat, captured thirteen Spaniards on land, and sent them to the king with news of what had happened.

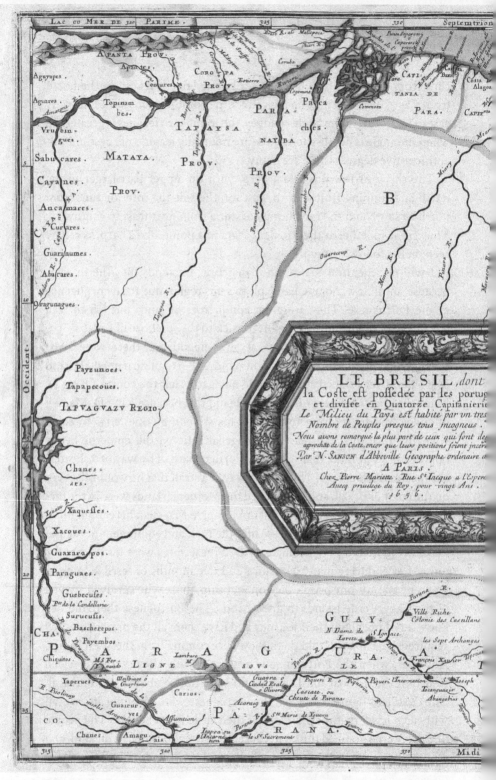

Figure 1. Map of South America showing the Rio de la Plata, Amazon, and Orinoco rivers joining at the Lacus Eupana. Also shows another mythical lake, Lacus Parima (or Lake Parime). Cartographic elements include some topographical details, names of settlements,

degrees of latitude and longitude, and scale. Decorative elements include sea monsters or fish and ship. —T. Cotes, for Michael Sparke and Samuel Cartwright, 1635. ©John Carter Brown Library.

The king at the time was D. João III because his father, King D. Manuel, had died a year before on December 13, 1521. The king sent four caravels to search for the Spanish ship, but, in spite of moving as quickly as they could, they received news that it had reached Seville.

The king's councilors determined that the best course of action was to send a letter to the emperor demanding all the spices the ship had brought from the Molucca Islands, since these were within the Portuguese sphere. The letter also stated that the king did not want any reasons to break the peace negotiated between them and to which they had agreed. This is what the king wrote to the emperor. The king had sent Luís da Silveira as his ambassador to Castile to negotiate marriages and alliances. He ordered him to alter his mission and to deal exclusively with this issue. The emperor did the same with his secretary, Cristóvão Barroso, in Portugal. The emperor ordered his ambassador to speak with the king of Portugal right away, and he sent his ambassador a letter for the king in which he discussed these issues and made many complaints; chief among these issues was that the king would demand the spices from his nau, since these goods were from an area within the Spanish sphere of influence. Furthermore, they had been obtained without the Spanish entering a port in Portuguese India. The emperor claimed that this was a breach of the peace treaty between the two kingdoms. Portuguese ships that entered Spanish ports were well provisioned throughout his kingdoms. The emperor asked the king to free the prisoners and to punish those guilty of capturing them in Cape Verde. The king responded to each of these complaints in turn and set things right according to justice.

All of these negotiations would have collapsed into warfare had the two marriages not taken place previously. King D. João III married Queen D. Catarina, the sister of the emperor, and the emperor married Empress D. Isabel, the sister of the king of Portugal. This made them in-laws twice over and brothers, and, as a result, they lived in peace and friendship.

King Francis of France was also eager to reap the rewards that they said came from this land. He began to raise new doubts about the agreement between the kings of Castile and Portugal, which excluded him, even though he had sought these lands several times. He was now sorry about the renunciation he had made. Because of the dislike he harbored for the kings of Portugal and Castile dividing the world between them and making the boundaries as they liked, the king of France allowed his subjects to sail so freely on the seas that they not only robbed other ships but claimed these lands and attempted to colonize them. This was especially true regarding Brazil, as we shall see.

CHAPTER 4
The Weather and Climate of Brazil

According to Aristotle and other ancient philosophers, the tropical zone of the earth was uninhabitable because the sun passed over it twice annually for the tropics.[1] It seemed to them that no one could live there with such great heat. The opinion was confirmed because the sun heats *uniformiter diformiter* with its rays, closer rather than further distant. Because of this, during the winter there is less heat because the sun is further away.

In the temperate zone, where the sun never enters, men die of heat when there is an excessive amount in the summer. It follows then that the tropical zone, where the sun never leaves, has to be deadly hot.

However, experience has demonstrated that the tropics are habitable and that in some of its regions men can live with greater health than in all the temperate zone. This is especially true of Brazil, where there is never any plague or other contagious disease, just pox every now and then, which effects the *negros* and the natives of this land.[2] These only occur once and never appear a second time on those who have had them. Some get ill from specific sicknesses, but this is caused more by their own disorders than the unhealthy nature of the land. Even though Brazil is warm because it is in the torrid zone, it is also very humid. At night, there is so much dew that within four hours after sunset the plants are wet. If someone sleeps outside, in the morning when he awakes, he is as wet as if it had rained.

Because of this humidity, it is impossible to store salt or sugar no matter how carefully it is done; it is too humid. Iron, swords or knives, in spite of being carefully cleaned, will begin to rust. This same humidity is the reason why the heat is tempered in this land, and it promotes a good complexion. Another reason is the east and northeast winds that blow from the sea all summer from around midday until midnight more or less. These sweep the land clean and are refreshing.

The last reason this land is so healthy is that the days and nights are the same length. As philosophers claim, longer duration makes the sensation more intense. If you slowly moved your hand over a modest fire burning hemp or straw, you would be burned more than if you quickly passed your hand over a hot fire. Because of this, in Portugal where the heat is less, you feel it intensely as it lasts longer and the days are longer than the nights in the summer. Even though the heat is more intense in Brazil, it does not last as long, and it does not get as hot as it does cold at night. The heat does not continue from one day to the next.

This is the response to the theory put forth by Aristotle that the sun heats the torrid zone more than the temperate zone but that it does so intensively but not extensively. This intensive nature is lessened by the fresh winds from the ocean and the humidity from the land as well as the dew that covers everything. In this manner, those who live in the tropics do so happily. The theory of the philosophers is correct regarding dead things, since meat can be exposed to the air in temperate areas for three or four days and not spoil as can fish, but here, after twenty-four hours, they have spoiled.

CHAPTER 5
The Mines of Metal and Precious Stones in Brazil

In the third chapter I began to criticize the negligence of the Portuguese and how they have failed to take advantage of the lands they have conquered in Brazil. It is now necessary for me to continue in this vein regarding the mines in Brazil. Brazil borders Peru, and the only division is an imaginary unbroken line. The Castilians have discovered so many rich mines there, yet here no one has taken the first step. When people go into the interior, it is to search for wild natives and bring them back by force or with lies to make them serve them. They sell them with much on their consciences. These excursions make the people so greedy that, even though they see evidence or hear news of mineral wealth, they do not attempt to dig, explore, or claim it.

A reliable soldier told me that on an expedition into the interior of São Vicente that he made with others, they made their way inland for many leagues. They captured many natives there, and at one stopping point, one native told him that three days' journey from there was a mine with a lot of high-quality exposed gold. It was possible to take pieces of ore. However, he feared for his life if he showed him the mine because another native had died showing white men its location. Telling him not to be afraid, because he would pray to God to save him, the native then agreed to show him the way. They planned to leave the next morning because it was already late in the day. At that point, the native went to his camp, and the next morning, they found him dead. As all the natives willing to show the location of the mine had died, there was no one willing to seek that treasure, which Mother Nature herself (according to the native) had opened for all to see.

António Dias Adorno, from Bahia, made another excursion into the interior, where he also saw all kinds of precious stones. He brought some examples of these with him, and lapidaries examined them.[1]

We know for certain that in a specific place in the mountains of the captaincy of Espírito Santo there are large deposits of emeralds. Marcos de Azeredo took some of these to show the king, and the specialists who examined them said these were from the surface of the earth and were burned by the sun. If they excavated there, at a deeper level they would find clear and very fine stones. The king then made Azeredo a member of the Order of Christ and gave him 2,000 *cruzados* to return to the site, but he did not do this. He was old and died; since then, no one has returned there.

There are also copper, iron, and nitrate mines, but if no one mines for gold or precious stones, they would hardly mine these.

I do not blame the king for this because I know that regarding these matters there have been some false reports. Aristotle says that the punishment for those who lie is that no one believes them when they tell the truth. In the same way, it does no good if the king orders something and his ministers fail to obey him, as what happened with Marcos de Azeredo and his emeralds.

CHAPTER 6
The Native Trees of Brazil

In Brazil there are great stands of wild forests of cedar, oak, yellow wood, *angelins*, and other trees unknown in Iberia.[1] There are trees with very strong wood with which equally strong galleons could be made. In addition, they make a fiber from the bark to caulk ships and cord for rigging and cables. Shipbuilders could use all these if they wished to construct ships, and the king could take advantage of this if he ordered them built here. However, the boats the natives make are canoes, made from only one log. They work the log using fire and iron. Some of these logs are so large that the interior cavity measures ten spans from one side to the other and so long that twenty rowers can work each side.[2]

The various types of wood in Brazil are useful for constructing houses because they are so strong. With the wood also grows something to bind them together: very strong willow twigs grow at the base of these trees. They are called *timbós* and *cipós* and they climb to the top of the tallest of these trees.[3] They appear to be masts of ships with their sails. With these, the rafters are bound, as are the shingles, and all the wood in the house that would normally use nails. This saves a lot of money, especially for fencing large pastures for oxen on the sugar mills.[4] These prevent the oxen from eating the sugarcane stocks and retain them in the pasture when they are required for powering the mill. These enclosures are made with pickets and railings held together with these *cipós*.

At the edge of the sea, and in some places extending into it, there are large stands of mangrove trees. Some of these are straight and narrow and are used for boards and rafters for houses. Others have branches that extend down to the roots at its sides. From these, new trees grow and extend down from these new branches. It creates a wonder of roots and branches, branches and roots, occupying a large area; it is amazing to see.

No less full of wonder is a plant that grows on the branches of any tree. It produces a large and very sweet fruit called *caraguatá*.[5] All summer long, there will be very cold water retained between its leaves, which are large and strong. This plant is a source of water for travelers when there are no springs.

There are many types of palm trees from which you can eat the hearts or fruit, which you can collect in bunches of coconuts. From these, you can make oil for cooking and for the lamps. The palm fronds are used as roofing for houses.

Brazilian woods are as strong as they are beautiful. They come in all colors: white, black, red, yellow, violet, pink, and sprinkled with green and yellow. Other than the yellow wood, which is the Brazil tree, and the other yellow tree called *tataiúba* and the pink tree called *araribá*, none of the other trees produces a dye.[6] These woods are highly regarded for their beauty when made into beds, chairs, desks, and sideboards as well as when oils are extracted from them for perfumes and medicines. There is a very large tree that stands very straight and tall called *copaiba*. When it is cut with an ax in the summer or drilled with a bore at its base, a valuable oil is extracted from its fibers. This oil can cure all the illness caused by cold humor, and it relieves the pains they cause.[7] It heals any wounds, especially recent ones, when placed on the scabs. It leaves no scars after healing. At some times, there is so much of this oil and it is so easy to extract it from the tree that when you remove the bore from the base, it pours out like olive oil from a pipe. But this does not happen to all the trees, only with the trees that the natives call "females." That is how they differ from the male trees since otherwise they are very similar. It is not just the oil that makes these trees special, but also that animals will rub against them seeking a cure for what afflicts them.

There are other trees called *caboreíbas*, which produce a very smooth oil for the same cures and His Holiness, the pope, has stated that it can be used for anointing the sick or at confirmation.[8] When it is used this way, it is mixed and consecrated with holy oils when those from Persia are not available. This is also extracted from the tree by striking it and sticking little pieces of cotton in these cuts to collect the oil. These are then pressed, and the oil is saved in coconut shells to sell later.

Other trees are appreciated for their delicious fruits, even though they are wild. These are everywhere, and they provide fruit in the fields and back country. There are so many types that I can only mention the main ones.

These include *sasapocais*, which provide the axles for the sugar mills because they are so hard, straight, and as big as the pipes that hold wine.[9] Their fruit is shaped like a covered urn, filled with delicious kernels. After these are opened and eaten, the shell can be used as a mortar to crush spices or anything else.

Maçurandubas produce the most common wood used for the beams and frames of houses because it does not decay. Its fruit is like cherries but larger and sweeter and has a liquid similar to rotten figs.

Genipaps provide the wood for ship oars just as the beech tree does in Iberia.[10] It has a round fruit as large as an orange. When it is not ripe and squeezed, it produces a juice as clear as fresh water from a jug, but whoever washes with it will become as black as charcoal. This will take more than a few days to remove. The natives use this to paint themselves for their ceremonies, and they are as happy to be naked as if they had a nobleman's fancy outfit. When ripe fruit is eaten, nothing is spit out.

Giitis is another fruit, which is ugly to look at, so it is called *coroe*, which means *knotty and pitted*. Even so, it has such a wonderful flavor and smell that it seems to be more complex, as if it were made from sugar, eggs, and musk.

The cashew trees produce fruits, which are similar to pears but contain more juice. These are collected in December in great quantities and held in such high regard that no one wants anything else as a gift, or to eat or drink. They make the juice into wine, and the nuts are added to the bread. White women also value these nuts very much and keep them dried year-round in order to make almond cookies and other sweets that call for almonds. The tree also produces a gum, like that from Arabia. The tree and its fruit look like the following:

Another plant has the same thing: the plant that produces the pineapple has a fruit that exceeds all others in the world in its aroma and taste. A small piece of this can be put on an open wound; it is very sour to eat, and it removes all the bad humors in the body. Before anything else, its beneficial qualities are that it removes bad humors and expels them from openings, as is the case with those who are ill from kidney stones. It turns them into sand, which is expelled in one's urine. It even cleans the rust from a knife. The plant looks like the following: (see next page)

Palm trees with large coconuts are grown, and these are gathered. They grow mostly along the ocean, and they only drink the coconut water inside the nut without using the meat the way they do in India. Father Frei Gaspar in his *Itinerario* on page 14 says that palm trees alone supply all the provisions a nau needs to sail. (see page 16)

There are fields of all sorts of beans, and the dry beans are better than those in Portugal because they do not have bugs nor are their shells as hard. The green beans are just as good. Their branches grow like the willow tree, and they grow without supports to form a large covered area with their branches and leaves.

Passion fruit grows in a similar manner in the wild. It is also cultivated on trellises on porches and patios at estates. It provides fruit of four or five different types, some larger and some smaller, some yellow and some purple. All of these have a wonderful smell and taste. What is most notable is its flower because in addition to being beautiful and colorful,

LES SINGVLARITEZ

Figure 2. Native Americans harvest cashew apples and nuts. One man, in the tree, drops fruits down to another while two more men express juice from the apples into a vessel. Includes feathered headdress. —Woodcut by André Thevet 1558. ©John Carter Brown Library.

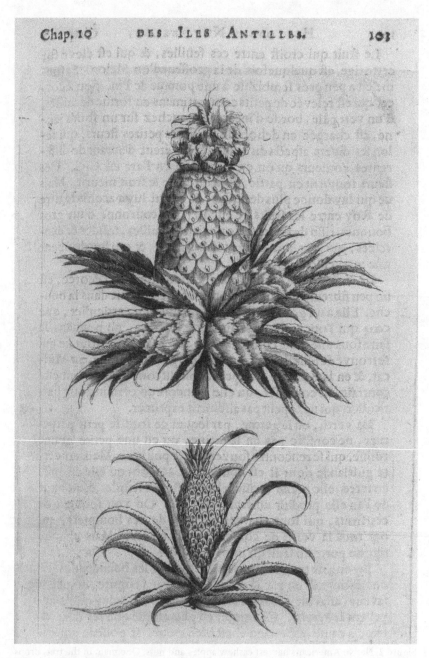

Figure 3. Two kinds of pineapple of their stalks —Engraving by Charles de Rochefort 1658. ©John Carter Brown Library.

it is mysterious. It begins at the tip with three little leaves, which bloom into a circle, representing the three divine aspects of one God. Others say these represent the three nails used to crucify Christ. Below this circle, it has another five leaves that form a purple crown, representing the five wounds and crown of thorns of Christ Our Redeemer.[11]

Of the plants and fruits grown in Portugal that were brought to Brazil, those hardest to grow flourish here to the point that every year there are oranges, lemons, cedrates, and sweet limes in great abundance.[12] There are also pomegranates, quinces, figs, and grapes grown on trellises, which are harvested twice a year. On these same trellises (if they so desire), they have flowering grapes, some not ripe and others mature, if they plant them at different times of the season.

There are many watermelons, squash, and other kinds of melons all summer. These are as good as those from Abrantes with the added advantage that of one hundred grown there, not two will be good, but of one hundred of those grown here, there will not be two that are bad.[13]

Lastly, all the vegetables that grow in Portugal grow in Brazil: greens, dill, coriander, savory, lettuce, beets, borage, turnips, and cabbages.[14] It is only necessary to plant these cabbages once in a little hole, and after they begin to bloom, they will flourish for many years, and in a few days large cabbages will grow. In addition, there are local cabbages called *taiaobas*. They also eat the cooked roots of these, which are like small potatoes.

CHAPTER 7
Medicinal Uses for Trees and Herbs and Their Other Hidden Qualities

In addition to the very useful balsam and the oil of the *copaía*, which I mentioned in chapter 3, there are others that produce resins and gums for pharmacies. Another tree is called *sassafras* or tree of fennel because it smells like that. Its roots and wood are used for cold humors, and it is as good a medicine as the wood from China.

There are trees of wild *canafístula*, called this because they grow in the forests, and there is another planted variety, the same as the one from the Indies.

There are other trees called *andaz*, which produce excellent chestnuts for purging oneself, and others that produce pine nuts with the same effect. These have this mystery: taken with the subtle tasting peel, they induce vomiting, but taken without the peel, they only induce diarrhea. The effects of the potato or *mechuacão* are better and easier, and there are many of them in the forest.

Along the seashore there is an herb that if it is not greenbrier, it looks like it, and if taken when you are sweating it will have the same effects.

The herb *fedegoso* the natives call a folk healer because of the many illnesses it cures, especially insect parasites, which are deadly diseases.[1]

The *ambaíbas* are wild fig trees that produce figs that are almost two spans long and a bit thicker than a finger. These are edible and very sweet. When ground and placed in a fresh bleeding wound, the buds of this plant will heal it marvelously.

The leaves of the *figueira do inferno* when placed over a tumor or infection relieve the pain and heal it.[2] Leaves of the *jurubeba* heal wounds, and its roots are an antidote for poison. The *caroba* heals buboes, and *cipó* heals diarrhea. To sum up, there are no illnesses that do not have herbal cures in this land. The natives have no other remedies, nor do they use any other medicines.

Other plants have hidden qualities. Among these is one very admirable herb called *live herb* that could be called *sensitive* if we do not consider philosophy, which teaches us that sensation divides plant from animal. This is how an animal is defined: a living sentient body. However, countering this we see that when a hand or anything else touches this herb, it closes and withers as if it felt the touch. Later it reopens its leaves as if it forgot the injury done to it.[3] This must be due to an unknown property, such as the rock that attracts iron. We do not know anything more about it.

CHAPTER 8
Staple Crops Grown in Brazil

Brazil has more staple crops than there are other lands in the world because it grows foods from all these places.

Wheat grows in São Vicente in great quantities, and it grows elsewhere, but it exhausts the land because of its energy.

Rice also grows throughout Brazil, which is the staple of India, and a lot of corn, which comes from the Antilles in the West Indies. Large yams also grow in Brazil, which are staples of São Tomé and Cape Verde, and small ones too, as well as many potatoes. Planted with these just once, the ground becomes full of potatoes.

However, the common and main staple of Brazil is what is made from cassava, which has larger roots than turnips.[1] They are a wonder because if you eat them raw or [improperly] cooked, they are deadly poisonous. Grated or milled into flour, they make small cakes. When cooked in a basin or an earthen vessel, they are called *beijus*, which are really good for you and easy to digest. The same flour can be mixed in a bowl with sweets, and if this is prepared well, it lasts longer than the *beijus*. Because of this, it is called *war flour*. The natives carry it with them when conducting warfare far from their homes, and sailors take it to sustain them when they leave here for Portugal.

Another flour is used without cooking it as much, and for this (if you want to make something delicious) you let the roots soak in a sauce until they soften and then squeeze them. These large, whole roots are dried in the sun and called *carimã*, and they are smoked and stored packed in reeds for a long time. Once ground, they become a powder as white as wheat flour, and they make bread with it once it is kneaded. If mixed with milk or corn and rice flour it is very good, but the dough is also very slippery and smooth. They taste best when made into *papas*, which are made with sugar for those who are sick, and they are more effective than *tisanas*. For the healthy, they are used to make fish or meat stew or they are cooked with water. This is the best remedy for all bites and infections. Because of this, they say these roots have admirable properties. Raw they are deadly poisonous, but with just a little water and salt they become food and a healing remedy. In my opinion, this plant has another more admirable property, and that is that these roots can be fed to pigs and horses to fatten them, but if they squeeze them and just drink the juice, they will immeditely die. Since this liquid is such a poison, if it is left to sit, it curdles into a paste called tapioca with which they make the most delicious flour and *beijus*, better than cassava. Raw, it is an excellent starch for collars.

There is another type of cassava called *alpins*, which can be eaten raw without causing any harm. When cooked, it is like a chestnut from Portugal. With all of these, it is not necessary to use the seed when planting, as with wheat. Just plant branches cut into pieces about a span long and stick them into furrows in the earth, and they will grow many roots. It is not collected in granaries where the bugs will eat it, as with wheat.

Instead, it is harvested little by little from the field as it is needed, and even the crushed leaves are cooked and eaten.

CHAPTER 9

Brazil's Animals and Insects

All the domesticated animals in Iberia also thrive in Brazil: horses, cows, pigs, sheep, and goats. They have two or three offspring when they give birth. Pork is eaten year-round in winter and summer and is given to the ill, as is chicken.

There are also wild pigs similar to the *javelins* of Iberia, which move in packs. If a hunter injures one, he must immediately climb a tree. Once the others see that they cannot reach the hunter, they jostle the injured pig and any others that are wounded and are so fierce they will not leave until three or four are dead. Then they leave in peace as does the hunter with his kill.

There are other animals that have navels on their backs, and these must be removed with a knife before they are cut into pieces. Otherwise, the meat will stink and only be fit for foxes.

There are other animals called *capybara*, which means *eaters of leaves*.[1] They are always in the water and are captured when they graze along the riverbanks. Some people raise them at home out of the water, and they taste more like meat than fish.

Other animals are called *antas*, which look somewhat like mules but are not as big.[2] Their snout is narrower, and their upper lip is longer, in the shape of a tube. Their ears are round, and their bodies are gray with white on their bellies. They go out to graze only at night, and as soon as the sun comes up, they hide themselves in thick grasses, where they remain all day. The meat of these animals has the flavor and texture of beef. The tanned hides of these animals make excellent leather for clothing and for defense from arrows and spears. Some of the animals have stones in their stomachs, which are like bezoars but smoother and more even.[3]

There are other types of deer, rabbits, agoutis, and pacas, which are like rabbits but fatter and tastier.[4] These are not skinned but rather eaten whole and are similar to suckling pig.

There are *tatus*, which the Spanish call *armadillos* because they are covered in a shell. The shell is not one whole piece like the turtle but consists of several pieces like layers, and when grilled its meat is like chicken.

The *tamandua* is an animal the size of a sheep.[5] It is gray with some white markings. Its lower snout is long and narrow and not as wide as the other animals, but small and round. Its tongue is as thick as a finger and almost three spans long. Its claws are like chisels; its tail is full of bristles and is almost as long as a horse's tail. All these things are necessary to protect its life. Since it only eats ants, it uses its claws to dig into ant mounds until they leave the hole, and then it sticks its tongue out to catch them. Then once it is full of them, it retracts its tongue. The animal does this several times until it is full. When it wants to hide from those hunting it, it covers itself with its tale, and its bristles cover its body. You cannot see its feet, head, or any other part of its body. It does the same when it sleeps, and it enjoys a slumber so deep that even cannon fire or a falling tree making a lot of noise does not awaken it. What will rouse it is a whistle no matter how faint it might be; it will stir right away. The elderly natives eat the meat from this animal, but not the younger folk because of their superstitions and prophecies.

There are also a great many dangerous animals that are not eaten, such as the wildcats and tigers that kill bulls, and, if hungry, they can take on an army. However, if they are full, they not only avoid bothering anyone, but they also do not defend themselves and allow themselves to be killed with ease.

There are foxes and howling monkeys, and among these monkeys are large ones, called *guaribas*.[6] These have facial hair like men, and they chew each other's beards. They move around in groups in the trees, and if a hunter aims at one and misses it, all of them burst out laughing. However, if the hunter hits the monkey and it does not fall from the trees, the others pull the arrow from the wound and throw it at the one who caused the injury. Then they flee higher in the tree, chew leaves, and place them in the wound. These leaves check the bleeding and cure the wound.

There are other monkeys that are not as large and are only able to make faces, but they smell. Other little ones are called *sagüins*; some are gray, and others are red.

There is another animal called the *jaritacaca*, which has hands and feet like a monkey.[7] It is spotted with several colors and more of a joy to the eye than the nose, as those who want to hunt it discover. With just passing a liquid, the smell is so terrible that a hunter will flee and a hunter's neighbors will avoid him for days. The unbearable smell is how it leaves a mark as to where is has been and where it goes. Dogs will wash themselves in water many times and rub themselves in dirt without being able to remove the stench.

Another animal is called a *perguiça* because it is so slow in moving its feet and hands that in order to climb a tree or walk a space of twenty spans, it will take half an hour.[8] Even if it is prodded, it will not run any faster.

Another animal is called *taibu*.[9] After it gives birth to its young, it collects them in a pouch on its chest and carries them there until they are grown.

There are also many types of snakes, and some are so large that they swallow a whole deer. The natives say that after the snake is full, it leaves its skin and its flesh rots and another develops from the spine. They say this because they found one captive in a vine that ensnared it. This cannot be but rather it was near the vine when it shed its skin, and the vine became entangled in its body. After that, the snake regenerated and the vine became entangled. So, it is not possible to say that the animal died (as the natives do) but that the snake is alive after shedding and it is not brought back to life but healed. Some of these snakes are sixty spans in length. In Pernambuco, one of these snakes wrapped itself around a man who was walking along. If he had not had a dog with him, a dog that bit the snake many times making it release him, the snake would have killed him without fail. Even so, after this experience, he failed to regain his color and previous strength.

A trustworthy woman, also from Pernambuco, told me that after she had a baby, some nights a snake would come and suck on her breasts. It was done with such tenderness she thought it was the baby. When she understood her error, she told her husband, and he lay in wait for it the next night and killed it.

Still others are called *cascavéis* because they have rattles on their tails.[10] They make a rattling noise with their tails wherever they want to go. Every year, they add one more rattle. I saw some with eight rattles. They are so poisonous that it is a miracle to live after being bitten. Another snake is called *two-headed* because it bites with its tail and head.

Brazil has unlimited types of ants that eat tree leaves. In one night, they can graze through an entire orange tree if the owner neglects to put water in pots at its base.

Another type is called *copis*, and they make covered paths where they go.[11] They gnaw the wood in homes, books, and the clothes they encounter if there is not a lot of vigilance.

There are no lice or bedbugs in Brazil, nor as many fleas as in Portugal. However, there is an insect similar to the flea but as small as chicken lice that burrows in the toes and soles of feet of those who walk barefooted. They become as large and round as *camarinhas*.[12] Those who know how to remove them whole, without damaging them, use the point of a needle, but those who are unfamiliar with them will break them apart, leaving matter inside.

CHAPTER 10
The Birds

In addition to birds that are raised at home, such as chickens, ducks, pigeons, and turkeys, in Brazil there are many chickens living in the wilds of the interior, ducks in the lagoons, wild pigeons, and birds called *jacus*, which by their appearance and size are almost like turkeys.

There are partridges and turtledoves, but the partridges have some differences from those in Portugal.

There are eagles in the interior living in the high mountains, and they are as large as those in Africa. Some are white and others have black spots. Without lifting themselves off the ground, they raise one wing high, like a Latin sail, and they fly with the wind like caravels. In spite of this, the natives catch them while hunting in the meadows.

There are many herons along the edge of the sea and other birds called *guarás*.[1] When these first get their feathers, they are white, but they later turn gray, and finally they turn red like grain.

There are five or six species of green parrots, some bigger, some smaller, and all will say what they are taught. There are also macaws and *arará-canindés* with curved beaks like parrots, but they are larger and have more beautiful feathers.[2]

There are some other birds that, in order to keep snakes from entering their nests and eating their eggs and little ones, hang their nests four or five spans under the branches of trees. The path to the nest is blocked with so many little dry sticks that it would be possible to cook a pot full of meat with them.

There are other birds called *tapeis*, the size of blackbirds, and all of them are black with yellow wings. They mimic the calls of all the other birds perfectly, and they weave their nests in sacks.

There are many large whales, which in the middle of winter, come to give birth in the bays and deep waters of the rivers along this coast. Sometimes they push a lot of ambergris to the coast, which they pull up from the bottom of the ocean when they eat.[3] This happens with frequency along the beaches, so birds, crabs, and the many other living things there come running to eat it.

There is another fish called *espardarte* because of a sword that it has on its snout.[4] This sword is six or seven spans long and one span wide with many points on it that it uses to fight whales. It splashes the water so high when it fights that the water can be seen from three or four leagues away. There are sailors who have seen the fish out of the water, according to the natives, and some have died while fishing [for them], but these fish only eat the eyes and noses of people. When that happens, we know it was not sharks that ate the people, because there are many of those in this ocean. They eat legs, arms, and the flesh.

In the captaincy of São Vicente in 1564, a sea monster came on the beach, and a young man named Baltasar Ferreira, the son of the captain, saw it. He went to examine it with a sword in hand, and the fish stood up on the fins of its tail. The young man thrust his sword into its stomach, which knocked it down. It stood up again and opened its mouth to devour the man, and he stabbed it in the head, stunning it. Right away, some of the young man's slaves came to help him finish killing the animal. The young man passed out and was nearly dead after exerting himself so strenuously. This monster fish was fifteen spans long and did not have scales but rather fur, as can be seen in the figure below: (see next page)

There are some small fish all along the coast called *majacus*, which are smaller than one span. When they sense they are caught on fishhooks, they cut the line with their teeth and flee. If they [the fishermen] bind the bait and catch one, they [the fish] calmly come up to the top of the water where, with a funnel-shaped net, they can be caught with no resistance. As soon as they are out of the water, they puff up so much that they become round like a bladder full of air. If you kick them, they burst and sound like a musket. Their skin is very colorful but also poisonous, as is the spleen. However, if they are carefully cleaned, they can be eaten grilled or baked like any other fish. Another fish has the same name, but it is larger and covered with sharp spines like porcupines. These fish are migratory and come from time to time. One year, there were so many in

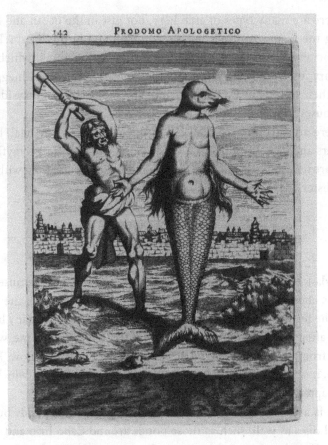

PRODOMO APOLOGETICO

142

Figure 4. A man [native American?] attacks a sea monster or merman with an ax or hatchet. The monster has a tail like a fish, webbed hands and a head with bristling mustaches. Includes view of a settlement, fortifications, and a fish.—Engraving by Giuseppe Petrucci 1677. ©John Carter Brown Library.

this bay that the homes and mills were lit for a long time with the oil from their livers.

Seafood is here in great numbers: oysters, some that live in mangrove thickets, others among the rocks, and bigger ones in the mud. In the sandbars, there are others that are round and flat where you find small pearls, and they say that larger pearls can be found by diving at greater depths.

There are cockles, clams, mussels, and trumpet shells like snails, and others so large that once the flesh is eaten, they make little trumpets from the shell, which can be played and are heard from a great distance.

There are many types of crab here, not just in the ocean and beaches among the mangrove trees but also on land and in the brush. There is a blue crab called *guaiamus*.[5] With the first winter rains, which are in February, when they are fatter and the females are filled with eggs, they leave their holes and wander out into the roads and countryside going into houses to seek something to eat.

There are shrimp here, not just in the ocean as in Portugal, but also in rivers and lagoons with fresh water. Some are as large as crayfish, and those are here as well. They are caught on the tidal reefs along with octopi and lobsters.

CHAPTER 11
The Other Things on the Sea and Land of Brazil

"Abundance makes me poor," the poet says, and it is true because where there is abundance it requires loss. This is what occurs with the harvest from the fertile vine heavy with fruit; there will always be many bunches found after a second look. That is what has happened to me with the things from the ocean and land in Brazil, which I deal with now. For this reason, it is necessary to take a second look at some of these, which are in this chapter, but it is impossible to discuss them all.

Salt is available in Brazil not just from artificial salt ponds but from natural ones as well, such as those ponds around Cabo Frio and beyond the Rio Grande, where it forms many large very white rocks.

Lime is also present in Brazil, from both rocks from the sea and from land as well as from shells of oysters eaten long ago by the natives. These are found in mounds covered with groves of trees. They can be unearthed and baked with ease in between layers of wood.

There is *tucum*, which has leaves that are nearly two spans long.[1] With just your hand, not using anything else, a very hard fiber can be collected. Each leaf produces a handful of fibers.

There is another plant called *caraguatá*, which looks like aloe, but each leaf is as long as an arm. When these are soaked and crushed, they become a flax with which you can make thread and cord and from these, cloth.

There are trees of soap because with the shell of the fruit it is possible to wash clothing. The fruit is a bead so round and black that it appears to be carved ebony. All you need do is bore a hole through them, string them, and use them as a rosary for prayer.

There is a lot of indigo and glass herb that do not need to be cultivated.[2]

There are many springs and rivers rushing with water that turn the sugar mills. There are other rivers where the tide enters very wide and deep entrances with good sandbars and harbors for ships.

If someone wanted to imagine a city that was well stocked and abundant, and this city had its doors shut and bolted, it would mean it was self-sufficient. This is the significance of the psalm urging the heavenly city of Jerusalem to praise God: "Praise the Lord, O Jerusalem, praise thy God, O Zion, for he strengthens the bars of thy gates" (Ps. 147:13).[3]

However, others would immediately describe another vision of a city with its doors open and carts loaded with supplies entering them and claim that this was better supplied with greater abundance. An authority for this view is not lacking in the same psalm, saying that God loves the gates of Zion: "The Lord loves the gates of Zion more than all other dwellings of Jacob" (Ps. 87:2). That is, he loves Jerusalem not because its gates are closed but rather because they are open to locals and foreigners, whites and blacks all with their dealings and business: "Behold the foreigners, and those from Tyre, and the people of Ethiopia, these were there" (Ps. 87:4).

All this is in keeping with the praises of the land of Brazil, first because it can sustain itself with its ports closed and without help from other places.

Rather, I ask, does wheat come from Portugal? The wheat from here is sufficient. Wine? The wine from sugar is very smooth, and for those who want it strong, cooking it for two days will make it as strong as wine from grapes. Olive oil? It can be substituted by that from coconuts from palm trees. Cloth? It is made from cotton here with less effort than linen and wool are made in Portugal because the cotton plant allows the spinner to collect and spin. Nor does Brazil lack dyes to use. Salt? Here there is both natural and man-made sources, as stated earlier. Iron? There are many iron mines, and in São Vicente there is a mill where they make excellent ironworks. Spices? There are many types of pepper and ginger. Almonds? These can be substituted with cashews, and so on.

If they told me that a land cannot sustain itself when it lacks wine from grapes and wheat flour for conducting Mass, I would agree because this divine sacrament is our true sustenance.[4] However, beyond these things, Brazil produces enough in São Vicente and the interior of São Paulo, as stated in chapter 9. With all these goods, it is settled that Brazil has its doors open. Ships enter daily past the great harbor entrances and into bays, loaded with wheat, wine, and other rich merchandise, which they leave in exchange for goods produced here.

CHAPTER 12
The Origin of the Peoples of Brazil and the Diversity of Their Languages

D. Diogo de Avalos, from nearby Chuquiabue in Peru, tells us in his *Miscelânea Austral* that in the mountains of Altamira in Spain there used to dwell a savage people who frequently were at war with the Spanish.[1] They ate human flesh, and because of this the Spanish grew tired of dealing with them and united to fight them in Andalusia. The Spanish defeated them and killed many. The few survivors could not sustain themselves by remaining there on land, so they abandoned Andalusia and set out on boats to where chance would guide them. They landed on the Fortunate Islands, now known as the Canaries, and made their way to the Cape Verde Islands and then landed in Brazil. Two brothers were the leaders of this group, one called *Tupí* and the other *Guaraní*. Guaraní left Tupí and his group to settle Brazil and went to Paraguay to settle his group there and in Peru.

This theory is not proven, and other theories are even less certain. I will not mention those since they are not based on anything substantial. What is true is that these people came from somewhere else, but we do not know where because they have no written records nor has any writer from antiquity discussed them.

What we see today is that all of them have brown skin and do not have beards. The only difference among them is their degree of savagery: some are more so than others (but all are savage enough). The most savage are known collectively as *Tapuias*, which are composed of many different groups with various names and different languages, and they are enemies of each other.[2]

Because they are less savage, the others are called *Apuabetê*, meaning *real men*. They also consist of various groups with different names. Those who live in the area from São Vicente to the Rio de la Plata are *Carijós*. Those living around Rio de Janeiro are the *Tamoios* while the *Tupinamba* live around Bahia. The *Amaupiras* live in the region of the São Francisco River. The *Potiguarás* live from Pernambuco to the Amazon River. All these peoples speak the same language, which the missionaries learn in order to instruct Christian doctrine. They use the *Arte de Gramática*, written by Father José de Anchieta, an exalted and worthy saint of the Jesuit order.[3]

Theirs is a very comprehensive language and has some words that do not exist in Portuguese. We call all brothers, *brothers*, and all our uncles are *uncles*. However, they call their oldest brother by one name and the other brothers by another name. Their father's brother has one name and the mother's brother another. Some vocabulary is only used by women; other words are only spoken by men.

Without fail, they are very eloquent, and some are so proud of this that they will begin speaking at first nightfall and continue all evening until the morning, walking the streets and squares excitedly urging others to observe the peace or war or to work or whatever else occurs to them. When one speaks, all the others remain quiet and listen to him

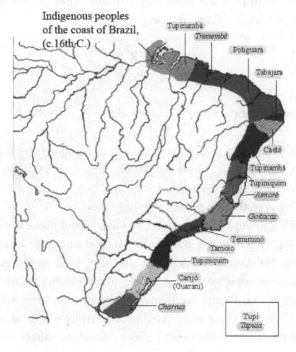

Figure 5. Distribution of indigenous peoples on the cost of Brazil in the 16th C. —Map by unknown 2011. Wikimedia. CC BY-SA 3.0

with attention. However, they cannot pronounce any words with f, l, or r, neither their own words or ours. When they want to say "Francisco," they say "Pancicu," and if they want to say "Luís," they say "Duí." Worse still is that they are lacking *fé, lei,* and *rei;* that is, *faith, law,* and *king.* They mispronounce these words as they do the others.

They have no faith, nor do they worship a god. They have no laws or rules, nor do they have a king who rewards those who obey him. Rather, they have a captain, more for conducting war than for peacetime. This captain is the bravest and shares the most relatives of the group. When he dies, if he has a son who can govern, the son takes his place. If not, then it falls to one of his close relatives or a brother.

In addition to this, there is a leader of the entire village, but each house has a headman who is also the bravest and has the most relatives and women. However, the natives do not provide any tribute or service to this headman nor to the village leader except to invite him to drink with them when they have wine, which they greatly enjoy. They make wine from honey, grains, potatoes, and other vegetables. Young women chew these and then put them in water until they ferment. They do not drink this while eating but while talking, dancing, or singing.

CHAPTER 13
Native Villages

There is a particular group of Tapuias called *Aimorés* who do not make houses where they sleep. When they reach a place where they want to sleep, they clear a space under the trees, rub sticks or arrows together to make a fire, and lay a deer hide over some forked sticks. They all sleep [under it] with their feet toward the fire. They have nothing more but are warm and dry even though rain might cover their bodies.

All the other groups of natives live in villages and make huts covered with palm leaves. These are arranged in such a way as to leave a space in the middle for dances and festivals, and they hold meetings there at night. The houses are large enough that seventy or eighty couples can live inside. There are no rooms inside the houses, just the supporting poles, and between two of these is a space for the family of one couple. The headman of the house is the first to invite one of the others to share his catch when he returns from hunting or fishing, sharing his catch with him and then with all the others. He keeps nothing more from his hunt than what he eats, regardless of how large the catch of fish or animal that is hunted.

When someone comes from far away, the old women from that house come to visit him in his quarters, weeping and wailing. They do not come all at once but in sequence, one after the other.

In their weeping, they tell him how they have missed him and the suffering they have endured in his absence. He cries as well, every now and then, making a sobbing noise but without saying anything. When the wailing has concluded, they ask him if he has come to see them and he says yes, and then they bring him food. The Portuguese who visit their villages also do this, mostly those who speak their language. The natives then tell the Portuguese how unfortunate their grandparents and other ancestors were to have never known people as worthy as the Portuguese, who are lords of all the good things from the earth. In the past, these things were rare, but now they have them in abundance, such as axes, scythes, fishhooks, knives, scissors, mirrors, combs, and clothes. In the old days, they cleared the land with wedges of stone, and it took many days to cut down a tree; they fished with spines, they did their nails and hair with pointed stones, and if they wanted to see their reflections, they needed a shallow bowl filled with water. Past generations lived this way, working hard, but now the natives finish their work and other things with ease. Because of these things, they have a lot of esteem for the Portuguese. This greeting is used with great frequency by the natives. It is always used, and, if omitted, it would be astonishing unless they are swayed by some evil deed or treachery against them, such as someone going from village to village visiting them or trying to capture them.

At night they have a fire to keep them warm because they sleep in hammocks in the air without blankets or clothes. They sleep naked, a man and his wife in one hammock, each with his or her feet next to the head of the other. The headmen sleep alone in their hammocks because they have many women. When they desire one of them, they go to her hammock in view of the others with no embarrassment. When it is time to eat, those who are eating will sit around squatting, but the father of the family will be in his hammock. Everyone eats from the same shallow bowl or gourd, which they call *cuia*. This is their tableware, and the gourds are highly valued because they act as plates for eating, pots, cups for water and wine, and spoons. Because of that, they keep them in a cage made of reeds called a *jirau*, where they also preserve their greens by smoking them to keep them from spoiling. They have no chests or locks, and the area where they eat has no doors. Everything is open. These people are so loyal to each other that no one will take or handle anything belonging to someone else without permission.

They only live in a village until the palm fronds on the roof begin to rot. This is a period of three to four years; then they move elsewhere. First, the headman determines the new locale after consultation with the elders. The new site must be on high ground, with breezes, near water, and near land suitable for cultivation. They say it must be land that has not yet been cultivated, because it is less work to clear trees than to weed plants. If these villages are near some of their enemies and they conduct warfare, they erect a wall around the village using very strong wood and mud. Sometimes they build three of four circles of walls, each with small openings for defense. Between the circles, they dig trenches and cover them with grass. These have pointed stakes at the bottom and other traps with heavy beams that fall on those caught there.

CHAPTER 14
Native Marriages and Raising Children

The headman might have many women, so it is not possible to determine which is the true and legitimate wife. They make no agreement, and the headmen easily leave some and take others. However, we can guess that it [the legitimate wife] is his first love, and this leads her to attend to her in-laws. She fishes for them, hunts, cultivates the fields, and brings wood for their fire.

However, the father-in-law does not surrender his daughter until she has finished her menstrual cycle, and then she must be tied with a cotton cord around her waist and one cord on each of her upper arms so that all can see. After she is deflowered by her husband or anyone else, the cords are broken as a signal this has occurred. They believe that if they hide this, the Devil will take them.

The husband receives his wife, and after the marriage is consummated, one thinks she is the legitimate wife. When they are not legitimately married, the man may marry his sister in law, the wife of a deceased brother, even if they have a child. Or he may marry his niece, the daughter of a sister. He will not marry his brother's daughter since they consider her to be a daughter. When any of these women are the first to marry the man, be they a niece or sister-in-law, they are married in a ceremony by religious figures who remove the sin. After the natives are baptized, the priests solve the impediment of being too closely related by providing a dispensation. They have a special right to do this.[1] They remove all the other impediments, marrying the others. These women continue to have sentiments for their first husbands because they usually remain with their oldest wives.

After giving birth, the mother goes to the river to bathe, and her husband lays down in his hammock, all covered up to protect himself from the wind. He remains on a restricted diet until the baby's naval dries. At that point, his friends will come to visit him as if he were ill. There is no power to remove this superstition because they say that it keeps them safe from many sicknesses. The baby is placed in another hammock with fire underneath no matter if it is winter or summer. If it is a baby boy, right away they place a little bow with arrows in the top of the hammock and if a girl, a spinning stick with cotton.

Mothers nurse their children for seven or eight years if they do not have other children in the interim. All that time, they or the fathers carry the child around, mostly when they go to work in the fields, which they do daily after breakfast. They do not eat while working but only later at night when they return to their homes. The husbands clear the land, burn the undergrowth, and clean it for the women. The women plant, clear weeds, collect fruit, and take it home in large baskets made from the palm tree, which they carry on their backs. It is a load large enough for a mule. The husbands carry the firewood on their shoulders and their bows and arrows in their hands. They make the arrowheads from shark's teeth or with sharp bamboo canes called *taquaras*. They are skilled shooters and teach their young children to shoot their targets. They rarely shoot at a little bird without hitting it, as small as it might be.

They also teach their young how to weave baskets and other practical things, at which they are highly skilled if they wish to learn. If they do not want to learn, they are not forced to, and no one punishes them for their errors or crimes, no matter how great they may be. Mothers teach their daughters to spin cotton and make hammocks from cords and ribbons for their hair, which they value greatly. They make up their hair and apply oil from wild coconuts to make their hair long, thick, and black.

For their festivals, they all dye themselves with genipap. If the dye is not in their hair, they look like the blacks from Guinea. The husbands dye themselves as well and remove the hair from their beards, if they have any, as well as from their eyebrows and eyelashes. They see this as very elegant. They also make holes in their lower lips and some also on the sides of their faces. They have pins or plugs of green stone in each of these holes, making them appear like demons.

In this chapter, I have discussed the matrimonial practices of these people, and I will discuss their other practices as well. However, I will not be verbose for the reader. The works that experts have written called *de Contractibus* cannot resolve all disputes, since human greed daily invents new ones.[2] But these do not impact these people. They are happy exchanging one item for another without thinking about their greater or lesser values. Thus, they will trade a baby chick for a chicken.

They do not use weights or measurements, nor do they have numbers beyond five. If counting has to exceed five, then they will use their fingers and toes. These factors explain their lack of greed. This being said, they want something as soon as they see it, but, as soon as they have it, they give it up easily or for very little.

CHAPTER 15
How the Natives Cure Their Sick and Bury Their Dead

Among these people, no one identifies himself as a doctor except for their folk healer, who lives alone in a house apart from the others. This house has a very small door, and a person entering it cannot be heard and he or she will not touch anything belonging to the healer. If someone takes anything or fails to give what the healer requests, he will say: "Go, you are going to die." This is called *being cast to die*. These natives are so barbaric that they will go to their hammocks and not want any food, and amazingly will be left to die; no one suggests they could escape. These folk healers should be called *quacks*; they do not cure the ill but trick them, sucking on the painful spot and then producing spines or old nails they had with them. Showing these to them, they say that these are what was causing the harm; and they will now be healthy, but they remain as ill as they were previously.

There are other more effective doctors. These are the prudent ones. When faced with the same illnesses, they give herbs or other medicines to make the ill feel better, and they cure them. However, if the illness is prolonged or incurable, there is no one who can help them, and they are abandoned. I witnessed one native I found in Paraíba at the edge of a road with his hands and feet numb. He asked me to give him water, saying he was dying of thirst. His own people, who passed by every hour, did not want to give him anything. Rather, they told him to die because he was already wasting away; he had no purpose but to eat bread belonging to the healthy. I ordered some people with me to find water. While waiting for them to return, I instructed him in the catechism since he was not yet a Christian.[1] In that way, his thirst awakened the salvation of his soul. When the water arrived, I wanted to baptize him before he drank it. A few days later, he died in a fire in a village where he was sent. No one was willing to remove him from the burning house, and he could not use his legs, nor did he have the strength to escape. This demonstrates the little charity these natives have for the weak and sick as well as the mercy of the Lord and the effects of His eternal predestination. This has been demonstrated not only here but in many other ways many times, ensuring that religious figures detour from their intended paths to find thatched huts or cabanas filled with the ill in agony. These people welcome the sacrament of baptism and will enjoy good fortunes in heaven.

As soon as someone dies, he is buried in the hammock in which he slept. His wife, children, and relatives, if he has any, go to the grave wailing, with their hair hanging loose in front of their faces. After the wailing, the wife continues with her hair like this for many days. However, if one of the important figures in the village dies, they anoint him all over with honey and over that they place colorful feathers. On his head, they place a cap of feathers with all the other ornaments that he normally wore for festivals. They dig a deep and large grave in his place in the house. They place him in his hammock in the grave with his bow and arrows, spear, and *tamaracá*, a gourd with some little stones inside with which he played music. They make a fire along the length of the hammock to warm him and place some food in a shallow bowl and some water in a gourd. In one hand, they place a *canguera*, which is a tube, made from the palm tree, filled with tobacco. Then they cover the grave with wood and earth so it does not fall on the deceased. The wife in mourning cuts her hair and dyes it with the fruit of the genipap, wailing about her husband for many days. Those who come to visit do the same. They wait until their hair grows to the length of their eyes, then they cut it and dye it black to end mourning and hold a festival with their relatives, drinking a lot of wine.

The husband, when his wife dies, also dyes his hair with genipap, and when the mourning period ends, he dyes it again, cuts it, and arranges large rowdy gatherings with singing, dancing, and drinking. During these festivals, they sing of the exploits of the deceased and the end of the mourning period. If the son of one of the chief figures dies, they place him in an earthen pot in a squatting position, his knees tied to the chest. Then they bury the pot in the floor under the spot where he lived in the house and cry for many days.

CHAPTER 16
How the Natives of Brazil Conduct War

These natives are naturally so warlike that they spend all their efforts waging war against their enemies. They hold a council in the village square with the village headman and the leaders of each house and other wise natives. Afterward, they rest in their hammocks, which they arrange on some poles, and the group grows silent to listen. These people have no secrets; the headman makes his proposal. Everyone listens carefully; once he is done, each of the elders responds individually until they reach a conclusion. Meanwhile, they make toasts smoking holy herb, which they use in serious ceremonies. If they decide to wage war, right away they prepare a lot of war flour and their bows and arrows, their defenses or round shields, and swords of charred wood. Once these things are ready, the night before their departure the headman of the village walks around proclaiming to the people where they are going, and the obligation they have to wage this war. He urges them to victory, so that they will remember it, and those in the future will be able to speak of their exploits.

The next day after their first meal, each one takes his weapons in his arms and his hammock where he will sleep on his back and a *paquevira* of flour. This is a tied packet, as much as he can carry, made with rigid, unbreakable leaves that are waterproof. They do not prepare any other foods since they can use their arrows to hunt along the way and find fruit in the trees and honeycombs.

The headmen take their wives with them, and the wives carry the flour and hammocks while the men only carry their weapons. Before they set out, the headman appoints a trailblazer to lead the way. This is a great honor among them. He decides where they will camp. They walk in single file on a narrow path like ants and know no other way of walking. They know the land well and not just the paths they have previously walked. They correctly guess the way in unfamiliar places, no matter how impass-able they may be.

As soon as they leave their own lands and enter those of their enemy, their spies have already gone before them. These are young swift men. Some have such a good sense of smell that they can pick up the scent of a fire half a league away even though there is no smoke.

Once they are two days away from the enemy village, they stop making fires to avoid detection. They then organize themselves so they can enter the village in the morning and surprise their enemy before being detected. Then they enter the village making a lot of war cries, blowing on trumpets, and banging drums, which creates a frightful racket. With-out exception, in their first encounters with either leaders or lesser ones, their wooden swords break their heads open. Killing has no value unless they bash open an enemy's head, even if it is in revenge for the death of others. The number of smashed heads is the number of names they acquire, taking away what the parents of their victim gave them at birth. These are names of animals, plants, or whatever they conceal. The name they take they do not discover (even though they steal it) until they hold large parties with wine and songs praising their valor. They cut and scar themselves with a sharp animal tooth, and then they put charcoal in the bloody marks. These remain imprinted on them for the rest of their lives. They consider this great daring because these marks and their differences indicate the number of broken heads.

If their enemies are prepared for war and already have defensive walls in place, they make another circle of poles stuck in the earth with bunches of needles tied together, which they call *caiçara*. When these are young, nothing will break them. From there, they boast and banter with their enemies, until one side or the other breaks away or leaves to conduct warfare in the open ground. All of their warfare is like a riot, running and jumping from one place to another because they do not stop and aim at their enemies.

CHAPTER 17
War Prisoners

Those captured in war are sold to the whites, who buy them for either an axe or a scythe. They are real captives, not just because they were captured in war, because that justice does not count, but because of the life that they are given, which is better than liberty [leading to death]. If the whites do not buy them, their first masters will keep them in prison tied around the chest and waist with thick strong cotton ropes. Each is given a woman, the most beautiful young woman in the house. She provides for his happiness and feeds him to fatten him for their feast.

Meanwhile, they plan for a great festival and gathering of relatives and friends called from thirty or forty leagues away. The night before and the day of the sacrifice, they sing, dance, eat, and drink with happiness. The prisoner does as well. After they anoint him with honey, over which they place feathers of various colors, and in some places they dye him with genipap and dye his feet red. They place a sword in his hand so he can defend himself as best he can and take the now timid captive to a space outside the village. They place him between two stakes in the ground about twenty spans apart. These have holes in them, and the ends of the cord around the prisoner are tied to each stake. He is captive and held like a bull. The old women sing to him that if he is tired of seeing the sun, soon he will see it no more. The prisoner responds with courage, saying there must be great vengeance.

Meanwhile the relatives and friends of the executioner go to his house where they find him all covered in dye from the genipap and a feather cap on his head, bone bracelets on his arms, large strings of beads across his chest, and a string of feathers hanging down from his waist. He has a heavy wooden sword in each hand and both hands are dyed. Seashells are stuck to the swords with wax, and great bunches of feathers are at their hilts and tips. They escort him dressed in this manner while singing and playing their horns, flutes, and drums, calling him fortunate to receive such a great honor. With this racket, they enter the space where the captive is held. The executioner tells him to defend himself because he has come to kill him. He then attacks him with the two swords, and the captive defends himself with his and sometimes stabs the executioner. However, since he is tied with the cords, he cannot escape the blow on his head from the executioner. The executioner then takes his name, which he later reveals in the ceremony discussed in the last chapter.

As soon as the captive is dead, the old women cut him into pieces, remove his intestines and other innards, rinse them, and cook them in a stew. They distribute the meat to all the houses and to all the guests who came to this slaughter, which they eat grilled and cooked. However, they save one very dried and grilled piece, called *moquém*. It is placed in cotton balls and put into tubes and smoked so that their hatred can be rekindled, and they can hold more festivals. They fill large earthen cauldrons with this stew, adding crumbs and little pieces of bread made from cassava. This is to stretch the supply of meat and ensure enough for everyone.

The executioner eats none of the captive's flesh. Rather, he goes to lie down in his hammock and lances and cuts himself, being sure that he will die if he does not drain the blood from his body. He does not cut his hair for another seven or eight months. After that, he drinks a lot of wine, and his friends frequently ask him to drink and dance. With that festival, his hair is cut, saying it ends the period of mourning. These people are so cruel to their captives that they not only kill them, but if they have a child with the women provided for them, they force her to give the child to her closest relative. The child is then killed in nearly identical ceremonies. The mother is the first to eat the flesh of her child. However, because of the love they have for them, the women sometimes hide their children and free the prisoners, leaving with them for their lands or other places.

BOOK 2
The History of Brazil at the Time of Its Discovery

CHAPTER 1
How the Discovery of Brazil Continued and
Orders Were Issued for Its Settlement

King D. Manuel I, when he heard the news about Brazil's discovery by Pedro Álvares Cabral, was preoccupied with conquests in the East Indies because of the promise they held. He was also thinking of the conquests in Africa, where his vassals attained such glory and honor. In spite of this, he did not delay when he had the opportunity to send a fleet of six ships headed by Gonçalo Coelho to explore this entire coastline. He spent many months sailing along the coast, discovering harbors and rivers. He sailed into many of these and erected already completed pillars with the king's seal on them, which he brought with him for this purpose.[1]

However, because of the little knowledge anyone had at that point of the coastal currents and winds needed to navigate, this was very difficult. He faced many misfortunes. He was forced to return to Portugal after the loss of two caravels. By that time, King D. Manuel had died in the year of Our Lord 1521, and his son, King D. João III, was ruling. He [Coelho] presented his findings to him [King D. João III]. Learning this, the king felt that it was important to send another fleet led by Captain-Major Cristóvão Jaques, a nobleman of his court. In this task, Jaques had very good luck discovering how to navigate the coastline, and he continued the task of leaving pillars in accordance with his instructions. As he was sailing along this entire huge coastline, he encountered a bay, which he called *Bay of All Saints* because he entered it on the first of November, the feast day of All Saints. He sailed into the bay and observed the expanse of shoreline and

rivers. In one river named *Paraguaçu* he found two French naus anchored
where they were trading with the natives. He opened fire on them and
sank the ships with all hands and goods on board. He then returned to
Portugal and informed His Highness of everything that had occurred.

His Highness then considered this information as well as additional
reports he had from Pedro Lopes de Sousa, who also had been surveying
the Brazilian coastline with an expedition. He ordered that this province
should be settled, dividing the lands among those who would agree to
conquer and settle them at their own costs. Each one would receive a par-
cel of land of fifty leagues of coastline and its interior. They were to be not
just lords but captains, and these would be called *captaincies.*[2]

He awarded them jurisdiction over crimes punished by being tied with
rope, public announcement, public whippings, and the death penalty
in cases involving peasants and up to ten years of exile for nobility. In
civil cases, the captain had jurisdiction over cases up to 100,000 *réis*; he
appointed judges and city council members, or his superior court judge
could act for him. He could also appoint public and judicial notaries, city
council and judicial secretaries, and the judge and secretary for orphans,
bailiffs, and rural judges. The head judge appoints the judge of the jail, and
the king appoints those royal officials of his treasury such as the supervi-
sors and his bailiffs, customs officials, doorkeepers of the customs house,
and marine guards. Even though the donataries distribute their land as
they wish to residents, should there later be any doubts regarding the
grant, the donataries would not be the judges, but rather the judges would
be the treasury officials. Those who receive land grants are not liable to
pay more than one-tenth of their harvest to God; this they give to the king
in his role as the commander of the Order of Christ. The king will then
give the donataries one-tenth of what he collects from these taxes or one-
tenth of the tax of one-tenth. The donataries also collect one-twentieth of
all fish caught within their captaincies. Donataries also own all the water
that powers the sugar mills. The mill owners will pay them two or three
arrobas of sugar for each one hundred they produce or whatever number
agreed upon between the owners or their lawyers. These taxes are not
paid in Bahia, Rio de Janeiro, Paraíba, and other captaincies held by the
king. They only pay the 10 percent tax. On those matters relating to civil
law and crime, the king later severely limited these, as we shall see in the
first chapter of book 3.

CHAPTER 2

The Captaincies and Lands That the King Awarded to the Brothers
Pero Lopes and Martim Afonso de Sousa

Because Pero Lopes de Sousa had already been exploring Brazil, it fell to him to make the first selection of lands before the others, and he did not take his fifty leagues all together but in two parts. One section of twenty-five leagues was in Itamaracá, which we will discuss later, and the other twenty-five were in São Vicente, which borders the lands of his brother Martim Afonso de Sousa. These lands are so close that there were bound to be legal questions and doubts about the borders. At the beginning, when they settled there and built forts, it was fortunate that they were so close and could defend each other against the enemy. This was demonstrated many times in the frequent wars the residents had with the natives and the French. They attacked them on land and assaulted them at sea using their canoes. Many times, they were surrounded, but they defended themselves very well. This would have been impossible had their towns and forts not been so close.

It is really true what Scipio Africanus said before the Roman senate, that it was necessary to continue the wars in Africa because without them there would be civil wars between neighbors.[1] This is what happened between these two, even though they were brothers, after they defeated the natives.

To be specific, the reason for doubts that these gentlemen had, or that their heirs have, regarding these captaincies I believe is based on the boundaries of their captaincies. They are the north and south banks of the São Vicente River. This river has three sandbars formed by two islands in the middle. One island goes along the coastline, and the other runs within the river. This can be seen in the drawing below and the confusion as to which is the boundary will be evident.

On the outer island, there was a village called *Santo Amaro*, but nowadays there is nothing left of it except a chapel dedicated to the saint. On the southern shore there was another village called *Conceição*. On the island in the middle of the river there are two villages, one called *Santos* and the other *São Vicente*, like the river. It was here that Martim Afonso de Sousa personally built the town and settled it with some very noble people. In that way, the town flourished in a very short time.

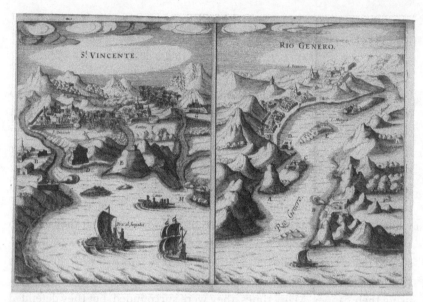

Figure 6. [left] Bird's-eye view of San Vicente, present-day São Vicente, Brazil. Items are lettered for identification in the text. Includes palisaded city of São Vicente, sugar factory, redoubt, fortifications, European ship, native American canoe, and native American sail boat. [right] Bird's-eye view of Rio Genero, present-day Rio de Janeiro, Brazil. Includes several fortifications, church, dwellings, sailboat, and stag or deer. Items are lettered for identification in the text. —Engraving by artist unknown 1624. ©John Carter Brown Library.

It was from São Vicente that he departed in 1533 to explore more of the coastline and rivers, and he went as far as the Rio de la Plata. He sailed for many days and lost a few ships and their crews in the shoals of that river. Then he returned to his captaincy, where he was summoned by His Majesty to be the captain-major of the navy in India, where he served for many years and later governed India.[2] He then returned to Portugal to be on the council of state until the reign of King D. Sebastião, when he died.

In the interior nine leagues from the São Vicente River is the town of São Paulo, where there is a Jesuit monastery and another for the Carmelites.[3] We have a site selected for our angelic order, where for many years we have requested to erect a building and made many requests and heard promises. If this were not sufficient encouragement, we have a lay brother from our order buried there in the Jesuit church, a Spaniard who was murdered by a secular Spaniard because he rebuked him for swearing. He was a religious man who led a holy life that was confirmed by God after his martyrdom with a miracle: a woman ill with the flux of the blood sat down on his tomb, and when she stood up, she was healed.

Around this town are four villages of friendly natives who the Jesuit fathers teach Christian doctrine, in addition to many other natives who come down from the interior.

The weather in these two captaincies is cold and moderate like that of Iberia because they are beyond the torrid zone at twenty-four degrees south latitude or more. This means that the land is very healthy and fresh and has good water. It was here where sugar was first produced and from here that plants were taken to other captaincies. Nowadays, they do not produce a lot of sugar but instead grow wheat, which grows well there as does barley. They also have great vineyards from which they collect many pipes of wine, which are hardened with fire.

Others raise cattle, and cattle do well there. The meat is fatter than in Iberia. Their feed is made from corn and wild pine nuts from the many stands of great pine trees. These trees are so fertile that they produce cones as large as jugs; each seed is like a chestnut or acorn from Portugal.

There are so many horses that each is worth five or six *tostões*. However, the best of all is the gold, which we will discuss later when we consider Governor D. Francisco de Sousa, who by royal orders attended to the mines.

A few years ago, a resident from these towns, a Castilian, took his wife, a Portuguese woman from São Vicente, to live on an island called *Cananéia*. It is located further to the south on the way to the Rio de la Plata. His wife was very beautiful, and the man was driven by jealousy. He lived without his fears for only a short time because, when word got out about the fertile land, many people moved there with their families, and the town grew to be as large as these others.

CHAPTER 3
The Lands and Captaincy That the King Awarded to Pedro de Góis

Pedro de Góis accompanied Pero Lopes de Sousa while he was exploring the coastline of Brazil. Góis was an honorable nobleman, very much a gentleman. Because of his love for this land, he asked the king to award him a captaincy. The king granted this, a captaincy of fifty leagues of land along the coast or the lands between the captaincy of Martim Afonso de Sousa and that of Vasco Fernandes Coutinho. Góis took possession of that captaincy with a large fleet that he assembled in Portugal at his own cost. It had many people and all the supplies they would require. At the mouth of the Paraíba River, which is at twenty and two-thirds degrees south latitude, he built a fortified town where they lived safely for the first two years. Then the natives rebelled, and they were at war for five or six years, sometimes making peace treaties and then breaking them. Góis and his people were so hard-pressed that they had to evacuate and move to the captaincy of Espírito Santo in ships sent by Vasco Fernandes Coutinho. Pedro de Góis stayed there; his entire fortune was gone as were the many thousands of *cruzados* provided by Martim Ferreira to start many sugar mills.

This region and captaincy is the land where the *Aitacases* live. It is all lowland and marshy, and these natives live more like sailors than people on land. Because of this, they could not be conquered, even though the Portuguese tried several times with people from Espírito Santo and Rio de Janeiro. When they tried to lay their hands on the natives, they ran off into the lagoons, where there they could not follow on horse or on foot. They are great fishermen and swimmers, and they catch fish with their hands, even sharks. With sharks, they put a stick about a span long more or less straight into its mouth with one hand; the shark remains with his mouth open because he cannot close it with the stick in it. With their other hand, they gut the fish, take its life, and then carry it to shore. They do this primarily not to eat the shark but for its teeth, which they use for the points on their arrows. These are deadly and their arrows are strong and swift, as when used to kill deer in the countryside, rabbits, even tigers and jaguars and other wild animals.[1]

These and other incredible things are said about these people. Believe them if you wish, but what I know is that none of their captives ever escaped with his life to tell us anything. The truth is that nowadays there is additional news about them. A cruel disease of pox befell them, which required that we find and befriend them, as we shall see in book 5 of this history.

CHAPTER 4
The Lands and Captaincy of Espírito Santo That the King Awarded to Vasco Fernandes Coutinho

Vasco Fernandes Coutinho was as busy as the other captains, tending to his captaincy. The king awarded it to him for his many services to the crown in India, giving him fifty leagues of coastline. He readied a large fleet at his expense, which he used to transport people and conquer the land. He brought D. Jorge de Menezes, of fame in the Molucca Islands, and D. Simão de Castelo-Branco and other nobles.[1] Together, when they spotted the Mestre Álvaro Mountains, which are large, tall, and rounded, they entered the Espírito Santo River at twenty degrees south latitude. There on the south side of the river, they established the town of Vitória, which today is called *Old Town* because another town was established one league upriver on Duarte de Lemos's island out of fear of the natives.

Because of his great vision, Vasco Fernandes ordered the construction of four sugar mills and returned to Portugal in preparation for an expedition into the interior. He had received news of silver and gold mines. He left D. Jorge de Menezes in charge as his deputy, and the natives conducted a cruel war, burned the mills and goods, and killed him with their arrows. This was in spite of being such a great captain, who in India and the Moluccas and elsewhere, had great skill with war.

The same thing happened to D. Simão de Castelo Branco, who was next to rule the captaincy. The natives surrounded the [Portuguese] people, threatened them to the point they could no longer resist, and they [the Portuguese] went elsewhere. When Vasco Fernandes Coutinho returned to his captaincy from Portugal, as hard as he tried to confront the natives and to get revenge, he lacked the power to do it. He required soldiers and war supplies, and the natives were arrogant because of their victories. He lived for many years struggling against the natives on that island; the two cities developed slowly.

In the end, he spent the many thousands of cruzados from his days in India, all of his inheritance from Portugal, and ended his days living on charity. I do not know if he had linen to be wrapped in when he was buried.

His son had the same name and also lived in great poverty in the same captaincy. This is not because the land is poor; on the contrary, it has some of the most fertile lands in Brazil. It produces a lot of good sugar and cotton, and they raise oxen, cows, and so many staples, fruits, vegetables, fish, and seafood that even Vasco Fernandes called it "my rustic village of abundance."

There are also many balsam trees that the women mix with crushed pieces of its bark. They make strings of beads and send these to Portugal and elsewhere. However, what these people failed to do after the wars was to explore the already-known gold and silver mines. It would seem that their descendants inherited this inattention. After a mountain range containing crystal and emeralds was discovered in this same captaincy, which I mentioned in chapter 5 of the first book, they did not explore it any further. In addition, they failed to build a fort to defend themselves against pirates. The river there is straight, and it could be fortified easily. Turning to spiritual matters, Francisco de Aguiar Coutinho, the current donatary, told His Majesty that he had a fort at the entrance to the river defending his captaincy and nothing more was required. This is the chapel of Our Lady of Penha. Two of our brothers from the São Francisco monastery in the town of Espírito Santo go there each Saturday to say Mass. We pay for this.

In truth, its location makes this chapel one of the wonders of the world. It is built on a large rocky outcrop at the top of a hill. In order to reach the chapel, you climb fifty-five steps carved out of the same rock. It is flat at the top, where the church and chapel are located. They have vaulted ceilings, and there is a space around them where the processions pass, surrounded by a chest-high wall. It is impossible to look down without feeling dizzy.

In the past, there was a hermit who lived in this chapel, a lay brother of our order from Asturias called Brother Pedro. He led a very saintly life as was confirmed at his death. He foresaw his death and went out to say goodbye to the faithful. He told them that after the celebration of Our Lady, he would die. This happened and they found him dead on his knees with his hands lifted up as during prayer. In moving his bones from that church to our monastery, there were many miracles. Few sick people can touch these bones with devotion and not have their fevers immediately expelled as documented in the archives of this same monastery.

CHAPTER 5
The Captaincy of Porto Seguro

This captaincy was the first in Brazil discovered by Pedro Álvares Cabral, while on his way to India, as stated in the first chapter of the first book. The king made a grant of fifty leagues of these lands, as he had done with the others, to Pero de Campo Tourinho. He was from Viana do Castelo and very skilled at sailing.[1] He organized a fleet of many ships at his own coast and left Viana with his wife, their children, some relatives, and many friends. They disembarked at the Porto Seguro River, located at sixteen and two-thirds degrees south latitude. He built a fort at this same place, which is now a town, the capital of this captaincy.

Tourinho also established the town of Santa Cruz and a second town called *Santo Amaro*, where there is a chapel to Our Lady of Ajuda on a high mountain. Halfway to the chapel, there is a miraculous fountain performing God's works. It gives health to the ill who drink its waters. This miracle began after the Lord suddenly blessed this site after a prayer from a Jesuit, as they say, reflecting his qualifications. He was a grandson of this same Pero Campo Tourinho and had his same name. The Jesuit was a fellow student of mine, who also studied the arts and theology and later became dean of the Cathedral of Bahia. After the death of his grandfather, he went to live with his grandmother and mother. With the king's permission, his mother, Leonor do Campo, sold the captaincy to D. João de Lencastre, the first Duke of Aveiro, for an annual pension of 100,000 réis. He immediately sent a captain to rule in his name, constructed a sugar mill at his own cost, and gave orders to build others, which they did. However, later they were abandoned because of the lack of oxen. No cattle can live in this region because of a deadly plant that grows in the pastures. They also faced many assaults from the native Aimorés, who killed their slaves. In addition, they lost many residents who left for other captaincies.

However, in spite of this, this area has many attractions, suitable for being settled. At the Rio Grande, where it borders the captaincy of Ilhéus, there are many Brazil trees, and on the Caravelas River there are many shells, which are used as currency in Angola. These are tiny little shells, many casks full of them, which could be traded for ships full of negros. The lands around this river and along the other rivers up to the border with the captaincy of Vasco Fernandes Coutinho are good for raising cattle and producing a lot of sugar on many mills.

CHAPTER 6
The Captaincy of Ilhéus

When King D. João III divided Brazil into captaincies, he awarded one of them, with fifty leagues of coastline, to Jorge de Figueiredo Correia, secretary of his household. This captaincy starts at the southern sandbar in the Bay of Bahia, called *São Paulo Hill*, and continues from there.

Jorge de Figueiredo organized a fleet of ships with all the people and supplies they would need. The expedition was directed by a Spaniard, a great gentleman, a man of strength and experience named Francisco Romeiro. When Romeiro arrived at São Paulo Hill, he started to lay out a town. However, unhappy with the site, Romeiro went to the location of the town of Ilhéus, which is called *islands* because it faces the sandbar. After making peace with the native Tupinaquim, the captaincy grew a lot, and that was when he sold it, with permission of His Majesty, to Lucas Giraldes, who invested a great deal of money building eight sugar mills. Even though the agents (as they normally do in Brazil) only credited him upon presentation of receipts. They sent very little or no sugar. Because of this, Giraldes wrote to his agent, a man from Florence named Thomas, who was paying him with very eloquent letters, "Thomazo, whatever you say send sugar and stop with the words." He then signed the letter saying nothing more.

But this was not the misfortune of the captaincy but rather it was the curse of the wild Aimorés who made the people flee from the mills with their cruel assaults. It may be that they are now living in peace, but the settlers are so ruined without their slaves or buildings that they survive by growing just enough to eat.

However, along the Camamu River and on the islands of Tinharé and Boipeba, which are in this captaincy and are closer to Bahia, there are some good mills and estates. On the Taipé River, which is only two leagues from Ilhéus, Bartolomeu Luís de Espinha has a sugar mill and next to it is a lagoon with sweet water. It has a lot of good ocean fish, manatees, and an orchard with quinces, figs, grapes, and thorny fruit.[1]

CHAPTER 7
The Captaincy of Bahia

This captaincy has the name *Bahia* or *bay* because it has one. This has become the common nickname for it and was adopted with good reason. It has a large semicircular bay with more islands and rivers emptying into it than all those known in the world. Today it has fifty sugar mills; for each mill, there are more than ten sharecroppers bringing sugarcane. Each one has his creek and private dock. There is no other land that has so many sailing passages.

There are thirty-two islands inside the bay, counting both the large and the small. There is only one at the entrance, but it cannot defend the bay from pirate attacks because there are two entrances or mouths to this bay, one inside the other. The first entrance is to the east from Padrão Point to São Paulo Hill, which is twelve leagues. The second inside entrance is from the south of that sandbar and Padrão Point to the island of Itaparica and is an opening of three leagues.

This bay is at thirteen and one-third degrees south latitude and encompasses the best lands in Brazil. It is not as sandy as the lands to the north, nor does it have the rocky outcroppings as in the south. The old natives compare Brazil to a dove. Bahia is its heart, and the other captaincies are its wings because they say that Bahia's land is like the juicy part of a fruit. It produces the best sugar we have in Brazil.

It is also an old tradition among the natives that they saw the well-traveled apostle Saint Thomas come to Bahia. They say he brought cassava and banana plants from the island of São Tomé, which we discussed in the first book. These natives wanted to kill and eat him in repayment for his instruction to adore and serve God and not the Devil, have only one wife, and not eat human flesh. They chased him to a beach where, in one step, the saint jumped to an island in the tide, a distance of half a league, and from there he disappeared. He must have been on his way to India. He who can take such large steps could visit all of these lands, and those who chase him would need to take such large steps as well.

However, since these natives have no writings, there is no additional proof or evidence except a footprint made in a rock on that beach where they claim the saint stepped on his way to that island. In memory of this, the Portuguese constructed a chapel on a hill there dedicated to Saint Thomas.

To the north, this captaincy borders that of Pernambuco at the São Francisco River. This river is worthy of not just one chapter but of many because of the great things they say about it. However, I will only mention them in passing, as I have with other places, because people do not believe such descriptions about Brazil. I do not know if this is still true or if people want to read about them.

This river is located at ten and a quarter degrees south latitude. Its mouth is two leagues wide, and the tides only affect the river for two leagues upriver. From that point on, it has sweet water and so many fish that in four days you can fill many large caravels. It is possible to sail upriver twenty leagues, even though the ship might be carrying fifty tons.

In the winter, the river has less water than during the summer, and the current is not as strong. At a point twenty leagues upriver, there is a waterfall where the water makes a sheer drop, and this makes navigation impossible. However, from that point upriver it is possible to sail on boats supplied there to a whirlpool, where the river goes underwater for some ten or twelve leagues. After passing the whirlpool, it is possible to sail up the river eighty or ninety leagues, even on large boats, because the river is very calm; there is hardly any movement. The Amaupirás travel on it using canoes.

We have not yet reached an agreement with these people. It is said that they can be tempted with some pieces of gold, which Duarte de Albuquerque Coelho, Lord of Pernambuco, used in conquering this land, but this did not work. Neither have the lands along the river been settled until now, with the exception of some cattle ranches and wheat farms near the sea. This land can support large towns because there is a lot of brazilwood and land for sugar mills.

I will not mention the Sergipe River or the Real River or others within this captaincy to avoid being tedious but also because there may be room for them elsewhere in this work.

King D. João III awarded the captaincy of Bahia to Francisco Pereira Coutinho, a very honorable nobleman of great fame and bravery in India. He organized a large fleet at his own expense and came in person to Bahia in the year of Our Lord 1535. He left the ships where the stone marker of Bahia is located inside the bay and fortified the site, a place now called *Old Town*.

They were at peace for several years with the natives, and he started two sugar mills. Later, the natives rose up and burned these and made war for seven or eight years. He and the people who came with him were forced to flee in large caravels to Ilhéus. These same natives, driven by the lack of trade with the whites, asked them to return and sign a peace treaty, which they did with much joy. A storm came into the interior bay of the island of Itaparica where these same natives killed those who returned and ate them except for Diogo Álvares. He had the nickname *Caramuru* given to him by the natives because he could speak their language. I do not know if this is sufficient proof that the natives are cannibals, but he would have been devoured by these companions had he not fallen in love with the daughter of one of the native leaders. She took his side and defended him. In this manner, Francisco Pereira Coutinho's life ended in spite of all his valor and strength, and his captaincy went with him.

CHAPTER 8

The Captaincy of Pernambuco, Which the King Awarded to Duarte Coelho

The fifty leagues of land of this captaincy begin at the São Francisco River, which I discussed in the last chapter, and extended to the Igaraçu River, which I discussed in the second chapter of this book. This is the captaincy of Pernambuco, which means *broken sea* because of a break in the reef where the sea enters.[1] The reef starts on the island of Itamaracá. Because of this, *Recife* is the name of the main port of this captaincy, which is the most famous and busiest of all ports in Brazil. The entrance through a break in the stone reef is so narrow that only one nau can pass at a time, and ships must form a line. Near the entrance there is a deep spot to anchor, and this is where the large naus come to load and the smaller ships of one hundred tons or less move back and forth from there to a village with two hundred inhabitants forming the parish of Corpo Santo. The sailors are very devoted to this image. The village has many shops and taverns and the sugar yard, which is a large covered enclosure where they store the large crates of sugar until the ships depart.

Recife is at eight degrees south latitude and is one league from the town of Olinda, the capital of this captaincy. It is possible to reach Olinda by sea or by land via a bridge formed by a spit of sand. The seawater passes along this bridge to the east, while a river passes on the other side to the west. Many little boats and barges ride the tides on this river, bringing goods. They careen their ships near the customs house.[2]

The name *Olinda* was given to this town by a man from Galicia, a servant of Duarte Coelho.[3] He was walking with some other people in the brush looking for a site to build a town; he found this place on a high hill and cried out in happiness, "O'linda."[4]

King D. João III awarded this captaincy to Duarte Coelho in recognition of his many services in India, the capturing of Malacca, and services performed at other times. Because he had such commitment and energy, he provisioned a large fleet with which he left Portugal with his wife D.

Beatriz de Albuquerque and his brother-in-law Jerónimo de Albuquerque. They sailed to the Igaraçu River, where they landed. This place is called *Marcos* because this marks the dividing line between the lands of his captaincy and the next one of Itamaracá and the other lands awarded to Pero Lopes de Sousa. A royal warehouse for brazilwood and a wooden fort were there already, which the king allowed him [Coelho] to use. He lived there for several years, and his children were born there: Duarte de Albuquerque Coelho, Jorge de Albuquerque, and a daughter, D. Inês de Albuquerque. She later married D. Jerónimo de Moura and had a son. The three of them died there, the two of them and their son, in one week.

From Marcos, Duarte Coelho gave orders to build a town one league upriver and named it *Igaraçu*. It is also known as the town of Saints Cosmas and Damian after its main church and patron saints. Many people visit from Olinda, which is four leagues away, and others come from more distant parts. Our Lord performs many miracles through the virtue and intercessions of these saints.[5]

Duarte Coelho placed an honorable man from Viana do Castelo named Afonso Gonçalves in charge of this town. He had accompanied him from India. From this town of Igaraçu or Saints Cosmas and Damian, Gonçalves sent to Viana for his many relatives, who were very poor, and they arrived with their wives and children. They began to work the land with the others who were already there. They planted staple crops and sugarcane for which the captain had already started a mill. In all these efforts, the peaceful natives helped them; the natives moved freely in and out of town with or without their goods as they wished.

After some drinking on one occasion, a few natives started to stab and kill each other, and it became necessary for the captain to send some white people with their slaves to separate them. This was against the advice of those who knew their language who said we should let them fight and bust open each other's heads. They felt that if we assisted them, as they always feared the white man, there was a danger our men would be captured; the natives would rise in revolt. This is what happened. They united in one group and turned on the whites with the same fury they previously had for each other. This did not abate until the captain sent more people to make peace. The worst aspect was that some of those who did not partake in the original drinking went running to their villages. They caused more trouble, claiming the whites had discovered them with the others and had captured, killed, or injured those in town. They went from village to village spreading this lie. To prove it, they took one of the dead, the son of the village headman, who had his head split open, saying they could now see this was true. Once the headman and the others saw this, they armed themselves and attacked the captain's slaves who were cutting wood in the forest. They killed one and the others fled to the town to tell what had happened. It was not sufficient that the captain sent word that the natives had killed each other after drinking and that the whites only intervened to separate them and that the whites were their friends.

The natives were not convinced, and the headman summoned help from other native villages. He and his people shared with them pieces of the captain's dead slave in order to nourish them. In this way, an infinite number surrounded the town, frequently attacking it and killing some of the inhabitants. Among those killed was Captain Afonso Gonçalves, slain by an arrow that struck him in the eye and went into his brain. The townspeople took his body and buried him in such secrecy that the enemy was unaware of his death for the two years of the siege. Rather, there was such energy and planning inside the city that it seemed that a great leader was directing it. Everyone rose to the occasion and fought together. Even the women guarded their part of the fortress while the men slept.

One night while the women were on duty, the enemy thought that the total silence meant no one was there. They began to climb the walls and enter through the portholes for the firearms. The women heard them scaling the walls and were awaiting them with pikes in their hands. As soon as they were halfway through the holes, they stabbed them in the chest and elsewhere. One woman, not content with this, took a firebrand and lit a cannon. This caused the other natives to flee and awakened our men. It was a heroic deed for the women to work in such silence and with such valor.

The greatest danger in this siege was hunger because they could not collect their crops from the fields, nor could they reach the sea to fish or look for shellfish. If the people on Itamarcá Island had not supplied them using a boat on the river, they all would have died of hunger. The natives tried to obstruct this assistance by various means, threatening those on the island, attempting to draw them into warfare, waiting for the boat to pass, and pelting it with many arrows from land. Because of this, it was necessary to heavily shield those on board, but, in spite of this, some of the rowers were injured. At one point, the natives planned a trap to sink the boat and all those in it. In order to accomplish this, they partially cut a large tree overlooking where the boat had to pass. The natives tied a rope around the tree, holding it until the boat arrived. Then they would free it and it would fall. But it pleased God to catch them in their own trap because the tree did not fall into the water. Instead, it fell toward the land, ensnaring some of them, injuring and killing many.

The Lord performed many other miracles during this siege because of the blessed Saints Cosmas and Damian, patrons of this town. If this were not true, they never would have received the many necessities they required.

Even Duarte Coelho could not come to their aid since the natives were continually attacking the town of Olinda and the natives controlled the roads. All he could do was send some boats to collect the children and others who could not fight so they would not drain their resources, no small feat at that time. Once the Lord wanted these enemies to tire of fighting, they became quiet and returned to peace and friendship with the whites, who then returned to their estates.

CHAPTER 9
How Duarte Coelho Sailed the Coastline of His Captaincy, Conducted War against the French, Made Peace with the Natives, and Returned to Portugal

The siege that Duarte Coelho faced during this time in the town of Olinda was challenging, as I have mentioned. Several times, the natives surrounded his tower. The shots he fired did nothing for his hunger and thirst, but they did kill many natives and Frenchmen. The Lord God moved the heart of Rahab, the prostitute, to hide the spies of the Israelites, thus making her an instrument of victory against Jericho (Josh. 6:17 and 6:22–25). This same spirit moved a daughter of one of the village headmen who had fallen in love with Vasco Fernandes de Lucena and already had sons with him. She secretly went among her own people, praising the whites and frequently bringing gourds of water and foodstuffs that fed our people.

Vasco Fernandes de Lucena was so feared and esteemed among the natives that the headman was honored to have him as a son-in-law. They considered him a powerful folk healer. At one point when the siege was tightened and those inside feared the natives would enter, he left alone and began to proclaim in their language that they were friends of the Portuguese. He said the Portuguese were their friends and that the French were not their friends because they had tricked them and brought them there to be killed. He then drew a line in the earth with a staff he carried and warned the natives not to cross it and head for the fortress because all those who did so would die. The natives then all started laughing and ridiculing this. Seven or eight angry natives then came forward to kill him, but when they crossed the line, they collapsed and were dead. When the other natives saw this, they fled, and the siege was lifted.

I would not believe this, even though I read about it from someone who did, if I did not know the exact location of that line. It was in front of the tower where they later built a magnificent church dedicated to the Savior, the main church in Olinda. This is where they have holy celebrations with solemn ceremonies. Therefore, this cannot be attributed to folk healers but to Divine Providence that wanted to use this miracle to indicate the site and impregnability of His church.

Because of this and many other victories, achieved more through divine miracles than human efforts, Duarte Coelho had more ambition than to be contented remaining in his peaceful town. He sailed in one of these ships south along the coastline as far as the São Francisco River. He explored every harbor in his captaincy and found the French and their naus collecting brazilwood from the natives. He expelled them from these ports and captured a number of their sloops. He and his men escaped danger, but many were injured. He was hit by cannon fire and needed a long time to recover. Even with all of this, he did not want to return until he cleaned the coast of these thieves and made peace with the remaining natives. Once he achieved this, he returned to his town with many slaves the natives had given him. They obtained them in their wars with each other. These slaves made the natives around Olinda very fearful and respectful of Duarte Coelho, saying he was some sort of an immortal devil. They believed this because he was not content to fight with natives and the French around his town, but he sought to fight others who were distant.

In this way, more out of fear than free will, the natives gave him lands for a mill one league away from town for himself and for his brother-in-law, Jerónimo de Albuquerque. They also gave land for sharecroppers to grow foodstuffs and sugarcane that the natives would harvest. The natives brought many chickens, game, and wild fruit, fish, and shellfish, which they exchanged for fishhooks, knives, pruning knives, and axes, which they greatly valued.

He also constructed larger caravels and sloops in which they traded with these coastal natives, with whom they had made peace. They exchanged the same tools and other trinkets of little value for many male and female slaves who served them and married with some of the free natives, serving them as slaves as well.

Seeing that his land was at peace and the inhabitants contented, Duarte Coelho decided to return to Portugal with his children, leaving his brother-in-law Jerónimo de Albuquerque to govern the captaincy with the company of his sister.

His intention in returning must have been to request an award for his services, which in truth were great, even though both he and his descendants benefited. Today the captaincy provides his successors nearly 20,000 cruzados. It pays the king much more; just in *dízimos* it annually renders 60,000 cruzados, not counting the brazilwood and taxes on sugar.[1] These are substantial; there is a lot of sugar in this captaincy since it has one hundred mills. However, at that time it did not have that many nor was it so lucrative. There must have been some people telling tales to the king that he should retake the captaincy. When Duarte Coelho went to kiss the king's hand, he withdrew it. The king gave him such a cold reception that Duarte Coelho went home and became ill because he was so disgusted. He died several days later. When Afonso de Albuquerque went to the palace in mourning, the king knew for whom he mourned, and he said to Albuquerque, "I am saddened that Duarte Coelho has died because he was a good nobleman. This death was the payment for his services, which is very different from the way God will receive him, which is that he will be rewarded with dignity, which is no more than those who serve Him deserve."

CHAPTER 10

How Jerónimo de Albuquerque Governed the Captaincy of Pernambuco in the Absence of Duarte Coelho; What Occurred Then

The natives of this captaincy had good reason (if they had the ability to reason) to cease warfare during Duarte Coelho's absence, but instead they rebelled. Duarte's wife, D. Beatriz de Albuquerque, was there, and she treated everyone as if they were her children. Jerónimo de Albuquerque, her brother, had a gentle manner as well as many children with the daughters of the headmen; he treated all of the natives with respect. However, since these are people driven more by fear than by love, the longer the one they feared was absent, the more they returned to their ways. They began to kill and eat whites and negros, their slaves, when they encountered them on the roads. The worst part was that this did not stop them from coming to houses with their goods, claiming they did not do this but that it was done by scoundrels who needed to be severely punished.

Jerónimo de Albuquerque had difficulty in understanding this and did not know what to do. Because of that, he called a meeting of the town officials and others to hear their opinions. The meeting was held at his house. Each one then said what he felt. Most thought that the natives should be punished and that they should go to war with them. Jerónimo de Albuquerque did not agree with this plan. He dissolved the meeting without reaching a decision, and each person returned to his home. Only a few who felt otherwise remained behind, among them Vasco Fernandes de Lucena, a credible and very knowledgeable man, who knew a lot about the natives of Brazil. He spoke their language and knew the tricks they used. He told the governor that it was not a good idea to wage war on these people without first establishing who was guilty. It did not make sense to punish the innocent for the actions of the guilty. He said that he (if the governor would give his permission) would organize a trap in which the natives themselves would discover and accuse each other. This would create internal divisions and mortal enemies, which was the most important thing. Once their kingdom was split, it would be destroyed. They would destroy it themselves, without our having to wage war. When necessary, we would assist by helping the other side. This was the easiest way to wage war and how the Portuguese conducted it in Brazil. In order to achieve this, the governor should order a lot of wine, invite all the headmen from the villages to come drink, and leave the rest to him.

Those present thought this was a good plan, and the governor swore them all to secrecy since that was necessary. He ordered them to make wine, and when it was ready, he invited the headmen from the native villages. When they arrived, he welcomed them through interpreters, saying that he would join them in drinking so that they would not fear the wine was poisoned and would drink with good cheer. After they were full of wine, Vasco Fernandes Lucena told them the governor had invited them because he wanted to wage war on their enemies the Tabajaras, who were another native group. He did not want to do it without their help. Some of them were scoundrels, as they themselves had confessed. They killed and ate the Portuguese and their slaves whom they encountered on the roads. They did this while the Portuguese were present; he feared that in their absence the scoundrels would enter their homes to kill their women and children. As a result, before leaving it was necessary to identify and punish these people and reward those who had been good.

Since these natives never speak the truth except when they are drunk (this is one of wine's many virtues), they began to name the guilty, and this led to slapping, hitting, and shooting arrows at each other. They were hurting each other until the governor ended it by grabbing them. After figuring out who had killed the whites, he tied some of them over the mouths of cannons and fired these in front of the others so they could see the guilty natives fly into pieces. He gave those remaining to their accusers for them to kill and eat in the main square, confirming them as enemies. They acted as if this had been going on for many years. They were divided into two groups. The accusers and their followers, which were a larger group, remained where they had been before, between the town and the stand of brazilwood. This is where the Portuguese had room to expand and construct their sugar mills and estates. The Portuguese also moved into the cultivated land of Capiguaribe, which is the best land in this entire captaincy, as well as the land extending to the town of Igaraçu. The guilty or accused natives left for the backlands of Cape Santo Agostinho, praising the Portuguese for their justice.

From there, however, the guilty natives frequently waged war against our friendly natives. They encircled them in the hills around the fields of Capiguaribe on its south side, called *Guararapes*. It was necessary for the captain-major, Jerónimo de Albuquerque, to assist these allies with some whites and more than ten thousand native volunteers. Since there were so many and those encircled only numbered six hundred archers, it was with great confidence that these allies attacked on all sides, thinking they had already won.

However, those surrounded were in better positions to defend them-selves. They did and attacked, killing and wounding so many that, after many hours of fighting, the leaders were forced to withdraw behind a thicket of dead branches. This was some twenty-five *braças* away from their enemies.[1] All night there was bantering and swaggering from one side to the other as they normally do. The natives said they did not want to ally themselves with the whites but wanted the friendship of the other natives who were surrounded. They demonstrated this the next day when the Portuguese and their allies were off guard, thinking that the enemy would not be seeking them. The enemy attacked with the force of two hundred archers from another village. They moved with such speed and force that many of our forces did not have time to defend themselves. Without weapons and in chaos, they began to flee, except for the captain-major, Jerónimo de Albuquerque, who was making an orderly retreat with the Portuguese. This did not save him for he was hit in the eye with an arrow from this first attack. Afterward, the others did not want to follow him, except for the negros who fled with him. Later, they killed many in revenge for this when they returned with Duarte de Albuquerque Coelho. He came with his brother, Jorge de Albuquerque, to rule this captaincy after the death of their father. They waged war on these people of the cape, as we shall discuss later.

CHAPTER 11
The Captaincy of Itamaracá

We have already mentioned in chapter 2 how once the king awarded Pero Lopes de Sousa his fifty leagues of coastline, he selected it in two sections. One was twenty-five leagues from São Vicente to the south and the other twenty-five were from the captaincy of Pernambuco to the north. This last area was called *Itamaracá* because of the island there with this name. It was here that he established a town called *Conceição*, with a main church with the same name and another church of the Misericórdia.

The island is two leagues long, or perhaps a bit more, and five rivers empty around it. Of these, it is the Igaraçu River that forms the boundary of this captaincy, with Pernambuco at seven and one-third degrees south latitude. This river flows next to the island on its south side, where the town and the harbor are located. There are buoys and red barrier markers, and if ships enter from the northeast to southeast, they can easily pass the sandbar. There is another sandbar at the north end of the island where large caravels enter.

The other rivers that come from the interior and empty around this island are the Araripe, Tapirema, Tujucupapo, and Gueena. The lands around these rivers all have very good sugar mills, especially this last mentioned Gueena, where there is another parish.

It was on this island of Itamaracá that the French constructed a fort and presidio with more than one hundred soldiers, a lot of weapons, and artillery. This is where the crews from the ships were sheltered when they came to load brazilwood. The natives cut it and brought it on their shoulders to trade for tools and other items of little value that the French gave them. The natives also brought spun cotton and ready-made nets in which they slept, monkeys, parrots, pepper, and other things from the land. These were very profitable for the French. This was why the French here in this port and elsewhere in Brazil traded with the natives, and they turned them against the Portuguese. They told the natives not to allow us to build towns, but rather that they should kill and eat us. The French said this was why the Portuguese came to Brazil and what they planned to do with the natives. When King D. João III became aware of this, he ordered a well-provisioned fleet of ships to come to this island first. He supplied it with all that it might require, and it was led by Captain Pero Lopes de Sousa. From here, it was to sail to all the other ports, expel the French, destroy their forts and trading posts, and construct new ones. This would be where brazilwood would be stored for his accounts, since the crown reserves brazilwood for itself.

This fleet departed from Lisbon and had a good voyage until the island of Itamaracá was in sight, and they saw a fully loaded French nau leaving for France. They feared that it would escape, so the captain sent a swift caravel after it led by Captain João Gonçalves. He [Gonçalves] was from his [de Sousa's] household and someone in whom he had great confidence. He [Gonçalves] had fought with him [de Sousa] against the pirates along the coast of Portugal and Castile. Since the caravel was very light and the French nau was heavily loaded, the French cast much of the brazilwood overboard. In the end, the caravel reached the French ship, and it turned to defend itself. The caravel shot a metal chain, which wrapped itself from prow to stern, stripping off the tackle on one side of the French ship. This killed a couple of Frenchmen, and the other thirty-five surrendered with the nau and eight pieces of artillery.

With haste, Captain João Gonçalves returned to the island where the captain-major had been for twenty-seven days. They had information that another nau would be arriving from France with supplies and goods, and he ordered they await the arrival of two caravels. These two caravels were led by Captains Álvaro Nunes de Andrade, a nobleman from Galicia, a descendant of the Andrades and Gamboas, and Sebastião Gonçalves Arvelos. They entered with the same tide as João Gonçalves, and this caused the Frenchmen in the fort to become weaker and lose hope, much more because the natives began an uprising. Some of the Portuguese that the French had taken captive were walking among the natives, since they knew how to speak their language, and they urged them to revolt against the French. If Pero Lopes de Sousa had not prohibited it, the natives would have killed the French and ate them. Natives are very changeable and attracted to novelty. The leaders approached Pero Lopes de Sousa to serve him in whatever he ordered. He received them in a warm and welcoming manner and told them not to harm the French because all were brothers. Even he would not harm them, if they did not resist, but rather support them.

Once the French were aware of this (which they heard about right away), their leader offered to surrender since they all wanted to be their captive prisoners if they would only spare their lives. The French captain did this and, not waiting for Pero Lopes de Sousa to arrive at the fort, brought him the keys. He met him while he was on his way to the fort with all his men, now disarmed. He [de Sousa] told them to turn over their supplies and remove the artillery from the fort with whatever else was there. He then leveled the fort and built another very strong one in town and a second one at Marcos to protect the royal factory. His Majesty gave this second one to Duarte Coelho, and from there they sent a great deal of brazilwood on ships.

While these things were being done, one night the captain-major had his lamp lit and his window open, and two arrows were fired at him from outside. One brushed his nightgown with its feathers, but both struck some utensils in front of a wall. He suspected the Frenchmen were responsible, and in the morning, he ordered that they all be hung. He was ready to begin the executions when two of them came forward. He had taken these two to the fort since they were bombardiers. They told him the others were innocent; they said in loud voices that they were the guilty parties. They had shot the arrows when they were certain of hitting their target; none of the others was guilty. He stopped the execution of the others and ordered the hanging of these two. However, many had already been hung, and the natives ate all of them. By doing this, the natives held the Portuguese in higher esteem and worked their lands and estates. They cut, carried, and loaded trees on royal ships. For all this, they were paid in a manner they especially liked.

The ships from the fleet were all fully loaded, and they departed for Portugal. The captain-major and some others explored the coastline as the king had ordered. They entered many bays and burned some French naus that they found, but the Frenchmen fled into the interior with the natives, where we later did them much harm.

In the end, the captain reached São Vicente, where he found his older brother, Martim Afonso de Sousa, building forts in his captaincy and giving orders to do the same in his own captaincy to the south of São Vicente. He then returned to Itamaracá. He acquired some good information from Francisco de Braga, who spoke the language of Brazil very well and whom he had left in charge. He turned over all his powers to him and returned to Portugal to inform the king what he had done. He then left for India as the captain-major of a fleet of four naus in 1539. When he was returning to Portugal, his nau sank, and nothing more was seen or heard about it again.

CHAPTER 12
What Happened in the Captaincy of Itamaracá after the Departure of Donatary Pero Lopes de Sousa

Since Captain Francisco de Braga knew how to speak the natives' language and was so well-known among them, they did whatever he wanted and ordered. This captaincy easily attracted many settlers. However, at that time, Duarte Coelho arrived to settle his captaincy. Because he built a settlement right at Marcos, this proximity caused some differences. This led to Duarte Coelho cutting Francisco de Braga's face with a sword. Captain Braga, knowing that he could not get vengeance, left for the Spanish West Indies, taking everything with him that he could.

So the captaincy was left in confusion and lost, like a body without a head. Things turned even worse when news arrived of the death of Pero Lopes de Sousa on his return from India, where the king had sent him as captain-major of the naus. However, his wife, D. Isabel de Gamboa, ordered that a pinnace be readied for immediate departure. Captain João Gonçalves had just arrived on it, and he had been with her husband. She ordered that it leave quickly without waiting for the other three ships that were still conducting business, so it left. However, those ships that left last had arrived. The first ship to leave was driven off course to the West Indies and the coast of the island of Santo Domingo with its masts broken, but its crew survived.

When Pedro Vogado, who was the captain-major of these three ships, noted that Captain João Gonçalves had not arrived at the island of Itamaracá, he loaded brazilwood on the ships and readied them to return. He informed D. Isabel what was happening and that he was temporarily in charge. D. Isabel ordered instead that, rather than continue as captain, someone better suited to be a captain should replace him, while he, Pedro Vogado, had acted so honorably. They left and went from this captaincy south (as Braga had done). They left this captaincy on the verge of being depopulated had it not been for one honorable resident named Miguel Álvares de Paiva, who was made a captain. He never wanted to leave the island. He decided along with others to not evacuate the women and children, which some wanted to do. They were afraid of the natives surrounding the town of Igaraçu. Now the natives were attacking them, and they had to respond. As we have stated in chapter 9, he was the captain who supplied those under siege with boatloads of supplies. He also transported soldiers and arms between the land and the island to stop the enemy from passing until the natives finally stopped fighting. Captain João Gonçalves then arrived from the West Indies, and there were a lot of celebrations. The natives held him as highly regarded as Pedro Lopes de Sousa while he was there. They called him *the old captain* and father of Pedro Lopes, and, in truth, he appeared that way because of the zeal with which he served and sustained the captaincy. He did not allow anyone to injure the natives but rather displayed kindness to all of them. As a result, they were so contented and servile that of their own accord they offered to work for the whites and till their fields for little or nothing. This was especially true one year in Paraíba when there was a famine and they came to work for the whites in their homes and serve them in exchange for food. As a result, there was no white man in this captaincy, as poor as he might be, that did not have twenty or thirty of these negros to serve him as slaves and wealthy whites had entire native villages.

What can I say about the trade they conduct? For a scythe, a knife, or a comb they trade loads of chickens, monkeys, parrots, honey, wax, and cotton string. Even the poor have these things!

Still today the old people call this a golden age, and it lasted as long as the "Old Captain" was alive. When he died, others came to destroy what had been created. They initiated so many problems and vexations for the poor natives on their own lands and villages that the natives began to rebel. This included those who sided with us in friendship and rejected the French. Had it not been for some others from the coast, those in the interior would never have allowed them to join them nor would they have traded with them. Afterward some of them joined them, and we conducted so much warfare against them that the residents began to feel it personally and it impacted their estates. This impacted the donatary as well when he had many losses and no gains. In the end, the king took a large part of the captaincy, which is a large part of Paraíba, since he liberated it from his enemies at the royal expense and that of his vassals, as we shall see in book 4.

CHAPTER 13

The Lands and Captaincy That King D. João III Awarded to João de Barros

At the edge of the twenty-five leagues of land of the captaincy of Itamaracá, which the king awarded to Pero Lopes de Sousa, the king awarded João de Barros, head factor in the Casa da Índia, fifty leagues of coastline.[1] In order for him and his friends to profit from this, he organized a fleet of ten ships with Fernand Álvares de Andrade, the chief treasurer of Portugal, and Aires da Cunha, who acted as captain of this expedition. With them he sent two of his sons, and together they numbered some nine hundred men. They brought with them everything they would need for the journey and to establish their new town and left Lisbon in 1535. However, they lost their way in the currents and the winds, and the ships went ashore in Maranhão and were lost in the shoals.

Many people survived this shipwreck. Together with the sons of João
de Barros, they settled on an island, at that time known as the Island of
the Cows, but now known as São Luís. They made peace with the natives
who lived there at that time, the Tapuia, trading for supplies and other
necessities. These peaceful relations were such that some Portuguese had
children with the Tapuia. This peace was not only because they grow
beards, which they discovered later. Their descendants still have them
today, like their fathers and grandfathers, but the peace came from the
love they have for the Portuguese. This love is so strong that the Tapuia
do not want to have peace with any other natives or the French, saying
that these were not real *perós* (a term they use for the Portuguese, which
seems to originate from someone named Pedro). Even in 1614 when our
people entered Maranhão, the natives made peace with them as soon as
they saw them, saying these were the *perós* they had hoped would come
and from which they are descended.

However, the lands the king awarded to João de Barros were not Maranhão, as some believed, but rather those lands beginning at the Paraíba
River bordering those belonging to Pero Lopes de Sousa. If he had been
awarded Maranhão and his children and the other survivors arrived there
and found the land so benevolent and peaceful, why would they not have
established a settlement?

This is established because all the captaincies awarded at that time were
contiguous and these donataries were in the order stated in the preceding
chapters.

It will be confirmed in the next chapter that Maranhão was awarded
to Luís de Melo da Silva, who discovered it. The king should not give
something to someone when he has already given it to someone else.

Even João de Barros in the first *Década*,[2] book 6, first chapter, where
he discusses his captaincy, does not mention Maranhão. He only says that
in the division of the province of Santa Cruz, which is commonly called
Brazil, King D. João III awarded him one [a captaincy]. This captaincy
cost him a great deal to outfit a fleet, headed by Aires da Cunha, etc., and
the fleet (as we have said) was wrecked and lost in Maranhão. And he
says, he set out in other ships to seek his sons and this left him in such
poverty and debt that he could not settle his lands. Now these belong to
His Majesty, by whose orders and finances they were conquered and the
native Potiguará peoples were won over.

CHAPTER 14

The Lands and Captaincy of Maranhão That
King D. João III Awarded to Luís de Melo da Silva

Maranhão has a huge bay facing the ocean. Its mouth opens to the north at two and a quarter degrees south latitude. It lies between Pereá Point to the east and Cumá to the west. In the middle is the island of São Luís, which is twenty leagues long and seven or eight wide. This is where Aires da Cunha and the sons of João de Barros camped after the shipwreck as mentioned in the previous chapter. This island sticks out of the bay like a tongue with Araçuagi Point in the north toward the mouth. There are many other islands in this bay, and the largest of these is six leagues long. Five rivers empty into this bay with lots of water and all are navigable. They are the Monim, the Itapucuru, the Mearim, the Pinaré, which they say begins near Peru, and the Maracu, which originates from many large lakes.

All of these rivers have very good water and fish and are bordered by excellent lands with many different woods, much fruit, and good hunting. Because of this, there are many natives living there.

At the time that Brazil was being discovered, Luís de Melo da Silva, the son of the captain of the fort in Elvas, came to explore Brazil on a caravel sailing along the coast. He was looking for a good captaincy to request from the king. Not being able to sail past Pernambuco, he became lost in bad weather and ocean currents, and he entered Maranhão, which he liked very much. He learned the language of the natives. Later, on the island of Margarita, he heard some soldiers, who had been with Francisco de Orellana, claim they had seen some impressive sights and that there were many things made of gold and silver in the lands of the interior.[1]

Motivated by this news, Luís de Melo went to the king in Portugal to request that captaincy in order to conquer and settle it. Once it was awarded to him, he got organized in Lisbon and departed with three naus and two caravels. Once he arrived in Maranhão, he lost these and most of the people on board to the shoals in the bay. He escaped danger in one caravel with some others and eighteen men from the island of Santo Domingo who arrived in a little boat. Among these men was my father, who is now with God in his glory. When he was a young man, he fled his stepmother, and since he was from the Alentejo, just like the captain, a descendent of the Palhas family, with a few beans to sustain him for the voyage, he left for Maranhão and later for here, Bahia, where he married and had me and other sons and daughters.

After Luís de Melo had been in Portugal, he left for India where he accomplished many valiant deeds and returned to Portugal a very wealthy man with a desire to return to this undertaking. He ended his trip aboard the nau *São Francisco*, which disappeared with no further news. There were no more Portuguese who administered Maranhão, since the French tried to make inroads there, as we shall see in book 5.

Now that we are at the end of this book, I should tell you two things: The first is that I did not list the captaincies or towns here in chronological order but rather organized them according to their location, from the south to the north. I will not do this in the following books; I instead will follow a chronological order. Second, I did not mention the captaincies of Rio de Janeiro, Sergipe, Paraíba, and others. These were conquered later and settled at the royal expense by the king's captains and governors-general, and they will have their places when we discuss them in the following books.

BOOK 3
The History of Brazil from the Time Tomé de Sousa Governed to the Arrival of Manuel Teles Barreto (1549–80)

CHAPTER 1
How the King Again Ordered the Colonization of Bahia by Tomé de Sousa, the First Governor General of Brazil

After the king became aware of the death of Francisco Pereira Coutinho, he decided to establish a city in Bahia. It had many qualities for colonization: the fertility of the land, its good breezes, and excellent water. It was also in the middle of the other captaincies; it would be like a heart in the middle of a body from which all would receive assistance and be governed.

In order to make this possible, he ordered a large fleet prepared with everything needed for this undertaking and appointed Tomé de Sousa, one of his counselors, as the captain-major in charge and governor of the entire state of Brazil. He gave him powerful jurisdiction in written instructions, ending the powers awarded earlier to the donataries. He had given them too much authority in both civil and criminal matters, as noted in chapter 2 of book 2. The king now ordered that criminal cases before the donataries had to be heard by the head justice of Brazil, and that in civil cases, the highest fine could be 20,000 réis. He further ordered that the head justice had the right to enter the lands of the donataries to preside in court and could review old cases and hear new ones. This was not done previously. In order for this to happen, he appointed Doctor Pedro Borges, who had been a magistrate in Elvas, to serve as the head justice, António Cardoso de Barros as the head of the treasury, and Diogo Moniz Barreto as the judge of the town they would be building.[1] These people were joined by some of the king's servants who were appointed to other posts, six Jesuit fathers to teach and convert the natives, and other regular clergy. They departed Lisbon on February 2, 1549. They also brought with them some married men and one thousand soldiers, among them four hundred convicts.

All these people arrived in Bahia on March 29 of this same year, and they left the ships at the old town that Francisco Pereira had built at the entrance by the sandbar. This was where Diogo Álvares Caramuru was found, who was discussed in chapter 7 of book 2. He escaped death because of the daughter of a native leader who was in love with him. After that, he fled in a French ship loaded with brazilwood. The ship had just set sail and he swam out to it. When they arrived in France, she was baptized with the name *Luísa Álvares.*[2] They married and then returned with the French in the same ship, and Caramuru promised the French that his in-laws would load it with brazilwood.

Then they returned to Bahia and cast anchor in the Paraguaçu River next to the Island of the French; they cut their anchor line and drifted along the coast.[3] Everything they had with them had been taken, and all of them were killed and eaten by the natives. Luísa Álvares, who was their relative, told them those people were their enemies and only her husband was their friend. She said they had returned to find them, and they wanted to live with them, which they did until the arrival of Tomé de Sousa and for many years afterward. I met her after her husband had died. She was a very honorable widow and someone who frequently made gifts to the poor and did other charitable works. She founded the Hermitage of Nossa Senhora da Graça next to the old town on a spacious site and petitioned His Holiness to obtain indulgences for its frequent pilgrims. She awarded the administration of this chapel to the Benedictine fathers, who visit it every Saturday to say Mass.

She died at a very old age. In her lifetime, she saw all her daughters and some granddaughters marry the most important Portuguese in this land, which they richly deserved as descendants of Diogo Álvares Caramuru. It is out of respect for him that I have made this digression. It was he who held on to this land for all those years and through his efforts that Governor Tomé de Sousa was able to make peace with the natives and have them serve the whites.

In this manner, Tomé de Sousa built, populated, and fortified the city, which he named *Salvador* in the place where it is located today. It is one and a half leagues from the entrance to the bay, where the port is calmer and provides more shelter for ships. Men from his time said (and I met some) that Tomé de Sousa was the first to crush stones for plastering and that he helped carry the rafters and lumber for the houses on his shoulders. He thus showed everyone that he was good company and amiable (very necessary traits for those who govern our cities).

With this, everyone delighted in his work and each one practiced the skills he possessed. Some worked at agriculture while others raised cattle, and they practiced all manner of skills, even those that were new to them. All this caused the land to greatly prosper, and it was accelerated by the money the king spent so freely. After three years of governing, he had spent 300,000 *cruzados* from the king's treasury on salaries for soldiers and officials, construction of the cathedral and the Jesuit residence, embellishments, bells, artillery, cattle, clothing, and other necessities. He did not do this to obtain his rights and taxes that were awarded to him by the Supreme Pontiff, with the obligation of supplying the churches and their ministers. It was for the pleasure in making this state grow and turning it into a great empire, as he said.

Nor did he forget that if someday it should happen that (and may God forbid it) Portugal were occupied by foreign enemies, as has happened to other kingdoms, and the king should be forced to flee with other Portuguese to another place, no land would serve him better than this one. If he were to flee to the islands [the Azores] (as they say and as D. António, the pretender to the throne, did in the year of Our Lord 1580), not only are they very small but they are very close to Portugal. Enemies could reach you there, and before you could recover, they would find you.

Even though India is a large place, it is so distant, and reaching it is so dangerous that by fleeing there all hope of returning and recapturing Portugal would be lost.

However, Brazil is so large, is located at such a safe distance, and is so easily reached that it would be very easy to come here and return when the king wished or to stay here. The people who live in the less than one hundred leagues of land that is Portugal would have plenty of room here in Brazil with more than one thousand leagues. This would become a great kingdom by having these people, for where there are bees there is honey. Here there are not just flowers but herbs and cane to reap honey and sugar. From other foreign kingdoms, merchants would come here to trade their goods that do not exist here. In the same manner, the spices from India would be closer from here and the journey shorter and easier since these are the only items they [merchants] bring to Portugal. Bread, cloth, and other similar items are not lacking in Portugal. All this esteem and high regard for Brazil ended with King D. João, who treasured it so.

CHAPTER 2
The Other Two Fleets That the King Sent to Bahia with People and Provisions

In the beginning of 1550, the king ordered another fleet with many people and a lot of supplies with Captain Simão da Gama d'Andrade at the helm of a famous old galleon.

This nobleman was very public-spirited in Salvador, and he died many years ago of inflammation and sores on his leg. In his will, he left instructions for Masses to be said for him in the Church of the Misericórdia, where he is buried with the epitaph that says, "For the great charity of Christ on the cross, here Simão da Gama Andrade is buried to be resurrected."

Bishop D. Pedro Fernandes Sardinha came on that fleet, a person of great dignity and an outstanding and eminent preacher. He brought with him four Jesuit priests to assist the six already here in teaching and converting the natives. He also brought other members of the clergy and embellishments for his cathedral.

In the next year of 1551, the king sent another fleet headed by Captain António de Oliveira Carvalhal to be the military commander of the old town. He brought with him many young ladies supported by Queen Catarina and from the Orphans' Shelter to ensure the governor found them suitable husbands. He did this by awarding some with dowries of municipal offices as well as dowries that he provided from his own estate.[1]

Tomé de Sousa was a wise and prudent man, a veteran of the wars in Africa and India. Where he had been, he had shown himself to be a valued gentleman. However, things here were so rough and he grew tired of struggling with convicts, seeing as they were not like the peach:

> That apple which once came from Persia's field,
> On alien shores, now gives a better yield.[2]

He repeatedly requested the king for permission to return to Portugal. Against this background, there is a story of something that Tomé de Sousa said (among many things that were very elegant) when this permission arrived.

It is customary here for the harbor captain to greet arriving ships and to inform the governor where they are from and what they bring. On this occasion, Tomé de Sousa had guessed that his successor as governor had arrived, and he was very happy. He asked for the good news because his wishes had now been granted, and the new governor was in the harbor. The governor responded after a few minutes, "Do you see this captain? The truth is that I wanted this very much and it made my mouth water to think of going to Portugal, but I do not know now what makes my mouth so dry that I want to spit but cannot." The captain did not respond to this, nor will I because the readers can make of it what they will.

CHAPTER 3

The Second Governor-General the King Sent to Brazil

The king had been moved by the pleas and misfortunes of Governor Tomé de Sousa, so when his three-year term ended, he sent as his successor D. Duarte da Costa. He left Lisbon in 1553 on May 8, bringing his son with him, D. Álvaro, and Father Luís da Grã, who had been the rector of a faculty at the University of Coimbra, two more priests, and four Jesuits. These included Father José de Anchieta, who later became the provincial here and who can be called the *Apostle of Brazil* because of his deeds and miracles, just as Father Saint Francis Xavier was known in India.[1]

As soon as the governor arrived, he worked hard to fortify and defend the new city of Bahia against the barbarous natives who had been restless and committed great assaults. He resolved some with prudence, while others were punished with force, killing them and capturing them in battle. The governor's son, D. Álvaro da Costa, acted as captain of these expeditions and performed very valiantly in all of them. The king did not forget to offer the governor support during his rule by sending fleets with many soldiers and settlers.

The bishop helped him as well, working without stopping in the conversion of souls to the divine cult, administering the sacraments, and all other spiritual matters, which the king wanted to promote as much as temporal matters.

However, the Devil, he who disturbs peace, began to stir up the pot, causing conflict between the heads of the church and the secular authorities. There were so many differences between them that the bishop had to leave for Portugal with his treasures; however, he never arrived because the nau was lost with those on board on the Cururuípe River, six leagues from the São Francisco River. Those lost included António Cardoso de Barros, who had been the head superintendent, two canons,[2] two honorable women, a number of noblemen, and many others, all together totaling more than one hundred people. Those who escaped with their lives from the sinking boat did not survive at the hands of the native Caité, who at that time ruled that coast. They were robbed, stripped of their clothing, and bound with cords. One by one, they were killed and eaten, except for two natives from Bahia and one Portuguese man who spoke their language.

I do not know whether this incident encouraged more discord later between the governors and the bishops. I will discuss these incidents in their appropriate places and note who is guilty if I know the reasons. I cannot state anything here other than to just note my misgivings, because I do not know the cause.

I can only tell you what I heard from people who traveled from this bay to Pernambuco and saw the location where the bishop was killed (because the road passes right by it). They said that the spot was never again covered with vegetation, unlike the surrounding lands. It is as if his blood calls to God against those who spilled it. God heard this, because afterward the people of Bahia went to war against those natives and extracted their revenge, as we shall see.

CHAPTER 4

Regarding a Ship Bound for India, Forced to Dock in Bahia during the Rule of Governor D. Duarte da Costa

During May of the second year of the governorship of D. Duarte da Costa, which was the year of Our Lord 1555, a nau bound for India, the *São Paulo,* was forced to dock in Bahia because of a lack of water. It had been in a fleet of five ships led by Captain-Major D. João de Menezes de Sequeira, and this ship was captained by António Fernandes, its owner. Many sick people arrived on that nau, and the governor ordered them sheltered in the hospital. The healthy were fed for five months while the nau's officials and those in Bahia considered the best course of action. (This included the governor and D. António de Noronha, nicknamed *o catarraz*, who was going to serve as captain of Diu.[1]) They agreed that if they left in October, they could complete the journey to India, which they did. In less than four months, they arrived in Cochin where they found the nau led by Captain-Major D. João de Menezes.[2] The next day they set sail for Goa and were very contented to bring the news of their return. Everyone feared they had been lost.[3] But in that year of 1555 they were dismayed by the news of the death of the illustrious Prince D. Luís, the Duke of Beja, supreme commander of the army of Portugal, the Lord of Serpa, Moura, Covilhã, and Almada, and governor of the priory of Crato.[4] Among his many virtues was his zeal for Christianity and military science.

There were only a few wars in which he was able to participate; however, with the knowledge that his brother-in-law, Emperor Carlos V, was going to wage war in Africa, he went to join him. He did this without permission and lacking any company because he knew that his brother, the king, would forbid this as he had done on previous occasions. However, his brother immediately gave permission for several noblemen to follow him and ordered a fleet already there to follow his orders. The captain of the fleet was António de Saldanha, and for all the money he spent, he [the king] generously repaid him. It was in this manner that a beautiful cavalry of nobles from his kingdom assisted the illustrious emperor in the conquest of Goleta and Tunis. Prince D. Luís had suggested these conquests, contrary to the opinions of many of the older veterans who told the emperor the opposite.

Our prince could not abide the slightest appearance of cowardice and forcefully insisted that the emperor change his decision to lift the siege. The others in his council wanted him to do this, but instead the emperor decided to proceed as the prince suggested. The prince fought under the emperor's banner and showed himself to be a soldier worthy to fight under such a leader. The emperor was fortunate to have the shrewd opinion of that soldier, who was like Nestor in his council and Achilles in battle.[5]

The prince was always pleasant to foreigners and kind to other Portuguese; he was generous to all, and for that he was loved and praised. He never married nor did he have children except for one out of wedlock, Lord D. António. Because his parents were not married, D. António could not be the king of Portugal, although in some places they proclaimed him king.

Also in that same year of 1555, the emperor Carlos V retired to a religious life in the Convent of S. Jerónimo de Juste. It was a healthy and comfortable place to distance himself from governing and from the troubles of this world. He left these to the very Catholic Prince D. Filipe, his son.

CHAPTER 5
Another Ship Bound for India That Cast Anchor in Bahia

In 1556 the king ordered five naus to sail to India and gave the leadership to D. Luís Fernandes de Vasconcelos who selected the nau *Santa Maria da Barca* on which to make the journey.

When all were loaded and ready to set sail, a hole large enough to sink the ship opened on the nau, and it began to take on water quickly. The officials tried to help but could not do anything because they did not know where the leak was. Seeing that time was fleeting, the king ordered the other four naus to set sail and this nau to be unloaded, which they completed in April. They quickly and completely emptied the nau and searched it from the stern to the bow without finding the leak. The fishermen of the Alfama were murmuring a lot that God allowed this to happen because the archbishop had taken away their ancient ceremonies to celebrate the fortunate Father Saint Pedro Gonçalves.[1] They take a statue of him to the fields in Xabregas accompanied by a lot of spirited dancing, offerings, and other signs of happiness and then bring him back with crowns of fresh coriander.[2] All of them dance and sing around him, accompanied by musicians.

The archbishop heard this complaint. He was good friends with the nobleman, who was disheartened because he could not make the journey that year. The bishop was also moved by the great faith and devotion shown by the fishermen and sailors for this saint. Because of this, he restored their rights to the festival as they had previously celebrated it. Meanwhile, they continued to look for the leak in the nau and use pumps and buckets to bail the water. One sailor found a hole in the keel that had been missed and needed a spike and caulking. He only covered it with tar, which they removed [and permanently fixed the hole] later. It was here that the water was entering, and they repaired it with great happiness. Then the nau was reloaded because the officials said there was still time to complete the voyage. It set sail on May 2, following its course, but along the coast of Guinea it was becalmed for seventy days. They pondered what to do, deciding to winter in Brazil because it was very late to make their way into the Indian Ocean, and they sailed for Bahia, where they arrived on August 14.

The governor, D. Duarte da Costa, received the captain-major and the others arriving on the nau, who were Luís de Melo da Silva, D. Pedro de Almeida, who was sent as the Captain of Bassein, D. Filipe de Menezes, D. Paulo de Lima, Nuno de Mendonça and Henrique de Mendonça, his brother, Jerónimo Correia Barreto, Henrique Moniz Barreto, and other nobles.[3] The governor freely wined, dined, and sheltered these people as well as all the others on board the entire time they were here.

The next year was 1557, which was very significant because of the death of Emperor Carlos V who died at the age of fifty-eight and seven months. He had abdicated his kingdoms to his son Filipe. To his brother Fernando he left the title of Holy Roman Emperor after he retired to a monastery, where he died peacefully.[4] It is also significant because of the death of King D. João, who died on June 11 at the age of fifty-five after ruling for thirty-five years.

It was in this year that the governorship of D. Duarte da Costa ended and his successor arrived.

In addition to being a loyal servant of the king, D. Duarte da Costa had another virtue, and I will not remain silent about it because it is very important for those who govern. That is, he patiently endured complaints, working to correct the problems rather than punishing those who complained. An example of this occurred one night while he was making the rounds of the city. He overheard a resident inside his home complaining about him in a very loud voice, and after he heard a good bit, he said from outside, "Gentlemen, speak softer or the governor will hear you!"

They recognized his voice and were very fearful he would punish them, but he never spoke about it, nor did he ever show them any ill will of any kind.

CHAPTER 6

Mem de Sá, the Third Governor of Brazil

D. Duarte da Costa was followed by Doctor Mem de Sá, who with good reason could be a shining example for the governors of Brazil. Not only did he have an education and will; he excelled in warfare and justice.

In 1557, he landed on shore, and the first thing he did was promote Christianity. In order to do this, he called for the leaders of the native villages around Bahia and made peace treaties with them with the conditions that they stop eating human flesh, even that of captured enemies or those killed in a *just war*.[1] He also insisted that they allow Jesuit fathers or other religious figures onto their lands to build houses where they would live. In addition, the priests would construct churches for Mass for Christians, teach the catechism, and freely preach the faith. Because of the greed of the Portuguese, some of them had captured as many natives as they could, justly or unjustly, and the governor prohibited this with severe penalties. He also ordered all those unjustly captured, who were now treated as slaves, to be set free.

He retaliated for the injuries done to the Christian natives by their neighbors and killed some of them. He asked them to turn over those who had committed murder and he would pardon the others. However, they felt so secure in their large numbers that they mocked his petition; for this, he responded in person on their lands. He killed many and burned more than sixty villages. He weakened them to the point that they sued for peace, to which he agreed, with the same conditions imposed on the others.

When he was not waging warfare, the good governor was administering justice. In addition to being the one who is honored by reigning and governing, as David says, "The king's honor loves judgment."[2] The governor was particularly keen about this role since he brought with him a special decree from the king that no new action could be taken without the governor's permission. The king had ordered this because he had learned about the many usurious transactions at that time committed by merchants selling on credit. In order to avoid exposing the usury, losing the debt, and having more penalties imposed by fines, many merchants did not take their debtors to court. They awaited payment for as long as they liked. They only pursued action against legitimate debts, which the governor immediately ordered paid. If the debtor was poor, the governor paid it himself or arranged for the creditor to wait for repayment, since it was clear that the debtor had no funds to repay him [the creditor].

In this manner, the suits ended and when Doctor Pedro Borges, the Superior Court magistrate, held a court session, there were no cases; he raised his hands to the heavens to thank God. However, this good period did not last very long because when Doctor Brás Fragoso arrived as the new Superior Court judge, he brought with him a provision that contradicted the governor's. The lawsuits and the cases of usury returned, and they were not disguised but very public. If a slave was worth twenty *milréis* paid in cash at the moment, merchants would sell him on a year's credit for forty. Because of that, they would not want to sell for ready cash but on credit, and no one was paying attention to this injustice.

CHAPTER 7

How the Governor Sent His Son Fernão de Sá to Assist Vasco Fernandes
Coutinho and How He Was Killed There by Natives

At this time, Vasco Fernandes Coutinho had been in great danger because of the natives of his captaincy of Espírito Santo. He sent word to the governor in Bahia, Mem de Sá, asking for help, which the governor provided at once, ordering five ships loaded with people, with his son, Fernão de Sá, as the leader in the galley *São Simão*. Diogo Morim the elder and Paulo Dias Adorno were the captains of the other ships.

They all arrived in Porto Seguro where the local people told them that most of the natives waging war on Vasco Fernandes were on the Cricaré River. They offered to accompany them, saying they should seek them out. Captain Diogo Álvares and Gaspar Barbosa escorted them in their caravels.

They sailed up that river for four days until they saw the native enclosures next to the water. They put the bows of the ships on land because it was high tide. The soldiers left the ships and attacked while the sailors moved the ships to the middle of the river to avoid their being stranded at low tide. The bombardiers fired the cannons from there. The fight began, which at first threw the natives into disarray; however, they regrouped with such vigor that our forces were dispersed among the enemies; cannon shots from the ships did not defend them but rather injured and killed them. The sailors turned the ships around to collect them, but they were in the deepest waters. Our forces had to swim to the ships, and the injured were on some rafts. Among the injured were the two captains Adorno and Morim, while the captain-major remained in the rear with his second lieutenant João Monge. The native forces grew larger, with people from additional villages coming to their aid, and their arrows killed the captain-major and his lieutenant.

In this manner, the life of Fernão de Sá ended after his great military deeds against a multitude of these barbarians in this fight, in others in Bahia, and elsewhere. The survivors left for Espírito Santo, where Vasco Fernandes received them in sorrow, learning of their defeat and the death of Fernão de Sá. He sent them with as many people as he could gather to fight some natives that he had almost surrounded. These natives had rebelled and killed some of our people, among them Bernardo Pimentel the elder, whom they killed while he was entering a house.

Once this was done, they returned to São Vicente and then to Bahia where the governor refused to receive them, knowing how they had left his son to die. Even though they were not guilty, we should not blame a father for being so distraught by the death of such a son.

CHAPTER 8
The Arrival of the French in Rio de Janeiro and the
War Waged by the Governor

Rio de Janeiro is located at twenty-three degrees below the Tropic of Capricorn, and it is inaccurately called a *river*, but in actuality it is a bay where the sea enters through a small opening that can easily be defended with artillery. Inside this is a bay or gulf, where many rivers enter, and there are almost forty islands. The largest of these islands are populated, and the smaller ones grace the landscape or serve as ports where ships can shelter.

These features and many others about this river and bay along with the fertility of the land made the area worthy for settlement when the rest of Brazil was being colonized. This area was within the donatary awarded to Pero de Góis, who did not confront the natives as we said in chapter 3 of book 2. Either for this reason or because of some unknown misfortune, it was ready to be colonized until Nicolas Villegaignon, a nobleman from France, Knight of the Order of São João, was informed by the French to go there to trade with the Tapuia. He was determined to colonize the area. In order to do this, he organized a fleet in which he came with many soldiers, entering Rio de Janeiro in the year 1556. He fortified the entrance and sought out the natives, making alliances and friendships with them. For better defense, on one of the islands in the bay he constructed a fort with stone, brick, and plaster. The natives volunteered to help him, while additional assistance came from France daily.

We were into the year 1559 when Queen Catarina ruled because of the death of her husband, King D. João. Her grandson, the future king D. Sebastião, at that time was not more than five years old. When the queen became aware of what had happened in Rio de Janeiro, she wrote Governor Mem de Sá, pressing him to attend to this task of the French presence, sending a well-provisioned fleet to assist him with it. With this fleet and some other naus the governor could amass, he, the leading Portuguese in Bahia, and as many soldiers as they could recruit, both whites and natives, departed for Rio de Janeiro. This was in the year of Our Lord 1560. After destroying the forces blocking the entrance to the bay, they entered it, and captured a French nau. From this, they learned that Villegaignon was not there; he had been called to Malta but had appointed his nephew as captain of the fort. The governor wrote the following to him:

The king of Portugal, my Lord, knowing that Villegaignon your uncle has usurped this land, has complained to the king of France, who responded by saying that "if he is there, make war on him and throw him out because he is not there with my authority." Since I do not find Villegaignon here and you are in his place, I admonish and demand by God's will and by that of your king and mine that you immediately leave this land that is not yours and that you leave in peace without learning of the injuries that occur in war.

The young man responded that it was not his decision to whom the land of Rio de Janeiro belonged but his duty to do as his uncle Lord Villegaignon had ordered. This was to maintain and defend his fort, which he had to do even if it cost him his life and that of many others. He further said that he did not want to kill but rather live in peace.

This dialog took ten or twelve days while our fleet prepared for war, and once they received this answer, they responded with artillery and shots from harquebuses aimed at the (seemingly) impregnable fort. While others were engaged in the heat of combat, Manuel Coutinho, a mulatto,

Afonso Martins Diablo, and other brave Portuguese soldiers scaled a section of the fort that appeared impossible to scale. They entered the castle
and unexpectedly took the enemy's gunpowder.

The French were disheartened by the loss of their gunpowder and the
unexpected daring of the Portuguese. They abandoned the castle at midnight, taking with them all the arms it contained. They retreated to their
naus, and some of them returned to their homeland. Others remained
with the Tamoios (this is the name of the local natives) to wage war again
and to show they were right to fight the Portuguese. They also wanted to
continue their lucrative trade with the natives.

Having obtained such an illustrious victory, the governor dismantled
the fort since he could not leave anyone there to defend it and to colonize the area. Many people had died in the fighting. He sent his nephew
Estácio de Sá in a captured French nau to inform Queen D. Catarina of
what had happened.

CHAPTER 9

*How the Governor Returned to Bahia from Rio de Janeiro and the Fortune of a
Ship Bound for India That Provisioned There*

The governor returned to Bahia from Rio de Janeiro in June of that same
year of 1560 and continued governing the region. His presence and guid-
ance were so sorely needed that the few times it was necessary for him to
visit his sugar mill in Sergipe, he left at night and had a servant wait on
the stairs and tell anyone asking for him that he was busy. This was not a
lie because wherever he was, he was busy. He did this so that his absence
would not cause any disruptions. Even though the mill was eight leagues
away from the city, he was not detained there for very long.

In that year of 1560, the nau *São Paulo* sought safe harbor in Bahia as
it had done previously at the time of Governor D. Duarte da Costa when
its captain was António Fernandes as we said in chapter 4 of this book.
This time the ship's captain was Rui de Melo da Câmara. The captain
understood that if he spent the winter here, it would add seven or eight
months to his journey, and the water and sea worms would soon weaken
the wood on his nau. He called a meeting with his pilots and those pilots
on shore along with the governor. They discussed whether there was still
time to continue their voyage and winter in India. The collective opinion

was that there was sufficient time, if they left in September and sailed into the northerly latitudes in the Indian Ocean to find Sumatra. That way, they could return from there in February with the monsoons that brought naus from Malacca and China to Goa. Taking all the supplies they needed from the city, they left on September 15.

Encountering good weather, they reached sight of the Cape of Good Hope by the end of November, and their journey continued to the island of Sumatra with mild winds until January 20, the day of blessed Saint Sebastian. It was nightfall when they found themselves running too close to the land because of the strong current. As hard as they tried to move away from the land, God determined this was where the nau would run aground with all on board. In the morning, they launched a little boat and landed it without knowing anything about the local people there, who were miserly and so used to trading that they tried right away to sell them some things.

But this did not happen, and there were seven hundred men from the nau, all in such good health and armed that they could cross the entire island. Right away, they constructed some huts to provide shelter, and they removed supplies from the nau: wine, olive oil, and everything else they could. Then they disassembled the nau, removing all the nails, wood, rope, and everything else they could use, and outfitted two boats along with the little boat. Everyone worked with great zeal and speed, working as blacksmiths, timber cutters, carpenters, and all the other trades as if they had always done these. Within no time, they launched these in the sea, stocked an ample water supply, and then gathered all the falconets and minions. The little ships could not carry bigger pieces since they were more or less like pontoons.

One of these pontoons was led by Diogo Pereira de Vasconcelos, a nobleman traveling with his wife, D. Francisca Sardinha, one of the most beautiful women of her day. The other pontoon was led by Rui de Melo, captain of the nau, and the third was commanded by António de Reyfoyos, a very honorable gentleman who had been sent as the captain of Quilon.[1] No more than 170 men could fit in each of the ships, which left 170 who could not be carried,[2] so it was decided they would walk on land within sight of the little boats so the men on them could help those on land if needed.

They divided the pistols among themselves and began walking along the coastline with the little pontoons always in view. As soon as it began to get dark, they found a place to rest and put the pontoons ashore. They did the same at mealtimes. In this manner, they continued walking without encountering any big problems. After a few days, they spied four ships that were doing their best to flee. One of our pontoons shot at them with a falconet, and the shot whistled past their ears. The crews were so fearful and startled that they jumped into the water and swam to shore. This left the ships loaded with palm flour (which is the main staple of all those islands), which supplied our forces. Those who had been walking boarded these ships and were more comfortable.

They were now at three degrees south latitude, and they gathered at a beautiful river that they encountered. The crews left their ships to enjoy themselves and sleep there several nights. They felt as relaxed and secure as if the land were theirs. Even Diogo Pereira de Vasconcelos and his wife left the ship. When the Manancabos, who are the people there, saw her beauty as well as her magnificent clothes, they wanted to take her to their king. That is what they did one night when the group stopped and they killed seventy people and kidnapped D. Francisca Sardinha. The ship's master did heroic things to defend her until they killed him. Diogo Pereira saved a daughter of his, named D. Constança, who later married Tomé de Melo de Castro, and other women whom he sheltered on his ship. He was disheartened about this misfortune that had occurred because of his excessive confidence.

From there, they left and moved along the coastline, which was very open. They were much more cautious because that disaster made them wary of the locals. They then spied the Sunda Straits and went to the city of Patani, where they found four Portuguese naus led by Captain Pero Barreto Rolim, which were loading pepper.[3] All these people were welcomed and were divided among the naus and given food and shelter. Some of them went to China, where Pero Barreto Rolim was headed by order of the viceroy, D. Constantino.

CHAPTER 10
How the Tamoios of Rio de Janeiro Afflicted the People of the Captaincy of São Vicente and How the Governor Ordered a Second War against Them

Seeing that they were freed from the war waged by Governor Mem de Sá, the Tamoios fortified their positions in Rio de Janeiro and went along the coast all the way to São Vicente, attacking the newly converted natives, imprisoning, killing, and eating as many of them as they found.

These troubles lasted for two years with no force able to stop the boldness of the insolent barbarians, which grew daily with the help of the French. It escalated to the point that they were not content with the evil inflicted on other natives but also threatened all the residents of São Vicente with cruel warfare on land and a fleet of canoes to fight them at sea.

Father Manoel da Nóbrega, the first leader of the Jesuit order in Brazil, wanted to remedy this great evil.[1] As a result, he set forth to understand the motivations of the barbarians in order to pacify them and have them live in harmony with us.

In this effort, he took with him his companion, Brother José de Anchieta, and António Luís, a secular man. They left on a nau owned by Francisco Adorno, an illustrious man from Genova, a very well-known man in that land, and a wealthy and devoted friend of the Jesuits.

When they spied the Portuguese nau, thinking it might have come to fight, the natives ran to their canoes and came out to meet them, armed with arrows. However, Brother José de Anchieta, in a brief and loving talk that he delivered in their language, calmed them and blessed the timing of his arrival and later gave thanks for other blessings. It was largely the many sermons and the example he set in the three months he lived among them, and the two months he was with Father Nóbrega, that allowed him to pacify the natives before he returned to São Vicente. The peace applied to all except for one group that disagreed with the others. Bolstered by the firearms they obtained from the French, this group continued the war against the Portuguese.

Queen D. Catarina had predicted these events when she read the letter from Governor Mem de Sá describing his victory in Rio de Janeiro. Even though she was grateful and felt she had been well served by him, she still thought it strange that he had dismantled the fort and that no one remained there to defend and colonize the area. She ordered that he do that immediately to prevent the enemy from creating a base threatening all of Brazil. Cardinal D. Henrique, who ruled the kingdom with her, wrote to him saying the same thing. In order to accomplish this, they sent the governor's nephew Estácio de Sá with the news, a fleet of six caravels, and the galleon *São João* and a nau from the India run called *Santa Maria a Nova*. The governor added as many ships as he could to these. He wanted to go in person, but the townspeople did not agree, so he sent his nephew in the year 1563.

Going with his nephew were the Superior Court magistrate Brás Fragoso and Paulo Dias Adorno, commander of the Order of James, in a small galley with ten oars on each side and other captains. When they all reached Rio de Janeiro, they found a French nau there fleeing upriver, but our forces chased it. The first to reach it was the galley led by Paulo Dias Adorno, and with him were Duarte Martins Mourão and Melchior de Azevedo. After that, Brás Fragoso arrived as did the others. When they boarded the French nau, they found a lot of bread, wine, and meat, which they took to the flagship *Santa Maria a Nova* and the galleon. The leader of this expedition, Estácio de Sá, had made António da Costa its captain.

However, there is no good thing in this life that is not diluted. One morning three little boats of ours were collecting water along the shore of the Carioca River, and nine enemy canoes ambushed them from where they were hiding. Three canoes attacked each of our boats. On the boat from the *Santa Maria a Nova*, they killed the boatswain and his mate and another two sailors.[2] On the little boat from the galleon, they wounded Cristóvão d'Aguiar, the young man, with seven arrows and another seven men, and they captured them and the boat, but Paulo Dias Adorno hurried back to his galley to their rescue and fired a shot from the falconet, which made them abandon the lifeboat.

After the dead were buried on an island, Estácio de Sá called the captains to a meeting, and they agreed that, if they went to São Vicente to locate canoes and friendly natives, they would be better able to wage war against these barbarous enemies.

They left one morning with the captured French nau leading and with a large caravel belonging to Domingos Fernandes from Ilhéus. At the sandbar, they encountered many canoes filled with native enemies and Frenchmen mixed together. When the enemy reached the large caravel, they made a hole in it with axes and sank it, while killing four men and injuring Domingos Fernandes with six arrows. He swam for the nau, which the natives also reached. The enemy also reached it and made a hole in it. However, an Indian from India, a servant of Brás Fragoso who was traveling on that nau with his master, was under a cover and killed a Frenchman through that very hole. With that, or perhaps in fear of the fleet arriving from behind, the enemy left immediately. The nau did as well, making its way to São Vicente, where they told the captain-major and everyone else what had happened.

At that time, the village of São Paulo, which is in the captaincy of São Vicente, was at war with the natives, and the village was in danger of being overrun. Estácio de Sá came with many people to assist them, and when the natives saw this, they immediately asked for peace. He negotiated a lasting peace with them.

Meanwhile, Captains Jorge Ferreira and Paulo Dias arrived with the canoes and natives, and as soon as they did, they went to Cananéia. Once they stocked the ships with all the provisions they needed, they again left for Rio de Janeiro in the year 1564, on the day of Saint Sebastian, whom they adopted as their patron for this journey.[3]

They entered Rio at the beginning of March, anchored in the bay, went on shore, and made some straw shacks where they could live. This was where the old part of the city is now, at the foot of a rocky outcrop that reaches to the clouds known as *Pão de Açucar.* They fortified the site as best they could with bulwarks and trenches of wood and earth from which they went forth to fight the barbarians. God helped them there for two years so that in almost all of their encounters they emerged victorious and those injured by the deadly enemy arrows healed quickly. Others not wearing armor and wounded in the chest by shot from a French harquebus felt nothing as if they had been wearing a breastplate and the gunshot fell to their feet.

The Tamoios were tired of such a prolonged war and disheartened by their lack of success, because it normally ended with their enslavement. The natives decided to focus all their strength on one battle directed by the French, and, without a doubt, the battle was designed to achieve its intent. However, Divine Providence was on the side of the righteous.

The Tamoios had added a number of new canoes to their usual fleet to total 180. These new canoes were secretly made far from where the Portuguese ships were anchored. They made a trap with this fleet of canoes, hidden in an inlet made by the sea. From that spot, a small number of them set forth and our general ordered five of the nine new canoes that he brought from São Vicente to fight them. Our allied natives were tired of warfare and had already set out in the other four canoes.

The Tamoios had not really begun the fight before they turned their backs, which was their plan to catch us. Our forces boldly followed them into their trap where the remaining enemy canoes came forth and quickly surrounded our forces on all sides. However, even this did not cause the Portuguese to lose their courage. Rather, they resisted valiantly, aided by Divine Favor, who knows how to extract success from events that appear adverse. We saw this here when the gunpowder in one of our canoes caught fire and singed several of the enemies who were aboard. With all their noise as well as that from the exploding gunpowder, the wife of the head Tamoio native let forth with screams and yelling, frightening the others. Her husband was the first to flee and went with her; all the others followed. This left our people free to return home and give thanks to God for such a large gift of freeing them from such a great danger with the voice of a weak woman. Later, those same enemies said that was not the case. They saw a strange warrior, notably large and beautiful, boldly jumping among their canoes, and this filled them with fear. Based on this story, the Portuguese believe it was the blessed Saint Sebastian, whom they had adopted as their guardian in this struggle.

CHAPTER 11
What Occurred on Jorge de Albuquerque's Journey
from Pernambuco to Portugal

At this same time, there was no lack of warfare in Pernambuco because of that victory the natives of Cape Saint Agostinho achieved over Jerónimo de Albuquerque, whom we mentioned in chapter 11 of the preceding book. The natives became so arrogant and aggressive that they never ceased to attack the slaves the Portuguese had on their lands and plantations. They especially attacked other natives in the bush who were allied with us and whom they considered their mortal enemies. The natives living around the São Francisco River did the same, attacking the boats going there to trade. At first encounter, they exchanged goods with the Portuguese and showed friendship, but in secret they captured several Portuguese who were off guard, killed them, and ate them.

Queen D. Catarina, who ruled Portugal, was aware of all of this and was just as prudent sending help for these wars as she was for those in Rio de Janeiro. She ordered the immediate departure of Duarte Coelho de Albuquerque, who inherited that captaincy, to go to their aid. He understood that he would need the help of his brother, Jorge de Albuquerque, and he asked the queen to order this, which she did. Jorge obeyed, both to serve the queen and the king, her grandson, as well as to please his brother and help him.

As soon as they arrived in Pernambuco in 1560 and Duarte Coelho de Albuquerque was able to take charge of his captaincy, he immediately called a council of the local leaders. They all decided that their general would be Jorge de Albuquerque. He accepted the position and began at once to attack the natives at Cape São Agostinho. Many of the natives were dead or wounded after these encounters, and the whites began to feel free to live on their farms, such as those along the São Francisco River. It was there that he went with his brother. That military campaign lasted five years, and they suffered hunger and thirst many times. He also lost a lot of blood from many enemy arrows. He reached a point where he was more disgusted with the internal quarrels of his friends, the Portuguese, than with these natives; he decided to return again to Portugal. He boarded a new nau of two hundred tons named *Santo António,* which was loaded at the port in Recife and destined for Lisbon with André Rodrigues as the master and Álvaro Marinho as the pilot.

Once the nau was loaded, it left on Wednesday, May 16, 1566.[1] It was not quite past the reef when the wind died. The situation became difficult because the tidal currents were emptying the bay and they pulled the nau to where it was grounded and four waves washed over it. They were in danger of losing the nau if the waves had been bigger. In order to help them, many lifeboats and other ships quickly set out and saved all the people and goods.

Even after it had been unloaded, it was not possible to free the grounded ship without cutting the masts. The ship was forced to return to port to be repaired and reloaded, which took a month and a half, until June 29, the day of Saints Peter and Paul. Then it was ready to depart with its entire company, in spite of friends who had predicted all along that the voyage would not be a success. It was one of the worst and most dangerous voyages that the sailors had ever seen. At a stop at the Azores on Monday, September 3, while the pilot was taking the sighting, he spotted a French pirate nau armed and in good condition as they usually are. Our ship was defenseless, with just a falconet and a small piece of artillery. The sailors on our ship decided to surrender to the French.

To this, Jorge de Albuquerque responded that God would never desire or allow the nau on which he was traveling to surrender without fighting or attempting to defend itself as best it could. For that to happen, everyone needed to pitch in and assist in the fight. With the help of Our Lord, with just the falconet and small artillery piece they possessed, they hoped to defend themselves. However, since the nau was so unprepared for war and the others were of such weak hearts, Jorge de Albuquerque thought that no one on board would help, other than the seven men who offered to do so. With their help and against the opinions of the others, they began to shoot the little cannon, their harquebuses, and arrows at the French ship. This lasted for nearly three days until the ship's captain and the pilot saw the great damage inflicted both on their nau and on those aboard from the French artillery and gunfire. Jorge de Albuquerque was not going to hand the ship over, and immediately ordered the sails lowered and began to shout at the Frenchmen boarding the nau. Some seventeen Frenchmen had come on board astern armed with their weapons drawn, with their swords, shields, and pistols. Without giving any answers or the Portuguese being able to stop them, they took command. When they realized that there was only a little cannon and some artillery pieces on board, they were very surprised and were even more so when they were told about the handful of crew members who fought them.

When the French captain heard that Jorge de Albuquerque was the one who defended the nau all that time, he came up to him and said, "I am not surprised at your strength since all good soldiers have this, but I am surprised at your audacity of defending an unarmed nau with such few crew members and few military supplies. But do not grieve. Because you are a good soldier, I will be a good companion."

And the captain was, and he would not eat until Jorge de Albuquerque had eaten first; and he had him sit at the head of his table. One day, the captain asked Jorge de Albuquerque to give a blessing in the manner of the Portuguese, and he did, making the sign of the cross, as we normally do. When he did this, some of the Lutherans present reprimanded him and he, reproached but not defeated, gave the blessing saying that he had to embrace the sign of the cross as long as he lived and with it he hoped to save the souls of all his enemies. After that, he asked the captain for permission to refrain from eating with them and to eat in his room. Even though the captain was displeased with this, he gave his permission, and he sometimes ate with him.

The nau was now at forty-three degrees north latitude, and it was a Wednesday, September 12; suddenly the worst windstorm ever seen hit them, and the nau lost its rudder, sails, and masts and was almost level with the water.[2] When everyone realized the great danger they were in, they were shocked and beside themselves, fearing this would be the last day of their lives. This fear drew them to a Jesuit father on board by the name of Álvaro de Lucena. They went to him to give their confessions, and afterward they all asked each other for forgiveness. Then they all kneeled to ask for mercy from Our Lord, which those French who had remained on our nau did as well. Their ship had disappeared as soon as the storm started. The Frenchmen asked for forgiveness from the Portuguese, saying it was because of their sins the storm had come. They asked the Portuguese to pray to God for them because they were at death's door; everyone could see the condition of the nau.

However, Jorge de Albuquerque began to speak in a loud voice, urging one and then another to do his part to help. Some manned the pump while others emptied the water from the deck. He said he hoped for the divine intercession of Our Lady, the Virgin, which would save them from their current danger. After he had said that, everyone saw a great shining in the middle of the extreme darkness around them and sank to his knees. They asked the Virgin for help and for mercy from God, which caused the storm to abate. Also, right away, the French nau appeared, and it was also very damaged but not so heavily that it could not provide rigging, sails, and supplies for us, but they did not want to. They unloaded some supplies, took their people, and left for France. They left the Portuguese only two bags of spoiled sea biscuit, a bit of spoiled ale, to which our men added a small container they had, two *canadas* of wine, one flask of *agua de flor*, a few coconuts, some handfuls of cassava war flour, and six slices of manatee.[3] Jorge de Albuquerque distributed this to thirty-odd men during the remainder of their voyage. He ordered them to make a sail from some napkins and towels they found on the nau, which they added to a small sail the French gave them. From two oars, they made a yardarm, and on the base of the main mast they attached a piece of wood two *braças* high and made some rigging from pieces that remained and some rope and cord tied to cloth. Only one nail held the rudder in place, and they attached some cords to make it work.

In this manner, they continued their voyage, asking the Mother of God to be their guide. They had no compass or astrolabe to use since the French had taken everything. She miraculously guided them to her church of Pena between the Berlenga Islands and Sintra.[4] The next day they were very close to Cape Rocha, and the nau was heading for the coast. A caravel passed by headed to Pederneira, and they asked the men on board to help them for the death and passion of Our Lord, saying they would be well paid if they picked them up and took them to land.[5] They responded by saying that they worshiped Jesus Christ but could not spare any time on their voyage. They left without showing any piety or perhaps because of fear of what appeared to them to be a ghost nau. Never before had they seen a nau in such unnavigable condition as the wreck in which these people sailed.

However, others on their way to Atouguia were not afraid or so cruel to ignore them after their first shouts (which was a miracle because they were very distant), and they towed the nau to Cascais at sundown.[6] Prince D. Henrique, the cardinal, ruled Portugal at that time, and he ordered the ship moved upriver in front of the Church of São Paulo. That way, all could see how the many prayers to God had saved those who sailed on it from the numerous dangers they faced.

And so, even though this voyage forms such a part of the history of Brazil that I am writing, because it is a starting point and comes from a captain from these parts who suffered on this journey, I beg those who read this chapter to give the Lord the same grace and prayer and maintain the same firm faith so he can save them from danger.

CHAPTER 12

How Governor Mem de Sá Returned to Rio de Janeiro and
Founded the City of Saint Sebastian de Rio de Janeiro and the Other Things
He Did There until Returning to Bahia

Of course, Governor Mem de Sá was not idle in Bahia, and the thoughts of events in Rio de Janeiro had not left him. Putting aside everything else, he prepared a fleet and, with Bishop D. Pedro Leitão, prepared to visit the captaincies in the south. All these at that time were in the bishop's diocese, and with all the splendor this city could muster, they set sail and soon arrived in Rio de Janeiro. On Saint Sebastian's Day, January 20,

1567, they finished expelling the enemy from the bay and followed them into their lands. They established their authority over the people and destroyed two places the French had fortified. One of these was a village of a native leader named Ibura-guaçu-mirim, which means *little large stick.* They wounded his nephew Estácio de Sá with a deadly arrow shot, which killed him.

Being able to relax and put warfare aside, the governor selected the location for a new city, which he ordered fortified with four castles. At the entrance to the bay, he ordered two more. It was called the *City of Saint Sebastian,* not only because it was the name of the king, but in gratitude for the assistance the saint had offered in the victory on his saint's day two years before. That was when Estácio de Sá had left São Vicente for Rio de Janeiro and started the war, asking for the saint's help. The Portuguese clearly recognized his assistance in the naval battle with the canoes as well as on other dangerous occasions.

In memory of that victory of the battle of the canoes, each year they reenact it in that bay on Saint Sebastian's Day. It is a mock battle with canoes and a lot of yelling from the natives who row and pretend to fight. It is really a sight to be seen.

The site that Mem de Sá selected for the city of Saint Sebastian was on the summit of a mountain, which could easily be defended from enemies. Later, when there was a peace, the town grew down to the valley along the sea and the beach became the main street. When Afonso de Albuquerque was captain-major, one morning they found a dead whale there in front of the door of the convent of Carmo. It had washed up overnight. It is here also that the canoes dock, coming from the lands and farms of the nearby residents. Each one comes ashore near the front door of the owner's house and unloads. That way they do not need carts as they do for those houses on the hillside. If the main church and the Jesuit church were not up there, the residents would not go up there year-round. This is especially true for the women. Because of these churches, some people live up there.

Once the city was founded by Governor Mem de Sá on this hill, he ordered the appointment of officials and ministers for the military, justice, and treasury. Because there had been some merchants who came with the fleet, and among other goods they brought some pipes of wine, the governor ordered that it be sold as it was in taverns. The merchants wanted to sell a *canada* for an excessive price. He [the governor] cut off the top in anger and said, "Yes, but this will now be the *quartilho*."[1] That is how it was, and even today where they craft the measurements, they are so large that the largest earthen vessel does not hold more than five *quartilhos.*

Among the first Frenchmen to come to Rio de Janeiro in the company of Nicolas Villegaignon, whom we discussed in chapter 9 of this book, was a heretical Calvinist named João Bouller. He fled to the captaincy of São Vicente, where the Portuguese welcomed him thinking he was a Catholic. They included him in their conversations believing this, since he was very eloquent and fluent in Spanish, Latin, and Greek and he knew something of Hebrew and was versed in some sacred literature. With all this, in his own way, he disguised his message and hid his poison from those who heard him. Several times, they heard him take a stab at the authority of the pope, the sacraments, the value of indulgences, and the worship of images. Even with this, there were some who saw the truth (since nothing can hide from the light of faith). He was denounced to the bishop, who condemned him as his errors merited. Because of his obstinacy and failure to retract his beliefs, he was turned over to the governor, who ordered his death by the hangman, in full view of the others captured in the last battle.

Father José de Anchieta was there to assist. He was already a priest, ordained by the same Bishop D. Pedro de Leitão. Even though at the beginning they thought the Frenchman was a rebel, Divine Providence would not allow the loss of this sheep from the flock of the Church. The father, with his clear reasoning, but chiefly by the power of grace, brought the Frenchman back to the Church. The father was very pleased with this victory and, as a result, apprehensive of losing the Frenchman. The father noted that the hangman was not very skilled at his profession and took a long time to execute the guilty, causing a lot of anguish. This put the Frenchman in danger of denying the truth to which he had already confessed. The father reprimanded the hangman and instructed him how to quickly perform his job. The father chose to place himself in danger of ecclesiastical punishment, for which he would be absolved, rather than risk the eternal damnation of that Frenchman's soul.

Cases such as this explain the need for divine dispensation and charity within the law. All the same, they are to be admired rather than imitated.

Once the administration was orderly and the land colonized and fortified, the governor entrusted his nephew Salvador Correia de Sá to govern
it.[2] He returned to Bahia.

CHAPTER 13
How the Governor Returned to Bahia and a Ship Bound
for India Sheltered There

Once Governor Mem de Sá returned to Bahia, right away he wrote to the
queen and to Cardinal D. Henrique, who were ruling Portugal, informing
them what he had done in Rio de Janeiro. He asked that in reward for his
services they send a successor for his office so that he could return to Portugal. His daughter was there, D. Filipa, and she later married the Count
of Linhares, D. Fernando de Noronha. Meanwhile, he continued with his
usual obligatory duties as governor.

At this time, Francisco Barreto arrived on a ship from Arrábida [out-
side Lisbon] seeking shelter. He had been the governor of India and was
going to [Mozambique to] conquer Monomatapa.[1] Governor Mem de Sá
gave them all he could to aid their journey. Many people from the ship
remained behind, including a soldier later found guilty of murder who
at one time had some differences with someone in Portugal. They had
reconciled and both were there. One day they went to enjoy the countryside where they lay down in the cool shade of a tree. One fell asleep, and
Medeiros (that was the name of the murderer) killed the other man with
a sword.

Francisco Barreto very badly wanted to punish this treachery by his
soldier, but he could not seize him. After he departed, the Superior Court
magistrate Fernão da Silva captured him and prepared his case, and he
was sentenced to death.

The day he was to face justice, those who remained from the ship asked
that the rope be cut so that he would fall on the gallows, and this is what
happened not once but three times.[2] The brothers of the Misericórdia,
who had accompanied him to see justice done, as they normally do,
asked the judge to not execute this sentence because it appeared to be
against God's will. He was returned to his cell, and the governor was
informed what had happened. The governor was an educated man and
upright about justice. He reprimanded them, stating that was a very pious

opinion, but it had no bearing in this case: the truth was well-known and the treachery notorious. The same governor one morning then ordered the prisoner removed from his cell and made the doorway his gallows, where they hung him and the rope did not break.

With these and other similar things the governor was occupied in Bahia while awaiting his successor. The wars did not stop in the captaincies in the south or in the north, as we shall see in the following chapters.

CHAPTER 14
After the Governor Left, How the Tamoios and the French Went from Cabo Frio to Rio de Janeiro to Capture a Village and What Followed

Since Governor-General Mem de Sá had expelled the enemy Tamoios from Rio de Janeiro before returning to Bahia, they gathered at Cape Frio, which is eighteen leagues from Rio de Janeiro. From there they built forts and assaulted São Vicente with the help of the French, who also helped them cut Brazil trees to load onto their many naus there.

These natives became so bold that, together with eight French naus and all the canoes they could muster, they sailed one by one into the bay of Rio de Janeiro, within view of the city of Saint Sebastian, to a nearby village one league away. This was the village of some of our native allies, whose leader was a great source of courage and strength. In past wars, he had accomplished great and heroic exploits in defense of Christianity and the Portuguese. His native name was *Araribóia*, and when he was baptized he was called *Martin Afonso de Sousa*. This was the name of the lord of São Vicente, who became his godfather when he arrived in his captaincy in 1530.

The Tamoios and their French allies came to attack and capture him and his people so that they could have a large banquet of their flesh. This was the message they sent to the captain-major, Salvador Correia de Sá, who feared the capture of this village would threaten the city. He quickly fortified it and armed its inhabitants and soldiers. No less concerned about his native friend, he sent for help from the Portuguese. Even though there were only a few, they were courageous and led by Duarte Martins Mourão, their captain.

Now aware of the situation, the brave native Martin Afonso de Sousa surrounded this village with earthen trenches and ordered all those who could not fight to leave. They hid in a safe place. He courageously awaited the arrival of the enemy. When the enemy came, they left their boats and were filled with the promise of victory and did nothing that day, postponing the battle for the following day. Our forces came to help. Assisted by the darkness of night, they placed a minion in a good position. They had brought it in a large canoe, and they would use it to eliminate the enemy.

The brave natives were revived with the arrival of this assistance, and his [Martin Afonso de Sousa's] people were filled with confidence. He [Martin Afonso de Sousa] filled in the trenches with his people, called in the name of Jesus Christ and Saint Sebastian, and charged his enemies before they could get organized. The natives were heartened by the sound of their leader's voice and encouraged by the example of the Portuguese. They surrounded their confused enemies, who, even though they were larger in number and put up a stiff resistance, turned their backs and fled. They were unable to withstand the combined force of the Portuguese and their native allies.

Our forces followed them, and with few injuries, they killed them in great numbers. The French had docked their naus too far ashore, and when the tide receded, they were stuck on dry land. The falconet rained a storm of stones down on them wounding and killing many sailors on the ships. By the time the high tide returned, many Frenchmen had been killed or injured. The barbarous natives were defeated and departed in their canoes with difficulty; gone was their boasting, and their forces were undone. Together with the French naus, they left for Cape Frio, and those carrying weapons left the lands of our ally, threatening to tear Martin Afonso to pieces with their teeth. They left many of their men scattered on the ground for the birds to rip apart with their beaks.

The French repaired their naus, loaded them with brazilwood, and returned to their country.

CHAPTER 15
The Wars in Pernambuco at That Time

Duarte de Albuquerque Coelho realized that many people from Portugal, as well as from other captaincies, wanted to flock to his captaincy of Pernambuco to build sugar mills and plantations. However, the most fertile and best lands were those around the cape where enemy natives lived, and he decided to wage war to clear them from it. For this purpose, he raised companies of soldiers. Those from Igaraçu were led by Captain Fernão Lourenço, who was also the captain of that town. Those in Paratibe were led by Gonçalo Mendes Leitão, the brother of Bishop D. Pedro de Leitão and son-in-law of Jerónimo de Albuquerque. The men from Capiguaribe had Cristóvão Lins, a German nobleman, as their captain. Those merchants and residents in the towns of Recife and Olinda, because they were from different places in Portugal, were organized into three companies. Men from Viana were led by Captain João Pais; those from Porto had Bento Dias de Santiago as captain, and for those from Lisbon, the merchant Gonçalo Mendes d'Elvas was captain. Among these six companies, twenty thousand negros were assigned, most of them native peoples from the countryside with Brazil trees, enemies of those at the cape.

The captain of the island of Itamaracá also sent a company of thirty-five white soldiers and two thousand native archers led by Captain Pero Lopes Lobo. He turned them over to Duarte Coelho to use where needed. He wanted them in the exploratory company of single young men.

In charge of all these troops as general was Duarte de Albuquerque Coelho, accompanied by D. Filipe de Moura and Filipe Cavalcanti, sons-in-law of Jerónimo de Albuquerque, and other noble and honorable men. Everyone wanted to serve under their command. The only people remaining in town were Jerónimo de Albuquerque with some old men who could no longer fight.

All of these people left, led by Duarte de Albuquerque Coelho, and marched until they first battled the enemy, who had been awaiting these first encounters. Some were killed and injured on both sides. However, seeing that it would be impossible to resist such a large force, the natives quickly fled, and our forces followed right behind them. There was no time to destroy the native villages and fields, so our forces did this when they returned later from the bush. However, Duarte Coelho guessed what his people were thinking and ordered some villages burned while creating presidios in others.[1] He told them to confiscate all the local foodstuffs, which forced the natives to agree to peace. He outlined the conditions that would improve their lives, and distributed lands to people who immediately began to work them. These lands demanded a great deal of work to plant, but then it was only necessary to eat the food grown and replant it in the same furrows.

In this manner, planters grew sugarcane and built sugar mills, and many became wealthy because the land was very fertile. Just one person, named João Pais, from the cape built eight mills, which he divided among his eight children, each receiving his own.

The lands around the Cirinhaen River, which were across from the island of Santo Alexio, six leagues from the cape, were also very fertile. These lands were occupied by another group of natives, enemies of those who had just been subjugated and pacified. It was from there that these natives attacked the others. Duarte Coelho told them via interpreters that they should stop this because these natives were friends, and if they did not, it would be necessary to defend them and extract vengeance for the insults and injuries they inflicted. These natives responded in a very arrogant manner that they had no quarrel with the whites or with Duarte Coelho. Rather, their quarrel was with those natives, who were their ancient foes; if the whites wanted to side with them, they still had arms to defend themselves one from the other.

When our interpreters returned with their message, Duarte de Albuquerque Coelho called for a meeting of the town council and other officials to decide whether this cause merited waging a just war and capturing all of these people. With this decision, they formed another army. Filipe Cavalcanti, a Florentine nobleman, was made captain of those at sea, and Jerónimo de Albuquerque was to lead those who marched on land. Duarte Coelho wanted to go alone as a soldier in the company of the adventurers. As soon as they arrived at the enemy villages and fields, they had large battles and met much resistance because the enemy was numerous and our forces suffered some defeats. Our men banded together right away and defended themselves with great courage and valor against other attacks.

When the natives saw assistance arriving on the ships and there was nothing they could do to stop them from unloading, of course, they attacked them energetically. Later, they lost hope and fled to the interior with their women and children leading the way and the warriors in the rear. They never turned around to attack our forces or our native allies. Our forces followed the enemy for many leagues until they arrived at a large enclosed area, where they stayed one afternoon. It was there, on some of the high places, that some of these natives appeared. They were boasting so loudly and showing such signs of defending themselves that our forces thought they were going to be captured. They did not know the reality until the next morning, when they were ready to fight, each one energized and ready for battle. However, that morning they quickly discovered that the natives had fled. Only a little boy and girl came out of the bush, and these were captured children from the allied natives. The children told them that at the same time those who were boasting appeared at the edge of the field, all the others were secretly fleeing to another area. They said there was no need to waste their energy following them further because they were going very far away and would not return. This is what happened. Our people returned to where they left the others and found them pulling up and destroying the fields of those who had fled. Then, feeling very contented, they all returned to Olinda, some by sea and others by land.

The fame from these two victories spread among the native peoples all the way from the coast to the São Francisco River and made them so fearful that they attached themselves to the whites as if they were their sheep. People sailed along the rivers with boats loaded with goods to sell for two *cruzados* or 1,000 réis each, which is the price of a sheep. People did not do this if they feared God, but rather it was those who placed more importance on interests in this life instead of what they should give to God who did this. There was one member of the clergy, commonly known as the *Priest of Gold,* who went to that captaincy boasting of being a great miner. Because of this, he was held in high regard by Duarte de Albuquerque Coelho, who sent him to the interior with thirty white men and two hundred natives. More men were not necessary. Whenever this priest arrived at a native village, no matter how large it might be, how well fortified or populated, he would pluck the feathers from a young chicken or the leaves from a branch. He tossed these into the air, and the same number of black demons would appear from hell expelling fire from their mouths. Just the sight of them scared the poor natives, both men and women, until their hands and feet were trembling. The natives would flock to the white men with the priest, who would then bind them and take them to the boats. Once those natives were gone, others would appear. Duarte de Coelho de Albuquerque, as many times as he was reprimanded by his uncle and brother, Jerónimo de Albuquerque, from Portugal, never put a stop to this great tyranny. I do not know if this was caused by his interest in selling the natives or if the priest had put a spell on him.

This was the reason King D. Sebastião ordered him to return to Portugal and where he went to die fighting with him in [the campaign in North] Africa.[2] The captaincy passed to his brother, Jerónimo de Albuquerque Coelho, who also fought in Africa and was injured, captured, and crippled in both legs. However, he was ransomed and lived for many years married to the daughter of D. Álvaro Coutinho de Almourol. They had two children: Duarte de Albuquerque Coelho and Matias de Albuquerque, who we will discuss in book 5. The Priest of Gold was also taken prisoner and put on a ship bound for Portugal. It stopped in the Azores for supplies, and he disappeared one night with no further news about him.

CHAPTER 16

How D. Luís Fernandes de Vasconcelos Was Killed by Pirates on His Journey to Become the Governor of Brazil

In the year of Our Lord 1570, D. Luís Fernandes de Vasconcelos started the journey to Brazil as its new governor. He left on a good fleet, but on the second day out of Lisbon, it ran into a storm that scattered the naus. One of them was discovered by some powerful pirates, who murdered forty Jesuit priests who were on board along with their leader Father Inácio de Azevedo. He had been the first Jesuit inspector in Brazil, and they killed him along with everyone else on board. The nau carrying D. Luís was damaged in the storm and sheltered on the island of Madeira. It was repaired after sailing two thousand leagues here and there. With great effort, it continued to Brazil and arrived within sight of the coast of Brazil. As hard as they tried to put ashore, they were forced to seek shelter on the Spanish island of Hispaniola, which is in the Spanish West Indies. They spent the winter sheltered there and then left for Portugal. The ship was in poor condition and lacked supplies, so they had to stop on the island of Terceira in the Azores. In the port, D. Luís heard the news of the disastrous death of his son, D. Fernando, who had been killed in India at the hands of the Muslims.

D. Luís went to another nau and waited until the time was right for departure for Brazil and then left alone. That week, he and his crew encountered three pirate naus of Lutherans. They did not have the weapons to defend themselves and did not want to surrender, so they fought valiantly, but D. Luís was killed in the battle.

D. Luís Fernandes de Vasconcelos (in addition to his other fine attri-
butes, which are worthy of a better venture) was very curious about maritime science. He was so knowledgeable about it that he could compete
with the most experienced and skilled pilots. In spite of this, he had very
poor luck on all his voyages.

The first time he went to sea, he was sent as captain-major of the India
fleet. The naus were all loaded and ready to sail when his ship developed
such a large leak that it could not leave with the others. It had to depart
later, alone, and wintered in Bahia as we discussed in chapter 5 of this
book. Even worse was his return voyage from India to Lisbon, when he
was in a very miserable shipwreck and saved himself and some thirty others on the lifeboat, leaving more than three hundred others on board to
drown. He had so much grief in his heart that the only thing he could do
was cover his eyes with a cloth to avoid witnessing such a sad spectacle.
After escaping the sinking of that nau, a few days later the Lord allowed
him to see the island of São Lourenço, inhabited by cruel barbarous peoples.[1] Their lives were equally at risk there, and they were far from other
lands, with no ship or supplies. Divine charity ordered that by chance a
nau passed by on its way to India, where D. Luís found yet another ship
bound for Portugal. After a journey of more than three years, he arrived
in Portugal after his long voyages, which cost him so dearly and only provided him with the debts, struggles, and dangers he faced. He had no time
to rest nor did his fortunes change when he was appointed governor of
Brazil, and all the unfortunate events we have related occurred. At the
end of these was his death, which ends everything.

CHAPTER 17
The Death of Governor Mem de Sá

In the same year that D. Luís Fernandes de Vasconcelos was killed at sea at
the hands of enemy pirates, which was 1571, Governor Mem de Sá died of
an illness. He had been waiting to return to the kingdom of Portugal, but
Our Lord took him to a better kingdom, which is heaven, in recognition
of his life and death and especially because of divine charity, on which one
can depend.

He was buried in a chapel of the Jesuit church that he had helped build
through his charity. In his will, he gave all his belongings to his daughter,

the Countess of Linhares, with the provision that if she died with no heirs, his mill and lands in Sergipe would be divided into thirds. One-third would be given to the Misericórdia of this city of Bahia and the other two-thirds to the Jesuit fathers, one for them and the other for payments and dowries for orphan girls.

Even though the countess died with no children, she left these lands to the fathers of Saint Anthony of Lisbon and ordered a chapel built. The Jesuit fathers here did not agree with this decision and filed their lawsuit jointly with the Misericórdia.

It was not just Governor Mem de Sá who died happy with his victories (if worldly things can bring happiness even at death) but there were other victories that year of his death, the fourteenth year of his government. Catholics achieved a great victory over the nonbelievers. These were the greatest victories seen in the world.

One of these victories was achieved by the Portuguese in India against three kings who banded together to expel them. To achieve that, they all attacked at the same time, Ali Adil Shah attacked Goa, Nizam Shahi assaulted Chaul, and forces from the kingdom of Aceh harassed Malacca.[1] However, since there were Portuguese defenders in all these places, resistance was equal in all of them.

Many people had the opinion that Chaul should be abandoned because it was not walled, and it lacked people to defend it against the power of Nizam Shahi. To send Chaul help from Goa would place both cities in danger. However, the Viceroy D. Luís de Ataíde, against the opinions of all, said that nothing would be abandoned. Leaving only 2,000 men in Goa, he sent D. Francisco Mascarenhas to Chaul with 600 selected soldiers in addition to many nobles and captains. Some of these provided ships at their own costs, such as D. Nuno Álvares Pereira, Pedro da Silva de Menezes, Nuno Velho Pereira, Rui Pires de Távora, and João de Mendonça. Other soldiers went to help and found passage on these ships. They could not find passage on other ships because they had secretly departed without the viceroy's knowledge. With just these few people, God was served by the viceroy's win against Ali Adil Shah. He laid siege to Goa for five months with 35,000 cavalry, 60,000 foot soldiers, 2,000 armed elephants, 200 pieces of field artillery, and more gigantic artillery pieces.

D. Francisco Mascarenhas, along with those he brought to help and troops already there led by Luís Freire de Andrade, the head captain of

Chaul, which totaled 800 troops, was able to kill 12,000 Muslims led by Nizam Shahi. He had 100,000 infantry and 55,000 cavalry with which he laid siege to Chaul. They were so unsure of victory that after nine months of the siege, he agreed to peace with D. Francisco Mascarenhas.

Ali Adil Shah also agreed to peace with the viceroy, both making mutually agreeable conditions maintaining their own, as well as the king's, honor. Those from Aceh did not fare any better, since on their way to Malacca, they encountered Luís de Melo e Silva in a naval battle, which he won. Thus, he was able to thwart their efforts.

With this victory accomplished, Viceroy D. Luís de Ataíde arrived in Portugal on June 22 of the next year of 1572, since his successor D. António de Noronha had arrived in India. King D. Sebastião went to the city of Lisbon to give thanks to God the next Sunday in a solemn procession from the cathedral to the monastery of São Domingos, where he spoke and informed the people of the viceroy's deeds, offering his right hand to the viceroy before all the other princes and lords who had accompanied him in this procession. This was a great honor and one that was well deserved and earned for such heroic achievements.

The other victory that year of 1571 was achieved by D. João of Austria, general of the Christian League, with Marco António Colona, the general of the galleys of Pope Pius V, Sebastião Veniero, general of the Venetians, the princes of Doria, Parma, and Urbino, and other lords fighting under their control. It was a Sunday, October 7, in the Gulf of Lepanto, where they defeated the pasha general of the Turks, killing him and taking his two children captive. They killed 30,000 Turks and took 5,000 captives, captured 250 galleys and galleasses, and liberated 15,000 Christian slaves rowing the oars of the Turkish fleet. Some of our forces also died in this battle—7,500 soldiers including some famous leaders.[2]

When the sultan Selim heard the news of the loss of his fleet, he was out of his mind, saying this was the beginning of the end of his empire. He was consoled by Luchali (Uluch Ali), who had escaped with fifteen galleys, and he showed the sultan the standard of Malta that he had captured in the battle. Counseled by his people, the sultan constructed another fleet and made Luchali the general in charge of it. Luchali was very contented with this new position and pressed for the rapid construction of new galleys, casting new artillery pieces, stockpiling ammunition, and preparing foodstuffs, all for the next year.

When the Holy Pontiff became aware of these plans, he discussed the creation of a new league with Christian princes. He also asked the king of Portugal, D. Sebastião, if he wished to join it as well as accept marriage to Margarita, the daughter of King Henry of France. They had already discussed this marriage, and D. Sebastião did not wish it. When D. Sebastião heard that the same king of France had refrained from joining the new league against the Turks, he declared that he would accept the marriage and did not require a dowry—just her father's entry in the league. He offered to harass Turkish forces in the Red Sea and Persian Gulf with his fleets, which had been victorious, and would do so with all his power and might.

So zealous was King D. Sebastião in honoring God and fighting for him against the infidels that this was the reason he accepted the marriage (which he did not desire) and wanted no other dowry. However, this marriage never occurred because of so many bad things and strokes of ill fortune. Margarita married Henry of Bourbon, the Duke of Vandoma and Prince of Biarne. King D. Sebastião continued with his wars, which was what he wanted most in this life, until he died in one of them.

CHAPTER 18
How King D. Sebastião Appointed Cristóvão de Barros as Captain-Major to Govern Rio de Janeiro

King D. Sebastião, after he assumed the throne and ruled in his own name, was so attentive to his colonies (if only God had allowed him to not be so), that, knowing of the events in Rio de Janeiro, he sent Cristóvão de Barros there as the captain-major and governor. He was the illegitimate son of António Cardoso de Barros, the first head of the treasury in Brazil, who had departed Brazil for Lisbon accompanied by the first bishop. Their nau landed on the coast next to the São Francisco River, and they were killed and eaten by the natives, as discussed in chapter 3 of this book.

Cristóvão de Barros was a wise and prudent man, fortunate in warfare. After he arrived in Rio de Janeiro, he was victorious in all his battles with the Tamoios. He pacified them so that along the rivers and bay, the iron of lances was turned into scythes, and swords became axes and hoes. The people were only concerned with their work and their lands. He also built a sugar mill next to the Magé River, where there is a fishing place called *piraiqué,* which means *entrance of fish.* It is so notable that it is hard to pass it by without commenting on it.

This is a river of sweet water, but the tides enter it for a distance of a league, more or less. In the abundant waters during June, which is the height of winter, there are so many of these *fataça* or *corimã* fish (as the natives call them) that they use two hundred canoes full of men to capture them. After throwing crushed *barbasco* weed upriver at the edge of the high tide, they string a net folded in half across the mouth of the river.[1] The fish try to leave with the outgoing tide but cannot because of the net, nor can they hide in the depths of the water because the drug in the water makes them stop moving and swirl. They flip on their stomachs and move over the water half dead. With a funnel-shaped net, they remove the fish two at a time just like a ladle used in a pot, until the canoe is filled. They immediately remove the heads and scale the bodies and salt and dry them on the many rocks. From the cooked heads, they extract oil, which is used for light all year.

During July, they conduct another *piraiqué,* or fishing done in the same manner as the earlier one, but the *fataças* are not as fat because they are all filled with eggs, which are large and delicious. These are salted, pressed, and dried to eat and taken to be sold in Bahia and elsewhere.

I mentioned this because this fishing is done on the Magé River, where Cristóvão de Barros built his mill. In his day and even a couple of years later, a public crier went around the city on the day of the fishing. Anyone who wanted to participate could go, and few declined since it was a chance to obtain fish as well as for some recreation.

CHAPTER 19
The Fourth Governor of Brazil, Luís de Brito de Almeida, and His Journey to the Real River

When news of the death of Governor Luís Fernandes de Vasconcelos, whom the pirates murdered, reached Lisbon, the king immediately appointed Luís de Brito de Almeida governor. He had been the secretary of the Misericórdia during a year when there had been many cases of the plague in Lisbon. The head of the charity and its members had been helpless, and the hospital was filled with fear of the contagious illness. Nevertheless, he always attended the sick, seeing to their needs. Because of this, the king turned the government over to him. After he arrived, he dealt with peacetime issues, which had become disorganized because of the death of his predecessor. Then he turned to matters of war.

The first of these was to expel the enemy natives from the area of the Real River and colonize it as the king had ordered. The king was well informed about the region, and the name of the Real River was known and full of promise.

This river is located at twelve degrees south latitude, and its mouth is half a league wide. It has two channels where coastal ships up to fifty tons can sail. The river is very deep, and it forms a bay that is more than a league long where there are many manatees and all sorts of fish.

The tide enters the river for seven or eight leagues and from the edge of the salty water upriver the land is very good for growing sugarcane and other plants. There is a lot of brazilwood, and for all these reasons, the king ordered the area colonized. However, because there were hostile natives there, the governor first had to clear them off the land with the help of many residents of Bahia. Some came on land and others arrived in the ships with the supplies. They had a great victory over a leader named *Sorobi,* burning their villages and killing and capturing many. Because another leader named *Aperipé* escaped with his people, they followed him fifty leagues into the interior without overtaking him. This is where they found two impressive lagoons, one is five hundred braças wide and one hundred long, and its water is saltier than the ocean and it is surrounded by parsley. The other lagoon is right next to it, and is six hundred braças long, and its water is very sweet. Both have a lot of fish, and the governor ordered they catch a lot of fish, which supplied them on their return to Bahia. He placed Garcia d'Avila in charge of the village where he had his house, estate, and many pens for livestock. It is twelve or thirteen leagues from there to the Tatuapará River. They began to colonize it, but that never happened. Instead of people, it has a lot of livestock.

CHAPTER 20
The Expeditions into the Interior at That Time

The residents of Bahia did not regret accompanying the governor on his journey to the Real River, even though they did not find the natives they were seeking to capture and have serve them. They had been filled with more of this greed than zeal to begin the new town the king wanted them to establish. But they were able to achieve their original intention, telling the governor that since the natives had fled from war, as he could see, and as they had done with his predecessor, and they were more than sixty leagues away from the sea, it would be better to bring them in using peaceful means of persuasion. They could do this using their *mamelucos,* who knew the language and who were related to them (because mamelucos are children of white and native parents). They would follow them easier than using firearms.

For these reasons, or to oblige those asking, the governor gave them the permission they sought to go into the interior and collect natives using mamelucos. These residents did not have total confidence in the mamelucos persuasive eloquence, so they also brought many white soldiers and allied natives and friends with their arrows and firearms. With these, if peaceful means or free will failed, they would bring them in forcefully using war. However, usually the mameluco relative speaking to them was sufficient. They discussed with them the abundance of fish and shellfish there and the liberty they would enjoy, which they would not have if they were captured in war.

With these deceptions and with a few gifts of clothes and tools for the leaders and trade for goods in exchange for those that were captured and ready to be eaten, they persuaded entire villages. Once they reached sight of the ocean, children were separated from their parents, brothers were separated from each other, and sometimes wives removed from their husbands. The mameluco captain would remove some, the soldiers others, the ship owners others, those who asked for permission would take some, and others who received permission would take others. All of the natives worked for them on their estates, and some were sold. However, they made the statement that these were natives of conscience and that they were selling the labor only. Those who purchased them, after their first error or effort to escape, would brand them on the face, saying they cost them money and they were theirs. Preachers wore out their pulpits speaking against this, but it was like preaching to an empty desert.

Among these excursions into the interior, one was made by António Dias Adorno. The governor asked him to search for minerals, and he entered the interior by way of the Contas River, which is in the captaincy of Ilhéus. He followed its current, which comes from afar. He explored a great deal of the countryside and found emeralds and other precious stones, which he brought to show, and the governor sent these to Portugal. Lapidaries there examined them and said they were of a very high quality. In spite of this, they did not seek out more gems but rather went there to find natives. They brought seven thousand native Topihuárens some two hundred leagues, without bringing any foodstuffs for them. They had to walk slowly because there were many women, children, and old people. They survived by eating wild fruit, hunting, and honey; they found so much food that they never experienced hunger, arriving fat and full of energy. In a place where we can see that the land is so fertile, it would be very easy to return and look for precious stones, which we know are there, as well as to discover others.

The same governor ordered Sebastião Álvares to the São Francisco River along with some skilled workers with all the provisions they would require to sail upriver and seek minerals. To this purpose, the governor wrote to one of the great native leaders in the interior named *Porquinho,* asking for his assistance to provide natives and anything else he could. He sent him some scarlet-colored clothes and a shepherd's staff to carry in hand.

Diogo de Castro carried these gifts. He had already stayed with Porquinho in his house and knew how to speak the native language well. Along with him went someone else who knew the language and who had been a Jesuit, named Jorge Velho.

Porquinho was flattered by the governor's requests and never failed to help the whites. The captain received his assistance in navigating the ship and they stopped where the river was no longer navigable because below that are the waterfall and whirlpool. It was there that a letter arrived from Governor Lourenço de Veiga, who had succeeded Luís de Brito. The letter ordered that he return at once to give an account of the royal funds he had spent. He obeyed, and after he came back he did not find his people who had joined the others from Pernambuco to seek natives. He collected some natives, and everyone was done with his work there.

Not only in Bahia but also in Pernambuco and Ilhéus, they were making other expeditions into the interior.

In Ilhéus, Luís Álvares de Espinha was the leader, and he went to the interior with the pretext of waging war on several native villages thirty leagues away. These natives had killed several whites; however, he was not satisfied to simply capture all the people in those villages but pushed further inland to capture an infinite number of natives.

In Pernambuco, Francisco de Caldas was the supervisor of the treasury, and along with Gaspar Dias de Ataíde and many soldiers, he went to the São Francisco River. They were joined by Braço de Peixe, who was a great native leader of the Tabajares; his people are very robust and warlike. They moved forward into the interior for many leagues, killing those who resisted and capturing the others.

Returning to the coastline with seven thousand captives, they decided to repay Braço de Peixe by bringing him and his people bound. He understood what was happening and did not fail to provide them with food from his fields and game they hunted. He assigned two hundred hunters to ensure the supply of game. After they were secure and no one was watching them, and there appeared no reason to do so, he called another leader, a relative of his called *Assento de Pássaro*, who came to his village with archers. He told his hunters who were among the whites that they should be alert the next morning. When they heard his usual roar, they should attack us, and no one would escape with his life. That was how it was. They found our forces sleeping and off guard and suddenly the natives sprang into action with such force that our forces did not have time to arm themselves or to flee. They killed all of them. They freed the captive natives, and all celebrated their liberty by eating the flesh of their masters. Then they allowed the former captives to return to their lands or go wherever they wished. The only one on our side who escaped was a mameluco man, hidden by a young girl, the sister of the leader Assento de Pássaro.

The news of this was brought by the ships that had been awaiting them in the port and then came to Olinda. It impacted everyone; widows mourned their husbands and children their dead fathers. The evil did not end with this. The murderers, fearing vengeance from the whites for these killings, were Tabajares and enemies of the Potiguarás. However, they formed an alliance with them in Paraíba and befriended them so they would help them in their battles with us, as we shall see later.

CHAPTER 21

The Differences between the Governor and the Bishop regarding a Prisoner Sheltering in a Church

Because of the death of Bishop D. Pedro Leitão, his replacement, Bishop D. António Barreiros, came to Brazil to govern this bishopric. He had been D. Prior of Aviz. He was a kindly man, charitable, and someone graced with many virtues. However, he had not been in Brazil for many days when a situation developed into differences and unpleasantness with the governor. The occasion was the following:

There was in this land a man named Sebastião de Ponte who was honored and wealthy but also cruel in some of his punishments for those who served him, be they whites or negros. Among other punishments, he branded a white man on the shoulder with a cattle iron after giving him a good whipping. Feeling the effects of this, the man embarked on a ship for Lisbon. While there, one morning he waited for the king to pass on his way to chapel. He let his cape fall and showed the king the brand on his shoulder. With many tears, he asked for justice.

Once the king was informed about the case, he sent a letter to the governor ordering Sebastião da Ponte arrested and sent to Portugal under guard.

Sebastião da Ponte got word of this, and he sought shelter in the chapel of Our Lady of Escada, which is next to Pirajá, where he had been living. In addition, he claimed to have entered minor orders.[1] He walked around with a habit and tonsure because he was not married, and for these reasons, the bishop asked the governor not to arrest him. But this did not work. He began right away to proceed to a censure, and finally this business resulted in people carrying arms. The ignorant and fickle people rushed to the bishop in fear of censure and then went to the governor trembling at capital punishment, which had been publicly announced with drums. Furthermore, even the governor's own children, who were studying to be ordained, sat next to him with stones in their hands destined for their parents. They were supported by the bishop, the clergy, and others in the church.

In the end, *jussio regis urgebat,* or "commandment was urgent," and the prisoner was sent to Lisbon as the king had ordered. He was put in Limoeiro jail and punished as his crimes merited.[2]

Also at the time, the nau *Santa Clara* hit a large rock on the coast of the Arambepé River while on its way to India. This was the distance of a shot from a little cannon from Recife, and more than three hundred men were lost, including Captain Luís de Andrade.

The river where this nau sank is five or six leagues from Recife, and many people went there to help. They pulled a lot of money from the bottom of the sea, and the divers and swimmers kept money for themselves and many people who could not swim. To this, the bishop replied with excommunication based on the Bull of Ceia, which forbids taking the goods from a shipwreck.[3] I do not know whether they were able to profit from any of this. I only heard from someone who had lived there for many years that it was a golden time for Bahia because of all the money that flowed and the many natives who came from the interior. It is accurate that it was a golden time and not a time of gold because, for that, other things are required.

CHAPTER 22
The Beginning of the Rebellion and Wars with the Natives of Paraíba

The Paraíba River, which on the sailing charts is called São Domingos, is at six and three-quarters degrees south latitude. Its mouth is a league wide, and the channel in the middle, which is called the bar, is a quarter of a league long. All the rest is very even from one side to the other. The bottom is clean sand, and because of this, it is a better port and capable of sheltering larger ships than Pernambuco's port, from which this is twenty-two leagues north along the coast.

One league upriver, there is a beautiful island covered with trees. The island is one league long and one-third of a league wide. In front of it is an anchorage for naus, which is able to shelter many from all winds. The tide reaches five leagues upriver, allowing large caravels to navigate it. Along the river, there is a flat field that stretches more than fourteen leagues and is two thousand braças wide. It is divided by salt marshes and rivers cascading with sweet water. Nowadays this area is filled with sugarcane and mills, and salty mangrove firewood comes from these marshes to cook the sugar and ash to cleanse it.[1]

More than twenty French naus entered this river each year to load brazilwood with help from the native Potiguarás. They used to rule all the land of Paraíba up to Maranhão, which is some four hundred leagues. The Portuguese in the neighboring captaincies of Itamaracá and Pernambuco used to help the natives after they made peace, as was mentioned in chapter 12 of book 2. But the natives faced many vexations and irritations that made them rebel.

I will just relate one of these, which was one of the last ones, the most recent in these series of rebellions. There were many mamelucos going among the native villages. There was one from Pernambuco trading captured natives and other things and under this pretext robbing them with violence and tricks. Since he was the son of an honorable man, he was more akin to his mother than his father. He went to a village in the Copaoba Mountains to trade. He was entertained at a dinner hosted by a great leader named *Iniguaçu*, which means *Great Net.* He fell in love with Iniguaçu's daughter of fifteen, saying he wanted to marry or live with her. He said he wanted to stay with them in their village and not deal anymore with the whites. The daughter and father both agreed to this, believing he would act as he promised. However, after Iniguaçu returned from a hunt that lasted several days, he did not find the man or his daughter because they had left for Pernambuco.

Iniguaçu was very saddened by this, and he sent two of his sons to find their sister. Since the mameluco would not let her go, one of the brothers went to António de Salema, who was the judge visiting Pernambuco. Before he left for Bahia, he ordered the father of the mameluco to present the girl, which he did, and the judge handed her over to her brothers. He passed a provision that no one should impede these natives, or they would be charged with a crime. Furthermore, he ordered that the whites on their return path should provide them with all the assistance and help they required to proceed. He advised the brothers not to allow mamelucos in their villages. He also advised the head captain of the island, Afonso Rodrigues Bacelar, to forbid such people from going into the interior.

The negros were very happy to see their sister and also later with the reception they were given by the whites on their return path, who obeyed the legal provision that they carried. This lasted until they reached the home of Diogo Dias, who was the last white person, living on the border of Itamaracá captaincy. He welcomed them with signs of affection but had many more for the sister. He sent her to join the other serving women without giving anything to the porters or any of the others her father later sent for her. When her father knew what had happened, he asked Diogo Dias to return his daughter, but he did not wish to. The father went to speak with the captain-major of the island to explain the situation, but nothing happened because he was Diogo Dias's friend, and he ignored the case.

Once the news spread among the native villages, they immediately wanted to take revenge on the merchants in their villages and take them captive, but the leader said that it would be wrong to punish the innocent for the crimes of the guilty. He only made them leave the villages and return home, as Judge António de Salema had ordered.

This negro was so well disposed toward the Portuguese that he would not have taken vengeance even on the guilty party if he had not been provoked by other Potiguarás, especially those living along the coast. The French interacted with them for their commerce in brazilwood; it was important to them that they retained ties with their kin in the interior.

At this time there were three French naus loading in the bay of Traição. The captain-major of Itamaracá had led an assault that had killed some Frenchmen and burned a lot of their brazilwood. Diogo Dias had also participated in that attack, and he said many things to the good Iniguaçu, that he agreed to attack Dias's house and lands, which were a mill he had started on the Taracunhaen River. He knew that Dias had many people, slaves, a large fortified wall, a strong house inside, and some pieces of artillery. He cautiously decided to come with all the natives from the interior, on the one hand, and Tujucopapo, who was the leader of those from the coast, came with his people and with the French, on the other hand, and that is what happened. Even though there was an infinite number of them, they did not send everyone into the enclosure, but rather only some entered on the sly, while the others hid. Our forces began to wound those who entered with arrows and gunshots, and they turned as if they were fleeing. When Diogo Dias saw what was happening, he mounted his horse and left the enclosure with his slaves and followed them. However, as soon as they saw him outside his enclosure, the others who had been hiding came out for the trap. With a great cry, they surrounded him and prevented him from returning. He and his people were killed there, and the natives entered the enclosure. No negro or white was left alive, not the big or the small, neither man nor woman. They were all killed and quartered.

This was the war with the Potiguarás, when Luís de Brito governed Brazil in the year of 1574, and it continued for another twenty-five years.

CHAPTER 23
How the King Divided the Government of Brazil, Sending Doctor António de Selema to Govern Rio de Janeiro and Porto Seguro and the Other Southern Captaincies, and Governor Luís de Brito to Govern Bahia and the Other Northern Captaincies and How He Conquered Paraíba

When King D. Sebastião learned all that happened in the previous chapter, he feared that the French would establish themselves in the area of the Paraíba River. He ordered Governor Luís de Brito de Almeida to survey the area and select a site for a fortified city that could be defended against the French and the Potiguarás. In order to help him focus on this, and so that the captaincies from Porto Seguro south would not be lacking in leadership, he placed their government in the hands of Doctor António de Selema.[1] He had been a judge in Pernambuco and held that position in Bahia. He left Bahia in 1575 and was warmly greeted in Rio de Janeiro by the captain-major Cristóvão de Barros as well as all the other Portuguese and native leaders who called on him. The first among these and most important was Martin Afonso de Sousa, whose native name was Araribóia, whom we discussed in chapter 14 of this book. The governor offered him a chair, but he sat cross-legged as was his custom. The governor told him through an interpreter that this was improper when speaking to the king's representative.

The native unfortunately answered angrily and with arrogance saying: "If you knew how tired my legs are from fighting in the wars in which I served the king, it would not be too much for you to allow me a small rest. However, since you find me so discourteous, I will return to my village, where we do not pay attention to such things, and I will never return to your court."

Nevertheless, he never failed to be with his people on all public occasions.

After the governor had been there a few days, organizing things and attending to justice, as the good educated man that he was, he was told that at Cape Frio there were many French naus bartering with the natives and that each year they came to load brazilwood. He determined right away that he would expel them and to do that, he joined with Cristóvão de Barros, four hundred Portuguese men, and six hundred allied natives. They attacked the French with vigor, but since the French had fortified their positions with their Tamoio allies, they defended themselves with a lot of energy. In spite of this, our forces were able to bear down on them so hard that for their own good, they surrendered. The Tamoios who escaped were shocked at what they saw and abandoned that entire coast. For those captives who demonstrated a willingness to accept the faith, Governor António de Salema settled them in two villages along the bay in Rio de Janeiro. The first of these was called São Barnabé and the other São Lourenço. He entrusted these natives to the Jesuit fathers to teach them the catechism and the mysteries of our faith.

CHAPTER 24

How Governor Luís de Brito Ordered the Superior Court Magistrate Fernão da Silva to Lead the Conquest of Paraíba and How He Later Went in Person but Could Not Reach It because of Contrary Winds

Because Governor Luís de Brito could not go in person to conquer Paraíba, which the king had entrusted him to do, he assigned Doctor Fernão da Silva, Superior Court magistrate and head superintendent of that state, to accomplish this. He was leaving for judicial rounds in Pernambuco. With him came those on foot and on horseback, as well as all the natives from Pernambuco and Itamaracá. These forces were mustered to punish the rebel Potiguarás. This group saw itself as very powerful and did not listen to advice to wait. They only went as far as the mouth of the Paraíba River, where they laid claim to the land in the name of the king in a solemn and recorded act. After that, they were very satisfied and returned to Pernambuco. After concluding the duties of his office, the judge returned to Bahia. However, the Potiguarás have no understanding of such legal acts, nor did they see any evidence of this, since they did not see any pillars or people bringing them. They continued to rule the land as before but with greater energy and strength.

Meanwhile, Boaventura Dias, the son of Diogo Dias, and Miguel de Barros from Pernambuco, a wealthy man who had many natives, built a sugar mill in Guiana. This was where António de Cavalcanti would later have his mill. To better defend it, they constructed a fortified house made of wood and mud, two hands thick. From the inside, the Portuguese used firearms and the natives had bows and arrows to defend it from some assaults and sieges from the Potiguarás. One day, they became aware that the patio entrance was open in one section lacking a finished wall. While some natives fought, others secretly filled this area with straw and set it on fire. It began to burn the wood above it, but the defenders could only see smoke, which blinded them without their knowing its source. When two women went to open a trap door to locate the fire, large flames immediately sprang up and engulfed them. The men saw this, and since the house was surrounded by enemies, they decided to make a last stand in the open fields. They surrendered their lives, but this was not in vain because they killed so many of the enemy.

CHAPTER 25
An Excursion from Pernambuco into the Interior

In the year of Our Lord of 1578, when Lourenço da Veiga governed this state, an expedition into the interior was organized in Pernambuco. Heading it was Captain Francisco Barbosa da Silva, who left in a large caravel to sail to the São Francisco River. Because there were too many people to fit into the boat, seventy men went by land, led by Diogo de Castro. He spoke the native language well and had traveled to Bahia and made other excursions into the interior.

This second group, after they passed the Formoso River, was attacked by a band of mountain pigs. The pigs were filled with such fury and made such a roar, showing their teeth, that it made the group fearful. However, since some of them had their pistols loaded, they fired at the pigs and made them retreat. They killed seven pigs, which provided them with food for the journey.

Nine days' journey from there, they reached Lagoa, where they spied a French nau anchored three leagues offshore, near the São Miguel River. Ten Frenchmen had left the ship and were in a palisade bargaining with some natives.[1] In the morning, our forces fell upon them while they were sleeping and killed nine. This left only one. Before he was killed, he valiantly defended himself with a halberd and, in spite of the wound on his leg, he was able to kill one of our soldiers, Pedro da Costa.

There were not many natives there, and Diogo de Castro told them he was only seeking Frenchmen, so the natives left without offering any resistance. Our people continued their journey until they reached the mouth of the São Francisco River, where the large caravel had arrived with its captain and the others on board. Since they lacked natives to carry their supplies and purchases, they sent for some from the native leader named *Porquinho* as well as from his enemy named *Seta*. This was in case one did not offer his assistance, the other would. They were both so obedient that they both came. In order to keep everyone happy, the captain went with Seta and his people and Diogo de Castro went with Porquinho and his folk.

After Seta had the captain in his house, he told him that he wanted to trade a village of his enemies that was nine or ten leagues distant.[2] If the captain accompanied him, he would hand it over to him. The captain accepted, and, as he left, he placed Diogo Martins Leão in charge to stand guard with twelve men. He then left with the others to where Seta took him.

Five of those who had remained with Leão went to nearby villages to look for food because the natives there had told them they were friends of the whites. However, the natives killed them for no reason whatsoever, and then they went to the house where Diogo Martins Leão and the others had remained. They planned to capture and kill them all and take their trade goods. Once our people understood why these natives had arrived, they quickly loaded their pistols and began to valiantly defend themselves.

Diogo Martins then quickly wrote a note to Diogo Castro asking for help, and he sent it with a Romani man. This man, when he saw the danger they were in, sent a copy to Porquinho. Porquinho immediately began to preach to his people that they always had been friends of the whites and would remain so until they died because it was the whites who brought them their farming and planting tools and other good things. For that reason, he would start on his way to help them, which he did. Within twenty-four hours, he was at the site of the siege with 1,500 natives along with Diogo de Castro and eight other white men. They were divided into two divisions and used a bugle to signal an immediate attack on the enemy. They attacked them with such force that the enemy could not resist and began to flee. However, since they had surrounded them with their divisions, the enemy fell into their hands, and they killed more than six hundred.

This was before daylight, and when the morning arrived, after greeting them and giving thanks for being freed from the siege, they asked

Diogo de Castro if the captain knew about the rebellion of those people, and when he said no, he wrote him two notes and sent them to him with haste because it is not wise to have one's forces scattered with so many enemies present.

One of these notes was carried by a mameluco, and he did not arrive because enemies killed him on the way. The other note was carried by a native and did arrive. When the captain read it, he put aside his initial fear and excitement to tell Seta and the others with them that it was necessary to return to help the whites because Porquinho had laid siege to them. They returned as far as a river that was four leagues away. The rebels had made a trap and were guarding the area. They sprang out and engaged in a battle that continued until nightfall. In the morning when they were ready to start fighting again, Diogo de Castro and Porquinho arrived, and this support bolstered the captain's spirit more than anything. With some fighting in front and others battling in the rear, they killed more than five hundred of the enemy.

They then held a meeting and decided to be done with the rebellion for good and to head for a large fortified enclosure on top of a mountain twelve leagues away where they had sheltered before.

They began to march, and on the second day, they arrived at a river that sprang from a rocky outcrop. It was there that they found the body of the mameluco sent with the note for the captain. His arms and legs had been cut off. From there, they sent a white and two negros as spies who encountered two enemy spies. They killed one and brought the other back alive. From him, they learned that the native encampment was two leagues away and contained a group of forty-three native leaders with their followers, wives, and children.

When our forces came within sight of this group, they did not want to give themselves away but rather just let them see Porquinho and his men, who now numbered two thousand from his villages. When those in the enclosed group saw these men, more left. Porquinho and his men fought and then pretended to flee and stopped at a good distance from our forces in the enclosure. Then the captain and his men went forth with a volley of gunshots aimed at the enemy's backs, and Porquinho and his men turned around and shot arrows at them. They were caught in the middle, and our forces killed three hundred of them. The others could not return to their enclosure and ran into the bush.

This enclosed area was 3,236 braças in circumference, and their drinking water was just one braça away. Our forces decided to take that first, and of course those inside defended it with a lot of energy for six days. On the seventh day, it was taken, and the enemy began to die from thirst. They attacked with many forays, and their last offer was that they would turn over a village of their enemies if the whites would accompany them to it, which they did. Entering the village, they announced that they had given them to the whites because they were enemies and by doing so had shown great mercy in not killing them nor had they traded them to other natives who would kill them or mistreat them. They gave them to Christians, who would treat them with mercy. The headman of the village, named *Araconda*, responded by saying that they, Seta's people, deserved captivity and death and not his people, since Seta's people had killed whites and his people had not and had never harmed whites. He then turned to the captain and said, "White man, I never mistreated your relatives, nor can these people give me away, but I will go with you willingly as your captive."

The captain thanked him and told him to present himself within fifteen days for the journey, which they did. There were so many that, walking in a single file (as they normally do), the line was a league long.

I do not know what sort of justice or reason Christian men, who say they follow these ideals, employ to make the innocent pay for the crimes of the sinner. They captured people who had done no harm to anyone and ignored those who gave them away, giving them their liberty, even though they were the rebels and killers who had conducted so much warfare and treachery. However, these people were the ones who would pay because no sooner had they left when Seta and his people decided to go redeem them and they sent spies ahead. When Araconda's people were hunting in the wild (which is how they sustained themselves on the journey), Seta's spies told them that their people were bothered by their guilty consciences and they wanted to redeem them from the captivity in which the whites had placed them. In order to do this, they would wage war, and they told them not to defend themselves, but when the battle started, to flee and return to their lands. Porquinho and his people had left, and there was nothing to fear. This was all conducted in great secrecy, but a native woman among the captives overheard it. She told her husband, and he told others, they said they would only believe it when they saw it, and they did not believe this communication. Their enemies had attacked their rear guard, killing eleven men, and those in front could not help them because they were so distant. Araconda's people were occupied defending the captain, and none of the rear guard was able to escape with their lives. They sent two negros to see whether they were dead or alive. When these two saw themselves surrounded and in such great danger that they were ready to collapse, they called for help from Saint Anthony. One used his bow and arrows and the other his sword and round shield. Together they were so devastating that this little battle gave strength to their friends, frightened their enemies, and made them flee. Those people from Pernambuco could not follow after them and returned to their homes poorer than when they left them.

There was one thing about Governor Lourenço da Veiga. Regardless of how busy he was, he never failed to go to Mass. He always came and went by horseback, so that no one would be obliged to accompany him.

CHAPTER 26
The Death of Governor Lourenço da Veiga

When King D. Henrique ruled following the death of his nephew King D. Sebastião, he was of such an advanced age of sixty-six when his reign began that there began to be debates as to who would succeed him. The claimants were the Catholic king, D. Filipe II of Castile, the Duchess of Bragança, the Prince of Parma, the Duke of Savoy, and Lord D. António. They all sent their supporters to court to inform the king of their legitimate claim, asking him to select the one with the best justification as his successor.

They all claimed to be nephews and nieces of King D. Henrique, children of his brothers or sisters, and were all equal in their relation to him. The Catholic king was the son of the king's sister, Empress D. Isabel, and Emperor D. Carlos V. The Duchess of Bragança was the daughter of Prince D. Duarte, the king's brother, and D. Isabel, the daughter of the Duke of Bragança, D. Jamie. The Prince of Parma was married to the Princess D. Maria, also a daughter of the same Prince D. Duarte. The Duke of Savoy was the son of Princess D. Beatriz, the king's sister, and D. Carlos, the Duke of Savoy. Lord D. António was the illegitimate son of Prince D. Luís, the king's brother. All were grandchildren of King D. Manuel I, the father of their parents as well as of this same King D. Henrique.

The king was at first inclined to favor the claim of the Duchess of Bragança, mostly because she was a woman and the Catholic king was a man, as well as for other reasons. He decided to leave the throne to her, but he did not want to make a formal declaration or mention it in his will. He thought it was better for claimants and for the kingdom of Portugal for them all to be informed at the same time.

At that time, the king was very frail and suffered with illness to the point that he died the same day he turned sixty-eight. He was the last king of Portugal through the masculine line; the first king of Portugal had been named Henrique, as was the last king.[1]

Once the king had died, the regents he named were the archbishop of Lisbon, Francisco de Sá, the head of the king's chamber, D. João Telo, D. João Mascarenhas, and Diogo Lopes de Sousa, president of the Council of Justice. Even though they did not have the desire to resist the Catholic king, in order to satisfy the people, they planned a number of defenses for the kingdom. King D. Filipe was fully aware of these as well as the preparations that D. António planned in order to be named king. D. Filipe was sorry to have to resort to force, but he was assured by his conscience as well as by written opinions from theologians and scholars of canon law, that he could do it, and he prepared for it. First, however, he wrote to the regents, to the five main cities in the kingdom, and to the three estates meeting of the Cortes in Almeirim asking them to declare him king in accordance with his late uncle's will and his right.[2]

They answered saying that they could not until the matter was decided in the courts, and when the king heard this, he appointed the Duke of Alba as general of the army and ordered him to enter Portugal by land and sea.

The army numbered more than 1,400 cavalry, and the infantry, in addition to the regiments from Spain, had almost 4,000 Germans led by their colonel, the Count of Baldron, and 4,000 Italians led by their captain-general, D. Pedro de Medicis.

The Duke of Alba's advisors said he should ignore the tower of São Gião and head straight for Lisbon. He ignored their opinions and set upon it with twenty-four cannons. Even though this did not cause a great deal of damage, its captain Tristão Vaz da Veiga, the brother of Lourenço da Veiga, the governor of Brazil, decided to surrender it. Asking for a safe passage, he met with the duke in the open, and they arranged the surrender of the fort. He gave away what D. António had awarded him, and after it was done, he was put in a Spanish presidio. When Pedro Barba, the captain of the fort of Cabeça-Seca, saw this, he still, up to that point, did not want to surrender. However, the Marques of Santa Cruz, D. Álvaro Baçan, was entering the bay with Spanish galleys, he resigned and joined D. António, who had been defeated a few days before in Lisbon. D. António left Lisbon for Coimbra, and then Coimbra for Porto, where they acclaimed him as king. Sancho de Ávila was always right behind him, and he was finally forced to set sail from the Minho River dressed as a sailor. He went to the Azores and from there to other foreign kingdoms, where his life ended.

I have summarized these events not without a purpose but to explain the illness or occasion of the death of the governor of Brazil, Lourenço da Veiga. He honored the Portuguese side, and he was wounded by the actions of his brother Tristão Vaz da Veiga in handing over the tower of São Gião in the manner we have seen. When he heard the news, he became ill and then died.

In this way, Governor Lourenço da Veiga died, and with him we come to the end of this book.

BOOK 4

The History of Brazil When It Was Governed by Manuel Teles Barreto (1584–88) until the Arrival of Governor Gaspar de Sousa (1613)

CHAPTER 1

How Governor Manuel Teles Barreto Came to Rule Brazil and What Happened to Some French and English Ships in Rio de Janeiro and São Vicente

His Majesty, King Filipe, the second of Castile and the first of Portugal, was proclaimed king at the end of 1580. When he became aware of the death of the governor of Brazil, Lourenço da Veiga, he sent Manuel Teles Barreto as his replacement. He was the brother of António Moniz Barreto, who had governed India.[1] He was sixty and not only old but from a Portugal of long ago. Everyone spoke to him formally, and even when he visited the bishop, he left in grace, which is not the case for all older people.

As soon as he arrived in Bahia, which was in 1582, he wrote to all the captains to inform them that His Majesty [King Filipe II] was their king. This was important because a few days afterward, three French naus came to Rio de Janeiro and approached the defenses of the city, saying they had a letter from D. António for Captain Salvador Correia de Sá.[2] At that time, he had gone to the interior to wage war on the natives. However, the administrator, Bartolomeu Simões Pereira, who was governing in his absence, knew the truth because of his letter from the governor-general. He told the French to leave at once because he knew who his king was. Since there were few people in the city—only young students and some elderly men who could not fight in the war in the interior—he made a company from them. D. Inês de Sousa, the wife of Salvador Correia de Sá, organized another company of women. They wore hats and carried bows and arrows; they also beat drums and lit fires at night along the beach. This made the French think these were soldiers defending the city. So, after ten or twelve days, the French hoisted their anchors and departed.

At the same time, two English galleons of three hundred tons each went to the captaincy of São Vicente with the intention to colonize it and build a fort. They were aware of the gold mines and other metals in that land because of an account by a married resident Englishman. They had heard that the Catholic king [King Filipe II] was dead and that Portugal was ruled by D. António, who had offered great things to the queen of England. Because of the letter from the governor-general, the Portuguese remained firm in their support for the Catholic king and had no wish for the Englishmen to remain. However, the English threatened to enter by force and would have done so if, at that moment, three Spanish naus had not arrived and begun to fight with them. The English lowered their banner and asked for peace, but the Spanish did not agree. Rather, the Spanish trained their cannons on them all night because the currents would not allow them to board the English ships.

The next day, even though they left one nau in such terrible condition that it sunk, the English abandoned the venture and left the port with their naus in poor condition, without yardarms and with many holes in their ships. They had more than fifty dead and many injured, while the Spanish had thirty dead and fourteen wounded. The Spanish naus entered the port and were welcomed by the Portuguese, who praised His Majesty with one thousand blessings (even though it was by accident) for coming to their defense so quickly.

The details of how those naus came to be there will be explained in the next chapter.

CHAPTER 2
The Fleet Sent by His Majesty to the Straits of Magellan Led by
General Diogo Flores de Valdez and Its Success

In 1579, Francis Drake, an English pirate, passed through the Straits of Magellan into the southern ocean. D. Francisco de Toledo, the Viceroy of Peru, ordered Pedro de Sarmiento to follow him with Antão Paulo Corso as his pilot. These two passed through the same straits from south to north and arrived in Sevilla. They then went to Badajoz, where the king was directing his army into Portugal. After the king heard his report, and with the unease that the pirate had caused in Peru, Pedro de Sarmiento declared that the strait was sufficiently narrow to build forts on both sides. Once this was done, the artillery would easily impede ships from passing. However, there were contrary opinions saying that the strait was wider than Sarmiento calculated; in the sections where it was as narrow as he claimed, that alone would not stop ships from passing through because of the strong currents. One or two hits from artillery would not always sink a nau, and another one could pass in the interim. Among others who held this opinion was the Duke of Alba, D. Fernando Álvares de Toledo. However, the king ordered twenty-three large naus sent to Seville along with five thousand soldiers and sailors and the military stores for the construction of these forts. They would be large enough for three hundred soldiers and some settlers to assist in their maintenance. He named Diogo Flores de Valdez general of this fleet and Antão Paulo Corso as chief pilot. Pedro de Sarmiento was named governor of the forts and towns. This fleet left Sanlúcar de Barrameda, in Spain, on September 25 in the year 1581. It was in a great hurry because of the urgency of the Duke of Medina Sidonia, and it ran into foul weather. After three days, the fleet sheltered in the bay of Cádiz after losing three ships. The majority of the sailors had drowned, and the ships were so battered that they required more than forty days for repairs. Then they prepared to depart for Brazil with seventeen ships and arrived at the port of São Sebastião de Rio de Janeiro, where they wintered for six and a half months. Even though they arrived on March 25, which is spring in Spain, in these parts it is the beginning of winter, and it is impossible to sail through the straits. In order to keep the sailors occupied, they made pikes for defending trenches and supporting mud walls and cut wood to construct two storehouses for the supplies at the straits. The governor of Rio de Janeiro, Salvador Correia de Sá, gave them a great deal of assistance with all of this.

When it seemed the time was right to sail, they left Rio de Janeiro on October 2 with sixteen ships, leaving one useless ship behind. They set course for the straits, which are seven hundred leagues from this port, and they arrived at the Rio de la Plata. A great series of winds arose that were so strong that they were twenty-two days at sea being pushed sideways and unable to use the sails. It was here on the eve of Saint André's Day that the nau led by Captain Palomar was lost along with the 236 people on board.

There was nothing they could do to help. On December 2, the sea and winds became calmer and the captains and pilots agreed that Diogo Flores should turn back and seek a port where they could repair the naus. Five of them had been damaged by the storms, and others were in the same danger.

They went to the island of Santa Catarina, three hundred leagues distant. Even though it was unpopulated (because it was Portuguese land and the Portuguese do not know how to colonize or take advantage of the lands they conquer), it had a lot of water, fish, good hunting, firewood, and other things. At the end of the twenty-two days they were there, Diogo Flores de Valdez left three naus that could no longer sail on the high seas to the straits and left the treasurer, André Equino, in charge of them. They were ordered to return to Rio de Janeiro, and he placed D. Alonso de Souto Mayor, who was appointed as the next governor of Chile, in charge of three other ships to take people to Rio de la Plata and the port of Buenos Aires. From there it is only a twenty-day journey to Chile. This same Diogo Flores then left for the straits with the remaining ships on the Day of the Kings in the year 1583.

The three naus that remained on the island of Santa Catarina left on January 14. On the twenty-fourth, they entered the port of São Vicente, where they encountered the two English galleons attempting to occupy the land, had the Spanish ships not arrived and expelled them with their artillery, as we have related.

Diogo Flores de Valdez continued his journey to the straits, keeping land in sight on his right until he reached their opening at fifty-three degrees south latitude. They entered in good weather but after two or three leagues, a storm arose and pushed them more than forty leagues back to sea.

They sailed for eight days but were determined to reenter the straits; however, they could not because of the contrary winds. Diogo Flores did not wish to tempt fate any further, seeing his naus destroyed and his men ill from so much work. He returned to the port of São Vicente on the Brazilian coast. With the naus he had and with the two more he encountered there, they sailed to Rio de Janeiro where they found D. Diogo de Alzega, whom the king had sent with four naus, supplies, and other things. Diogo Flores believed the fleet was destroyed, with no surviving sailors or munitions, and he decided to return to Spain with D. Diogo de Alzega. His admiral, Diogo da Ribeira, would stay with five ships that remained and return the next summer to see whether they had better fortune entering the straits and colonizing them as ordered by the king.

Diogo Flores set sail with the other ships, which were now no more than seven, but had to seek shelter from a great storm that pushed him back two hundred leagues. He went to the Bay of All Saints at the beginning of June 1583 and attempted to stock the necessary supplies provided by the royal treasury. He sent supplies to Rio de Janeiro for Admiral Diogo da Ribeira to continue his voyage to the straits. Governor Manuel Teles Barreto fed all the captains and gentlemen splendidly one day and the bishop D. António Barreiros fed them the next. However, the person who provided the most was a citizen named Sebastião de Faria, who owned a sugar plantation. He offered them his houses and all his servants to feed them, their friends, and servants for the eight months they were here. He did this only to serve the king, without receiving any payment whatsoever, since such services when offered in Brazil are rarely compensated.

CHAPTER 3

On the Assistance Requested by Paraíba from Governor Manuel Teles and the Resolution regarding It

In chapter 25 of book 3, we mentioned how Governor Lourenço da Veiga refrained from conquering Paraíba when asked to do so by King D. Henrique. While he was in office, he entrusted this to Frutuoso Barbosa.

This man had left Pernambuco and had been to Paraíba to load wood on ships several times when there was peace with the Potiguarás. Because he was knowledgeable about the land and its people, the king placed him in charge of conquering it. The king made a contract that he would provide all the supplies needed for this as well as the naus and equipment. In exchange, once Paraíba was conquered, Frutuoso Barbosa would be its captain for ten years.

Frutuoso Barbosa arrived at the port in Pernambuco in 1579 in a handsome galleon and a *zabra* accompanied by other ships with many Portuguese, soldiers as well as married couples. They brought a lot of valuables, supplies, and ammunition needed both for the conquest as well as the settlement that would follow. They brought with them a vicar, to whom the king had awarded four hundred *cruzados* in salary, religious men from our angelic Franciscan order, and Benedictines with the supplies and funds needed for their work. This must have cost the royal treasury a great deal. In the seven or eight days they were anchored in port, they did not disembark, nor did they tend to the business for which they came. They then sheltered in the West Indies, where Barbosa's wife died, and from there they returned to Portugal. Barbosa left Portugal in 1582 by order of King Filipe and returned to Pernambuco to plan his actions with the people of Olinda. Simão Rodrigues Cardoso, the captain-major and magistrate for Pernambuco, would lead those on land, and he and his forces would leave by sea with others from the captaincy who would serve the king. When he arrived at the mouth of the Paraíba River with this fleet and some large caravels, he went upriver because he was informed that there were seven or eight French naus anchored there, beached and unattended. Most of the French sailors were in the bush with natives cutting wood to load on board. Quickly attacking these ships, our men were able to burn five after plundering them first, which was an honorable deed, and the others fled with almost all the Frenchmen.

This victory was achieved so easily and without spilling any blood that it made our people drop their guards. Some went ashore with the son of Frutuoso Barbosa, and suddenly the natives attacked them, coming from an island, fighting with them up to their lifeboats, where they had taken shelter. The naus did not come to assist, and it was tragic to see more than forty Portuguese killed, among them the son of the captain. With this same furious energy, the enemy attacked the smaller zabra where Gregório Lopes de Abreu was captain. The day before, he had moved to the front of the island and anchored there almost on dry land. Had he not defended the ship with such force, the natives would have captured it and everyone would have been lost.

Captain Frutuoso Barbosa was so afflicted and apprehensive with this chain of events that he hoisted anchor and moved the entire fleet to the mouth of the river, since it was not safe where he was. He was awaiting the arrival of the army. He was ready to set sail, since they seemed delayed, when Simão Rodrigues arrived with two hundred men on foot and horseback and many natives. On its way from the cultivated fields to Paraíba, this group had a victory over the Potiguarás. Those natives had been informed of our arrival and were awaiting our men. They revolted and made their attack. Had our allied natives not been there to assist the whites at this first encounter, the Potiguarás might have won.

They were so emboldened by their past victory that they engaged hand to hand with our men. But in the end, the Potiguarás were defeated, thrown into disarray, and with this victory our forces arrived on the north side of the mouth of the river, which bolstered those on the fleet. They were energized and, in the eight days they were there, they were able to fortify a site on the north side of the river, since the south side appeared impossible. This is an area called *Cabedelo*, and it is a poor site, lacking water. But they did not work on one side or the other but rather fled with great haste after seeing a large number of natives on the other side. They then sent the galleon to inform His Majesty what had happened, and Frutuoso Barbosa was totally despondent. He remarried on route to Pernambuco, and his new wife and her son replaced his lost wife and child. So everything returned to as it had been before: the natives were more arrogant than ever, and the neighboring captaincies were at risk of being depopulated.

They held out the hope of a rescue from those in Bahia. They had sent António Raposo there to make their case to Governor Manuel Teles Barreto, who did so by protesting against the Potiguarás voiding their promises. He made his case to the council in the governor's house, and with him were the bishop, D. António Barreiros; the general of the Spanish Army, Diogo Flores de Valdez; the Superior Court magistrate, Martim Leitão; and others who had an interest in this matter. They determined that General Diogo Flores and his men and Martim Leitão should lead, and they gave them all the powers needed to colonize Paraíba. They placed Martim Carvalho, a resident of Bahia, in charge of the fleet's treasury and supplies. Everyone agreed to this with great enthusiasm, particularly Diogo Flores. Because of Flores's misfortune in the matter of the straits, perhaps he would be able to seize this prize in his path.

CHAPTER 4
How Doctor Martim Leitão, Superior Court Magistrate, Was Sent by the Governor with General Diogo Flores de Valdez to Conquer Paraíba and Build a Fort at the River's Mouth

Continuing the subject matter of the last chapter, they made ready and departed from Bahia on March 1, 1584, with a fleet of nine naus, seven of which were Castilian and two Portuguese, and they arrived in Pernambuco on the twentieth of the same month. The superior crown magistrate immediately disembarked, and the ships remained outside the port. He went to a meeting with D. Filipe de Moura, whom Jorge de Albuquerque, the lord of the captaincy, had appointed as captain along with several other voting members of the city council. Among these was D. António de Barreiros, the bishop of Bahia. He had gone with the fleet to visit the churches of Pernambuco and Itamaracá.

Everything was finalized for a departure on Easter Sunday, with D. Filipe de Moura leading the men. There was much that the superior crown magistrate had to do. He started at once, asking each person and preparing people from Pernambuco. They gathered at the town of Igaraçu on the appointed day, where D. Filipe had arrived with those from Itamaracá at the sugar mill owned by his father-in-law, Filipe Cavalcanti, in Araripe until Martim Leitão joined their camp. After they left, an additional forty men joined them; D. Filipe had turned them over to Álvaro Bastardo. The first group reached the second one at the Paraíba River, where they fought the natives. They then crossed the river on the north side, where Simão Rodrigues Cardoso had crossed before, and they sought the sandbar of the river, where they found Diogo Flores. He had already burned three French naus, which he found beached on land. He climbed on one and an enemy in the bush fired an arrow and hit him the chest, but he was not injured because of his good armor.

Because the main aim had been to colonize the area, once they reached their encampment, Diogo Flores came forth, and after meeting with the captains, they decided to first build a fort for protection so they could build a town in its shadow. They proclaimed General Flores to be in charge of the fort and Francisco Castejon as infantry captain, with 110 Castilian soldiers with harquebuses and fifty Portuguese. The Portuguese soldiers selected a leader for the town they were going to build. Since most were from Viana do Castelo, they selected Frutuoso Barbosa, who was from there. They also kept in mind the offer by King D. Henrique that he would make him captain of Paraíba if he conquered it. Since it was a conditional offer, if he did not complete it, the king was not obligated to honor it. This was the opinion of the general.

They built the fort a league from the entrance to the river on its north side and directly across from the tip of the island. They did this so that the soldiers would not be carried away by the current in the middle and because it was a good site. The island was a poor site, low, with foul water.

Captain Francisco Castejon remained in charge of the troops, and in honor of General Diogo Flores they named it Fort São Filipe and São Tiago since it was on their day that the general left Spain and he was saved.[1]

While the others were building the fort, Captain Simão Falcão was watching an enemy village. One morning he attacked it, killed some natives, and captured four. Our forces used these four as interpreters, and since the army was not busy, they left for the interior to search for enemies. They went as far as a meadow called *the Oysters,* which is three leagues from the fort, and they camped there. Because it was the feast day of the Holy Spirit and people were ready to celebrate, they had a party and abandoned everything else for that day and for the eight days following it. D. Filipe explained these festivities by saying that he was waiting for his father-in-law, Filipe Cavalcanti, who had remained at the fort.

One afternoon, after hearing a trumpet and a lot of noise, ten men set out on horseback and another forty on foot with many natives under the command of António Leitão. They were very unorganized and pushed into the interior. They fell into a trap and were fearful until they reached the sight of the clearing. They had not made any arrangements for those there to assist them. Everything was so unorganized that when night came, they slept next to a great lake when they should have gone to the fort. Fleeing with wings of fear, they fell over each other, knocking at the gates of the fort. The captain in charge was disgusted when he saw them and did not open the gates but rather left them outside in the rain all night. This was a mild, but deserved, punishment.

When daybreak arrived, they attempted to talk them into once more seeking out the enemy. More than fifty men with harquebuses joined them from the fort, but they would have none of it and wanted to return to Pernambuco. That is what they did, and our forces saw them from the front of the fort leaving in boats. This was very difficult since it was winter. The entire return voyage was very difficult, and many horses and slaves died from deprivations.

CHAPTER 5
The Assistance Sent to Paraíba because of the Efforts of the Head Justice

So it was that they arrived in Pernambuco in the month of June, and right away the captain of the fort asked for supplies, as did Frutuoso Barbosa.

Because the enemy had been so victorious, they were threatening them, and only the fury of the artillery prevented the enemy from overtaking the fort. Finding the enemy in the open, they killed them. In skirmishes the captain had with them, he displayed his personal valor, as did the Spanish and Portuguese who followed him. This was in spite of Captain Frutuoso Barbosa, who had no patience for these skirmishes, and because of his demands, prevented them when he could. Both he and the captain of the fort were in foul moods, and there were fights and ugly words between them; they each wrote stacks of complaints about the other, which they sent to the Superior Court magistrate with requests for supplies. The judge was known as a dutiful royal servant, and this bothered him, but it was the responsibility of the superintendent of supplies, Martim Carvalho, who, on the other hand, was very negligent. Because of this, there was great discord between these two, always originating from the lack of supplies. The men were at the edge of fighting and suffered from a hunger that drove them to even eat their horses.

Martin Leão sent them twenty-four men by sea under the command of Nicolau Nunes along with some supplies provided by the superintendent of supplies. However, the provisions were so few and the attacks from the Potiguarás so frequent that in the month of September the captain of the fort went to Pernambuco to ask for help. This is where he found Pedro Sarmiento, whom the general had left with Admiral Diogo da Ribeira in Rio de Janeiro to colonize the Straits of Magellan and rule the town they would establish. They came all in shambles and also wanted supplies, which were given to them, so they could return to Spain. However, Captain Castejon was so slow in getting packed that Admiral Ribeira became impatient. One day (after many other days had passed) in the home of Martim Carvalho with all the judges and town officials present, as well as the bishop, the two exchanged a great deal of foul language. When that occurred, some people in the house forcibly separated them with the help of the captain's soldiers above [them]. Engaged in fighting as they were, they went out to the street, and many people came to help as did the Superior Court judge, who calmed them as best he could.

Because of this, the captain returned to Paraíba in October with few provisions and with every indication that they would be fewer each time because of the hatred between himself and the superintendent. However, his return was godsent because in that November, two French naus entered Paraíba. When they saw the fort, the large Portuguese nau, and two pinnaces left by Diogo Flores, they anchored three leagues distant at the mouth of the Bay of Traição. From there, they began to barter with the Potiguarás. The French came ashore from there to the fort, bringing with them some short cannons, which they trained on the fort, while making large trenches and walls of earth and sand so that our artillery would not strike them. With these and other cunning tricks, since they were well acquainted with our style of warfare, the captain of the fort lost the hope of being able to defend himself. He informed the chief magistrate of this and asked for supplies as well as those for Frutuoso Barbosa.

On the first day that he could, the judge went to pass the night in Recife, where he prepared a ship of seventy tons at his own expense. He manned it with many white men and seventy natives; Gaspar Dias de Morais was captain. Morais was an old soldier who had fought in Flanders, and he was given the post because he asked for it. In two days, he was being carried in a hammock because he was ill, and they left him on land. The judge supplied this ship and a galley belonging to Pedro Lopes Lobo, captain of Itamaracá. Lopes acted as captain, with a crew of fifty men and some natives. They arrived in Paraíba, where they were welcomed and appreciated like life itself.

When the Frenchmen saw that reinforcements had arrived, they returned to their naus in the Bay of Traição. When the captain of the fort discussed this matter with the captains who had come to assist, they determined that Pedro Lopes, the captain of the galley, should remain in the fort because of the many natives conducting the siege. They say there were more than ten thousand around their trenches and embankments. The captain and his galley and the nau that had come to assist went to seek out the Frenchmen, which they did. They captured them on the ocean, made them beach their naus, and then burned the ships, while killing several of Frenchmen. This was an honorable act since these naus were large and ready to fight. However, the nau that had remained at the fort, because it was very large and the coastal wind was pushing toward the Indies, was made to remain in the harbor. Most of the artillery they had taken from the French was on board that nau.

The ship and the galley returned from pursuing the French, and those on board quickly disembarked. They hit the enemy with such force that they gained ground, killing many of them. The natives kept a great distance, and our forces gathered the water the natives had collected. Those in the fort had more space than ever and were very happy. It was with great praise that the court magistrate returned to Pernambuco and Itamacá, but not before hearing the accounts about everything and receiving congratulations for making the journey. It had made a great impact, both on the bold actions of the French, who had been prevented from collecting wood, and on the Potiguarás, who could no longer trade with the French.

CHAPTER 6

How the Superior Court Magistrate Martim Leitão Went to Paraíba the First Time, How the Trip Was Organized, and the First Siege

The Potiguarás were left stewing with the memories of these offenses and the desire for vengeance. In January 1585, they gathered in larger groups than ever and laid three powerful sieges around the fort. The thick palm trunks defended the natives from the artillery, and every night they fought and gained ground. The captain of the fort immediately informed the chief magistrate of their situation. The captain feared that in this manner, the natives would get closer to the fort and attack it, and they would not be able to use their artillery. Nor would they be able to fight the natives, because there were many people who were ill because of the poor site, hunger, and bad water. Many had died, and thus the fort was in great danger.

On February 8, they made new requests with greater vigor, began to requisition everything, and prepared to evacuate everyone. They knew that the nau was their best possible escape. The captains were all in revolt when they heard this news, and it was all the more worrisome since the famous native leader Braço de Peixe had arrived to aid the Potiguarás, or as he was known in his language, *Piragiba*. We discussed him in chapter 20 of the previous book.

The Superior Court magistrate furnished the supplies requested by the captain of the fort and sent these with Captain D. Filipe who was working with Martim Carvalho. D. Filipe also took with him some other supplies requested by the fort's lieutenant. The lieutenant felt the matter was urgent, and all agreed, including the bishop and town officials. They asked the magistrate to personally participate in this war, and they made a solemn declaration to this effect. Realizing the importance of this matter, he agreed on February 14, with plans to depart before the month was over. He began the preparations with great speed, and it was remarkable how many people came forward to accompany him. However, there were no more than thirty ships in the harbor. There never had been such a demand for provisions, and it would not be possible to supply and dispatch the ships so quickly. The great diligence shown by Martim Leitão was also remarkable; he wrote to each of the nobles, urging them to join this expedition, providing good reasons for the journey, and preparing everyone. Everything in Brazil is purchased on credit, and they needed great quantities of supplies, which the merchants could not agree to supply on those terms. As a result, he had to provide these himself and to supply one and then the other without end. He also raised troops for the captains, which they later used in the vanguard since they trusted them so highly. There were many single people, mamelucos, and natives who are very effective in such operations. For these two companies, he paid for their rations and everything else they needed. He supplied their weapons, even though in the written preparations the superintendent said these would be paid for by His Majesty's treasury.

There were two captains of the guard, Gaspar Dias de Morais, who had been to Paraíba before to assist, and Micer Hipólito, who was an old hand and a very experienced local. In addition, they appointed nine others as captains: Ambrósio Fernandes Brandão and Fernão Soares, whom they called *captains of the merchants,* and Simão Falcão, Pedro Cardigo, and Jorge Camelo, who were appointed as company captains of the army. João Pais was the captain of Cape Saint Agostinho and very wealthy. He always took up the rear. João Velho Rego was the captain of Igaraçu, and there was Pedro Lopes as the captain of Itamaracá. Because there were 195 good horsemen, they organized three squads of thirty horses drawn from the best to assist wherever they might be needed.[1] These were led by Captains Cristóvão Pais d'Altero, António Cavalcanti, the son of Filipe Cavalcanti, and Baltasar de Barros. The son of António de Carvalho, another captain, went in his father's place because his father was ill, and his son did well in all his battles.

The second in command of this expedition, the person who really took charge, was Francisco Barreto, the son-in-law of the Superior Court magistrate Martim Leitão. He was called the field commander and was equal to many thousands of soldiers for his strength and skill.

This army, which was the most beautiful thing Pernambuco ever witnessed and for all I know will ever see, was led by General Martim Leitão (which was what he was called on this expedition). They went to camp in the field in Igaraçu, and in the middle of it, he raised his field tent with two other tents attached to it. One was for the Jesuit fathers who traveled with him, and the other was his pantry where his servants also stayed. Here he made great proclamations, enforcing severe penalties against all who fought or used their swords against each other. In particular, he urged that there should be friendship and order among everyone. He gave other good and necessary orders, and if such orders were customary here in Brazil, we would not experience so much damage and disorder. They waited there for three days for some others to join them, and he and other officials provided shelter.

On the fourth day (which was March 1) they left and went to camp on the other side of the Tapirema River, where he reviewed his forces. They had five hundred or so white men, and the general issued orders to all telling them what they needed to do. He formed companies and ordered one of the squadrons of cavalry to lead the way, the other to guard the rear, and the third to be in battle with him. They would alternate to prevent competition. The captain in charge of the rear guard would be responsible to leave one hour before dawn with some natives to find the way forward. In this orderly manner, trusted men always accompanied the mamelucos and natives leading the way. Flanks of the army were in the bush, and servants cleared the way. Their journey lasted five days and was the great campaign of Paraíba. Some participants remember people moving in such a tight formation that when the road was long and narrow, they did not pass the vanguard as a precaution. That day, because it was more important, Francisco Barreto led the way. However, the general wanted to move faster, and he galloped ahead to see what caused the delay. He thought it might be dense bush or that the servants had delayed clearing the way with their scythes. He ordered the vanguard to move faster with caution while he waited there to return to his usual place in the convoy.

The vanguard moved forward with the field commander leading it. Just as the sun was setting, they came across a large enclosed village of natives next to the Tibiri River. There must have been three thousand souls there. In spite of the number of natives, the developing darkness, and the strength of the enclosure surrounded by a wooden wall, our forces attacked like lions and entered the village, killing many enemies and making the others flee. Our forces were not badly injured because of the speed of the attack; the enemy did not have time to fire many arrows. Most of the army was with the rear guard, and they rushed forward to join the others in battle. They moved as quickly as they could, but it was all over by the time they arrived.

The entire army then entered the walled village, which Francisco Barreto had emptied with the forward troops. They all settled in and slept there that night. They found some prepared flour, guns, and gunpowder, which some captives told them the natives were planning to use to attack the fort.

CHAPTER 7
How Peace Was Attempted with Braço de Peixe and When He Declined,
How They Conducted War

Early the next morning, the natives began their bantering (as is their custom) on top of a steep hill in front of our enclosure, in spite of the marshy land there. Our people recognized them as Braço de Peixe's people and not Potiguarás but Tabajaras, their enemies. However, because they feared the Portuguese and wanted revenge for the deaths of more than one hundred at the hands of Gaspar Dias de Ataíde and Francisco de Caldas (even though they had good reasons), as we said in chapter 20 of the previous book, they had allied themselves with the Potiguarás. Because the Tabajaras were more industrious and braver, they did our forces great harm. Once this was known by General Martim Leitão, and in light of the importance of peace with the Tabajaras and separating them from the Potiguarás, he sent interpreters to explain that they were safe and that he only sought Potiguarás. The general said they never desired peace with the Potiguarás, but they did with his people. In addition, they told Braço de Peixe's people that the general was an honorable man from Portugal and did not employ the deceptions and evil ways of the Brazilians. Furthermore, he was well-informed about Braço de Peixe's former friendship with the whites. He knew the Portuguese broke the peace agreement, and if Captains Ataíde and Caldos were alive, he would send them to the king for punishment.

In this manner and by them offering wine, they agreed after exchanging hostages that Braço de Peixe would send his ambassadors after the evening meal to discuss peace with the general. Meanwhile, the general worked very hard to find an exit from the marsh at its top or bottom, but he did not find one because of its size and the thick brush.

At noon, three natives came to discuss peace, and the general listened to them in his tent as they were questioned by interpreters and shown all the necessary courtesies. Braço de Peixe and his people had many Potiguarás with them. That and his fear caused by his guilt meant that nothing would suffice to assure him of peace. As a result, that afternoon he would kill the hostages and war would begin. The enemy had underestimated our numbers but rushed to fire thirty-odd pistols and many arrows at our forces that afternoon. The general wished to end that. So, in order to fool the enemy, he ordered everyone to take positions between the enclosure and the swampy area. In order for this to succeed, they had cleared the area that morning. He also wanted to show them two short cannons that he brought on carts and display their power. He aimed at a cluster of dead trees and branches the natives had erected to defend themselves at the top of a hill above a burned area. They performed other menacing acts, but nothing made the natives want peace.

The general then resolved that the next day he would battle the enemy. That afternoon, he ordered that they make bundles of firewood from what they cut along the edge of the enclosure; by using the bridges the natives had in the swamp they could cross with these to the other side.

The general's preparations were not obvious in the enclosure, but they could be seen better in the council that night in his tent. There were various opinions and some confusion, and his gentle words convinced two-thirds of the men to remain in the enclosure with Francisco Barreto and the supplies. He would go on foot with the other third to confront the enemy on the hill.

They heard Mass the next day very early in the morning, and the general left with only the companies of the vanguard and one of the cavalry led by António Cavalcanti. He ordered that our forces cross the swamp through a burned bare patch so that they would not fall into a trap and the enemy attack them from the rear. Father Jerónimo Machado of the Jesuits carried a crucifix before them, and they encountered numerous obstacles, since the enemy had cut down many trees during the night to impede their path. Because of this, and since many soldiers were walking along the other side of the burned area with the bundles of firewood, they made slow progress. They were fearful, and the general had to reassure some. He ordered the company led by Ambrosio Fernandes to stay in the swampy area and not move until all the men were ahead. He pulled out his sword and swore that he would slay the first person who spoke, if all did not fight bravely. This and picking up the pace after all had caught up allowed them to quickly capture the hillside ahead of them.

After all the enemy had gathered in the enclosure, our forces went on foot up to them and put all of them in irons, yet they refused to surrender. When the general saw this, he pulled an Englishman forward that he had with him and armed him, and he climbed on his shoulders above the enclosure with a lance of fire. He waved it around and fired so many burning splinters that the enemy fled. Our forces pulled down two or three braças of the walled enclosure and entered. They pursued the natives a bit but were hindered by the terrible road and the obstacles the natives had placed on it. The natives are like wild insects that flee wherever they wish, and many escaped. God ordained that they remain for us. They have and we are now friends.

Moving as quickly now as our forces could, the general ordered the dead trees and wood in the enclosure to be burned. Once all was destroyed, they returned to their companions who had remained at the other camp. They came forward and greeted them with a hymn of praise to God.[1] The same day in the afternoon, there was a sudden attack by the edge of the Tibiri River, which some of the captains met in a disorganized manner. Because there were many people attacking, the general sent Francisco Barreto to organize our forces, and he did very well, establishing order. In this skirmish, some Potiguarás were killed, but none of our people were injured. Since there was no point in staying there another day, the general ordered the camp burned. With the entire army below the Tibiri River, they chased the enemy. They slept two leagues from there at a place now called *the Marés*. They took all the supplies they found, which was the greatest damage they could offer, burned two empty villages, and looked for a new camp made by one of the native leaders named *Assento de Pássaro*. Before they found it, they encountered so many obstacles along the terrible path that they had to cut their way through the bush and marsh with enemy spies surrounding them. As difficult as it was for the general to move forward, he passed the vanguard with the judge of the captaincy, Francisco do Amaral, who always followed him. They found the village, and it was large, strong, and empty except for some old men and women who could not flee. They fought our people. They stopped there that night and the next. Because of the many marshy areas and differing opinions about the unknown paths, they decided to return to the Paraíba River and follow it to find the way to the fort where they would relate what had happened.

Leaving that enclosure by another way, which was the main road, they encountered so many labyrinths that the enemy had created, so many pits they had dug, and trees they had cut down to block the path that it was a marvel. The enemy had no fear; a handful were able to block the path for many. However, Our Lord guided our forces and kept the enemy from misleading them.

After crossing the Paraíba River, in three days they reached the fort, which was pitiful to see, all damaged and in ruins, as well as the general state of the soldiers there. Their hunger and misery were obvious.

CHAPTER 8

How General Martim Leitão Arrived at the Fort and Ordered Captain João Pais to the Bay of Traição and Afterward Departed for Pernambuco

The afternoon they arrived at the fort, the general ordered that Captain João Pais quickly depart for the Bay of Traição with three hundred soldiers and cavalry, which they did the next morning at daybreak.

The general also dealt a great deal with Frutuoso Barbosa who wanted to go two leagues from the fort, next to Marés, where there were many supplies on the south side of the Paraíba River. He wanted to establish a village there, and, in order to do that, he was joined by eighty white men and as many natives as he could find. He offered to stay with them for six months, and Francisco Barreto, his brother-in-law, would stay with them an additional six. However, they were not ever able to finish with him. In the written statements they made, he said he wanted to abandon this effort in Paraíba and not continue it for one more hour. With all of this, the general decided to establish a town at that site (which all agreed appeared to be a good one). Pero Lopez and others agreed to do this but could not finish it. With the same energy, he decided to go to the beach with the same people and establish a place on the Bay of Traição next to João Pais. In that way, with one encampment above and the other below, there would be no room in between them. The enemy followed them for several days until engaging them from a distance. However, they planned to leave at low tide the next day, but very suddenly that evening forty-two people fell ill with odd stomach cramps and pains in the chest. Among these were Francisco Barreto, the Jesuit Father Simão Tavares, and other very important people; this delayed them for two days. Seeing that they were not improving because of the bad air and poor water at that site, they were forced to move upriver two leagues to a very beautiful field called *the field of oysters*. In the six days they were there awaiting João Pais, some recovered. Once he arrived and they were once again all together, knowing that their enemies would not be so bold as to attack them in the bay, they burned many villages and took their supplies. They had two or three meetings to determine what they should do. They knew for sure that the Tabajaras, Braço de Peixe's people, were on bad terms with the Potiguarás. They had begun to wage war on each other and would exhaust themselves. Everyone agreed that it was better to leave them alone. Before they expended all their energy, it would be best to inform Braço de Peixe that they would help him fight the Potiguarás, and he should not return to the mountains. In great secrecy, the general sent a native relative of his with a message of great promises if he returned and came to the sea.

After giving this order, staffing the fort with twenty more men, and placing Captain Pero Lopes in charge to replace Frutuoso Barbosa, the general provisioned the fort as best he could. He left sufficient supplies of flour, hardtack, wine, and sardines for two months.[1] Everyone left for Olinda in a happy mood, even though the Superior Court magistrate Martim Leitão (since he was now no longer called *general*) was not happy or content. He said he had not done anything since there was no town established in Paraíba, and the war had not ended, even though they had the strength for such measures in which Our Lord had so favored them.

In this manner, they entered the town of Olinda marching in order with drums, and everyone accompanied the magistrate to his home. They had the largest party and festival of triumph ever held in Pernambuco, which was on April 6, 1585.

CHAPTER 9

How Captain Castejon Fled the Fort and the Superior Court Magistrate
Apprehended Him and Provided for the Soldiers

On June 1, 1585, news arrived in Pernambuco that Captain Pero Lopes had arrived in Itamaracá. The magistrate Martim Leitão had left him and some Portuguese in the fort in Paraíba along with the captain in charge of the fort. The news was this captain wanted to desert with the Spanish, and he secretly sought a pilot to take him to the West Indies. Since the magistrate was so attentive to this matter, as soon as he heard the news, he went looking for Pero Lopes and spoke with him. In four days, Lopes agreed to return to supply the fort, and he would take some locals and natives with him who would remain with him until January. The magistrate agreed to pay him fifty cruzados monthly because it would not be possible to break his agreement with the king until he was informed and they proved who was responsible for abandoning the fort.

It was with great difficulty that Pero Lopes agreed to this because the impossible character of the captain of the fort, Castejon, made the people flee. Another major hurdle was the supervisor of supplies, Martim Carvalho (who until that point had very poorly supplied the fort). He now said publicly that he would no longer provide anything at all, leaving the fort defenseless. Things would have turned out even worse had the magistrate not resolved this issue by making loans. He immediately asked Captain Pero Lopes to make a list of the provisions required for one hundred men for six months, and once that was done, it totaled 3,000 cruzados. The magistrate sent the list to merchants who had these provisions, and they were satisfied by credit offered by the merchant João Nunes. Lopes boarded a ship and prepared to calm the Spanish in the fort. Lopes had the town council write letters and send gifts, telling them they were certain the fort would now be better provisioned since they were now free from Martim Carvalho, which pleased everyone.

The magistrate wrote the same things. Pero Lopes took these letters and went to his home on the island of Itamaracá to prepare for the journey. The ship and people were there ready to accompany him. In the meantime, he was to inform the captain of the fort, Castejon. Either the Devil drew him into his web, or I do not know why, but Pero Lopes did not inform those in the fort, nor did he send the letters, even though he was charged with this responsibility. He had them in his possession from June 8 until June 24 when everything was prepared for departure the next day by sea and by land for those on the island. They began to say that the Spanish had arrived there from the fort, and they said the captain [Castejon] was following behind them and they [Castejon's men] had destroyed everything.

On account of this (the news of which quickly spread) the entire town gathered at the time of the Ave Marias at the magistrate's house. There they decided to gather at the [Jesuit?] college, with the bishop, Captain D. Filipe, the town council, and superintendent Martim Carvalho, who did not rest in these matters. That same night he sent his officials to find Castejon quickly, which they did in good time. When questioned, his only reason for leaving the fort was hunger, which was a weak excuse because he admitted that after the war waged by the magistrate, the enemy did not return. He could have searched for provisions with the boats left upriver, and it would have been easy. However, they must have been uneasy since they took revenge by casting the artillery into the sea, sinking a nau there, burning the fort, and breaking the bell. After that, they came to town as if they had done nothing. That was what they later determined in Portugal, where the magistrate sent Castejon as a prisoner; he was set free and cleared of all charges.

The next morning, when the meeting had begun at the college, there were some doubts from the bishop and others about the poor response they would get from Portugal regarding something so important. It would make the effort of settling Paraíba more difficult; truthfully, it was now more doubtful than ever. There had been so many false starts, so many of our people had been killed, and the fear of the French always seemed to be present. Because of all this, they said that land could never be conquered without the king's strong support.

It was only the magistrate, filled with energy and passion, who persuaded the others, with many reasons, to select one from among them. He would go with 150 others and some natives, with the expenses and provisions they would require, to recover what was lost. If they did not agree, the magistrate and his friends were determined to go to our ruined fort before our enemies could get there and fortify it. Those who had the duty to protect it had left it defenseless. He made this case with so much energy, talking about supplies, protests, and threats from His Majesty that he shook them and made them wake up. They then selected Captain Simão Falcão, who seemed to be the right person. However, Frutuoso Barbosa did not want to accept this. Simão Falcão was immediately notified of his selection, and the magistrate gathered all the Spanish men in town who came from the fort. He used proclamations, effort, and great diligence to accomplish this. He formed two squadrons of forty-two men from these soldiers, housed them, and provided their daily rations from his house at his expense. Nor did he forget to ask religious figures to pray for God's assistance in this effort.

CHAPTER 10

How Braço de Peixe Asked for Peace and Assistance against the Potiguarás and
the Superior Court Magistrate Returned to Paraíba to Establish a Town

That month of July there had been some delays caused by the poor health of Simão Falcão, who had been in charge in spite of his illness. At the end of the month, two of Braço de Peixe's people arrived at the home of the magistrate asking for assistance in fighting the Potiguarás. When he and his people had responded to Leitão's message as we mentioned in chapter 8 and came to the sea, the Potiguarás had surrounded them and put them in great danger.

That same day, Martim Leitão gave the natives some clothes and went to Recife with João Tavares, the secretary of the town council and judge of the orphans. They spent the night there. Before he left, Tavares publicly stated his opinion that we should provide the help they requested, and Leitão agreed after hearing his pleas and being asked in the name of the king. They left with twelve well-armed Spaniards and eight Portuguese and a well-stocked caravel prepared for anything and stocked with some gifts. It left the port of Pernambuco on August 2, 1585, and on the third it arrived above the Paraíba River. They met Braço de Peixe and other leaders there, where our port and city are now located. They frightened some Potiguarás with gunshots, and the Potiguarás fled because they assumed we had more forces.

They sat down, made peace with Braço de Peixe, and exchanged gifts and pledges of peace, which Captain João Tavares concluded on the Day of Our Lady of the Snows.[1] Because of that, this became the name for the town they established, and she was made its patron saint and guardian. Under her watchful protection, they constructed a wooden fortress with its back to the river, and they sheltered in it.

The magistrate was immediately informed of this. All the townspeople and residents of these captaincies rejoiced with this news, since it seemed to them, with good reason, that their work was completed. After giving many thanks to God, the interpreters arrived by land with forty natives and the embassy of Braço de Peixe. The magistrate welcomed all of them to stay in his house and provided clothing and fed them. He sent word to Captain João Tavares as to what he should do and sent him an additional twenty-five men, native, mameluco, and white, since the Spanish were still very ill. He also sent fine clothes for the native leaders and other gifts to make them all very happy. He further ordered that there be no capturing of natives, since he was well acquainted with this and was opposed to it. This was with good reason, since enslaving them harms the natives in Brazil.

In order to ensure the peace, it seemed necessary to immediately build a fort, recover the artillery from the old fort, and establish a town. Everyone agreed that no one other than Superior Court Magistrate Martim Leitão could do this, which everyone asked him to do. He accepted as a service to God and king as well as for these captaincies, and he left for Paraíba on October 15 of that same year. The expedition consisted of some of his friends, officials, and servants and numbered twenty-five on horseback and forty on foot. They took with them stonemasons and carpenters and all the supplies needed to build a fort and other buildings. They arrived there on the twenty-ninth and were warmly received by the natives and whites who were there. The native leaders who came from a league away greeted him one by one with great festivity. He had the servants from his house dismount from the horses so that the natives could ride; some of them were fearful because of what had happened in the past with the whites, and it was necessary to help them into the saddle.

With this success, they rode through the middle of the native villages, which made some cry and others laugh with pleasure. Later that evening, they were told about the places where a town could be established and that they should seek what they would need to build it. Manuel Fernandes was in charge of the king's construction, and Duarte Gomes da Silveira,

João Queixada, and the captain were all informed in secret of this beforehand but were also aware of the various opinions about where to build
the town.

The next day, the magistrate heard Mass before sunrise (which he
always did when traveling on these expeditions). He went on foot to see
some sites, and in the afternoon, he went on horseback from the bank of
the Jaguaripe River to Cape Branco and other places. At night, he was certain this was the best site for the city: a plain more than half a league wide,
very flat, surrounded by water on all sides, dominating the port, which
the shot from a falconet could easily reach. The side facing the harbor was
so steep that from the prow of a sixty-ton ship you could step on land.
This was where a beautiful spring of fresh water emerged, which could
supply the ships. It was a beautiful scene of nature, and there was a lot
of limestone. Right away, they ordered an oven made from it and stones
quarried from above it.

Once all was surveyed and the shrubs were cleared, on November 4,
they began to build the fort. It was 140 spans long on each of its four sides.
It had two sentry boxes, which held eight large pieces of artillery at opposite angles to each other. Everyone worked on this structure following
his [Leitão's] example. He called each one to work in the morning, sending some for the limestone, and others to the forest with the carpenters
and woodcutters. Still others went with the stonecutters, and those who
remained prepared the lathing for the mud. Only the foundation and
corners were made from stone and lime while everything else was wood
lathe and mud, four spans wide. He right away ordered eight lathes so that
everyone worked. It was something to see the persistence and pride with
which he worked more than the others. The magistrate toiled from sunup
to sundown, only stopping for an hour at lunchtime. After two weeks of
work, the fort was ready for the artillery. In this brief time with a lot of
work and focus and with the help of divers brought for this purpose, they
were able to remove the artillery pieces from the sea without losing one,
which was a miracle. They were only missing the lower parts, but with
six that they brought from Pernambuco and two falconets, which were in
storage on the large caravels, they had all they required.[2]

Once the artillery was in place, in order not to waste time and to
prevent our native allies from getting cold, because the cold season had

already started, he ordered João Tavares and Pero Lopes and all the people to wage a good war at the Fraldes de Copaoba. This is a very fertile mountainous land eighteen leagues from the sea where there are many Potiguarás. Only leaving behind his servants and the officials working on the city and Cristóvão Lins and Gregório Lopes de Abreu, everyone else left with them. They only traveled thirteen or fourteen days, but they did not destroy more than four or five villages. The magistrate regretted their haste and decided to go in person. As quickly as possible, he finished building what he could of the fort, the captain's house, and the warehouse.

CHAPTER 11
How the Magistrate Went to the Bay of Traição

After everything had been arranged in good order by November 20, the magistrate left Cristóvão Lins there, a German nobleman, along with the various officials and the required number of people. He left with eighty-five white men and 180 native allies. They were sufficient and a mixed group; many tried to hinder their departure with bravado, saying that there were French naus in the bay. With their words, some began to forget to show the required respect, especially one who went beyond that, aiming his harquebus at Captain João Tavares's chest. The magistrate ordered him apprehended, and at the entrance to the fort in front of everyone, he was whipped. This was a gentle remedy because after that no one said anything. Thus, everyone left the fort and went to pass the night at Tibiri; from there, the next day they reached the Field of the Greens, where they met with our native allies. They only took six *alqueires* of war flour with them and the whites did not bring more than two days' rations. When the magistrate was informed of this, he happily said they would find their food among their enemies. Since their enemies were alive, they had to have food to eat. From there, they left for Jorge Camelo's spring, and, after the sun had risen, they reached the Mamanguape River, which is eight leagues away. Because they had to reach some villages on the other side of the river before the enemy natives they had encountered sounded the alarm, they took advantage of the low tide and went without supper, crossing at midnight all wet from the day's work. At daybreak, they walked in an orderly fashion together until ten o'clock and then fell upon the enemy with a frightful cry and made a great noise at the field and riverbank.

[The original text is missing this section, as mentioned in the introduction]

They crossed to the other side, and it was two hours before daybreak when they made a fire, which quickly dried their harquebuses. The magistrate right away ordered that they should seize the beach, which until that point was unknown. It seemed to many that it was very long and taking it would be a lot of work. However, the judge went with Duarte Gomes, António Lopes de Oliveira, and three natives leading the way. They walked until daybreak.

Those on horseback departed with some men with harquebuses to attack from the north, while the others went with our natives from the south. They attacked the fort held by the enemy with great cries, killed twenty natives, and captured their leader. Others swam into the ocean because the land had been captured and took shelter on the French nau. All the Frenchmen were on board with their guns, since the day before they had been warned by a native who escaped from Duarte Gomes. In the clarity of the morning, they began to search the beach where our forces were located with their artillery, and we drove them out of the village on high ground. Our forces found the village in shambles but with a lot of already prepared flour and beans that made for a feast along with the cashew nuts from the forest, which were just then ripe. In order to destroy all their supplies and separate the French from this place, they remained there for three days. In the afternoon, they pulled up all the cassava plants. That night, the magistrate ordered that three sets of blacksmith's works they found there belonging to the French be thrown into the ocean. It was important to take them from the enemy. This was how the French cooked their food. Removing them from the camp and taking away their ironworks was important; their presence meant the French were living there. They found more than seventy large and small cooking vessels, goods, and many tools, which our natives took.

The next day, the magistrate ordered twenty-four men with harquebuses to attack the French ship at low tide, and they fired three or four volleys at it. Even though they did no damage, the French were afraid our forces would approach or that more ships would arrive from Paraíba. They hoisted anchor and fired their cannons in the air. They took this news back to France, but our forces were very content to see them depart even if the view was only from the beach.

CHAPTER 12

How They Left the Bay of Traição for Tujucupapo and
Returned to Pernambuco

The third day, our natives loaded the spoils of this conquest and some supplies and left the Bay of Traição, always following the coastline. The captured natives spoke of nothing but Tujucupapo, the great leader of the Potiguarás, who was a celebrated shaman. On the fourth day after they left, they were feeling unconcerned because it seemed the enemy no longer sought them, yet they called out from the rear, "Potiguarás! Potiguarás!"

Shouting this did not frighten them, even though their numbers were few, because warfare in these parts is always conducted in the bush, and the natives always line up single file and follow a very rough path. Even though there were few natives, since they could not line up or make a battle formation, they occupied a very long space. Because of this, the warning cry from the rear affected each person where they were, and they started to walk faster. However, at that time, there was a Spanish soldier who asked Martim Leitão for help because the forces in the vanguard were falling back and there were injuries. He left at once just wearing pants and a doublet and took a spear from João Nunes and a shield for one of the natives, leaving Gregório Lopes de Abreu and António de Barros Rego in charge. He mounted a horse and went through the bush, which was the low ground. He arrived as three enemy squadrons burst from the bush, and they gathered their forces and went on the attack since this is their method of fighting. When our native forces saw so many enemies, they were astonished and quickly surrounded all our forces with branches to shelter them from whatever might happen. Once the magistrate arrived, they began to speak with him, telling him they were determined to build their homes there where they could live and later die peacefully and that their enemies' houses would be theirs.

Then yelling vigorously, "At them! At them!" the magistrate moved forward, directing João Tavares to another area. With his enemies in front of him, he avoided the many traps they had set and the heavy fortifications they had made. Their crops were still planted, and there were many dead. There would have been more had our forces not opened the path so all could pass. That way, the enemy had little shelter offered by the poor pathway and large swamp (where they usually flee for safety). There were many incidents of various people getting stuck in the mud, more than they wished, and they did not wish to follow the magistrate, their captain, after his horse fell down with him, and he led it by the bridle. He did this as a gentleman, although covered in mud, and he jumped onto the horse all disheveled and went after the enemies using another road. He went with two others on horseback and some natives, who were constantly saying things to humiliate their enemies. The same thing happened where João Tavares was fighting. The number of dead would have been countless if our brave natives had followed the enemy. However, seeing that the enemy were so many and they were so few, they reluctantly stayed near the whites.

After all this was over, they gathered after three in the afternoon in the large village near the swamp, where they rested for what was left of the day. They gave many thanks to God for this great victory. They were certain they saw more than twenty thousand Potiguarás that day brought by their shaman, who unfortunately escaped on a horse that he previously had obtained from the whites.

The injured were attended to, but there were no deaths. They were sufficiently pleased by this victory to remain there for one more day. They were twelve leagues on this side of the Rio Grande when they heard the news that all the native enemies had crossed to its other side. As the lords of more than four hundred leagues of coastline, it was not possible to use all of them. They returned to the fort, where they were received with great festivities. The magistrate continued the good work done by Cristóvão Lins and the other officials. Everything was completed on the fort, the towers, and the storehouse, with space for the captain and the tax collector. Also completed were the positions for most of the artillery. When everything else was done, they respectfully turned over the command to captain João Tavares and left him with thirty-five soldiers supplied for four months. Once this was done, they headed for Pernambuco at the end of January 1586. This was a short time to have done so many things and built so much, but in upright men the desire for honor makes this possible.

CHAPTER 13

The Arrival of Captain Morales from Portugal and the Return of the Superior
Court Magistrate to Paraíba

At the end of the following February, some letters arrived for the magistrate from the king asking if he had been well served in what was accomplished in establishing a town in Paraíba. The king further ordered that all related expenses be paid. These letters were brought by a disabled Spanish captain named Francisco de Morales along with fifty Spanish soldiers. They came to collect soldiers here with Francisco Castejon, and that was a very good thing, even though they had little effect, because Castejon did not amount to much as a captain. Morales left Pernambuco on April 2 for Paraíba, and he should have been under the authority of João Tavares, the captain of that fort, according to his guidelines. Everyone was under the authority of the magistrate. However, as soon as Captain Morales arrived, he threw João Tavares and the Portuguese out of the fort, treating all of them in a troublesome manner, and he enraged the natives in their villages to the point that each day they went to complain in Pernambuco.

They told him that he was wrong to take the fort away from someone who had sworn to protect it and that he should return it to the captain. He responded rudely to the magistrate, forgetting his duty and all the favors the judge had shown him in Pernambuco. He then separated himself from him, the town officials, and all the Portuguese. There were many charges against him, and they removed him and sent him to the king because of his many excesses, which had always been increasing. These were in addition to the slander he had been writing in letters about the magistrate, sending them from Pernambuco. He was an enemy of the magistrate, driven by his envy of his many successes. He wanted to defame him in Portugal as well as locally. The magistrate considered all these things until the end of September of that year. On the twenty-seventh of that month, news and letters arrived from Paraíba stating that five French naus had arrived at the Bay of Traição with many people and military supplies. They were determined to join with the Potiguarás to attack the fort of Paraíba. Along with this news came a long list of requests from Captain Morales and the residents. The letters asked for help from the magistrate, the captain of Pernambuco, and the town council.

Once Martim Leitão received this request, he called for a meeting at the [Jesuit?] college, to include the captain of Pernambuco, officials from the town council, the treasury officials, and the other wealthy and important people in town. They all agreed that in order to prevent this theft from growing and allowing a large army of Frenchmen to leave after they and the Potiguarás destroyed all that we had gained in Paraíba, it would be best to go to the aid of our forces there. No one could do this as well as the Superior Court magistrate, as he had done before. Everyone there petitioned him in the name of the king to do this, and he accepted. He immediately commandeered the use of two naus, there not being any more in port, and several large caravels. They sent 150 fighting men, in addition to the sailors, in these ships. Some cavalry went by land to join our forces in Paraíba, so that they could wage an effective campaign by land and by sea.

Once the ships were all prepared and everything was ready, news arrived that Francisco de Morales wanted to come from Paraíba, but Martim Leitão wrote him to refrain from that, and once he arrived there, he would supply him with all his needs as he always had done. However, if he insisted on coming now, he should not bring the king's soldiers. But nothing would keep Morales from leaving and bringing the king's soldiers with him. Some envious people from Pernambuco, enemies of the magistrate, persuaded him to abandon the fort and lose it. He spent some time in Olinda acting in a debauched manner before leaving for Portugal. On October 20, news arrived that two more French naus had arrived at the Bay of Traição to make a total of seven. To wage a better fight, they took one additional nau that arrived from Portugal. Cannons were mounted on carriages, and it was fortified against artillery fire as were the others; by the beginning of December, three merchant naus and two large caravels or zabras were also made ready. They were captained by Pero de Albuquerque, Lopo Soares, Tomé da Rocha, Pero Lopes Lobo, captain of the island of Itamaracá, and Álvaro Velho Barreto.

Once the magistrate had this in order, he and twenty-five men on horseback went as far as the mill belonging to Filipe Cavalcanti, which is seven leagues from the town of Olinda. At that point, he sent them on their way to Paraíba, and he returned to Olinda, promising them as he left that he would be with them the next week. He then went to Recife where he waited for thirteen days without being able to sail because of a huge storm from the northeast. The storm made a nau lose its anchor and pushed the ship to the riverbank. The magistrate was afraid of this delay and wanted to send a large caravel to Paraíba with the news, but the winds were such that they did not let up and blew from Cape Saint Agostinho to the island of Santo Aleixo.

With all this work, with everyone upset, and the magistrate believing he would not be able to make the voyage, Mauro de Resende arrived with a long list of needs, saying that all would be lost if the judge did not arrive there before Saint Thomas's Day.[1] They were surrounded by many forces, both French and Potiguarás, and they had attacked one of our native villages on the border four days back. This was the village led by Assento de Pássaro, our best native. They had killed eighty natives and two Spaniards, and all were assumed lost there.

The magistrate realized there was not enough time to sail to Paraíba, and he decided to go by land, telling the others to follow him. He left at daybreak from the Tapirema River, which is nine leagues from Olinda. On the second day, he encountered some thirty-two men who had left beforehand. The others were unreasonable in refusing to make the journey, so these were the only men to follow him on land. He and these men arrived at our village of Paraíba, which its residents call *Our Lady of the Snows*, on the day before Christmas eve, December 23. He began at once to organize everything and prepare for his departure, because he had to leave the next day for Copaoba, which he did. He had heard this was where all the enemy natives and some of the French were cutting brazilwood to load on their naus. Preventing this was the most effective warfare either side could conduct.

CHAPTER 14
How the Superior Court Magistrate Left Paraíba for Copaoba

From the City of Our Lady of the Snows, where the magistrate left Pero de Albuquerque as captain, after four days' journey he reached the great enclosure of Penacama, which was extensive and one of the main villages of the Potiguarás. This was where Duarte Gomes de Silveira had gone the previous October. After doing quite well there, on his return he lost eight or ten men, which was the largest loss this campaign in Paraíba had incurred after sending for Martim Leitão. He was keenly aware of this loss because, in addition to the warfare he conducted each year in person, he always ordered other attacks. Sometimes these were led by Duarte Gomes and other times by Captain João Tavares and others. This journey was filled with unending work, chiefly due to the lack of clean water. There was only a little available from very contaminated wells; it was so foul smelling that it was necessary for the men to hold their noses with one hand while drinking with the other.

From this village, they marched for Copaoba directly, and on the second day in the morning, they attacked another enemy village. Our natives let out their war cry, and many of the enemy fled as soon as we entered the area in spite of our forces killing many. We captured seventy or eighty alive. Those who had fled watched us from a spot more than a league away from a large empty village. Our natives wanted to rest there for two days, and that was necessary because of all the hard work they had endured on the way. They also found a river there, but there was some fighting because the enemy defended their positions. They were assisted by the lay of the land, because Copaoba, where they were, is all hilly and uneven with pits. This is not like most of Brazil. It is also *massapé* soil, which is very fertile. This explains why fifty Potiguar villages were there, all grouped together.

The next morning, the fighting began once again over the water. This was in spite of our forces being organized. They did not approach it except in groups at a given time to gather water and give some to the horses. They always went with ten or twelve soldiers with harquebuses to guard them. However, there were many of the enemy and they had piled up a nest of dead branches around the river, which the magistrate ordered Diogo Gomes and some others to remove. They had begun to shoot their arrows and retreat, and our forces decided with Braço to create a trap above them by linking it with the ongoing fighting. After taking their fill of water, they would turn their backs. Starting that afternoon, Braço hurried around the field and said there were many enemies at the water's edge.

The magistrate went out and saw that, along the shore at another part of the river, there were ten or twelve of our allied natives in great danger. They did not dare turn their backs, and they carried many arrows and a lot of gunshot. The judge ordered seven or eight men on horseback to assist them, led by Francisco Pereira, but only Simão Tavares went with him. They made the enemy flee and gathered our natives, including one who was dead and another who was at death's door. All were injured by arrows and pistols, and Francisco Pereira was even more badly injured. He acted like a good gentleman. João Tavares went to escort Braço de Peixe back to camp because he had sent word for help. On his way to set a trap for our enemies, he fell into one of theirs, and he was now in danger. After all this had passed, a great fear began to settle among everyone. That night, the magistrate was informed in secret by João Tavares that more than twenty-two of the outstanding soldiers were ready to flee. The judge responded with a speech urging their continued resistance as well as other measures, which put an end to the matter. They arranged an orderly response for their enemies that next morning, since the previous evening they had made ten shields out of some boards from boxes. The fearful could then use these to shield themselves in safety. Everyone sprang to life, and they set fire to everything, as they always do in these clearings and the villages they capture. That morning they sought out the enemy, who were within sight inside three stockades, one next to the other, and they were protected at their critical entrances.

The first of these stockades was protected by a gulch made by the river, and it caused a delay because of the resistance from the enemy. The judge went there and urged them on, as he understood its importance. After he arrived, they captured the stockade, and no one was wounded. With the same energy, they attacked the second stockade, which was covered in earth in a valley. They dangled a good net over a hill from above, with the other two nets remaining below. When the enemy saw three nets and the arms that moved them, they were afraid of everything. The enemy did not stop at the third stockade, even though our forces had approached it on hands and knees with great effort. If they had not used the nets, which was a clever order from the judge, they would not have had such success. On this occasion, the magistrate worked hard, and that morning, he changed horses three times because he wanted to be everywhere at once. God helped them, and they followed the enemy more than half a league until they came to a village where the enemy put up great resistance to save their women and children. This undertaking was slowing down, since our vanguard was nearly overtaken three or four times until the main body of troops arrived with the magistrate. They charged ahead vigorously to conquer the enemy in three or four more villages, which were destroyed that day. They went to rest on a hilltop where they saw some thirty-odd villages scattered around within a league. In fear, the enemy had abandoned these; they were burning. The enemy were a countless number, while our forces were only 140 whites and 500 native archers.

CHAPTER 15
Once Copaoba Was Destroyed, How They Searched for Tujucupapo

From there, our men went to find Tujucupapo, who had fled from them the year before. They walked for two days and reached the ocean on the third day. That morning, the forces in front encountered a strong wooden enclosure. They recognized from the flag and the drums that the French were there with the Potiguarás, and they informed the Superior Court magistrate of this. When the justice arrived, he spotted the troops under Captain João Tavares, and they were as energetic as always. Three of his men had died from wounds from chains fired from cannons. In spite of this, he had maintained his troops next to the enclosure. He and his sergeant Diogo Aires, a timid soldier, on this expedition had suffered fourteen arrow wounds between them, and each had overtaken an opening in the enemy's wall. Sometimes using their swords and other times their harquebuses, they had cleared out the enclosure.

In spite of the clouds of arrows and gunshots that the enemy constantly rained on them, the judge, along with some people who wanted to join him, crouched down as best they could and made their way to the end of the wall at its lower edge. At that place, the enemy had used the thick undergrowth as their defense, and it was a weak spot covered with earth and palm leaves. They began to pull it apart even though the enemy inside began to fight back with harquebuses and many arrows. These wounded the bailiff, Heitor Fernandes, and others. In spite of this, Martim Leitão was the first to break the wall by using his sword to cut the vines holding it together, creating an entrance. A cursed piece of wood wounded him in the hand as he entered, and his fingernails were dripping blood. Seeing him in this state, like a wounded elephant, Manuel da Costa, from Ponte de Lima, pushed his way inside to accompany him.[1] When the enemy spotted him, they wounded da Costa with two cursed arrows, and with another two they knocked off the judge's helmet, leaving it fastened only by the front strap. He had many arrows stuck in his shield, and he bent on one knee to remove them and cover his head. Suddenly, he was struck by the enemy, and they grabbed his hands. They did not want to kill him because they recognized him and wanted to show him alive as proof of their victory. They only injured him in one thigh from a distance. The judge, seeing this as a last gasp of life, got up and limped furiously to Manuel da Costa, his friend, to defend him and pull him away from the fighting. At that moment, others began entering the enclosure; the first among them was the mayor of Pernambuco, Bartolomeu Álvares, made of the same stuff as Martim Leitão. He did well that day, assisting as the valiant and strong soldier who fought in Africa.

The rest of our forces who entered after him did the same and acted with such valor and strength that the enemy abandoned the stockade, the French leaving first. When this happened, our people inside began to shout "victory," and our forces entered, by one way and another. They did nothing except embrace each other and shed tears of contentment over the blessing God had performed. They did not chase the enemy very much because once the fury of battle had passed, they needed to tend to the wounded. There were forty-seven injured and three dead among our forces. On the other side, one native was killed, and the natives carried him away, as is their custom. The French second lieutenant was also killed and was left stretched out in the stockade with his flag and drum, which our forces took to Paraíba. However, they had just begun to treat the wounded when it was necessary to stop because they heard a loud cry and clamor from Potiguarás who were coming to assist those in the stockade. Had they arrived a bit earlier, it would have been impossible to resist them, and they attacked our rear forces. However, when they saw that the others were gone and our forces were inside, they too fled.

There were many wounds caused by the enemy while they were in the stockade, mostly from the gunshots the French fired while allied with the natives. The remainder of the day was spent tending to the injured. The judge went among them showing great vigilance and charity, dispensing healing herbs and drugs. Out of respect for his men, the lack of gunpowder, and other shortcomings, he ordered them to burn the wood they found there. They returned in an orderly fashion via another path the next morning. It took some work from them to find their way to Paraíba,

guided by the sun, since no one knew their location. They took shelter
that first night, each as he could, along the edge of a small stream.

The second day as they were walking, at the break of day, they were
attacked twice by natives. The natives did this to thwart their progress on
the path. Our forces repelled them, and they fled with their wounded. Our
men were not injured on this trip, and they arrived in Paraíba, where they
received the welcome they deserved.

CHAPTER 16
*After Disbanding the People, How the Superior Court Magistrate Constructed
the Fort of São Sebastião*

Later that week, the magistrate prepared to sail to the Bay of Traição to
attack the French naus there. In order to do this, he ordered several large
caravels to join him so they could attack at night using just their oars.
It was not the time for the seasonal winds that would allow larger naus
to sail from Pernambuco to Paraíba. However, it was confirmed that the
French had burned their cargo of brazilwood and departed in empty naus,
so the head justice disbanded everyone. The only two remaining were
his officials, Pedro de Albuquerque and Francisco Pereira, who was still
recovering from his wounds. At the end of January 1587, they went to
the Tibiri River two leagues above the city along the flat fields of Paraíba
to construct a fort to protect the new royal sugar plantation as well as
to defend the village of Assento de Pássaro and other border areas. This
fort would secure that area and make it safe for people to live near the
fields, so the judge ordered its construction. They did a lot in a short time,
constructing a fort one hundred spans long, using large beams closely set
together. The walls were five spans thick and nine high. People could
fight and defend the fort using the outer wall, which was twenty-two
spans high and made with solidly packed mud walls. The upper scaffolds
were covered, and houses were around the outside where people could
find shelter. Two guard houses were back-to-back with a tower in the
middle and with large doors facing the Tibiri River.

Since construction had started on Saint Sebastian's Day, when it was
completed, the fort was named in his honor. The artillery was put in place
and the paths were opened, and everything was built as if the magistrate
would remain there for life or as if he had built it for his children. He left

for Pernambuco in the second week of February suffering from fevers, which his strength and unbending spirit had allowed him to endure. He arrived home, went to bed, and did not leave it for the next three months. This was not long, considering all the heat, rain, warfare, and work he had endured.

CHAPTER 17

The Great Treachery of the Natives of Sergipe toward the Men of Bahia and the War Conducted by the Governor against the Aimorés

It was with great contentment that Governor-General Manuel Teles Barreto received the good news about these wars and conquests, made possible by the leadership of the Superior Court magistrate Martim Leitão. However, as all such happiness in the world is mixed with grief, this was the case with the great treachery and deception employed by the natives of Sergipe. They said they wanted to hear the doctrine of the faith from the Jesuit fathers from Bahia, and they used a number of middlemen to ask the governor on their behalf. They asked for soldiers to protect them from their enemies along the way home if they attempted to stop them.

The governor called for a special meeting of the town council and other trustworthy officials to discuss this. The first to vote was Cristóvão de Barros, supervisor of the treasury. He said, as he was knowledgeable about the ways of these people, that if they wanted to go, they should leave at once; they would be welcomed and favored in everything. However, our forces would not provide them with any soldiers because they had not provoked any natives along the way, as they usually do. Those who knew these people best all voted the same way.

The intermediaries pushed hard and had sufficient authority to make their case. They claimed it was of great importance for the salvation of these souls, who wanted to join the society of the Holy Mother Church. The good governor came to concede what the natives requested and provided them with 130 white and mameluco soldiers to accompany them. The ambassadors happily left with this group and with some natives from the villages and Jesuit fathers, sending advance word to their people that they should meet them at the Real River. This is what happened, and they crossed the river on rafts. There were some cabanas there where they rested. The old women came to wail and cry among them, which is their sign of peace and friendship. Once the wailing had concluded, they offered our people their vegetable stews, game, and fish as well as the women they desired. Their parents and husbands did not object; however, they did become very jealous, which was a very bad sign. Some of the slaves told their white masters this, but it did not prevent the whites from accepting the women as if they were their legitimate wives.

In this manner, this group made short days and a relaxed journey to Sergipe, and they settled into the native villages, living in the native houses with such confidence as if they were home. They left their guns with their concubines and went from one village to the other with a rod in their hands. Meanwhile, the women stuffed their harquebuses with stones and tar and replaced their gunpowder with charcoal. After this was done, one morning they came running to our people saying they should arm themselves because their enemies were coming. But it was their own people who were pretending to be the enemy, and our people were so careless and defenseless that they were slaughtered like sheep or lambs. The only ones to remain alive were some of the native servants for the Jesuit fathers, who brought the news. The governor was so upset that he wanted to go personally to extract vengeance. He wrote to the head captain of Pernambuco, who at that time was D. Filipe de Moura, and the head captain of Itamaracá, to prepare all the men they could muster to fight them on one side and the other. However, his advanced age and health did not allow this; he wrote them again saying he would not be coming but they should assist those in Paraíba.

At this same time, another group of natives revolted, a people called the *Aimorés* in the captaincy of Ilhéus, which placed it in danger. When the governor was informed of this, he ordered Diogo Correa de Sande and Fernão Cabral de Ataíde, who had many slaves and villages of unconverted natives, to see whether they could attack them. He sent some soldiers from his guard led by Diogo de Miranda and Lourenço de Miranda, Spaniards and brothers. They all went from Jaguaripe by land to Camamu and Tinharé, and they set many traps. Since the enemy was treacherous and never came out to fight, they hid in the undergrowth. Very few were killed, and they shot several of our natives with arrows.

CHAPTER 18

The Death of Governor Manuel Teles de Barreto and How Bishop D. António Barreiros, the Head Superintendent Cristóvão de Barros, and the Superior Court Magistrate Governed in His Place

Governor Manuel Teles de Barreto was elderly; before seeing the definitive end of these wars, he became ill and passed from this life. Life is also a constant battle, as the saintly Job says, and the Lord wanted him for His triumph, where all is in complete peace, glory, and fame. This governor was a great friend of the residents and very much inclined to favor them. Whatever they wanted, he gave them, preventing merchants from seizing goods on their estates. When the merchants complained to him about this, he dismissed them harshly saying that they came to destroy this land and that after three or four years they took with them all they could of what was here. It was the residents who preserved the land and made it prosper with their work, and they had conquered it by spilling their blood.

Governor Manuel Teles died in 1587, and the officials opened the royal order he had brought with him. In the event of his death, the government should be in the hands of Bishop D. António Barreiros, Head Superintendent Cristóvão de Barros, and the Superior Court magistrate. Since this last mentioned was absent, the other two began to govern and the head accountant of supplies, António de Faria, was their secretary. The time they governed was prosperous because of the victories over our enemies, which we will mention in the next chapters. It was also because of the opening of commerce on the Rio de la Plata. Furthermore, the bishop of Tucuman sent the head treasurer from his cathedral to Bahia to seek students to ordain as well as for some other church business, all of which was completed. From that point on, there was never a year in which some royal or private ships did not dock with merchandise, which makes a lot of money for those in Portugal, and these goods are much in demand here, which is why they bring them.

Also in 1587, the Capuchins of our Order of Saint Anthony came to Brazil to establish monasteries led by the commissioner Brother Melchior de Santa Catarina. He was a religious figure of great authority and a good speaker. He had with him a letter from Pope Sixtus V and written authority from our very reverend father General Francisco Gonzaga, who wrote an entry at the end of the book about our angelic order. At the invitation of Jorge de Albuquerque, the Lord of Pernambuco, they established their first monastery there. Because of this, they established four monasteries there as well as the custodial congregation.

CHAPTER 19
Regarding Three English Ships That Came to Bahia at That Time

A short time after the bishop and Cristóvão de Barros began to govern, two English naus and one zabra suddenly entered this bay with a pinnace. The pinnace had left from here and was headed for Rio de la Plata with a Spanish merchant named Lopo Vaz on board.

As soon as they arrived, they captured the ships in port, among which was an *urca* owned by Duarte Osquer, a Flemish merchant who lived here. The ship had Flemish sailors who surrendered the ship to the English without a fight. After that, the English ships began to bombard the city with such ferocity that the inhabitants were disheartened and filled with fear; they fled to the interior. The bishop posted guards at the many exits from the city, and there were many of these because there was no wall. He wanted to prevent the men from leaving and allow the women to exit. Because of this, many men left at night, and some were cloaked as women. The few men left asked the bishop to do the same and leave. One venerable and wealthy man named Francisco de Araújo asked, for the love of God and king, for the bishop to remain. Not only was he the bishop but also the governor. If the people had fled, he and his men would stand and defend the city.

There was also a woman on horseback who carried a lance and shield. She was from Itapuã and chided those she encountered for fleeing from their homes and encouraged them to return.[1] Everyone ridiculed her for this.

At that time, Cristóvão de Barros was not present in the city because he was making the rounds of the sugar mills in the bay asking for donations for the Misericórdia.[2] He was the head of that organization that year. However, as soon as he heard the sound of the bombardment, he came with all the people he encountered along the way, and with those remaining in the city, they were able to fortify it. They sent people to various locations and punished some of those who fled and did not return. As an example of shame for the others, they placed one man at the pillory in a large basket with a woman's knitting needles around his waist.[3] The English did not dare to enter the city but were content to sail back and forth in the very large bay. It is also very deep, but not deep enough for them to bring their large ships close to the city, so they sent the zabra and the pinnaces to pillage the town. Cristóvão de Barros ordered a fleet of five boats, of the type that carry sugarcane and firewood to and from the sugar mills, to pursue them. These boats even without cover are strong and swift, and they prepared them, placing two minions and some men with harquebuses on each, led by their captains. These were André Fernandes Morgalho, Pantaleão Barbosa, Gaspar de Freitas, António Álvares Portilho, and Pedro de Carvalhais. A galley was led by Captain-Major Sebastião de Faria. They were to find the English wherever they landed and attack them.

They knew that the English were headed for André Fernandes Morgalho's ranch in Jaraguá to take cattle, and they had already left to fight on the fishing vessel. They engaged them, and there were deaths and injuries on both sides. Among these was Duarte de Góis de Mendonça who had been on the galley. He was shot in the head, and serious injuries from his shattered helmet brought him to death's door.

They also came ashore once again on the island of Itaparica, where António Álvares Capara, other Portuguese, and many natives killed several of them. At sea, one of our ships captured one of their lifeboats with four Englishmen who were rowing it and killed three. After seeing their few gains and the fact that Lopo Vaz, who they were holding for ransom, had escaped by swimming to the city, they hoisted their anchors and departed for Camamu to find water. But Capara did not let them get away; he killed eight of them and brought their heads to the governors. Thus, the Englishmen returned to their land after being here for two months.

CHAPTER 20
The War Conducted by Cristóvão de Barros against the Natives of Sergipe

Cristóvão de Barros, now that he was governing, was eager to avenge the treachery of the natives of Sergipe toward the men of Bahia, which we discussed in chapter 18 of this book. His father, António Cardoso de

Barros, had been killed and eaten there while about to leave for Portugal with the first bishop of Bahia. I have recounted this in chapter 3 of the third book. He called for many men from this land and from Pernambuco to come forward to help him, and they were anxious to accompany him as it was a very just war, given license by the king. They hoped to bring back many slaves.

The forward troops were led by Captain António Fernandes, and those in the rear by Captain Sebastião de Faria. They decided to follow the seashore, and they sent Rodrigo Martins and Álvaro Rodrigues, his brother, into the interior with 150 white and mameluco men and one thousand natives. They recruited all the Tapuia peoples they found along the way to assist them and brought three thousand natives with bows. With so many people, they did not wait for Cristóvão de Barros and attacked the enemy villages they encountered. The enemy fled and formed a large group, who resisted and this placed our forces in a siege. They sent four natives to inform Cristóvão de Barros of the danger they faced. With this news, he ordered they pick up the pace, and when they reached a hilltop, they saw some smoke. He sent Amador de Aguiar with some men [to investigate], and they returned with four spies taken from the enemy. They guided our forces to the encampment and arrived on the day before Christmas eve at two o'clock in the afternoon. As soon as the enemy saw them, they lifted the siege and fled but not before losing six hundred men, while we only lost six.

From there, they went to the village of Baepeba, who was the king and leader of all these people. Next to him were two other villages, which totaled twenty thousand souls. Our forces captured their defenses and took the enemy's water source. There were dead and injured on both sides but more on theirs.

They also attacked one of these enclosures, which the enemy immediately retook. The enemy attacked where Sebastião de Faria was, killing one man and injuring many. But our forces made them retreat, killing three hundred of them.

Finally, Baepeba decided to finish this battle for good, and in order to accomplish this, he sent word to those in the other enclosures to come and fight our forces. He came forth as well. Their plan was to round up our forces in the center and kill them. Three natives carried this news at four o'clock through our clearing. They had no other path, and only by killing them could they be stopped.

Upon hearing this news, the natives left their enclosures and our general came out with only the cavalry, which consisted of sixty men, and this made the enemy flee. He did not allow the cavalry to chase the enemy as they wished because the enemy from the main encampment of Baepeba had not turned their backs. On New Year's Eve 1590, seeing that they were alone and lacking water, they began to flee. The bravest led the way, sending forth clouds of arrows that made our forces scatter. However, the general was able to cross in front of them, and by shouting and using lances, he made them stop, turn around, and return to their enclosed village. Our forces entered after them and killed sixteen hundred and captured four thousand.

Once the victory had been achieved and the injured treated, Cristóvão de Barros armed some horseback riders as they do in Africa from the royal supplies he had brought for this purpose. He distributed the captives and the land, keeping for himself a generous portion of both with which he established a large cattle ranch there. The others followed his example. Because of the fertility of the pastures, these flourished to such an extent that they now provide the mills in Bahia and Pernambuco with their oxen and butchered meat.

Sergipe is located at eleven and two-thirds degrees south latitude. The French enter the harbor there with their lifeboats leading the way for their naus of over one hundred tons. They load their ships beyond the entrance because the harbor is only three fathoms deep at low tide. Cristóvão de Barros was not only able to avenge his father's killers but also able to take this bounty from the French as they were loading brazilwood, cotton, and local pepper. In addition, he cleared the road to and from Pernambuco and other northern captaincies to Bahia. Before he accomplished this, no one was able to travel safely on foot without being attacked and eaten by the natives. The same deliverance came to those at sea because it is here that the Gulf of Vazabarris begins, and this is where many ships were lost on the reefs that jut into the ocean. Those who survived a shipwreck did not escape the hands and teeth of the natives. Nowadays, it is possible to walk with ease and in safety, coming and going with written appeals and everything else, without having to wait six months for the monsoon as they did in the past. Many times, they receive the first responses from Portugal there, faster than here or in Pernambuco.

This was such a good undertaking, one worthy of praise and recognition, but what awaited Cristóvão de Barros when he returned to the city was the discovery that his positions were occupied. That is, he had asked the king if he could relinquish the post of head superintendent of royal supplies in order to attend to his estate of four sugar mills; however, he was also removed from his post as governor. While he was conducting this war, Baltasar Rodrigues Sora had arrived with a letter of appointment to direct royal supplies, which the bishop immediately accepted. However, when he wanted to assume the duties of governor, the bishop did not allow it, saying this was not in his letter of appointment. The other royal order placing Cristóvão de Barros as governor did not state that the superintendent of supplies was to govern, as was the case with the Superior Court magistrate, but rather mentioned him by name, and it was a personal appointment. In spite of this, the superintendent of supplies, Baltasar Rodrigues Sora, insisted and asked the bishop to bring this issue forward for legal discussion, which he did. He met with other educated men, theologians, and jurists at the Jesuit college, but they did not agree with the bishop's reasoning. Baltasar Rodrigues received the majority of their votes and began to govern. Cristóvão de Barros was undone by the arrival of Rodrigues Sora. His side of this case was not heard because he was busy conducting royal service when Rodrigues Sora made his plea. Barros then left for Portugal with his appeal and never returned.

CHAPTER 21

An Expedition into the Interior Seeking Natives Who Fled from the Wars in Sergipe and Other Natives

Once the victory was attained that we have described in the preceding chapter, Governor Cristóvão de Barros left for Bahia, leaving Rodrigo Martins in Sergipe to finish collecting the natives who had fled from this war. Many natives had crossed the São Francisco River, entering the captaincy of Pernambuco, where our forces went looking for them.

The first of these was Francisco Barbosa da Silva, whom we discussed in chapter 26 in the previous book. He returned in terrible condition from an expedition to the interior. This time it was even worse because it cost him his life, as well as the lives of those with him. He could not endure one affliction after another, and he finally died. Another person on this expedition was Cristóvão da Rocha, who came on a large caravel with forty men. He obtained permission from Tomé da Rocha, the captain of Sergipe, to join Rodrigo Martins in going to the interior to find these natives and any others he might find.

After walking for a few days and passing the whirlpool in the São Francisco River, they stayed in the home of a native named Tumã. According to Cristóvão da Rocha, this is where they began to question whether they had the permission of the Albuquerques of Pernambuco to go on this expedition. Without this, those from Bahia could not conquer or take prisoners in that region. For that reason, they had to clarify their rights. Those from Pernambuco, who were few in number, turned around, although Rodrigo Martins did not give his permission to do so. António Rodrigues de Andrade agreed to this departure. He had one hundred negros and some white men with him from Bahia. Captain Cristóvão da Rocha left with them because he had heard that Porquinho's people had killed four or five white men who had gone there with two Jesuit priests. They went straight to their villages, and the first thing they found was a mameluco named Domingos Fernandes Nobre who begged them to avenge the death of the white men. This was sufficient to stir up the natives and make them flee. It also frightened the four horses that came with our expedition; the natives fear horses. Seeing this, the captain sent word to one of their enemies to come help fight them, which they did.

I should not forget to mention here what a soldier related to me. One of the important natives who came to assist us went to the horse stables. He sat down and talked with the horse, saying that he would have him as his friend. He had heard that horses were very brave in war, and it was a good thing to have a man as a friend so that they would understand them and do them no harm.

There was a mameluco there who had taken care of the horses, and when he saw the man so taken with the horse and so sad because the horse had not answered, he offered to act as an interpreter. Pretending to speak into the horse's ear, he said the horse was happy to have his friendship and that he would recognize it when the correct time arrived. With this excellent answer, the native became even more fond of the horse, and he asked what his friend ate or wanted to eat because he would provide whatever he wanted. The mameluco answered that the horse normally ate hay and grains but that he also liked meat, fish, and honey. The native provided all these things in abundance, sending some natives to fetch grass, and others to hunt, fish, and extract honey from the trees. The interpreter lived on this, and the horse gained so much weight that he choked and died from being overweight. The native was very sad at his death, and he ordered his wife and family to weep and wail as they usually do for a deceased loved one. This was one of the leaders invited there by Captain Cristóvão da Rocha to hunt Porquinho's people who had fled into the interior in fear because of the mameluco's plea.

One of the natives came to talk secretly with Diogo de Castro, one of our soldiers, because he knew him and was his friend. The native said he was very surprised that they had come there to wage war because he knew what friends the whites were. There had been deaths of those who came with the Jesuit fathers, but the natives accompanying the priests spoke ill of the fathers and told the people not to listen to their sermons because they were there to fool them. Some of them thought this, but not all of them, and all should not be punished.

Diogo de Castro answered by saying that the peace and friendship between them was well established and they did not come there to break it, as the mameluco was saying incorrectly. They had only come searching for those natives who had fled the war in Sergipe, and he advised these people to return to their villages, assuring them they would not be harmed. The native still was not convinced until he heard these words from the captain's mouth. Once that was done, he went to persuade his people, and they were convinced within a few days. Among them was Porquinho, now very old and ill. He asked for the sacrament of baptism, and Diogo de Castro baptized him, naming him *Manuel*.

I do not know of anything else that was good that came of this expedition, since once Porquinho was dead, their enemies sold the others to the whites, and they were exchanged for some people they had captured. They took them captive to a certain stopping place along the São Francisco River, where they divided them among themselves. Captain Cristóvão da Rocha and those from Pernambuco took some and António Rodrigues de Andrade and those from Bahia took others.

They made their way through the Salitre Mountains and brought some pear-shaped gourds to show. They said there were many of them.

However, at that time there were many natives in that area, and they had treacherously killed Manuel de Padilha along with forty men. They had left from Bahia for those mountains, as did Brás Pires Meira, along with seventy men sent there by Governor Manuel Teles Barreto. The natives wanted to do the same to these people who had now arrived. They were saved by their keen vigilance along the way.

CHAPTER 22
On the Continued Wars in Paraíba against the Potiguarás,
Who Were Assisted by the French

The captaincy of Paraíba remained as it was described in chapter 16 of this book, and Captain João Tavares took charge and built a sugar mill. It was not far from the royal mill, and he built it together with Diogo Correia Nunes. The planters were very contented and began to plant their cane to mill and cultivate their lands. This [roças] is what we here call the lands under cultivation for fruit and other foodstuffs.

At this time, the Spaniard D. Pedro de la Cueva arrived. He had gone to Portugal at the order of Frutuoso Barbosa, requesting the king place Barbosa in charge of the town in Paraíba. His Majesty had agreed, and Cueva carried with him a royal decree awarding it to Barbosa. Cueva remained as an infantry captain in charge of all the Spanish who had remained there. This included Captain Francisco de Castejon as well as Captain Francisco de Morales. Cueva took command, and Frutuoso Barbosa assumed his role as governor in the city. D. Pedro went to a fort on the frontier constructed by Diogo Nunes Correia. However, these two captains (as if they were made to fight each other) began at once to have quarrels. This allowed our enemies to roam freely at will, attacking the fields and estates of the whites and the villages of our native allies. These attacks became so frequent that people stopped fishing or collecting shellfish because enemies could appear at any moment and kill them. These captains did nothing about this other than to write to D. Filipe de Moura, the captain-major of Pernambuco, and Pedro Lopes Lobo, on the island of Itamaracá, asking for them to come to their assistance. The captain of Itamaracá did this, bringing the people and supplies that he could.

Things in Paraíba reached such an extent that two additional infantry companies were organized, one led by Captain Pedro de la Cueva, with his Spanish soldiers (Diogo de Paiva remained in his place at the fort with fifteen men). Another company was organized of Portuguese men, with Captain Diogo Nunes Correia as head. These two companies joined the natives loyal to Braço de Peixe and Assento do Pássaro. Two of our preachers instructed the natives in Christian doctrine and went with Pedro Lopes Lobo to inspect the frontier. They always sent their spies and runners ahead until they fell upon a large enemy village, where there would be a lot of killing because they would find them unprepared. They captured nearly nine hundred people, most of them women and children. Once the other natives became aware of our forces, they were careful to pay more attention to fleeing rather defending themselves. When our forces arrived, they found these villages deserted and burned more than twenty of them. These events caused a great deal of harm and grief to the natives of Paraíba, as we have described.

When our runners were ahead of the others, moving from one area to another, they came across a very large village, fortified at one end. They could not see the other end because it was covered by undergrowth. They were so fearful in presenting the news that it made everyone afraid. However, Pedro Lopes, who was very experienced in these wars, motivated the others and energized them with reasons all night. The next morning, he divided the men into three equal squads and had them march to the enclosure. When he saw their fear and how slowly they moved, he grabbed his shield and sword and went to the enclosure saying, "Those who want to, follow me, and if you do not want to, remain here. I alone can defeat them." This encouraged everyone to fight, and without any delay they attacked the enclosure. They entered it, killing and capturing many of the enemy with none of our people being in danger, even though there were many injured by arrows. This was especially the case of some young native men from Itamaracá who entered first along with some negros. They entered from the side covered by bush where the fence was weak and was made of branches. They were the reason this victory was achieved so easily, since once they were inside, the enemy was so focused on them that they did not attack the others who entered elsewhere.

Our forces stayed in this enclosure for three days and found a lot of supplies, cassava, beans, many arms, bows, arrows, shields. They also found some French swords and harquebuses left behind by fifteen Frenchmen who fled.

On the morning of the fourth day, they left for the beach and walked along it to the Bay of Traição, where they took the inland path to Paraíba without encountering any enemies. When they entered the captaincy, no one could resist feeling excited by their recent victory.

Once in Paraíba, Captain Pero Lopes Lobo stayed in Assento's village along with the Jesuit fathers. He and the fathers tried to make peace between Governor Frutuoso Barbosa and D. Pedro de la Cueva and eventually were successful. However, after Pero Lopes returned to his captaincy of Itamaracá, the old hatred and differences resurfaced as did the war with the Potiguarás, and there was no one to blame. The king ordered D. Pedro to return to Portugal and Frutuoso Barbosa returned on his own. André de Albuquerque assumed his place, but relations had deteriorated to such an extent that he could not fix them in the short time he held that position.

CHAPTER 23

How Francisco Giraldes was Appointed Governor of Brazil but
Never Arrived, He Returned to Portugal and Died; D. Francisco de Sousa
Came as the Seventh Governor

When the king became aware of the death of Governor Manuel Teles Barreto, he sent Francisco Giraldes to replace him. He was the son of Lucas Giraldes, the Lord of Ilhéus, whom we discussed in chapter 6 of book 2. Had he arrived in Brazil, it would have led to good things for that captaincy. However, because his ship got too close to the coastline too soon and the waters off Paraíba flow northwest to the West Indies, he was forced there and returned to Portugal. He died there and never governed Brazil. With him came the High Court, which would have been something new for Brazil at that time. However, God was pleased to allow only four or five justices to arrive on other ships. One of these became the Superior Court magistrate; another became the judge for the deceased. Since the chief justice and the others did not arrive, the tribunal was not established. The king did not address this and only sent D. Francisco de Sousa as governor. He arrived on Sunday of Holy Trinity in 1591.[1]

Along with him came the inquisitor or visitor from the Holy Office of the Inquisition, Heitor Furtado de Mendonça. He was very ill when he arrived along with everyone else on board except the governor, who was in good health and had all he required. However, after his arrival and the usual welcoming ceremonies, he became ill and was taken to the Jesuit college where he was at death's door. However, God was merciful and spared his life. His first public appearance, even though he had not recovered completely, was to attend an auto-da-fé.[2] The inquisitor had announced this publicly and had given the public a grace period to denounce the guilty.

At that time, a caravel arrived from Portugal with letters for the governor informing him of the death of his wife. He announced that he would not return to Portugal but remain in Brazil until his death. He did not say this in an idle or trifling way, but rather it was very prudent. He was known as D. Francisco das Manhas; this policy allowed the governor to attend to the needs of the citizens and natives and for him to become one of them. It mattered little to say something but not put it into action; he became the most beloved governor in Brazil, along with the most respected and adored. Because he was so kind and likeable, he was able to admirably retain his dignity and authority. He was best known for his generosity and noble acts. Other governors collected and retained, but he was only concerned with what he needed to give and spend. He was such an enemy of greed, that in his haste to flee from it, he leaned toward the extravagant. He gave to those who were good and bad, the poor and the rich; they only had to ask. It was the custom then to say only a thief asked him for a little because he always gave much more.[3]

There was no church that did not get painted and he approved all the charitable brotherhoods organized for each one. He cleaned up the city with new plaster stucco, which fell down with time, and he constructed three or four forts from stone and lime, and these remain. The main ones are presidios with soldiers and captains paid by the royal treasury: Santo António at the mouth of the bay and São Filipe at Tapuípe Point, one league from the city. These are mostly to instill fear rather than to do anything since they do not defend the city or the port. The mouth of the bay is too wide at three leagues, and the bay is too big. He could do all this because he had the king's authority, and to ensure it, when his funds from the *dízimo* were insufficient, which is all the king spends here, he could borrow from any other source. There was a time when he taxed the crates of sugar leaving for Portugal at one cruzado each in the customs house. He borrowed funds from the estates of the deceased, which were due to their absent heirs. A nau called the São Francisco that sought shelter here on its way to India was purchased by the merchant Diogo Dias Querido for 30,000 cruzados, which he paid to the royal treasury in Portugal. No other governor was able to spend so freely, but what followed was rather a tightening of the budget to the point that old royal debts could not be repaid without new provisions nor were any extraordinary expenses possible. The king was so generous with D. Francisco because of the wars in Paraíba and because of the many pirates along Brazil's coastline, as we shall see in the following chapters.

CHAPTER 24
On the Journey Gabriel Soares de Sousa Made to the Mines in the Interior, Which Was Halted by His Death

Gabriel Soares de Sousa was a nobleman who married and remained in Bahia after participating with Francisco Barreto in the expedition to Mutapa. I discussed him [Barreto] in chapter 13 of book 3. He had a brother who explored the interior of Brazil for three years, where he found some samples of gold, silver, and precious stones. He did not return with these because he died about one hundred leagues from Bahia making his return trip. However, he sent these samples to his brother, who used them to spend some time at court and pay some of his expenses until the king sent him to Brazil. He left Lisbon on a Flemish urca named the *Grifo Dourado* on April 7, 1591, with 360 men and four Carmelites. One of these, Brother Jerónimo de Canavazes, was later their leader.

They spied the shore on June 15, and since they were not familiar with the bay, which was Vazabarris, they dropped anchor, but the southerly winds were so strong and the currents so swift that they broke two cables. At the advice of a Frenchman named Honorato, who came from the interior with two natives in a raft, they entered the bay with their assistance. The nau touched bottom and hit so hard that the rudder was dislodged and broke. That made some of those on board dive into the water and swim, but they drowned in the waves. The others escaped in a small boat sent by Tomé da Rocha, the captain of Sergipe. They also unloaded some royal property as well as some of their own, and Gabriel Soares de Sousa ordered it brought to Bahia on this same boat with twelve soldiers. Francisco Vieira was in charge, and the pilots were Pero de Paiva and António

Apeba. Soares de Sousa had come from the interior with five companies led by Captains Rui Boto de Sousa, Pedro da Cunha de Andrade, Gregório Pinheiro, the nephew of Bishop D. António Pinheiro, Lourenço Varela, and João Peres Galego. Julião da Costa was the field commander, and the sergeant-major was Julião Coelho.

They arrived in this city and were warmly received by Governor D. Francisco de Sousa, who allowed them to carry out the provisions in their royal orders. They were to take two hundred native archers from the villages controlled by the Jesuits and any whites who wished to join them to his estate in Jaguaripe. At that point, they re-formed two companies because Pero da Cunha and Gregório Pinheiro did not wish to go on this journey. One of these new companies was led by João Homem, the son of Garcia d'Ávila, while the other was assigned to Francisco Zorrilha. The chaplains were Jácome de Queiros and Manuel Álvares, who later became the vicar of Nossa Senhora do Socorro.

They left for Jaguaripe, and after fifty leagues, they arrived at the mountains of Quareru. They built a fort there, which was seventy spans long and had sentry boxes in the corners. The king ordered these constructed every fifty leagues.

The miners started working a vein of silver they found in the mountain and were able to extract some of it, but the general ordered it closed and left twelve soldiers there with Luís Pinto in charge. He had fought in Africa. They left with the others and went another fifty leagues to the source of the Paraguaçu River to build another fort. The water there was foul, and the game was even worse, consisting of snakes and lizards. Many became ill, including Gabriel Soares de Sousa, who died there in a few days, more or less in the same place where his brother departed this life.

He was buried with a lot of sorrow from his people in the fort they had built, and from there they returned to the first fort, which had better water and healthier air. The commander, Julião da Costa, informed Governor D. Francisco de Sousa what had happened, and he ordered their return to this city.

They came by way of Cachoeira, where Diogo Lopes Ulhoa went to meet them. After hosting them royally for eight days on his sugar estates, he sent them on his ships to the governor. He did not receive them and provided them with little, while Ulhoa had spent more than 2,000 cruzados on them from his own funds.

Gabriel Soares's intention on this journey was to reach the São Francisco River and to follow it to the Lagoa Dourada, which they say is its source. In order to achieve that, he took with him a native named *Guaraci*, which means *sun*. He went with them and died on the journey, leaving all the mines hidden until God, the true light, wishes to show them to us.

Gabriel Soares de Sousa's nephew, Bernardo Ribeiro, sent people to find his uncle's remains, and they are buried in the Monastery of São Bento. On his tombstone, there is a phrase inscribed from his will: "Here Rests a Sinner."

I do not know what other more truthful source he could have discovered for us had he lived, since as stated by Saint John, "If we claim to be without sin, we deceive ourselves and the truth is not in us" (1 John 8).

CHAPTER 25
How Feliciano Coelho de Carvalho Came to Govern Paraíba and Continue the Wars There

In May 1591, Feliciano Coelho de Carvalho arrived in Pernambuco. He was a nobleman raised in Africa as a child, a good and wise gentleman. He sent his things by sea and went by land to begin his rule of Paraíba. He found the city facing great difficulties caused by the continuing attacks of the Potiguarás on our fields and on the edges of town. He decided to rid the land of these people, and in order to do this, he asked Pero Lopes, the captain-major of the island of Itamaracá, to come with his men and personally assist him. He did this and arrived with fifty white soldiers, cavalry, and three hundred negros. They all left in unison; the Tabajara natives and as many whites as possible accompanied the governor. They were divided into companies with their goods and squadrons.

They then attacked a large village that their spies had found. Since the natives were unprepared, they faced our vanguard and put up some resistance because the enemy believed there were no other forces. However, after they saw those on horseback and the others on foot who were arriving, the enemy began to turn their backs and flee. It was too late because our forces were all unified, and they killed so many that it was pitiful to see so many dead enemies. Those who fled were followed by the vanguard; they resisted by firing many arrows. They fled for the safety of another village that was a quarter league distant. Those in this village came out and helped the enemy, making our forces halt. Here and there were many arrows and many were injured until Captain Martim Lopes Lobo arrived. He was the son of Pero Lopes, and he came with two more men on horseback, twenty men with harquebuses, and some negros. This gave our forces new energy, and they responded with fury. The enemy was afraid and fled into the bush, creating an entrance to the village. Our men slaughtered so many women, children, and old people that only one person was left alive. He had ducked under Captain Martim Lopes's horse, and the captain wanted to spare him to discover what the French and other natives were planning. At that time . . .

[***][1]

CHAPTER 30

[The original text here is missing a chapter title and text, as noted in the introduction.]

[. . .] had asked for assistance, bringing with him D. Jerónimo de Almeida, who had arrived from Angola a few days earlier along with many gentlemen who were in the captaincy. They were amazed to hear that so few had defended against so many, and the enemy had attacked as was described. Since they were no longer needed, they left there and returned to Pernambuco.

However, this assistance did not really help very much because a Potiguar native who worked for a married soldier was excited when he saw so many men on horseback. He told the lady of the house and she replied: "What you see now is nothing; many more will come, and they will kill all your family and the French among them. Look how few soldiers were needed at Cabedelo to capture so many people in ships, and now if these men go to the mountains along with those additional men coming, you will see if they leave anyone alive."

After hearing this, this Potiguar fled to his people even before Manuel Mascarenhas left Paraíba, and they found him getting ready to attack our forces with the assistance of Monsieur Rifot, whom we have recounted did a great deal of harm along this coast. He wrote a letter challenging Feliciano Coelho, placed it in a gourd, and put that on a road where our spies retrieved it. Feliciano Coelho responded by returning the gourd filled with gunpowder and gunshot and placing it where the letter was found, meaning this was how he would defend his people. Coelho again sent for help from Pernambuco, but greater help came from a *negra* whom they did not see. She told the natives they would all die because innumerable Portuguese came by horse and on foot from Pernambuco. When Rifot heard this, he assembled all the Frenchmen and Potiguarás in a multitude and asked if the Portuguese were as many as this. The *negra* answered that there were more Portuguese and threw six or seven handfuls of sand into the air saying there were more Portuguese than these grains of sand. The family members were filled with cowardice when Rifot said that in order to have that many people, it would be necessary to find them in France. With that, he said his goodbyes and left with his people for his naus in the Rio Grande and returned to his land. The Potiguarás spread out around their land and were filled with fear. This was related by three of them whom our runners captured in a field.

CHAPTER 31

How Manuel Mascarenhas Homem Built the Fort of Rio Grande and the Assistance Sent to Him by Feliciano Coelho de Carvalho

His Majesty was informed of the events in Paraíba and all the damage caused by the French in Rio Grande where they were trading with the Potiguarás as well as stealing our ships coming and going to Portugal. They were also robbing estates and selling people to the natives so they could eat them. In order to stop these great evil acts, the king wrote to Manuel Mascarenhas Homem, the captain-major of Pernambuco, urging him to immediately go there, build a fort, and establish a town. He did these things with the advice and help of Feliciano Coelho. The king also wrote to the governor-general D. Francisco de Sousa telling him to provide all the necessary supplies and pay for them from royal funds, and the governor did this, carefully preparing everything. The governor-general sent a fleet of six ships and five large caravels to await the others arriving by land in Paraíba. The captain-major was Francisco de Barros, and the admiral was António da Costa Valente. The captains of the other ships were João Pais Barreto, Francisco Camelo, Pero Lopes Camelo, and Manuel da Costa Calheiros.

Led by Captain-Major Manuel Mascarenhas, three infantry companies went by land. Their leaders were Jerónimo de Albuquerque, Jorge de Albuquerque, his brother, and António Leitão Marim. There was also a company of cavalry led by Manuel Leitão. Their arrival was staggered, and Manuel Mascarenhas was ordered to leave for Rio Grande by sea and to take Father Gaspar de Samperes, a Jesuit priest, with him to plan the fort because he was also a great architect and engineer. He went with his companion, Father Lemos, and our brother Friar Bernardo das Neves, because he was fluent in the native language and well respected among the Potiguarás. Because of this and out of respect for his father, Captain João Tavares, who had fought very hard alongside him, he took with him another priest from our order, a man called Friar João de São Miguel. Feliciano Coelho went by land with the four captains and their companies of men from Pernambuco and with another from Paraíba, led by Miguel Álvares Lobo. These totaled 178 men on foot and horseback, not counting our natives, who were ninety archers from the villages of Pernambuco and 730 natives from Paraíba. This last group was guided by their leaders: Braço de Peixe and Assento de Pássaro, Pedra Verde, Mangue, and Cardo Grande. This army began to move from the edge of Paraíba on December 17, 1597, with its spies and runners sent ahead burning several villages that the Potiguarás had abandoned in fear. This was related by several captured natives.

However, those who fled the enemy could not flee from the sickness of smallpox, which is the illness of Brazil. In the past, it was so common among our natives and locally born whites that ten or twelve would die every day. This forced Governor Feliciano Coelho to return to Paraíba so the sick could be cured, and the captains went to Pernambuco with those able to walk. They said they would return to continue the expedition when they had recovered from the sickness. The exception was Captain Jerónimo de Albuquerque, who left with Captain-Major Manuel Mascarenhas on a large caravel for Rio Grande in the fleet as we have said. On the way there, he saw seven French naus at the port of Búzios trading with the Potiguarás. When they saw our fleet, the French cut their cables and fled, but our ships did not follow them because it was late and they wanted to complete their trip.

The next morning, Manuel Mascarenhas ordered two large caravels to explore the river, which they did. Once it was safe, the fleet entered in the afternoon guided by sailors taking soundings. They disembarked there and cut some limbs from mango trees to begin the fort and defend themselves from the Potiguarás. It did not take them many days to appear;

one morning a countless number appeared with fifty Frenchmen who had remained on the naus in Búzios as well as some who lived there, married to Potiguarás. They surrounded our forces in their enclosure and injured many of our people with arrows and gunshots sent through the branches. One arrow hit Captain Rui de Aveiro in the chest as well as his sergeant and others, but they did not collapse. Like elephants at the sight of blood, they were enraged and defended themselves so valiantly against the enemy that they lifted the siege and left.

At that point, a native named *Surupiba* came wanting to make peace. He was from the lower part of the river and arrived on a raft made from branches. They grabbed him and put him in irons. Once captive, he displayed such arrogance; seeing the things Manuel Mascarenhas used and how he ate, he said he should be treated the same. So they gave him better treatment, and the Jesuit fathers, against the advice of our brother Friar Bernardino, who was familiar with their customs and tricks, persuaded the others to set him free. The native promised them he would bring everyone there in peace, and they gave him some clothing and other gifts for his people. They gave him these things twice; he sent for more saying he had pacified the people and they were coming. However, two of our lifeboats with twenty soldiers were leaving for Cape Bento da Rocha to cut mangrove trees, and they entered a gulf and began to cut wood. The enemy natives surrounded them while they were among the trees and planned to attack them at low tide when the lifeboats would be on dry land. All of our men would have been killed if the larger of the two boats had not left and discovered these enemies, alerting the men in the other little boat to quickly leave and put some distance between themselves and the enemy. The enemy all at once then left their hiding places and entered the water. They moved to a sandbar in the middle of the river, where they began boasting loudly, saying that now they had them in their trap, believing the lifeboat was stuck on land.

However, God wished to open a channel and allow them to leave and inform Mascarenhas so that he would no longer be fooled by these deceptions and tricks. This was especially true when, several days later, they saw the mountains filled with a countless number of armed enemy natives who immediately descended to again attack our enclosure. But our forces did not await them there, nor did they allow them to start a siege, but rather they awaited the enemy along the path, and a platoon attacked them from the bush. They captured them with such force that those in the rear fled, and our men followed them in the front to the river. Our Tabajara natives even went into the water killing them, not leaving one alive. They were so drawn into this battle that it was necessary to send the lifeboats to pick them up beyond the harbor entrance.

But even this did not stop the natives from making continued assaults that so threatened our forces that they could hardly go out and find water to drink from some little nearby wells. The water was foul, and they faced the same difficulties with their other needs. Had it not been for the arrival of Francisco Dias de Paiva, they would have lost the hope for rapid assistance from Paraíba that had been sustaining them and abandoned the structure. Paiva arrived in an urca coming from Portugal, supplied by the king with artillery, arms, and some provisions for the fort they were building. He was the leader of the captain-major's family and the man who raised him. As soon as the ill began to recover, Feliciano Coelho sent word to the captains in Pernambuco; when he saw they were not coming, he assembled his men and left from Paraíba to help on March 30, 1598, with one company of twenty-four men on horseback and two companies of infantry with thirty men with harquebuses in each. These were led by Captains António de Valadares and Miguel Álvares Lobo and 350 native archers with their leaders.

They found nothing along the way except abandoned villages and some spies, and we sent out spies as well and captured some of theirs. From them they learned that there was a large enemy village one league from the fort and that it was heavily defended. It was from this village that the enemy went forth to attack our forces, and the governor ordered they pick up the pace so they could attack this village before the natives were alerted. However, they found the village abandoned and large enough for all our forces to rest there.

The next day, Manuel Mascarenhas went to see the fort and discuss how to complete its construction because much was still needed. Feliciano Coelho said that he and his cavalry along with Braço de Peixe and his men would work one day and that António de Valadares and Assento de Pássaro's men would work the next day. Miguel Álvares Lobo would work with Pedro Verde's men the third day. This rotation would ensure that the work would get done and each group of natives would have a white man fluent in their language to encourage them. These men were Francisco Barbosa, António do Poço, and José Afonso Pamplona.

However, they retained some natives to explore the interior with some locally born whites, and this group found a village where they killed more than four hundred Potiguarás and captured eighty. From those natives, they learned that there were a lot of people nearby, both Potiguarás as well as Frenchmen, in six heavily fortified villages, and that they would have already come and killed our forces if not for the fact that many were ill or dead because of smallpox.

While they were building the fort, a ship arrived from Paraíba with beef, chickens, and other supplies sent by Pero Lopes Lobo to his lieutenant, Francisco Coelho. The ship's pilot brought the news that there was a French nau anchored at the port of Búzios unloading people on shore. Hearing this, Manuel Mascarenhas, all his cavalry, thirty soldiers with harquebuses, and many natives went there. They started with the little houses of the Potiguarás where the trade was taking place, killed thirteen, and captured seven as well as three Frenchmen because the others escaped in a lifeboat or by swimming. The captain-major Manuel Mascarenhas, seeing that they did not have the boats to attack the nau, decided to set a trap, pretending to go. He left a wounded Frenchman on the beach so they would come fetch him from the nau in a sloop, which they did. However, as soon as they saw the first person get out of the sloop, our forces came forward, but it was in such a haphazard manner that they only captured him. The others were able to return to the nau, and it set sail.

CHAPTER 32

Once the Fort at the Rio Grande Was Completed, It Was Turned Over to Captain Jerónimo de Albuquerque. The Captains from Pernambuco and Paraíba Returned Home; Their Battles with the Potiguarás along the Way

When the fort at the Rio Grande was completed, it was called *the Fort of the Three Kings*, and Manuel Mascarenhas entrusted it to Jerónimo de Albuquerque on the Day of Saint John the Baptist, 1598.[1] Albuquerque took the usual oaths of office. After leaving the fort very well staffed and stocked with artillery, weapons, supplies, and all that was necessary,

Mascarenhas and his men left to spend the night in the village of Camarão, where Feliciano Coelho was resting with his men. The next day, they all left for Paraíba in great friendship and peace, which is the best ammunition against enemies. This is what was applied to the first group they encountered at a large and strong walled enclosure six days after their departure. They sent one of their spies ahead, a very valiant native convert named *Tavira*. With only fourteen companions, he was able to kill more than thirty enemy spies, not leaving any survivors to inform the enemy. Our forces quickly attacked the enclosure at midday and fought for more than two hours without being able to enter, except for Tavira. He boldly climbed the walls and entered with a sword and shield; calling out his own name, he injured and killed the enemy until his sword broke and he was left with only a shield. He caught the arrows with the shield, and Captain Rui de Aveiro and his soldier Bento da Rocha saw this and using a hole in the wall, fired two harquebuses, making the enemy retreat from Tavira. This gave him sufficient room to turn and climb back over the wall, easily clearing it as if he were a bird. By this and other similar actions, this native has achieved such fame that among the enemy, just saying "I am Tavira" will make them all cower and fearful. Those in this enclosure were fearful after Tavira's actions, and our people were energized. Our people saw that if they could be captured at night with the enemy so close and others surviving elsewhere, they were at risk. So they once again attacked with great energy, shooting so many harquebuses and arrows that it put those inside in danger. This was clear when they heard the loud wailing and crying of the women and children.

Captain Miguel Álvares Lobo and his sergeant João de Padilha, a Spaniard, attacked an entrance into the enclosure and opened it, allowing others to enter. Captain Rui de Aveiro and other captains did the same thing elsewhere, forcing the Potiguarás to flee by way of other openings at the top of the stockade or elsewhere. In the end, more than fifteen hundred Potiguarás were killed or captured, and our forces only suffered three casualties among the Tabajaras. Some were injured, including some whites as well, such as Sergeant João de Padilha.

Four days later they were attacking another enclosed village, not as large as this first one but better fortified and filled with handpicked natives. There were no women or children to cry, just male warriors, including some ten or twelve skilled at using harquebuses. They did not fire unless they had a clear shot of one of our men. The archers did the same, and as a result they injured many people. It would not have been possible to sustain the attack on the stockade if a soldier from the Estrela Mountains named Henrique Duarte had not thrown a firepot inside and it burned a house.[2] When the natives inside saw the fire, they thought they would all be burned so they left the stockade. However, they did not flee or turn their backs but withdrew defending themselves valiantly against our men who followed them. Even though they killed 150 Potiguarás, the natives killed six white men. Among these were Diogo de Sequeira, the second lieutenant of Captain Rui de Aveiro Falcão, who was killed by a gunshot that first passed through the cap belonging to Bento da Rocha, next to him. When Rocha saw him dead and the flag down, he raised it and allowed it to wave next to him in the field among the gunshots and arrows. His captain-major, Manuel Mascarenhas, saw this and issued a certificate allowing him to request the awarding of a gentleman's habit with a large stipend.[3] Instead, he entered our angelic Franciscan order and had a stipend of poverty and humility by which he lived and died a holy man in this safekeeping.

They also injured Captain Miguel Álvares Lobo with two arrow wounds and Diogo de Miranda, the sergeant of Manuel da Costa Calheiros's company, was wounded in the arm by a native with a scimitar. The native struck his shield with such force that it cut the straps used to hold it, wounding Miranda's arm. He chased the native around the stockade, plunging a sword into his chest up to the hilt. This was not sufficient to stop the native stoutly holding on to him, and the native would have pulled him down if Jerónimo Fernandes, head of the squad of his company, had not hit him in the neck, which made him let go. Once the dead were buried and the injured were treated, they resumed their march until they reached the border of Paraíba. At that point, Manuel Mascarenhas bid goodbye to Feliciano Coelho and made his way with his men to Pernambuco.

CHAPTER 33
How Jerónimo de Albuquerque Made Peace with the Potiguarás and Began to Colonize the Rio Grande

After the others had left, Jerónimo de Albuquerque met with Father Gaspar de Samperes, a Jesuit, who returned to the fort since he was the engineer who designed it. They discussed what would be necessary to make peace with the Potiguarás. They came across a very easy answer by freeing one of their captives named *Ilha Grande* or *Large Island*, a native leader and healer, sending him to speak with his relatives.

The native was well prepared, knowing what he needed to say to his people. Arriving at the first village, he was very warmly received, especially after they understood why he was there. They sent messages to the other villages, along the sea as well as in the interior. These were the villages led by Pau-Seco and Zorobabé, the main leaders. Once they were all assembled, the messenger said:

All of you, brothers, children, my relatives, you all know me and who I am and how you relied on me in peacetime and during war. This is what now drives me to come from the white people and tell you all that if you want to have a quiet life in your homes and on your lands with your women and children, then you need to come with me. There will be no more discussion; we will go to the fort of the white men and speak with Jerónimo de Albuquerque, the captain there, and the priests and make peace with them. This will be a lasting peace, like the one made with Braço de Peixe and the other Tabajaras, and it has been done throughout Brazil. Those who join the church are not enslaved but rather are instructed in the faith and defended. The French never did this, nor will they now. Their way is blocked by the fort where they cannot enter without being killed, and the Portuguese sink their ships with artillery.

The native was able to give these reasons and many others with such energy in his words that everyone accepted his suggestion. This was especially true for the women, who were tired of carrying all their goods on their backs, fleeing into the bush without being able to enjoy living in their homes or eating the vegetables they planted. They threatened their husbands, telling them they had to talk to the whites since they would rather be their captives than continue to live with such fears from constant warfare and attacks.

As a result, the main native leaders soon came to the fort to make peace. There was little needed to make this happen, for the reasons already stated. From that point forward, our people traded with them in safety. Governor D. Francisco de Sousa was informed of all this by the captain-major of Pernambuco, Manuel Mascarenhas, who went to see him in Bahia. The governor ordered that this peace should be cast in solemn legal terms, which they did in Paraíba on June 11, 1599. In attendance were the governor of Paraíba, Feliciano Coelho de Carvalho, with officials from the city council, Manuel Mascarenhas Homem with Alexandre de Moura, who was to succeed him as captain-major of Pernambuco, Superior Court magistrate Brás de Almeida, and other people. Our brother Friar Bernardino das Neves was the interpreter because he was very skilled in the local language. He was well respected by the native Potiguarás and Tabajaras as we have stated. Because of this, Captain-Major Manuel Mascarenhas stayed by his side on these occasions, never leaving him.

Now that peace had been made with the Potiguarás, our people began to create a town on the Rio Grande, one league from the fort, which they called the *City of the Kings*. The captain of the fort governed the town as well, and the king continued to send a new captain every three years. They raised all sorts of cattle on this land since it was better for livestock than for growing sugar. They only created two sugar mills, and they could not create more because sugarcane needs *massapé* soil and mud and these lands are sandy. We could say they are the worst lands in Brazil; in spite of this, if men are focused and want to work, these lands can make them rich.

Just as they were beginning, the bishop of Leiria banished a man there, either in jest or in seriousness, writing in the sentence, "You are banished for three years to Brazil from where you will return wealthy and honored."[1] This man married a woman living there who was also from Portugal. He married her not for any dowry she might have had but rather because she was the only single white woman there. They knew how to farm, and in three years they were able to acquire 2,000 to 3,000 cruzados. They returned to Portugal with this money and shared a table with the captain-major of Rio Grande, João Rodrigues Colaço, and his wife D. Beatriz de Menezes. He spent his time with the captain, and his wife sat at the same level with this nobility. I saw this when they boarded the ship to depart from Pernambuco. They were given this honor because at that time there were no other white women in Rio Grande. The captain's wife gave birth, and this woman became a godmother and her husband became a godfather. They treated them as close friends. In this manner, the man completed the letter of the bishop's sentence, returning from Brazil wealthy and honored.

They were not the only ones to become wealthy along the Rio Grande; there were many others. Even though the land is the worst in Brazil, as I have said, many things will grow on it. Other farms produce a great deal, and there is good fishing from the sea.

The salt works are not far from there. This is where the salt collects naturally, and it is possible to gather great cargoes of it each year. As soon as the salt is collected from one bay, it begins to pile up in another. It does not hurt that ships from Portugal do not go there (except the occasional one from Arrabida), but it is sufficient that they go to Paraíba, which is only some twenty-five leagues distant, or to Pernambuco, fifty leagues away. The locals take advantage of what they have here, using their large caravels. Because of all these benefits, it was very important to colonize and defend Rio Grande to expel that nest of thieving Frenchmen.

CHAPTER 34

How the Governor-General Went to the Mines in São Vicente and Álvaro de Carvalho Continued Governing Bahia and the Dutch Who Came There

For many years, rumors circulated that there were mines of gold and other metals in the captaincy of São Vicente. This was the land King D. João III gave to Martim Afonso de Sousa, and there was some truth to these rumors since there was evidence of gold there. When Governor D. Francisco de Sousa saw these, he informed His Majesty and offered to investigate, leaving Álvaro de Carvalho to govern Bahia in the interim. The governor left for the south in October 1598, taking Custódio de Figueiredo, the High Court justice, with him. Figueiredo was someone who arrived with Francisco Giraldes, and he served as the judge for the deceased and absent.

On December 23, 1599, a fleet of seven Dutch naus entered this harbor. The lead ship was called *Jardim de Holanda* or *Dutch Garden* because it carried a garden of herbs and flowers.[1] This fleet took control of the port and the ships in it, burning and destroying those who resisted, as had occurred with a galleon belonging to the commander of Lessa. It came loaded with merchandise to exchange for sugar. Álvaro de Carvalho posted his own people on the beach and around town to defend it if the Dutch disembarked, but they did not dare to do so. They wanted to negotiate and asked for a hostage equal to their general, who wanted to personally attend these talks. So Estêvão de Brito Freire went to his captaincy as a hostage. The general went to the Jesuit college, where Captain-Major

Álvaro de Carvalho awaited him, and they negotiated for four days and were given what they needed.

However, at the end of four days, the general was told to sign the agreement because there would not be any other. With that, he left in a rage, and Estêvão de Brito was able to leave. In his anger, the general ordered a caravel he had captured in port and some pinnaces in the bay to rob and destroy whatever they could. They attacked the plantation of Bernardo Pimentel de Almeida, which is four leagues from this city. Not encountering any resistance, they burned houses and a church and even took the bell from the belfry. But the bell rang, and these men were punished by André Fernandes Morgalho, whom Álvaro de Carvalho had sent with three hundred local men. Still finding the enemy there, they vigorously fought with them, forcing them to board their ship. Many were killed in the skirmish and were left on land, while some were killed while boarding. Among the dead was a Dutch captain, whose death greatly saddened the enemy.

From there, they all returned to their naus, and now stocked with people and supplies, they went to the island of the Frades to get water, which they needed. André Fernandes knew this, and he had the Dutch in his sights. He went after them with his men in six pinnaces, entering the island from another bay between the island of Cururupiba and the mainland. It could only be reached at high tide; since they had not been discovered, they disembarked at another point on the island of the Frades. At the same time, Álvaro Rodrigues arrived from Cachoeira with his natives. They were then all together, crossing the island through the bush until they were near a lagoon next to the beach. This was where a boatload of Dutchmen had left the ship to search for water. What they found was salty, and they went back to their ship. Our forces left them alone, remaining hidden in this trap, thinking they would send others to find another spring. However, they did not; instead, they went to the island of Itaparica. When they got on land, they burned a sugar mill belonging to Duarte Osquier; it did not matter to them that he was Flemish since he was married to a Portuguese woman and had been in Brazil for a long time. Our captains, André Fernandes Morgalho and Álvaro Rodrigues, soon arrived and engaged them with such energy that they killed fifty of them. Those remaining boarded their ships and set sail, departing the port they had occupied for fifty-five days.

Upon leaving the entrance to the port, they captured a nau belonging to Francisco de Araújo coming from Rio de Janeiro with seven thousand or eight thousand *quintais* of brazilwood.[2] After loading the wood and the men from the nau on board their ships, they set it on fire, sending several women who had been on board to the mainland.

CHAPTER 35

The War with the Native Aimorés and How Captain-Major Álvaro de Carvalho Made Peace with Them

At that time, Bahia was not only attacked by enemies at sea but was under a much greater threat by land from the native Aimorés. They are wild Tapuias, whom we mentioned in chapter 15 of book 1. Since they have no houses or established hunting grounds, nor do they come out in the open to fight, they are like lions and tigers in the bush. It is from there that they spring onto the roads, or, without even showing themselves, they shoot arrows from behind trees and a handful cause great destruction. Having crushed those in Porto Seguro and Ilhéus, they started on those in Bahia. They cleared them from the Jaguaripe and Paraguaçu Rivers, and they have not crossed the Paraguaçu and come north. If they come that far, nothing would prevent them from coming right up to the city because there is bush up to its edges. Since the roads all pass their hiding places, no one could enter or leave without being killed or injured by these savages.

D. Francisco and Álvaro de Carvalho wanted to fix the damage caused by these people, and they met with Manuel Mascarenhas, who was here to discuss issues relating to Rio Grande with the governor before he left. All agreed that because they were dealing with these people, the forest dwellers that they are, a conventional war was not possible. Manuel Mascarenhas suggested using some Potiguarás from Paraíba, people already at peace. By doing this, the Potiguarás would be busy, distant from their native lands, and not in revolt. As soon as he arrived in Pernambuco, he gathered a large group of them led by the most rebellious and suspicious leader named Zorobabé. Álvaro de Carvalho sent them to Ilhéus with Captain Francisco da Costa to *hunt* the Aimorés; that is what we can call their style of warfare. But they became very fearful, and that was not all bad. This evil was not completely solved, and they had not made much progress before the Potiguarás returned to Paraíba. But God had another, better remedy by way of a female Aimoré captured with her people in an assault led by Álvaro Rodrigues da Cachoeira. She was taught the language of our Tupinambás and in turn instructed several people in her language. She was treated well and taught the mysteries of our holy Catholic faith, which are necessary in order to be a Christian. She was baptized with the name *Margarida*. After learning our ways and growing fond of us, she wore a cotton dress, which is the dress of our natives. She was given a hammock in which to sleep, mirrors, combs, knives, wine, and whatever else she could carry, and she was told to go tell her people the truth, as she did. She showed them the wine that we drink, which is not their blood as they believed, and the meat we eat is from cows and other animals, not human. We do not go about naked, nor do we sleep on the ground as they do, but rather we sleep in hammocks, which she tied to two trees. All of her people tried stretching out in one, combing their hair, and looking at themselves in the mirror. In that manner, they were sure we desired their friendship, and she dared some young men to come with her to Álvaro Rodrigues's house in Cachoeira on the Paraguaçu River. He brought them to this city to Captain-Major Álvaro de Carvalho, who dressed them all in red cloth and showed them the city. There was no house, tavern, or shop that did not invite them in and toast to their health. After that, they were convinced and abandoned their fears. We made peace with all the Aimorés along this coast. We pray that the Lord should maintain it, and they should not have another occasion to revolt.

CHAPTER 36

What the Governor Did in the Mines

After the governor left Bahia, he arrived in the captaincy of Espírito Santo in a few days. They told him there were precious metals in Master Álvaro's mountains and elsewhere; he ordered some excavations and samples, from which they extracted some silver. They also explored the area that yielded emeralds sent from Bahia by Diogo Martims Cão. They constructed a small fort made from stone and lime in which they placed two pieces of artillery to defend the entrance to the city. Once this was completed, the governor left for Rio de Janeiro, where he was greeted by the captain-major, who at that time was Francisco de Mendonça. All the people greeted him as well and applauded because governors-general never visited there. There were so many civil cases and criminal evidence that he would have been there a long time if he had to hear them all. So he sent for the Superior Court magistrate Gaspar de Figueiredo Homem, who had married in Pernambuco, to have him stay there.

Once the magistrate had arrived and the governor was prepared to leave, four pirate galleons appeared in the bay. Knowing that they would be leaving their ships to look for water along the Carioca River, they ordered men around it to set a trap. That is what happened: four pinnaces went out, and the men got off one of the ships and filled their water containers. The pirates were returning to their ships when our forces attacked and killed all of them except for two who badly injured the governor. When the men in the other pinnaces saw this, they returned to their galleons. A mameluco who had been captured in a canoe knew that the governor D. Francisco de Sousa was there and was determined to burn the ships. They set sail right away, leaving the port to resume their journey. The governor went to São Vicente, where after a little while another galleon entered the port. Its captain was a Dutchman named Lourenço Bicar who petitioned the governor, saying he was a good Christian and had never harmed other Christians and had come to sell his merchandise, not to harm others. He asked the governor for permission to unload his cargo and sell it, paying taxes to His Majesty. The governor responded by saying that if his motivation is as it appeared, he would give his permission. However, afterward there were some questions, and they believed that this ship had come with a large fleet to enter the Straits of Magellan but could not enter it because of a storm. Thus, the captain was separated from the others and had come here to find shelter. Our forces then sent six armed men out in a canoe. Under the pretext of wanting to see the nau, they were able to capture the gunpowder and firearms. Following them were many soldiers and native archers who immediately boarded and took control of the ship. Those on board could not defend it nor could they burn it, as they desired, because our forces had captured their gunpowder and firearms.

The treasury gained more than 100,000 cruzados from the merchandise on the ship, and it was spent as quickly as it was obtained. The governor left São Vicente for the town of São Paulo, which is closer to the mines. The men and women up until that time dressed in dyed cotton cloth. If someone had a nice cloak and a woolen cape, they would lend these to a couple for their wedding. After D. Francisco de Sousa arrived and they saw his fine clothes, as well as those of his servants, there being so many special clothes, women's headdresses, and thin silk capes, it seemed to be another place.

D. Francisco had spent a lot of money in Bahia on these clothes, but he spent even more in São Paulo because that is where there are fields like those in Portugal, fertile with wheat, grapes, roses, and lilies watered by cool streams. This is where he sometimes hunted or fished when free from the work of the mines, which was a great labor but which did not always produce results. The gold is obtained by panning; sometimes you obtain very little or nothing, while other times you find grains with weight and value. He strung a rosary of gold as he found the pieces: round, square, or elongated, and he sent it to His Majesty with samples of pearls found on the flat ground of Cananéia and elsewhere. He asked the king to pass a provision calling for the natives in the mountains to be used for this labor and for other tasks he required. King Filipe I never responded to this because he died. He was succeeded by his son, King Filipe II, who summoned him to Portugal after he ruled Brazil for thirteen years. The king sent Diogo Botelho to govern as his successor.

CHAPTER 37
The Eighth Governor of Brazil and the First Who Came via Pernambuco, Diogo Botelho; How He Brought Those Shipwrecked from a Nau from India on the Island of Fernando da Noronha

The eighth governor of Brazil was Diogo Botelho, who first arrived in Pernambuco in 1602. He was the first to travel this way, and this custom was followed by his successors. The reasoning (according to some) was that António da Rocha, the secretary of the treasury, persuaded him to do this. Rocha was married there and came with him from Portugal. Rocha had gone to Portugal with a suit against Captain-Major Manuel Mascarenhas. Rocha could also have mentioned the generosity of the people there, which could have sparked the governor's interest. With greater certainty, we can say that the governor wanted to see the land and forts he had sworn to protect and rule. I do not know what inconveniences exist for governors to bypass it on their way to Salvador, when stopping there only causes a brief delay.

The governor brought with him two serious religious figures of Nossa Senhora da Graça of the Augustinian order. The governor had a son in Pernambuco and wanted them to establish a house there, but the people did not agree. They said they were not able to support so many large religious establishments since they already had the Jesuits in Nossa Senhora do Carmo, the Cathedral of São Bento, and our angelic order of São Francisco. They were given a generous gift, which the governor was able to obtain from the sugar mill owners, and they returned to Lisbon.

At that time, the Dutch left some people on the island of Fernando de Noronha. They had been on a nau from India along with D. Pedro Manuel, the brother of the Count of Atalaia, and António de Melo, the captain. They were brought to Rio Grande in a lifeboat from the nau and a caravel sent by Governor Diogo Botelho. They were naked and hungry and brought nothing more than a few precious stones. Even these were not guarded by their owners but by some slaves from India. The Dutch were looking for them, so the slaves swallowed the stones to keep the Dutch from taking them.

When these people arrived, the captain of Rio Grande, João Rodrigues Colaço, was not there. He had gone to Pernambuco to welcome the governor. However, these survivors did not go wanting because D. Beatriz de Meneses, the captain's wife and the daughter of Henrique Moniz Teles from Bahia, hosted and fed them daily. To sustain them while on the uninhabited road to Paraíba, she sent her slaves with baskets filled with all they would need. Once they arrived in Paraíba, Captain-Major Francisco Pereira de Sousa sheltered and fed them as best he could. He gave some of his woven purple clothing to D. Pedro Manuel, who accepted it and thanked him for providing for him in his time of need.

From there, they walked to Guaiena, which is in the captaincy of Itamaracá. This was where a son of António Cavalcanti, who was at his father's mill, sheltered and fed them splendidly; he accompanied them as far as the town of Igaraçu. This was where they encountered the bailiff of Pernambuco, Francisco Soares, who had been sent by the governor to meet them with sweets and cold water. The governor was awaiting them a quarter league from Olinda and offered his house to D. Pedro Manuel, who could not accept and went to the Jesuit college. From there, Manuel Mascarenhas asked to take him to his house, which was highly decorated for the occasion. He handed over the house and his servants and left for another house in front of it. The next day, Manuel Mascarenhas ordered and paid for many pieces of silk and bolts of cloth from merchants. He also ordered tailors to make clothes for those who wanted them; no one refused because they were all in need. Only D. Pedro Manuel refused, because he was satisfied with the clothes given to him by the captain of Paraíba. He said that for someone who had lost so much in the shipwreck, these clothes would be sufficient until he reached Portugal. He knew that it was the person people wanted to see and not his clothes. He then married the niece of the archbishop of Braga, D. Aleixo de Meneses, whom he knew well, since Meneses was the archbishop of Goa. She had a large dowry, and His Majesty gave him many favors.

CHAPTER 38

The Expedition of Pero Coelho de Sousa to Paraíba and the Mountains of Boapaba, Done with the Governor's Permission

Pero Coelho de Sousa wanted to see if he could regain some of the losses he and his brother-in-law, Frutuoso Barbosa, sustained in Paraíba. He went with the understanding that once the king rules a land, it cannot be conquered. However, the lands beyond it can be conquered, specifically the mountains of Boapaba, which are heavily populated with natives. Sousa asked for permission to explore that area from the governor-general Diogo Botelho. After obtaining it, he sent three ships with provisions, gunpowder, and firearms to be held for him at the Jaguaribe River. He left Paraíba by land in July 1603 with seventy-five soldiers. The leaders were Manuel de Miranda, Simão Nunes, Martim Soares Moreno, João Cide, João Vaz Tataperica, Pedro Congatan, an interpreter, another French interpreter named Tuim-Mirim, and two hundred native archers. Their leaders were Mandiopuba, Batatam, and Caragatim, all Tabajaras; and Garaguinguira, a Potiguar. Walking along on this expedition, they came to the Jaguaribe River and found their boats with the supplies. From that point, Captain Pero Coelho sent a soldier with seventy natives to explore the interior. They found an encampment and one native walking around laughing. From him, they learned that his people were armed and ready to fight because they did not want peace with the whites. In spite of this, the captain gave him some scythes, axes, and knives to pacify his people, which he did. The next day he came looking for the interpreter to whom he had spoken before and who knew what to say. These were such simple and humble people that when leaving their homes and fields, they brought their women and children, saying they only wanted peace with Christian whites and to accompany them wherever they went.

The natives in the next village followed that example, and they all went off toward Ceará. A few days of rest were needed because they were traveling with children. They resumed walking to a hill, afterward called *Coconut Hill* because some seven or eight coconut trees planted there on their return had grown to be very large. From there, they went to the large village of Ambar and the bush of the colored wood, which they call *Iburá-quatiara*, and then to Camoci. It is at the foot of the Boapaba Mountains, where they went the next day. That was before daybreak on the eve of Saint Sebastian's Day, January 19, 1604. At dawn, they were seen by the enemy with room to form only two squadrons with their supplies in the middle. Another squadron was formed from twenty soldiers led by Manuel de Miranda and was ready to deploy where needed. Sixteen soldiers were guarding the rear, while nine were in front in the company of Captain-Major Pero Coelho de Sousa.

That was the order in which they were attacked half a league from the base of the mountain. They faced a hail of arrows and seven Frenchmen firing harquebuses, which did great harm. Our forces did not fail to leave some enemy dead on the field because our men fought with great energy and strength. After two hours of sunlight, our side had camped at the foot of the mountain and made a shelter of stones since there was no wood: none for a fire because the landscape was barren and even less wood for cooking. There was also no water. Some of the children began to die as a result. At night, some of the enemy returned to fire arrows and hurl stones at our people from above and these injured many. The enemy cried out that they welcomed our coming because they would be masters of white captives and other similar things. But Our Lord desired to send a large rainstorm at three o'clock in the morning, causing the enemy to cease their attack. Our forces were able to appease their thirst, and, to show even greater mercy, the Lord showed them a field with a stream. Our Christian natives saw this as a miracle and fell to their knees to thank God. The captain decided to slaughter a horse that they still had, to sustain the soldiers, since it was impossible to feed everyone; among the adults and children there were more than five thousand souls.

At ten in the morning those in the mountains began to play a home-made trumpet, which our Frenchman Tuim-Mirim answered on another. After requesting permission from the captain, he then went to a hill to speak with the Frenchmen. There he greeted three of them, and after these greetings, the Frenchmen said that native leader Diabo-Grande wanted peace if they would hand over Manuel de Miranda and Pero Cangatá. Those making this request were some mulatto and mameluco servants from Bahia who were greater devils than the leader they served.

Tuim-Mirim answered that the captain could not engage in such treachery because his king would disapprove. With that answer, they left, and at two o'clock in the afternoon all the natives from the mountain descended to fight until dark, when they returned to their camp on the hill, leaving many of their dead. We had seventeen dead and several wounded.

In the morning, the captain ordered the army to move up the hillside. He led the way with the bulk of the army, while Manuel de Miranda went another way with twenty-five men. When they got to the enemy camp, it was noon; a fierce battle began because those inside were assisted by sixteen Frenchmen. These men were firing their harquebuses from behind a stone barrier. When they saw that we were fighting in other places as well, the enemy came out from their camp, since we had killed and injured many of them. They opened the encampment and fled; only two of our soldiers were killed, while the others took shelter in the native houses. These were very well stocked with supplies, meats, and vegetables, all of which our soldiers really needed. They had finished the chestnuts, which were all they had.

They were there twenty days, at the end of which they waged war on another very strong enclosed village, led by Diabo-Grande. He had the help of another powerful leader named *Mel-Redondo* in another village a quarter league away. Even though they faced great resistance, our forces won and made the enemy flee to Mel-Redondo's village. It was heavily fortified with two rings of wooden fences. These were made with thick, strong poles, and one fence was inside the other, with three sentry boxes manned by the French. When Captain Pero Coelho de Sousa saw these, he ordered some large shields built. These were so large that it took twenty negros to carry one. Walking behind these with the supplies and some people, they were able to reach the walls; they fought for two days.

They killed three of our white soldiers and injured fourteen, not counting the many natives, but, in the end, the village was captured along with ten Frenchmen who were inside. The others had fled with the natives, whom our men pursued for four days as far as a river called *Arabé*. This was where our people camped and from where the captain ordered some attacks. Within a few days, they captured many people, among them a leader named *Ubaúna*. He was held in such high esteem in those mountains that, as soon as the others heard he was captured, they asked for peace with the condition he be released. The captain promised to do this and gave the negotiators some scythes and axes. The next day, their leaders all came in peace and took their beloved Ubaúna home.

In the end, three days later, Mel-Redondo and Diabo-Grande and all their people came to the entrance to the camp and laid down their weapons, signaling they wanted peace. Captain Pero Coelho had a scribe write a formal agreement promising the peace would be respected and maintained by both sides from that day forward.

From there, everyone went together to Punaré; Pero Coelho wanted to continue another forty leagues to Maranhão, but the soldiers did not agree to this since they were walking naked. Some of them were sufficiently upset about this that they wanted to kill him. So it was necessary for them to seek shelter in Ceará. From there, Pero Coelho left Simão Nunes as captain with forty-five soldiers, and he went to Paraíba to look for his wife and family and colonize those lands. When he arrived, he sent his report to the governor-general Diogo Botelho along with a gift of the ten Frenchmen and many natives. He also requested aid to continue the conquest, which the governor promised to send but did not. He had been informed that the natives had been captured unjustly and were brought to be sold. It was better to pacify them through prayer and instruction by the Jesuit fathers as was later arranged by the Jesuit leaders in Bahia. We will discuss this success in chapters 42 and 43 of this book.

CHAPTER 39
The Passion Shown by Governor Diogo Botelho in
Converting Natives Using Priests

The conversion of the native peoples is such a necessity for administering Brazil that governors have always been passionate about it, aiding the efforts of missionaries. If this were not so, it would cause great harm since these natives are very poor, have no possessions to lose, and are self-depriving. On the other hand, they are so changeable and inconstant that they can easily be led by anyone. They scatter very easily where they cannot respond to enemy attacks, unlike the manner in which they accept the doctrine of the faithful when priests have them grouped together.

[***]¹

[. . .] especially in regard to the negros of Guinea, the slaves of the Portuguese who daily rebel and rob on the highways. It is only their fear of the natives that keeps them from doing worse. A Portuguese captain leads natives into the interior to seek them [the negro slaves] out and bring them back to their masters as captives.

Governor Diogo Botelho understood this very well and urged our ministry, which was our instruction of the Tabajaras (which made the Potiguarás very jealous). We provided order and religious figures who instructed them in the faith since this was the main condition of the peace treaties concluded in Paraíba. It has been five years that we have had them among us, telling them first to build churches and create ornaments, bells, and everything else that was needed. Seeing how this sponsorship was on hold since there were no brothers skilled in their language, we wrote to His Majesty and to our leaders. Our head brother António da Estrela came to this land and saw how taxed we were. He ordered three missions to the Potiguarás of Paraíba in addition to the two we had with the Tabajaras, some of whom were married to Potiguarás as well. He assigned four brothers in each because there were so many natives. In addition to the villages where the brothers lived, they had many others to visit, and two brothers were needed to do this. They baptized the ill when they were near death, and this was more than seven thousand not counting the children and adult converts, which were forty-five thousand as shown in the baptismal registers when we were in charge.

I have to say that it is hard work dealing with the inconsistent natures of these people. In the beginning, it is a joy to see their devotion and fervor as they embrace the Church. When the bell rings for instruction or Mass, they run to it with an enthusiasm and uproar that makes them seem like horses. However, after a short time, they begin to cool, and it becomes necessary to bring them by force. They then move to their fields outside the village to prevent us from doing this. They latch onto all the festivals with any ceremony with great eagerness because they love novelty, such as the Day of Saint John the Baptist, because of the bonfires and crowns of leaves, or the Day of the Dead to pay their respects. They also love the Day of Ashes and Branches, mostly because of the suffering, which disciplines them. They interpret this as a noble deed. This is so much so that a leader named *Iniaoba*, after becoming a Christian he was called *Jorge de Albuquerque*, was absent during Holy Week. He arrived in the village on the eighth day after Easter saying that he had disciplined the big and the small. He spoke with me, since he was in charge, saying that even the young should learn discipline. Since he was such a brave man, how could it be that the blood remained in his body and he did not bleed? I told him that everything happened in its own time and that the lashings of discipline are reminders of the sufferings Christ endured for us but that now we celebrate his glorious resurrection with happiness. However, this answer did not quiet him. He asked me so many times, saying that he would be dishonored and seen as weak, that I had to tell him to do whatever he wanted. At that point, he immediately went around the village lashing himself harshly, bleeding from his back while the others were celebrating, filling themselves with wine.

CHAPTER 40

How the Governor Went from Pernambuco to Bahia and Sent Zorobabé to
Paraíba with His Potiguarás to Paraíba to Follow the Escaped Negros from
Guinea at Palmares on the Itapucuru River; How Whaling Began

After Governor Diogo Botelho had been in Pernambuco for more or less a year, he came to Bahia, and when he arrived, Álvaro de Carvalho left for Portugal. The royal palace, where the governor lives, is on the main square, which has a pillory in the middle. The governor immediately ordered it moved out of sight because he said the sight of it made people sad. He remembered being in front of another pillory, sentenced to beheading for following Lord D. António, but he was pardoned by His Majesty because he was married to a sister of Pedro Álvares Pereira, a court secretary. He was not the only one to have a hatred of the pillory because none of his successors put it back, nor does one exist in this city. This makes me recall reading that there was an earthquake and storm in Bassein and not a house or church was left standing but just the pillory, and, in the chapter house of the brothers, the wall was left intact where they kept the rods for discipline. This shows that punishments for wrong-doing remain, while people and cities do not.

When the governor arrived, Zorobabé was ready to leave with his Potiguarás for Paraíba. They had come to wage war on the Aimorés as we have stated in chapter 33 of this book. The governor learned that there was a runaway slave community or band of negros from Guinea at Palmares on the Itapucuru River, four leagues before the Real River, and he ordered the natives to capture the negros, which they did. It was no small thing to clean out that growing nest of thieves. However, few were returned to their owners because the natives killed many, and Zorobabé took some to sell along his way to purchase a tent, a drum, a horse, and some clothes, with which he made a triumphal return to his land, which we will discuss in another chapter. However, now we will discuss how whaling began here in Bahia.

There was a great lack of fish oil in Brazil for making boats or ships watertight as well as for lighting lamps in sugar mills where the work continues all night. If they had to use olive oil for lighting, they would use so much and the negros like it so much that all the oil in the world would not suffice. Some fish oil came from Cape Verde and from Biscay by way of Viana do Castelo, but it was so expensive and so limited that it was necessary to blend it with olive oil. Fish oil is bitter and smelly, and this prevents the negros from licking the oil lamps. The great lack of this oil was a real pity, especially seeing the whales, who have the same oil, swimming in this bay and no one was catching them. But God sent His help, by which prayers are answered, motivating Pedro de Ofrecha, a man from Biscay, who wanted to do this fishing. He came with Governor Diogo Botelho from Portugal in 1602, bringing with him two naus of others from Biscay. They began to catch whales, and once the Portuguese learned how to do this, they all returned with whales and did not have to pay any taxes for fishing. Nowadays they must pay a tax, and annually His Majesty sells the right to hunt whales to one person for six hundred *milréis*, more or less, for a five-year contract from his agents.

Because this type of fishing is something to watch, better than any jousting or games, I want to describe it here extensively.

Each June, a great multitude of whales enter this bay to give birth. Each whale has one baby, as large as a horse. At the end of August, they return to the ocean. Fishing begins on the Day of Saint John the Baptist after a Mass is celebrated at the Chapel of Our Lady of Montserrat at Tapuípe Point. Once this is completed, the priest blesses the pinnaces and all the equipment used in this fishing and then they leave to hunt whales. The first thing they do is harpoon the baby, which they call a *calf.* It is always on the surface of the water playing and jumping like a dolphin, so it is easy to harpoon it with a weapon that has shoots on it like a dart. When it is injured and restrained with poles, they pull on the rope attached to the harpoon and then tie it alongside one of the pinnaces. They use three in this effort. Then they harpoon the mother, who is never far from the offspring. Since a whale does not have bones, other than in the spine, and the harpoon is heavy and shot with force, it enters the whale's body halfway up its shaft.

Once the mother knows she is injured, she takes flight for a league, sometimes more. She races on the surface of the water, and the man with the harpoon lets out the rope and follows her until she tires. When the other two pinnaces appear, the three make a formation with the boat with the calf in the middle. The mother then knows they have come for her, and another boat with another man at the harpoon throws it with the same force as before. She is exhausted, and all men on the pinnaces throw spears with sharp points like half-moons. She is then injured to the point that she gives out loud cries of pain. When she dies, she exhales great quantities of blood through her vent, so much that it covers the sun and makes a red cloud turning the sea red. This is the signal that it is over, and she is dead. Right away, five very skilled men jump out with thick pieces of linen cord with which they bind the mouth and jaw to prevent water from entering. Then they bind the whale and bring it alongside the pinnace. All three boats then form a line and row to Itaparica Island, which is three leagues distant from this city. They go to a port called Cruz where they slaughter the whale and extract its oil.

Payment for those who hunt whales for the two months of the season totals 8,000 cruzados. Each man at the harpoon receives five hundred cruzados, and the smallest payment made to the others is thirty *milréis*, not counting the food and drink provided for all. However, the profit from this is great since they normally kill thirty or forty whales and each one renders twenty *pipas* of oil, more or less depending on its size. These pipas are sold for eighteen or twenty *milréis* each. This does not count the lean meat from the whale, which they cut into pieces and slices, salt, and dry in the sun. Then they put these in pipas and sell each of these for twelve to fifteen cruzados. The people working on the oil do not do this. [The work packing the meat] employs sixty men, whites and negros.[1] This work is for servants and negros belonging to the masters of the sugar mills and the sharecroppers. This is the food given to the negros, and they like it better than any other fish. They say that it cleanses them and cures sores and other diseases and weaknesses. When the masters come home injured from their drunken fights, this oil when heated cures them better than balsam oil.[2]

Even though they have killed many whales, they did not find ambergris in any of them, which they say is their food. What they did find was not the same kind. This was in a whale who died a few years ago here. In the stomach and intestines, they found twelve *arrobas* of very fine ambergris, and another *arroba* the whale had vomited on the beach.

CHAPTER 41
How Zorobabé Arrived in Paraíba and Was Suspected of Rebellion,
Imprisoned, and Sent to Portugal

Chapter 39 of this book describes how Zorobabé was returning to Paraíba from the wars against the Aimorés when the governor sent him to look for the runaway community of negro slaves. He killed some and took others captive, which he then sold to the whites and purchased a tent, drum, horse, and clothing to make his triumphal entrance home. Some Potiguarás went forty leagues to await him on the road, others went ten or twenty; all of them opened the path and cleared it with hoes.

Only Braço de Peixe, a Tabajar, remained with his people in his village, and since Zorobabé decided to pass by, he sent word for them to come out and greet him because of what he had done so far away. The old man answered that, even though he was an old man, he did not wait along the roadside except to conduct war or greet a woman. Since Zorobabé was not a woman nor did he come in war, he would not stir from his hammock.

With that answer, Zorobabé passed by that village and ate dinner at the Niobi River, half a league from his village. He sent word to our religious brothers that he wanted a dance of *corumis*, a dance done by the children of the school, and to see the church opened and decorated with branches so he could enter it.

The leader of the mission responded to his messenger, saying that the children were excited about his arrival and were scattered everywhere. The church was only decorated with branches on saints' days, but that the door was open. He came that afternoon on horseback, well dressed, with his flag and drum. He had a brave native walking in front of him with a drawn sword, swinging it, making all the innumerable people stay back.

With this grand entry he passed by the church without entering it, and he went to his house. A relative of his came right away, a Christian native called Diogo Botelho, who until that point had been ruling the village in his place. He asked the brothers to forgive his not entering the church but because he had arrived drunk he would come the next day, as he did. Before that, he ordered five chairs to be placed in the nave of the church. The chair in the middle, where he would sit, was covered with a striped cloth made of wool. His relative and the leaders of the other villages would sit on the other chairs. One of these was Mequiguaçu, the leader of another village. He was now a Christian and named *D. Filipe.* The religious brothers also went there to welcome him and then took him inside the school where the children are taught. The chairs there are logs and pieces of wood on which they sit. However, Zorobabé grew angry and wanted to leave, but the leader of the mission stopped him. They told him that all the people in Paraíba would be gathering, as well as many Portuguese, and they only came for one reason. According to what everybody said, it was to know what Zorobabé planned to do. The next day, which was Sunday, he would be preaching to them, and in preaching, it is only possible to speak the truth. As a result, he needed to know the answer to this special question and because of this, Zorobabé could not refuse him.

Zorobabé answered him saying it was his intention to wage war on Milho Verde, a leader in the interior who had killed his nephew. His nephew had become a Christian named *Francisco* and was formerly known by his old name of *Aratibá.* His brother, Pau-Seco, had ordered warfare. Zorobabé had come to rule because of the death of his brother and nephew, and he now wanted to extract his revenge. The leader of the mission told him that they were now vassals of the king of Portugal and they could not wage a just war without his orders and permission from the governor-general of Brazil. In addition, Zorobabé was well aware of the state of his people. As soon as war was declared, they would abandon agricultural work. Since women, the elderly, and children did not go to war, they would stay behind and die of hunger. So, if he agreed, they would preach that they clear and plant first. He would say this as well to keep everyone calm, and he agreed. The leaders were at peace and returned to their villages.

Zorobabé was also visited by many whites from Paraíba, who brought him clay jugs of good wine and other gifts. These visits were because of their interest in native affairs, their need for natives to work, or their fear from rebellion because he was so powerful. This fear was so widespread that the captain of Paraíba, urged by the captains of Itamaracá and Pernambuco, never ceased writing the leader of the brothers to keep an eye on him. They said natives were going to start a rebellion led by him, which the brothers did not believe at all. They found him very obedient. He only complained once, and that was that the brothers did not visit his house even though all the other residents of Paraíba did. The brothers answered that they did not visit because he was not a Christian and he had many women. He said he would quickly send them away and only keep one if he were baptized. For that celebration, he would raise many chickens because he was not so common as were the others. They ate beef and wild animals at their weddings and baptisms. At his feast, there would be chickens and feathered birds.

In spite of this, when Zorobabé drank he was restless and rebellious. Fear on the part of the Portuguese grew to the point that they apprehended him and sent him to Alexandre de Moura, captain-major of Pernambuco and from there, he was sent to the governor. They put him in prison and many times put poison in his wine and in his water, but it did him no harm. They say that he feared these liquids and only drank in the morning in his own cell, and with this solution he saved himself from the poison. In the end, they sent him to Lisbon, but because it is a seaport and ships leave daily for Brazil, he could return. So they sent him to retire in the city of Évora, and he died there along with the suspicions of his rebellion.[1]

CHAPTER 42

*What Happened to a Flemish Nau on Business in the Captaincy of
Espírito Santo Loading Brazilwood*

Flemish urcas normally come to Brazil after loading in Lisbon, Porto, or Viana do Castelo. They bring merchandise from their country as well as from Portugal to exchange for sugar. Among these ships was one that went to the captaincy of Espírito Santo. The captain of that ship asked the leader of the Jesuits, who instruct the natives there, if they would collect a cargo of brazilwood in the village of Reritiba, where they have a lot of it and a good port. The Flemish ship would return the next year to collect it and would in turn provide them with ornaments for the church or whatever they wanted.

The priest told the magistrate, who was there, all about this brazilwood contract, and with his permission, they cut the wood in that village. However, the king was told that since these Flemish urcas are stronger and better defended, everyone would want to transport their goods on them and Portuguese shipping would cease. If that happened, there would be no ships to form an armada and no experienced sailors. The king agreed and wrote to Governor Diogo Botelho and the other captains to forbid foreign ships from trading or any other business in their captaincies. He ordered them to sink the ships and pursue the crew as they do with enemies.

After this prohibition was issued, the Flemish urca arrived in Espírito Santo, and the Jesuit leader had been transferred to Rio de Janeiro. The new leader in his place knew nothing of this arrangement. They then went to the village for the wood, and the Jesuit fathers there would not allow them to load it. They took four natives on board and sailed to Cape Frio, where the captain disembarked. Using a disguise, he went on foot to speak with the superior at the Jesuit college in Rio de Janeiro. The Jesuit leader told the captain he could not do anything about this, because the king had prohibited it. Furthermore, he said the captain should return to the coast with great caution since, if Martim de Sá, the governor of Rio de Janeiro, found him, it would cost him his life.

The Flemish captain did not return with sufficient secrecy, and Martim de Sá discovered his presence. The governor sent five large canoes with many white men and native archers led by his uncle Manuel Correia to Cape Frio. They found some Flemish men on land loading brazilwood on their pinnace. The wood had been cut there. They apprehended all of them and took them to Rio de Janeiro. They did not find the governor's nephew because he had gone by land to Cape Frio. He arrived there and did not find the canoes with which to capture the nau, which was in deep water. He returned in a rage and prepared four ships that had been loading and left in search of the Flemish nau, which had already set sail. He sent their captain, whom they held prisoner, to tell the men on board not to fire on them and to allow them to board. They did this, and all their men were hidden under the cannons and netting.

There were some Portuguese who wanted to cut the masts and rigging, but Martim de Sá said the nau was now his and he did not want it damaged. It was now nighttime, and our people were comfortable walking around the deck when the Flemish sailors and some natives on board began to stick them with pikes from below. From bow to stern, the Flemish sailors fired two cannons filled with rocks, nails, and metal balls. This caused a lot of confusion, killing some of our people and injuring so many that it was necessary to leave the nau and seek assistance in the city. Once the Flemish men saw they were free, they sailed to the island of Santa Ana to get water, which they needed. The island is fifteen leagues north of Cape Frio. There are good springs there and safe anchorage for naus. Since they did not have a small sloop, they made a raft of planks, and five of them went onshore with the water barrels. One of them went to the high point on the island to keep an eye on the sea, while the other four filled the barrels, and they transported them one by one on the raft to the nau.

Only four men and two boys remained on board the nau because all the other men were in the canoes. When the natives became aware of this, and there were four of them as well, they each selected one white man. Using a knife and sword, each native easily killed a white man when he was not paying attention. The natives spared the two cabin boys, locking them in a room. The boys had not warned the others collecting water when they saw them, and they would be needed later to help sail the ship. When those who went to collect the water returned to the ship, the natives killed them, cut the anchor line, and set sail with the south wind. At the time, it was blowing from the stern, headed for their village. However, they did not know how to navigate, and once they approached their village, the wind shifted to the northeast, pushing them toward Cape Frio. They passed the cape and were close to the entrance to the harbor of Rio de Janeiro when the wind shifted again to the south. Because the coastline from Cape Frio to Rio runs east to west and a south wind intersects with the coast, it pushed the nau and smashed it into pieces. The natives were able to save themselves by swimming to the shore. They told Martim de Sá the news. He was no longer the leader because that very day, his successor, Afonso de Albuquerque, had arrived. With Albuquerque's permission, Martim de Sá went to see whether he could salvage any of the goods washed along the shore, but he was able to find little since most of it had been damaged or destroyed by the sea.

CHAPTER 43
Pero Coelho de Sousa's Disastrous Second Expedition to the Boapabé Mountains

Captain Pero Coelho de Sousa, whom we discussed in chapter 37, left Paraíba with his wife and children on a caravel bound for Ceará. This was where Captain Simão Nunes and the soldiers had remained in an earthen fort awaiting help from the governor for a year and a half. Since such assistance never arrived and there was a great lack of clothing and supplies, the soldiers wanted to relocate along the Jaguaribe River. It is closer to towns, and they could get aid from there. It is also easier to run away from there, which they did. Simão Nunes asked the captain-major for permission to cross the river with the soldiers to eat some fruit. However, they did not only collect fruit but scattered and fled. Once the captain saw this, he was left with only eighteen soldiers, and they were all injured, which was why they did not flee with the rest. There was one native remaining called *Gonçalo*; the other natives had all left as well. The captain then decided to return to his home, and after making this decision, with some soldiers with minor injuries, he made a raft from mango wood, and little by little all of them crossed the river. Once this was done, he ordered the five children to go first, the oldest of whom was not yet eighteen, then the soldiers, and then him and his wife. All were on foot. On the first day of this journey, they began to tire because as soon as there was a moment of calm, someone could not walk because the sand was too hot, the children began to cry, his wife began to moan, and the soldiers complained. The captain did his duty by motivating and encouraging everyone.

On the second day, the captain carried two of the smaller children on his back because they could not walk, and the complaints began about thirst. These were not solved until the next night when they found a well with sweet water next to two others with salty water. There was only a space of two braças between them. They stayed there for two days and Gonçalo, the native, filled two gourds with water, which they shared, and they were able to walk for a while. It was very difficult and dangerous because of enemy Tapuias all around; they saw smoke from their fires. The worst enemies were hunger and thirst, which started to kill the soldiers. The first was the carpenter. When he realized that he could not continue walking, he told the captain to leave him; he said that when he died his work would be done. However, the captain encouraged him to continue, saying that God would give him the strength to reach water and food. After hearing this, he got up and walked until someone else died. Then there was D. Tomásia, the captain's wife, who shed so many tears that it seemed that her heart would break. She had all her children around her clinging to her, the youngest to the oldest, saying they could not walk any further and that they wanted to remain there and die with the dead soldier. They said they could not endure any more thirst. While shedding rivers of tears, rivers that would have quenched her thirst if they had not been salty, she told her husband to go and save his life because she only wanted to die with her children.

Some of the soldiers burst into tears while others urged her to continue walking. The captain put aside as much of the pain as possible of what he felt and said that just a little ahead was a well. With that hope, they went forth to the well of the bitter water, which is what they called it because of its taste. When they reached it, no one could drink the water. They went on to another well, which they called the *tidal well*. They passed half a league beyond the mango trees in mud up to their waists where they found some crabs called *aratus*. Up to that point they had been surviving on tree roots and grass. They grabbed the crabs and ate them raw with great delight as if they were some delicious stew. Much later, they reached a well where they rested for a few days.

They walked from there in the salty marsh for many days. While there, they spied a passing ship carrying the Jesuit fathers, which was the assistance the governor had sent. However, they were not able to speak to the people on it. After they left the salty marsh, the captain's oldest son died. He had been the light of his parents' eyes. What they all felt I will leave to the imagination of the reader. It was here that the soldiers agreed with the children, saying they would go no further. Without a doubt, that would have been the case except for the captain's wife, encouraging and energizing them, urging them to continue walking. She did the same with the children, and they began to walk at her pleas. However, they were so thin that the wind battered them. They lay down on the beach. The captain went five or six leagues ahead with two of the bravest soldiers to search for water, and he returned with two filled gourds. This refreshed the children so they could walk a little more. On the beach, they saw some people. One was the head priest of Rio Grande who heard about them from the soldiers who fled. He had come with many natives, hammocks to carry them, a lot of water, supplies, and a crucifix in his hand. When he arrived, he gave the crucifix to the captain and the others to kiss, which they did with great happiness and many tears. The priest cried as well, seeing such a spectacle since they were all skin and bones, looking like death itself. With great charity, they took them to Rio Grande and then Paraíba, where Pero Coelho de Sousa left for Portugal to ask that his service be recognized. After spending a few years at the court in Madrid with no response, he went to live in Lisbon and never returned to his home.

CHAPTER 44

The Mission and Expedition by Two Jesuits Ordered by Governor Diogo Botelho to the Same Boapaba Mountains; How Different Orders Pray

The governor was not just eager to see the conversion of the natives who had made peace in Paraíba and asked for instruction, as we have said. He also wanted to extend this to those who wandered blindly in their ignorance. In order to do this, after he returned from Bahia, he asked the leader of the Jesuit order, Fernão Cardim, to send two fathers to preach in the Boapaba Mountains, where Captain Pero Coelho de Sousa was on an expedition. Conversions such as these make war and its related costs unnecessary; if they achieve their desired goal, which is to obtain the friendship and peace of the natives, it is possible to colonize the land. The Jesuit leader immediately agreed and sent Father Francisco Pinto, a deeply religious man of many qualities, a great preacher, and a man close to God. He understood the customs and languages of Brazil. The other priest was Luís Figueira, a well-educated, disciplined man of great kindness.

These two left Pernambuco in January 1607 with some converted natives, tools, and clothing the governor gave them as gifts for the natives. They began their trip at sea, following the coastline 120 leagues to the north to the Jagariba River, where they left the ship and began walking. It was very difficult, and they walked many leagues to the Ibiapava Mountains, which are many leagues this side of Maranhão, near the wild natives they were seeking. However, their way was blocked by other natives who were even more wild and cruel than the Tapuia. The fathers attempted to offer them gifts through their native companions, telling them they wanted their friendship and free passage to continue. However, the natives did not agree, and they killed the native envoys, sparing only one boy of eighteen to guide them back to the fathers' camp, which he did. Many of the hostile natives came with them. When Father Francisco Pinto emerged from his tent, where he had been praying, to see what was happening, he tried to calm the handful of his natives with words of love and benevolence as they tried to defend him with their arrows. But the wild natives fell upon them with fury and killed the bravest converted native; then the others were unable to resist or defend the priest. They hit the priest on the head so many times with a clubbed pole that they split his head open and killed him.

They wanted to do the same thing to Father Luís Figueira, who was not far away from his companion. A young boy traveling with them heard the noise of the approaching wild natives and warned the priest in Portuguese, "Father, Father, run for your life." The priest quickly went into the bush. Because he was guarded by Divine Providence, the wild natives could not find him, as hard as they tried. They were content with the spoils they found, the ornaments the priests use to conduct Mass, some clothing, and tools. After that, Father Luís Figueira had to collect his few remaining companions, who scattered in fear of their lives, and return to the site of this sacrifice. They found the priest's body stretched out, his skull broken, his face disfigured, covered in blood and mud. They cleaned the body and placed it in a hammock. His grave was at the foot of a mountain since they were not able to do more under their difficult circumstances. However, the Lord did not allow him to remain this way for long. Martim Soares, who is now the captain there, tells me they have placed his body in a church where he is venerated, not only by the Portuguese and Christians who live there, but by these same natives.[1]

CHAPTER 45
How Governor D. Diogo de Menezes Came to Rule Bahia and
Preside over the High Court

Governor D. Diogo de Menezes only remained in Pernambuco for one year because he learned of a galleon anchored in Bahia on its way to India.

The sergeant-major Diogo de Campos Moreno was ordered to provision the ship with all the supplies it needed, which he did, and this cost the royal treasury 9,000 cruzados. This was paid by the tax collector, who at the time was Francisco Tinoco de Vila-Nova. With all this happening, the governor felt his presence was necessary in Bahia to ensure the ship lacked nothing so it could continue its journey, which it did. However, because it was late in the season, the ship encountered contrary winds and landed on the coast of Natal. Only the number able to fit in a lifeboat were able to leave. The nau sailed to India. The sailors returned the next year in another nau, which was lost in this bay, which we will discuss in another chapter.

I turn now to the High Court, which arrived this year from Portugal and which the governor presided over as did subsequent governors. Gaspar da Costa came as the court chancellor. He died after a short time and was followed by Rui Mendes de Abreu. This was something new for Brazil because up until that time, justice was administered by local judges, with a Superior Court magistrate visiting Brazil every three years. When the seriousness of the case demanded it, the governor would sit with the justice as would the lawyer for the deceased, who was trained in law, as well as any others they wanted to join them. The general population did not hesitate to give their opinions (always ready to quibble about new things). Some said it was a good thing the High Court judges were here, while others said they never should have come. However, after experiencing their integrity in judging and their knowledge of the issues, something that one person previously could not achieve, I do not know anyone who could complain with any reason. The only exception might be their ecclesiastical cases, because in these matters the High Court has been excessive. In their quest to defend the king's interests, it has crushed those of the Church. God does not want that nor does the king. To prevent this, King D. Sebastião, who is now with God in heaven, ordered that throughout his kingdom, the decisions of the Council of Trent should be enforced. These call for bishops, when passing sentences against clergy and laypeople, to avoid the hasty use of excommunication.

When some scholar writes about this stating the opposite, that is not adequate. Another religious council (and it would be necessary to have one to discuss this) or king would have to revoke it. Why is it necessary to judge and sentence fornicators, pimps, usurers, and the others sentenced by religious judges? What if they do not obey their sentences even if they are censured? What is the effect of the Church's justice? Why are these cases called *mixti fori*?[1] If after preventing it the court then interferes and defends the guilty, are they not still guilty? Surely, this was why this is called *mixti fori*, if not because it would lead to strife rather than first punishing the person, correcting [this behavior], and eradicating it from the land?

I do not deny that when ecclesiastical judges proceed against the rules of law, then the secular arm should address the rights of the prisoner; beyond that, it should not interfere. It does not serve the king, nor does it serve God. It is not important if it impedes the correction of evil or if it disturbs the peace of those who should be encouraged. This is what happened after the High Court came to Brazil, in particular Bahia, where it resides. It is such a small effort to make a reasonable appeal. Without its being here, these appeals continued. The ecclesiastical courts have to go such a long way to find a solution to their summons, which is fifteen hundred leagues distant or more from here to Portugal. This is how Bishop D. Constantino de Barradas was unable to have the man he wanted to serve as vicar general.

There is one thing I noted in this material, and I will conclude this chapter with it (unless I am forced to return to it in another chapter). The bishop declared that a man was excommunicated; he appealed to the High Court and was found innocent. If he did not obey the order of excommunication and fled to avoid meeting or speaking with officials, the penalty was a fine of twenty cruzados for anyone caught speaking with him. This fine was not in place prior to the excommunication; those who wished to avoid speaking to him only did so because he was not a member of the clergy but a layperson.

CHAPTER 46
How D. Francisco de Sousa Came to Brazil to Govern the Southern Captaincies and regarding His Death

There was a lot of apprehension in Brazil because of the great sums of money that D. Francisco de Sousa had spent from the royal treasury. These were carefully reviewed in Portugal. However, because he took nothing for his own gain, but rather spent his own money first just like the other grand captain, the only manner in which the king treated him was to award grants. He had only asked to rule over the mines of São Vicente, so the king awarded him these along with the governance of Espírito Santo, Rio de Janeiro, and the other captaincies in the south. Those in the north were governed by D. Diogo de Menezes, as was done when Governor Luís Brito de Almeida assigned these to António de Salema.

D. Francisco brought his son, D. António de Sousa, with him. He had been in Brazil before and was now the captain-major of the coast. He also brought a younger son, a little boy, named D. Luís, and the court magistrate and member of the High Court, Sebastião Paruí de Brito. They left in two caravels from Lisbon and arrived in Pernambuco in twenty-eight days. In spite of this area not being his to govern and beyond his jurisdiction, they celebrated his arrival there.

From there, they went to Rio de Janeiro, and he began to govern on land and his son directed maritime affairs. Afonso de Albuquerque, who had been the captain-major until then, said that the only thing left to manage was the air. However, they quickly left him behind since D. Francisco went to the mines and D. António left for Portugal with samples of gold. He took a cross and a sword made of gold for His Majesty, but the pirates at sea took these. The governor did not have the chance to send replacements because of the great illness that occurred in the town of São Paulo, which killed him. He was so poor at the time that a Jesuit priest who was with him when he died said he did not have a candle to hold in his hand, so he had him taken to the Jesuit monastery. However, God wanted him to shine at that time of gloomy anguish, as he had done so with so many others, because of D. Francisco's many acts of charity and piety.

Even though he was young, the people wanted his son D. Luís to govern, which he did until he left for Portugal. He left by way of Pernambuco, and there he married a daughter of João Pais. That was the end of the business about the mines since there were individuals charged with visiting them whenever they wanted to extract gold and pay the tax of the royal fifth. They extracted gold, not only from riverbeds but by digging in the earth. By panning, they separate the gold; they also use mercury to do this.

CHAPTER 47
On the New Invention of the Sugar Mill

The main business of Brazil is making sugar, and in no other activities are mills and the skills of men applied more than in inventing machines, which they call *mills.*

I recall reading an old book about the nature of things. In the past, they cut the sugarcane with a knife, and the juice ran out from the cuts and was solidified by the sun into sugar. There was so little of it that it was only used as a medicine. Later, many devices and mills were invented to make greater quantities. All of these were used in Brazil, such as cylinders, grinding stones, and axles. This last one was the most common, using two axles, one over the other moved by a water wheel or by oxen. In a large open space, it turned something called a *flywheel*, which, when it picked up speed, made four others turn as well as the axles that milled the cane. In addition to this machine, there was another with two or three seesaws made of long boards thicker than barrels. After the cane was pressed in the mill, these would squeeze it. A building 150 spans long and fifty wide was needed for the kettles where the liquid was cooked to make the sugar. It took a lot of time and money to build it and the mill.

Recently, when D. Diogo de Menezes was the governor, a Spanish cleric came here from Peru; he showed people an easier, simpler, and cheaper method, which is used today. This is using three rollers on end, all together. The middle roller is connected to a water wheel or to a pole turned by oxen or horses, and it turns the other two. The cane is pressed twice, extracting all the juice with no need of a seesaw or anything else before cooking it in the kettles. There are five large kettles at each mill, and each holds more or less two pipas of *mel*.[1] This is not counting some large pots where the sugar is also produced. The sugar is dried in clay molds in a cooling shed and then taken to the purging shed, which is very large. The molds are placed in rows, and a hole is made in each to allow the impurities to drain, making the sugar very white. I saw an example of this when a chicken jumped onto one of these molds and his feet were covered with mud. The rest of the sugar was dark, but where his feet had touched the sugar, it was white.

Because these mills have three rollers, they are interlocked and are not as complicated or as expensive as previous mills. Those have been taken apart and replaced with these, and all new mills use this design. In Rio de Janeiro, where in the past they were growing [cassava to make] flour for the Angola trade rather than sugar, there are now forty sugar mills. In Bahia, there are fifty, while in Pernambuco there are one hundred. In Itamaracá there are eighteen or twenty and many more in Paraíba. What good is it to produce so much sugar that it lowers its own price, rendering so little profit that it does not pay for itself?

These mills and cogs that they now use, powered by water or oxen, look like the figure below.

At this same time that Governor D. Diogo de Menezes ruled Bahia, a nau from India entered the harbor because it was taking on a lot of water. Its captain was António Barroso. The ship's master, António Fernandes, came ashore in a lifeboat with the bad news. He asked for help because the nau was split open in three places and there were fourteen spans of water inside. The governor immediately sent two caravels with experienced pilots to bring the ship to port. This was to prevent the tidal currents from beaching the ship on the bottom of the bay. To prevent greater damage, they cut the masts and quickly unloaded the ship. After everything was unloaded, seeing that the ship could not be repaired, D. Diogo ordered it burned, salvaging many nails.

These goods were turned over to the superintendent, who at the time was the High Court justice Pero de Cosceno. He was sent to Portugal under guard for this incident. He was injured in the foot, fighting at sea

Figure 7. Different stages of sugar production. Built environment includes open-sided evaporating furnace, two grinding mills one driven by a waterwheel and one by oxen, forms for sugar loaves. Workers gather canes in fields of sugar canes. Two ox carts carry canes to mill. Items in the image are lettered for identification in a key above. —Engraving by Simon de Vries 1682. ©John Carter Brown Library.

with pirates, and this made him lame. However, the goods were all taken. The king then ordered a search for them using a fleet of seven naus led by Captain-Major Feliciano Coelho de Carvalho who had been in Paraíba, and he was able to recover them.

Additional Section 1

[As mentioned in the introduction, these sections have been included here as was done in the Universidade de São Paulo edition of the text.]

Brother Agostinho de Santa Maria was familiar with this *History* by Brother Vicente do Salvador and he used much of it in his own work, sometimes citing it and other times not. This following passage from his *Santuário Mariano* appears to be one of the lost chapters of this Frei Vicente's work.

This fleet left France in 1595 when the governor of Bahia was D. Francisco de Sousa with the objective of capturing the city or damaging it as much as possible. They went by way of Arguin, where the Portuguese had a castle.[2] Even though the French assured them, giving their word they did not intend them any harm, they should never have been believed. They are heretics and enemies of God and the truth. They showed this by burning the church and taking a statue of Saint Anthony of Lisbon, placing it on deck to guide them. But this was all done in mockery and ridicule, with the Frenchmen saying, "Guide us Anthony, guide us to Bahia." When they said this, they cut it and slashed it with their swords, and they set their dog on it. However, God did not wait to punish them in the next life. He does this with others, sending them to hell and punishing them with eternal torments because they offended his images and those of the saints. In this case, he punished them with deadly diseases and sudden deaths.

The first to be punished was also the first one who committed the sin and who most mocked the saint, waving his sword at him and striking him with it. This fellow drank some water from a jug and suddenly fell down dead. While he died drinking, others died of thirst because the pipas where the water was stored were curved and made of iron and they burst, with the water emptying from them.

Due to the lack of water and many daily deaths, some of the ships had to be abandoned because there were not enough sailors. Those remaining from those ships moved to the flagship led by a French captain named Malvirado, and the other large nau had as its captain Pão de Milho or

Cornbread, because it was not all wheat.[3] This group did not want to join with Malvirado, whose advice was to head for Bahia and surrender to the governor. Malvirado believed the governor would not kill them, and they were all but lost now.

So Pão de Milho and his group parted ways with Malvirado and went to the Real River to collect water. He was spotted by some of our natives in Sergipe. They informed Captain Diogo de Quadros, who then captured Pão de Milho and the others who had disembarked.

Malvirado and his group went to Bahia, and from the sandbar at the harbor entrance they sent in a group in a lifeboat with a white flag. They asked the governor for mercy to spare their lives and in turn they would hand themselves over along with the nau, artillery, and everything else. The Portuguese could have everything, which they took. A captain named Sebastião de Faria was placed in charge. Before arriving in Bahia, the heretics and the captain had thrown the image of the saint overboard so that no one would see the damage they had inflicted on it.

It was really a miracle that, being it was December and the winds along that coast are northeast and the currents run southeast, the statue of the saint moved against the winds and currents toward Bahia for twelve leagues from the north, where they had thrown it in the ocean. It must have been that the fish, as they have done on another occasion, heard the Catholic doctrine the heretics rejected. To everyone's amazement, the fish took the statue and securely carried it on their backs. They placed it with great reverence at that spot where those coming from Sergipe with captive Pão de Milho and his Frenchmen would find it standing upright, like someone waiting for them. They took it to Bahia in triumph where they say they carried it.

These heretics could have converted after seeing this miracle, but their hearts were too hardened to allow this. The saint entered with a great festival from those who knew and revered him, and the statue was placed in the Church of Our Lady of Ajuda, which is known as the Church of the Merchants. They organized a solemn procession, which took place on the first Sunday of Advent, December 3, 1595, to the Church of São Francisco, where he was placed in a niche on a side altar dedicated to him.

This procession was ordered by the king (who had learned of this success), and the governor and the town council participate in it each year, although nowadays it is with less devotion. In this first procession, the governor ordered everyone to participate so that the imprisoned heretics could see our great veneration for the image of the saint, while they only dishonored and insulted it. While the procession was passing the square in front of the grates of the jail, they lowered the flags and fired guns as signs of their veneration.

After receiving an answer from the king, the governor ordered gallows constructed on this same square, where Pão de Milho, his pilot, and the others captured in Sergipe were hung. Those who turned themselves in were set free, although they did not deserve it.

When the news of this reached France, the next year they sent a fleet to avenge what had happened. This fleet encountered a Dutch fleet carrying salt and they fought. The Dutch won and destroyed the French ships. Those who could escape made their way back to France. However, it was not over this salt that they fought the war but rather over religious differences.

A fleet of French ships arrived in the town of Ilhéus. They were pirates and a worse plague than the Aimorés. Three of their naus could not enter the harbor, so they sent in ten small boats. This was in 1595.

The Frenchmen came ashore, and the handful of residents fled, except for Cristóvão Vaz Leal and a couple of men. However, they were also forced to retreat to the Chapel of Our Lady of the Snows, which is outside the town, because there were so many of the enemy and our forces were unprepared. Even though there was word about French pirates along the coast, they did not have time to construct a fort nor was there any artillery or firearms other than a falconet in the Fort of Santo António at the port where the Frenchmen landed. The artillery man Pedro Gonçalves had fired a shot with it, killing two men.

The Frenchmen followed our forces to the chapel, where, assisted by Our Lady, the Virgin, our forces were able to valiantly resist, killing three Frenchmen and wounding twelve men with harquebuses. The French forces retreated to the town and barricaded themselves in the houses belonging to Jorge Martins and began to plunder the other homes. However, our forces secretly positioned themselves inside some of the houses. The French entered thinking they would find gold, but they found lead instead. In the twenty-seven days the French were there, there was not one day these traps did not kill at least one of them; sometimes, they killed as many as fifteen.

Our forces were encouraged by this success and came out in the open to face the French. The infantry captain had not yet arrived since he was on his plantation some two leagues away, so they selected someone else to lead. He was not the most noble or wealthy man, but he was the bravest as he had shown in the attacks and traps. He was a poor mameluco (which are people of mixed parents) named *António Fernandes*. He had the nickname of *Catucadas* because this is what *stabs* or *thrusts* are called in his mother tongue. It was a wonder that our forces, consisting of only fifteen or twenty people armed with only bows, arrows, and swords, were able to kill fifty-seven Frenchmen while fighting in the open once the mameluco captain, António Fernandes, joined the fight. If they had redoubled their efforts, they would have killed all the Frenchmen and taken their ships. With this loss, the French fled, leaving the land and its harbor because of the valor of a young uneducated man who did not speak Portuguese. The French were not the only ones confounded by these events, but also the infantry captain, who never appeared.

BOOK 5

The History of Brazil from the Time of Governor Gaspar de Sousa (1613–17) until the Arrival of Governor Diogo Luís de Oliveira (1627)

CHAPTER 1

The Arrival of the Tenth Governor of Brazil, Gaspar de Sousa, and How He Came via Pernambuco to Organize the Conquest of Maranhão

When His Majesty was informed of the death of D. Francisco de Sousa, he reunited Brazil under one governor and appointed Gaspar de Sousa to lead it. The French in 1612 had colonized Maranhão, saying they had as much right to do so as the kings of Portugal because in his testament Adam did not leave more to one than to any other. With this pretense, they brought twelve religious men from our order of the Capuchins to convert the natives. This was a very effective method to easily pacify them and colonize the land. His Majesty ordered that the governor go to Pernambuco to organize the expulsion of the French from Maranhão and colonize and defend it. Maranhão is one of the territories ruled by the crown of Portugal. Since D. Diogo de Menezes, the previous governor, had returned to Portugal at the end of his three-year appointment, in the interim Bahia had been governed by Chancellor Rui Mendes de Abreu and the head of the treasury, Sebastião Borges. Because both men were very old and in poor health, the governor had appointed Baltasar de Aragão, a local resident, to act as the captain-major of the infantry. He did this because they had been informed that enemies were headed their way by land. In Pernambuco, going to Maranhão, Jerónimo de Albuquerque sent one hundred men by sea in four ships to find the enemy ports and what they held. These ships sailed along the coastline of Ceará to the Cove of the Turtles, and there they conducted a siege and established a presidio. From there, they sent one ship to Maranhão led by Captain Martim Soares

Moreno. Albuquerque and the remaining troops returned to Pernambuco to inform the governor about what they had done and to request more troops and supplies for this expedition. The governor delayed any action until Martim Soares returned with more information. Until that point, the governor was busy administering and dispensing justice. In doing so, he was evenhanded and fair; for this he was loved by the little people and feared by the powerful. He also built a number of important public works, such as the beautiful customs house next to the dockyard for boat repair. This is where they unload cargo from ships as well as wagons on cobble-stoned city streets. He also built another very long customs house on the road to Jaboatão. He built it there because the deep mud prevented some of the ox carts from delivering the crates of sugar from the mills to the customs house in the city.

In this interim, Martim Soares was exploring the bays, rivers, and ports of Maranhão. By way of the West Indies, he sent word to Portugal that Frenchmen were conducting business in Maranhão. When the king was informed of this, His Majesty ordered the governor to notify Jerónimo de Albuquerque of these developments.

CHAPTER 2
How the Governor Ordered Jerónimo de Albuquerque to Conquer Maranhão

Once Jerónimo de Albuquerque had been selected as captain-major for the conquest of Maranhão, as we have discussed, he immediately went to the villages of our pacified natives. Because he knew their language and customs well, he was able to recruit as many as he wished. I will relate how he did this in one village to show the ease with which these people can be led if one understands them. He made a pile of bows and arrows and next to it another pile of spindles and spools. Showing them these piles, he said, "Nephews, I am going to war, and these are the weapons of valiant and brave men who will follow me, and these are for weak women who need to stay home spinning. Now I want to see who is a man and who is a woman." His words had hardly left his mouth when all the men began to take hold of bows and arrows and pick them up, saying they were men; they would leave at once for war. He calmed them down and selected those he wanted. They made more arrows while they waited for the army at the Rio Grande, where they would meet.

The governor was not able to recruit the white soldiers he needed so easily. Other than a couple who volunteered, the others could not be persuaded even with the threat of jail time. Because they came from great distances through the bush from their mills and estates, at night they fled; when ten were recruited four did not appear. As a result, they created a very good ploy, which was to oblige the wealthy men and mill owners who had more than one son to send a second son as well. When this was ordered, they had more than enough people because no mill owner would send his son without a minimum of a white servant and two negros.

He also asked for two religious figures from our order, and the prelate sent him Brother Cosme de São Damião, a prudent man and one who carefully follows the rules of our order.[1] He also sent Brother Manuel de Piedade, a learned and skilled preacher who is very gifted in the native language of Brazil. Father Piedade is respected by the Potiguarás and Tabajares, as well as by his father João Tavares and his brother, Brother Bernardino das Neves. We discussed Brother Bernardino in the last book. The war was not going to be against only the natives but also the French. The French had constructed a fort already and were expecting an attack, so the governor also sent Jerónimo de Albuquerque and Master Sergeant Diogo de Campos Moreno. He was an experienced soldier in the wars in France and Flanders, and he knew very well how to form an army, as well as the strategies and devices of warfare.

Once this was done, they all departed on Saint Bartolome's Day, August 24, 1614, in a caravel, two pinnaces, and five large caravels. The captain-major and his son, António de Albuquerque, were in the caravel and his son led a company of fifty soldiers with harquebuses, with Second Lieutenant Cristóvão Vaz Moniz and Sergeant João Gonçalves Baracho. In one of the pinnaces the master sergeant of State Diogo Campos Moreno led forty men, while in the other Captain Gregório Fragoso de Albuquerque, who acted as admiral, led fifty armed men. His second lieutenant was Conrado Lins, and his sergeant was Francisco de Novais.

The large caravels were captained by Martim Calado with twenty-five men, António de Albuquerque's sergeant with another twelve, Luís Machado with fifteen, Luís de Andrade with twelve, and Manuel Vaz de Oliveira with another twelve. In addition to these white soldiers, there were more than two hundred native warriors, those whom Jerónimo de Albuquerque had selected from the villages in Paraíba and who had awaited them at the Rio Grande. Most of them were with their women and children, but others were loaded on board and distributed among the ships. The brothers made the single women remain behind, both the natives as well as other single women who came from Pernambuco.

From there they went to the Cove of the Turtles where they had left the presidio and where they had tried the hand of the French. The French had arrived on the nau *Regente* and two hundred of them had gone ashore with their captain. At two in the afternoon, Captain Manuel de Sousa e Sá and eighteen men with harquebuses came forward and killed some of them, making them board their ship. One of our men was killed and six were wounded. When the monsieur was asked why he retreated, he said that so many men were in the trenches after our men had left that he feared they would come to aid our forces and he would not be able to escape. He did not believe it was possible that so few men would have tried to attack so many unless they had their backs covered with many forces supporting them. The "many forces" in this case were twenty soldiers who had remained behind because they lacked gunpowder and ammunition. They placed a scaffold, which they had made on the beach, in sight above the trench to aid in the fighting. However, the best reason they said they won was that God wished it so. This victory foretold what was to happen in Maranhão, where Manuel de Sousa left with his soldiers and Jerónimo de Albuquerque made him captain of the vanguard forces of the army.

CHAPTER 3
The War in Maranhão and the Victory That Was Achieved

Our forces left the Cove of the Turtles on September 28, 1614, and sailed for four days when they came to the mouth of a river called *Aparéa*. There were some who thought they should build a fort there. Diogo de Campos thought they should not use their entire army to immediately seek out the enemy but rather to occupy the land little by little. Jerónimo de Albuquerque thought the land was too extensive and ordered the chief pilot, Sebastião Martins, with Captain Francisco de Palhares and thirteen soldiers to take soundings on the river and scout the land, as they did. After walking twenty leagues more or less, they entered the Bay of Maranhão on the south side and found a good port that they thought would hold the anchored fleet.

With this information, they set full sail for five days to where the lifeboat was and arrived at this port on the October 28, the Day of the Apostles Saint Simon and Saint Judas, where they left the ship for land. They began to construct a fort that they called *Santa Maria*. Even though it was made with sticks and poor supplies, the workmanship was better than the materials. It had a good design made by Captain Francisco de Frias, the chief royal architect in these parts of Brazil. This fort was constructed on the east side of the island of São Luís, the island where the French are located. When they saw our ships and learned from their native spies how few people were on board, they captured a ship one night along with some sailors remaining on board.

Eight days later, which was the feast day of Saint Isabel, the queen of Portugal, the French came from the island with more than forty-six canoes holding three thousand native archers. They landed at a spot directly under our fort, twice the distance of a large musket shot. They began to unload their canoes there as well as their larger ships. Their general was Daniel de Touche, Monsieur of Reverdière and a Calvinist. He was in one of the large ships in deep water, waiting for the high tide to unload with the others.

Our forces realized that if the French forced them to cease work on the fort and then established a siege, our fort was not sufficiently strong to withstand them nor did our men have the supplies to avoid hunger. As a result, they determined that the best course of action was to attack them at once. This is what Jerónimo de Albuquerque did with eighty men with harquebuses and one hundred archers, going up the mountain while Diogo de Campos came from the beach with the remaining people. Although there were fewer men with Campos, seventy soldiers remained in the fort with some natives led by Captain Salvador de Melo in case they were needed to support the others. The master sergeant was marching from the beach, and a French trumpeter in a canoe rowed by four natives who approached him with a letter from General Monsieur of Reverdière. The letter stated there would be a great threat if our forces wished to resist, and he would wash his hands in the blood that would flow because he had the right to conduct war and also had much greater forces. The sergeant then placed the letter in his hat band and sent the messenger to the fort with a blindfold over his eyes so they could hold him prisoner in the interim. There was no time for any other response but to await the reply from Jerónimo de Albuquerque. This was given with a loud cry from the natives leaving the bushes where they were hidden, and the enemy did not fear them and those on the beach moved forward as well. In the middle of our forces were our two brothers, Brother Manuel and Brother Cosme, each with a cross in his hand, urging and exhorting our forces to the victory that God was well served to award them. In a little more than half an hour, they killed seventy Frenchmen, among them a lieutenant, captured nine, and made the others flee. Our forces suffered only four deaths and some wounded; among these was Captain António de Albuquerque, the son of the captain-major. He had two wounds from a harquebus in his thigh.

The French general saw the slaughter of his troops and his natives, many of whom were dead or who had fled; this was the response to his arrogant letter. He returned to the island with his fleet and less arrogance.

CHAPTER 4
The Truce Made between Our Forces and the French in Maranhão

The next day, the French general sent another letter to Jerónimo de Albuquerque charging him for how poorly he had followed the rules of war in attacking him without first responding to his letter as well as taking his messenger hostage and threatening him. If he did not surrender the messenger with the other hostages he held, he would have to hang the Portuguese sailors in sight of Albuquerque and his men. These were the sailors from the captured boat, which he now held on the island. He also stated that the Portuguese should not be fooled by the victory they achieved because they would not have another. He still had many good soldiers, not to mention the others waiting for him in France and thousands of natives. With these forces, he could wage a cruel war and extract vengeance for what the Portuguese had done to his people. He signed the letter at the bottom, "Your mortal enemy Reverdière."

Jerónimo de Albuquerque responded to this letter saying that he, the Lord of Reverdière, was the one who had broken the rules and practices of war, taking ships with four unarmed sailors on board in a port belonging to His Majesty, with no letter written beforehand. Reverdière had attacked him on land next to his fort with his three hundred Frenchmen and three thousand armed natives when he had just begun to fortify it. There was no other response except that given in law, which is to meet force with force. If he hung the Portuguese prisoners, harm would come to those French prisoners he held. With these and other reasons he developed the letter, to which the Frenchman responded with a milder and politer one. This continued until they wrote to each other in that manner. Like card players, at the end, after raising the stakes, and seeing the bet, they came to an agreement. In order to reach it (there was a safe conduct pass for those involved), Captain Malharte and a nobleman who was a member of the Order of Saint John came to Fort Santa Maria; Diogo de Campos Moreno, a colleague of the captain-major, and Captain Gregório Fragoso de Albuquerque, his nephew, went to the French ships, where the general was waiting. After each one stated what he wanted and wrote it down, they agreed to the demands from the French general. They drafted the terms, and our messengers and theirs came and went back and forth. The next day Captain Malharte returned with the treaty written as follows:

Details of the Truce

These articles of truce are made between Monsieur Daniel de La Touche, Lord of Reverdière, lieutenant general of Brazil, appointed by the most Christian king of France and Navarra, an agent of Micer Nicolas de Harley, the Lord of Sansy, and of the council of state of the same king and of the private council, the Baron of Molé and Grosbués; and Monsieur Rasilli, between the two lieutenant generals of the most Christian king in the lands of Brazil with one hundred leagues of coast of all latitudes and Jerónimo de Albuquerque, captain-major of His Majesty King Filipe II of the military expedition to Maranhão and the master sergeant of the entire state of Brazil, Diogo de Campos, a colleague and relative of the captain-major, etc.

Item. First, the peace that has begun between the two parties will start today and last until the end of November 1615. During this time, all hostilities will cease as they have since October 28 until now. Hostilities between the two were caused by a mutual lack of understanding, and this resulted in a great loss of Christian blood and hostile feelings on both sides.

Item. It is agreed between the two parties that they will send two nobles to their most Christian and most Catholic majesties, that is, the French and Spanish kings, to know their wishes in regard to who should remain in these lands of Maranhão.

Item. While these messengers are involved in this task and until they return from Europe bringing the expressed will and orders from their majesties telling us how to proceed, no Portuguese will set foot on the island nor will any Frenchmen leave the island to the east without written permission from the generals, with the exception of the generals themselves and their servants. They can come and go on the island and the fort on land as many times as they desire.

Item. The Portuguese will not have any dealings with the natives of Maranhão beyond what is negotiated via the Lord of Reverdière, nor will the Portuguese go beyond two leagues of their forts or ports without the permission of this same lord.

Item. As soon as the notice arrives from their majesties, the people who must leave will present themselves to leave the land for the others.

Item. Those prisoners captured by one side or the other, Christians as well as pagan, will be set free and unhurt; however, if any of them wish to remain for some time where they are, this will be permitted.

Item. The Lord of Reverdière will allow free passage on the ocean for the gentlemen Albuquerque and Campos so that they may collect all the supplies they may need in total safety. If more troops arrive to help them, this will not alter the length of this treaty nor the other agreed conditions.

Item. No accidental action in contrary to what has been agreed by these gentlemen will result in breaking this contract of peace. There are many alliances between their majesties, and if any danger results in altering this agreement or in the event of some injury or wrong occurring between the Christians or the natives of one side against the other, the injured side will make its case to its general for redress. In regard to things of lesser importance, these gentlemen have not specified these because they have faith in their word, which will not fail them as they are men of honor. They do this for the security and steadfastness of all that has been declared above. All three will sign this and affix their seals with their family crests. Completed on the French fleet in front of the Portuguese fort on the Maranhão River, November 27, 1614.

The day after these terms were made public and read by our captains, Monsieur de Reverdière, Monsieur del Parte, Brother Ángelo, the leader of the Capuchins, three monks accompanying him, and other French nobles came to our fort of Santa Maria. They were very happy, as were our people, and the treaty was signed. The French stayed all day until the afternoon, leaving for their island with a salvo of celebratory artillery fire.

The master sergeant Diogo de Campos undertook this embassy to Spain, and as a security he took the French captain Malharte. In the same manner, Captain Gregório Fragoso de Albuquerque went with the ambassador to the French king, and he died there. The French brothers departed immediately as well, since they had been ineffective in their missionary efforts with the natives because they did not know their language. They left two brothers with us so they could learn the language and customs of the natives. They were surprised to see our observant brothers following the rules of our angelic order of Saint Francis in such a remote place. Our brothers were equally astonished to see brothers of such great virtue and authority in the company of heretics, but not all the French were heretics. Many were Roman Catholic, heard Mass, gave confession, and took communion. Manuel de Sousa also left in a large caravel with the news for Governor-General Gaspar de Sousa, but he was delayed in the West Indies and went from there to Lisbon. He returned with news and letters from His Majesty and orders as to what we should do.

CHAPTER 5
Regarding Francisco Caldeira de Castelo Branco Who Was Sent to Maranhão by Governor Gaspar de Sousa to Provide Assistance

The governor understood the need for assistance in Maranhão in the form of additional troops, arms, and supplies, so, in the next year of 1615, he sent another fleet there, commanded by Head Captain Francisco Caldeira de Castelo Branco. Admiral Jerónimo de Albuquerque de Melo joined them in a caravel, Captain Francisco Tavares went in a second caravel, and João de Sousa went in a very large caravel.

They left from Recife, the port of Pernambuco, on the tenth day of June of the year 1615, and on the fourteenth they arrived at the Gulf of Mucuripe, which is three leagues from the fortress in Ceará. They anchored there, and the people disembarked in order to bathe and refresh themselves. Some had become ill with measles, and this healed them. Those who were healthy fished with a net given to them by the lieutenant at the fort, and they caught many fish.

It was here that Captain Francisco Caldeira located the three men that Jerónimo de Albuquerque, captain-major of Maranhão, had sent by land to ask the governor for assistance. These were Sebastião Vieira, Sebastião de Amorim, and Francisco de Palhares. These first two continued their journey with the letters from Maranhão as well as other letters from here. However, Palhares boarded a ship partly to provide aid but also because the lieutenant said that a pinnace sent by the king from Lisbon would be leaving there in a few days with provisions, gunpowder, and other necessities.

On the seventeenth, our fleet set sail, and it anchored in the Cove of the Turtles on the eighteenth where the captain sent an interpreter and some natives to the village of Diabo-Grande. This was the name of the principal leader of the Tabajares. Meanwhile, the others were fishing on the beach and eating squash and watermelon, which they found there in abundance. These had earlier been planted by Manuel de Sousa e Sá and Jerónimo de Albuquerque when they passed by. After finding a native interpreter and adding four more natives sent by Diabo-Grande for the journey, they continued on their way to the mouth of the Apereá River, where they cast anchors on the day of Saint John the Baptist.[1] Upon entering the river, the pinnace, which carried the captain-major, hit a sandbar but miraculously was able to escape from it. There were only five spans of water and the pinnace draws ten. However, since it was under full sail, it cut across the sandbar like someone jumping over a bonfire on Saint John's Day and entered the river on the other side where it was deeper.[2]

From there they sent a boat with six sailors and three soldiers led by Captain Francisco de Palhares to tell Jerónimo de Albuquerque they had arrived and to send pilots to guide them. Albuquerque sent two pilots who thought it best not to sail up the river because there was little wind and many shoals. The trip would be risky and slow, so they decided to disembark and went on the shore. In two days, they anchored in our port by the fort of Santa Maria, on the eve of the day of the Virgin Mary's visitation.[3] This brought no small amount of contentment to Captain-Major Jerónimo de Albuquerque and the others suffering in great need, seeing how the Lord had blessed them that day with such great assistance. They celebrated that day by firing all the artillery and harquebuses from one side to the other. This made the French very sad since they knew that we altered the peace treaty made with them.

After they finished unloading the goods, provisions, gunpowder, and ammunition from the ships and submitted them to the royal customs official, the soldiers were assigned to the captain-major who reorganized the two existing companies and created two new ones. Each of these had seventy men, and Jerónimo de Albuquerque de Melo, his nephew, and Francisco Tavares were selected to lead these. They then called for the French general Monsieur de Reverdière, and after a beautiful display of their soldiery on the beach, where he was received with Francisco Caldeira, the three went inside the fort. The captain-major told the French general that Francisco Caldeira de Castelo Branco brought orders to fight from the governor-general Gaspar de Sousa. He did not wish to do this, but he was ordered to remove the French from Maranhão as well as their forts on the island of São Luís. The governor-general ordered this because he had not agreed to any peace treaty, nor was he even aware of one.

General Reverdière responded by saying that according to the treaty they concluded, they should await a response from their kings to whom they had written and not change or alter anything. However, he would return to his fort and inform his people what had happened and respond shortly. This is what he did four days later, asking Captain Caldeira and Brother Manuel da Piedade to explain to his people what had occurred. They would return with a final answer from the French. The two of them left for the French fort in the same pinnace that brought this letter; they disembarked on the island of São Luís and went to the fort named for the same saint. The French were there, and they remained there, debating the issue for thirteen days. Jerónimo de Albuquerque presumed bad intentions because of this delay, and he began to consider resolving the matter by force. This would have been very easy because he had all the natives in Maranhão ready to assist him against the French. However, the French decided to abandon everything with no additional struggle. The Portuguese allowed them to return to France, and our forces went to the fort on the island, which we named São José. We will have to leave them there for now because we must turn to other matters.

CHAPTER 6
How Captain Baltasar de Aragão Left Bahia with a Fleet to Fight the French and How He Lost

When Baltasar de Aragão was appointed captain-major of Bahia and became aware of the expected arrival of the French enemy, as we have discussed in the first chapter, he began to inspect the city and its beach and fortify them using wooden poles and dry mud. He was very diligent, working all the time with his slaves and servants. He did not call on many others to assist, just the carpenters and masons to build the wall and gate around the Carmo using stone and mortar. Until that time, the walls had been made of adobe with wooden frames. He restored and fortified the gates and paid for everything himself. He even brought almost all of the wooden poles used to fortify the beach on boats from his sugar mills.

Now that they were ready to meet the enemy, they knew there were six French naus off the coast near São Paulo Hill. Making the other ships ready, which were loaded with cargos, Aragão left in his ship, which carried three hundred crates of sugar. He took his woodwinds, silver plate, and the best carpets from his home because he decided to bring the governor on his ship from Pernambuco.[1] The best of the other naus was commanded by Vasco de Brito Freire, which was on the lead ship, while the other naus were captained by Gonçalo Bezerra and Bento de Araújo, who were royal officers living in Salvador, and Second Lieutenant Francisco de Amaral and one other person named Queirós.

The next day after they left, which was Saint Matthias's Day, they encountered the French, and both sides fought with great energy. Our side had a great advantage because we had captured a nau and the French flagship was so badly damaged that it sank the next day. Baltasar de Aragão only wanted to save the French captain's ship as a trophy of his victory. However, I do not know if it was the wind or if it shifted in the sails, but when he went to capture it, his own ship tilted so sharply that water poured in the open artillery hatches. So much water entered the ship that it and its owner immediately sank to the bottom of the ocean. They say he said at that moment, "This is my coffin."

More than two hundred other men drowned with him. Some of them were on board and others were swimming, but there was no one to rescue them. Our other ships had left, leaving the captain to easily claim his prize. Some men saved themselves by swimming to the enemy ships, where they were brought on board. One of these was Francisco Ferraz, the son of the High Court justice Baltasar Ferraz and nephew of Aragão's wife. The French left him on land seventy leagues on the other side of the Rio Grande toward Maranhão with two or three others. He died of hunger and exhaustion crossing a river. He died of want, while here in Bahia he had a family worth 50,000 cruzados. His father died shortly thereafter of grief, and everyone said it was God's punishment for an unjust decision that had been made shortly before. It was as follows:

Baltasar Ferraz had a nephew here who fell in love with a young woman married to an honorable young man. The nephew took her from her home and was accompanied by her wherever he wished. Finally, he sent her to Viana do Castelo, where he was born. The husband filed a complaint before the superior magistrate, Pero de Cascais, who bravely put the nephew in jail, but he was freed until his court date. His uncle worked hard sidetracking testimonies, recusing himself, and performing other cunning tricks in order for the High Court judges to then exonerate and free his nephew. Preachers said the plaintiff was ignorant and there never had been a more just decision made in this world. As a result, there was nothing more that could be done except to appeal to Our Lord Jesus Christ. As a righteous judge allowed the prisoner to leave with his cousin and relative, they all ended in disaster. His uncle, who did not leave with them, joined them in death.

Another young man named Agostinho de Paredes also swam to the enemy flagship. Since they were in a rage because their ship had been so badly damaged, they refused to allow him on board. Rather, they stuck him in his shoulder with a pike. After escaping the shipwreck and then the sharks that came after him while he was bleeding, he swam more than a league to land. He was at the brink of death, but he was healed in the hands of the surgeons and lived for many years.

CHAPTER 7

Governor Gaspar de Sousa's Journey from Pernambuco to Bahia and What He Did There

After the governor sent Captain Francisco Caldeira de Castelo Branco with supplies to help in Maranhão and learned of the death of Captain Baltasar de Aragão in Bahia, his presence in Bahia was more required than ever. He planned his arrival without the pomp and solemn trappings that are employed for the arrival of governors. He arrived in secret with only one servant, and he entered his house, saying that he did this out of respect for the death of Baltasar de Aragão.

The next day, he went to the cathedral. His first day presiding over the High Court with the other judges, he discussed the complaints he had heard about them. If he forgot any he had heard, he did not hesitate to later mention them.

His careful vigilance of all his ministers, officials of justice, the treasury, and army was astonishing. No error of the market clerk or any other official escaped his attention for correction. He took his job seriously and did not have time for the games or pastimes that other governors claimed warded off laziness. He excused them, saying they were more gifted than he, since he worked day and night on governing and yet he never finished resolving problems. However, he had little luck in Bahia since he was not able to enjoy living in the city for long. He had not been here four months when the king ordered him to Pernambuco regarding Maranhão. He created a committee composed of the High Court justices, the treasury officials, members of the town council, and architects to inspect the cathedral. They needed to decide whether the building should be demolished and rebuilt or whether they should only repair what was destroyed, which was an arch in the nave, a wall, and the main entrance. His was the only vote to repair the ruined sections, to enlarge the high altar, and to add a loft for the choir, which it did not previously have. The others all voted to build a new church, which they started to do. It will be completed someday or maybe never. After this was done, the governor departed for Pernambuco, and Chancellor Rui Mendes de Abreu and the head of the treasury, Sebastião Borges, were once again in charge.

CHAPTER 8

How the Governor Returned to Pernambuco and Sent
Alexandre de Moura to Maranhão

The governor left for Pernambuco in a Spanish caravel that was wintering in Bahia so that it could make its way to the Rio de la Plata in the summer. I decided to join him on this voyage to Pernambuco, and we made the journey in a few days. However, one day before we arrived, there was a terrible storm from the south, and the governor feared the caravel would sink under the large waves. He ordered the convicts on board freed from their chains. They had been sentenced to reside in Maranhão. He asked me for a relic to put in the ocean and for us to say our prayers to the Lord

God, which we did. My companion used the cord that was around his waist and hung it overboard until it touched the ocean. It pleased the Lord that the caravel became calm and the wind and currents turned tranquil, so that the following day we entered the port in fair weather.

When the Spanish saw this, they wanted to keep the cord, saying that they hoped to make it safely to the Rio de la Plata using it. This was not the first time, but rather there were infinite times, when the Lord used a cord from our angelic father Saint Francis to free sailors from shipwrecks and to perform many other miracles. By these acts, God shows his infinite mercy, for which he should be praised.

The governor conferred with Manuel de Sousa de Sá regarding what the king had written in his letters about Maranhão. Then he loaned him nine ships, four large ones, five smaller ones, and nine hundred white and native men. He also gave him plants and livestock with which to colonize the land and firearms to expel the French. These would be used as a last resort, since their expulsion was ordered by the king. By that time, Vasco de Sousa had arrived and was captain-major of Pernambuco because Alexandre de Moura had vacated the position; he placed Moura in charge of the entire expedition, giving him the power to appoint public and military officials as he saw fit.

The captain of the flagship of this fleet was Paio Coelho de Carvalho, who had also just finished his term as captain-major of Itamaracá. After going to Maranhão, he went to Portugal and became a brother of the Order of Saint Francis in Arrábida. The captains of the other ships were Jerónimo Fragoso de Albuquerque, Manuel de Sousa de Sá, Manuel Pires, Bento Maciel, Ambrósio Soares, Miguel Carvalho, and André Correia. The captain-major, Alexandre de Moura, took two Jesuit priests with him, and with the holy name of Jesus they left Recife on October 5, 1615.

The governor did not attend to administering and did not understand how to rule the land, as was done at the time of Alexandre de Moura. But Vasco da Sousa had less patience and became very irritated. He sent his brother, a member of our order, with a letter asking to serve the king in another position because he was idle there; the governor did everything. The king was convinced by his reasoning and sent an order making him captain-major of Bahia, which he then governed.

CHAPTER 9

Regarding a Dutch Fleet Passing by Rio de Janeiro for the Straits of Magellan
and a French Fleet Loading Brazilwood at Cape Frio

At that time, Constantino de Menelau was captain-major of Rio de
Janeiro; he had succeeded Afonso de Albuquerque. He discovered a fleet
of six Dutch ships anchored at the bay of the Marambaia River, which is
nine leagues south of Rio de Janeiro. Their general was named Joris van
Spilberg. Martim de Sá had a sugar mill nearby in Tijuca, and he knew
from his own experience that they were there because they needed water.
They would have to leave their ships. He wrote a note requesting the
captain-major's permission, which he received, and he went there with
twelve canoes filled with three hundred Portuguese and native men. They
left their canoes and hid them in the river. Since they found three lifeboats
on the beach, they believed the Dutchmen were on land, which they were.
Some were collecting water while others were distracted picking fruit.
They surrounded the Dutchmen and attacked them so quickly that, even
though they were thirty-six men who tried to defend themselves, they
could not. Our forces killed twenty-two and captured fourteen and their
pinnaces, while those on board the ships could do nothing because they
were so distant. The Dutch set sail right away to continue their voyage
through the Straits of Magellan into the Southern Sea and the coast of
Peru. They met several naus along the way and sank them. These would
appear to have been made of lesser-quality wood, not as good as those
they later met from Manila, one of the Philippine islands. They fought
those as well, but they could not capture them. According to a Dutch surgeon who was there, when cannonballs hit those ships, the holes sealed
themselves without any patching or sealant. The Dutch ships did not have
this wood, and two of their ships were sunk, one escaped, and the others
were captured. Our forces took them prisoners, making them rowers in
the galleys. The surgeon told me that they faced such hunger and hard
work they were near death.

Martim de Sá wanted to take charge of the others captured near Rio de
Janeiro and free them. He took one Dutchman named Francisco Duchs to
his house and gave him . . .

[text ends here, as noted in the introduction, the original is incomplete].

CHAPTER 18
How Henrique Correia da Silva Was Appointed Governor of Brazil but Did Not Arrive, Why This Occurred, and How Diogo Mendonça Furtado Came in His Place

Once D. Luís de Sousa had completed his three-year term governing Brazil and his wife, the Countess of Medelim, had been at court, she asked for leave for him to return. His Majesty appointed Henrique Correira da Silva to replace him, and he accepted with goodwill and eagerness. This was my impression after talking with him several times in Lisbon, where I was at that time. This was also when Duarte de Albuquerque Coelho, the Lord of Pernambuco, decided to send his brother, Mathias de Albuquerque, to govern his captaincy. Governors appointed after Diogo Botelho started the custom of going to Pernambuco directly from Lisbon. In order for them to not be detained in places of importance where everyone has selfish needs, the king passed a provision notifying Governor Henrique Correira that he needed to go directly to Bahia without stopping in Pernambuco. If his ship were driven into that port or if for any other reason he stopped there, then he had failed to obey the king. Henrique Correira responded that he would not be going to Pernambuco or to Brazil because he could not govern lands without being able to inspect their fortifications. He needed to visit all these lands to determine what they needed for defense and in order to govern them properly. He said that if His Majesty passed such a provision, then he should give the position to someone else, which he did right away. He appointed Diogo de Mendonça Furtado who had come from India and was married there. He had been at court asking for recognition for his services.

Diogo de Mendonça prepared for departure as quickly as he could. Some of the High Court judges who arrived with D. Diogo de Menezes had died, some had returned to Portugal with the king's permission, and still others were awaiting permission to leave. As a result, the king sent seven justices with the governor so they could join the two who were married and living here. Thus, the High Court would be completely staffed.

They all left Lisbon in August 1621, and when they reached the latitude of Pernambuco, where the ships bound for Pernambuco left those headed for Bahia, the governor sent a servant of his named Gregório da Silva with them, a man knowledgeable about Recife. The captaincy of Recife was vacant because of the absence of Vicente Campelo. Matias de Albuquerque created this post as captain of the royal fort only, separating the post from that of captain of the nearby town. He gave it to one of his servants, and, as a result, the positions were separated.

CHAPTER 19

The Arrival of Governor Diogo de Mendonça in Bahia and the Departure for Portugal of His Predecessor D. Luís de Sousa

Governor Diogo de Mendonça Furtado arrived in Bahia on Tuesday, October 12, 1621. It is a day that the common people believe is unlucky. He was the twelfth governor of Brazil. After he disembarked, he was escorted to the cathedral in a solemn procession, which then accompanied him to his house. Before taking the stairs to his house, he inspected the warehouse storing the gunpowder and firearms on the ground floor. This demonstrated that he valued soldiering and being a captain more than anything else. The truth is that at that time, these were the most important things because the truce between the Spanish and the Dutch had ended and new battles brought from across the seas were expected. These battles are how we pay for our sins and even for our improprieties, so it is necessary that those living on the islands and coastlines always be on guard.

It seems that Governor Diogo de Mendonça foresaw this when he inspected the military supplies before entering his house to enjoy himself and relax from his journey. His predecessor, before leaving for Portugal, established many friendships and received people in his home and greeted them in the churches. He was a great gentleman in his dealings with people. Once the ships were ready, he boarded a pinnace from Viana do Castelo called *Manja-Léguas* or the *League Eater* because it was a fast-sailing ship. Everyone was sad to see him depart because he had done no harm, not by act or word. He was very wealthy without taking what was not his. He brought a lot of wealth with him and made investments. He also loaned money, which was not repaid, and I do not know if he saw repayment later.

In his day, he built a beautiful building for the High Court next to his own. Previously, court was held in a rented building. A seminary that the king had ordered constructed, with the funds for four orphan boys to study, had fallen down. These buildings are made from packed earth and collapse. D. Luís started another building made with stone and mortar. However, no one has lifted a hand to complete it even though it was such a pious undertaking and he left 6,000 cruzados for its construction. May God wish that it be completed someday.

Pero Gouveia de Melo, the head of the treasury, and Francisco da Fonseca, a judge of the High Court, both went with D. Luís. They sailed by way of Pernambuco to join the fleet. He did not act as a captain since the ships were merchant vessels or because he did not have time to plan this with Matias de Albuquerque, captain-major of Pernambuco. The two did not always agree.

CHAPTER 20

How António Barreiros, the Son of the Head of the Treasury, Was Appointed to Govern Maranhão by Governor-General Diogo de Mendonça Furtado and Bento Maciel to Rule Grão-Pará; Captain Luís Aranha Was Sent to Explore North of the Cape by Order of His Majesty

When His Majesty was informed of the death of Jerónimo de Albuquerque, the captain-major of Maranhão, he appointed the Spaniard D. Diogo de Carcome as governor, to rule independently of the governor-general of Brazil. D. Diogo was married in Lisbon, and he delayed so long in making his preparations, or the king's ministers were so slow in making his appointment, that he died by the time it was made. He never left Lisbon. The governor then decided how to best serve the king until another appointment was made. His Majesty had awarded António Barreiros the position of head of the treasury for six years with the condition that, if he established two sugar mills in Maranhão, he would have the position for life. The governor then appointed his son, António Moniz Barreiros, as governor of Maranhão. Thus, he could use his position to facilitate the construction of those mills.

The governor also awarded the captaincy of the Amazon River to Bento Maciel Parente since Jerónimo Fragoso de Albuquerque had died. At this same time, which was in 1623, His Majesty sent Captain Luís Aranha de Vasconcelos in a caravel from Lisbon to explore the river from the north cape and sound its depths. They said that navigating this river would be a cheaper way to transport His Majesty's silver from Potosí.[1] His Majesty ordered the captains of Pernambuco, Rio Grande, Maranhão, and Pará to give the captain all that he required. As a result, Matias de Albuquerque gave him a sloop and seventeen soldiers and loaned the services of António Vicente, a pilot who knew the river well. He loaded a caravel with 8,000 cruzados worth of all sorts of supplies, paid by the crown, for the fort in Pará. It had been two years since payments or supplies had been sent there, and they were very much in need. André Pereira Timudo, the captain-major of Rio Grande, assigned him four soldiers. Pero Gomes de Gouveia, his second lieutenant, was one of these and Captain Luís Aranha placed him in charge of the sloop. The others were Sergeant Sebastião Pereira, Pero Fernandes Godinho, and a carpenter who was also important for this expedition.

António Moniz Barreiros in Maranhão assigned him fifteen soldiers. Among these was one from Flanders named Nicolau, whom the natives had captured in Pará when he left a Dutch fort there along with two others and seven negros from Guinea to plant tobacco. He had experience with that great river. Our forces left from Maranhão and arrived at the fort on May 14, 1623, where its captain, Bento Maciel, told them their caravel would not be able to sail against the current, so he gave them another sloop and some native canoes. He also assigned thirty white soldiers to them with their captain already appointed. Luís Aranha did not want to accept this; he wanted to appoint his own captain. He said that His Majesty asked officials to give him soldiers, not captains. He was satisfied with the natives and with Brother António da Marciana, from our order, assigning Brother Cristóvão de São José as the chaplain for this expedition. This man was so respected by the natives that in a few days of sailing upriver, forty canoes with more than one thousand friendly native archers followed them in goodwill. The natives were also motivated by the many gifts that the captain gave their leaders as well as other natives who brought our men offerings of game, fruit, and vegetables. He did not accept these without paying for them with tools, glass beads, combs, mirrors, fishhooks, and other things, as he said the king had ordered.

With this multitude of natives and handful of white soldiers from other captaincies, they continued their journey. It was not without encountering some great storms. The worst of these broke the rudder on the largest ship. In order to fix it, they had to put ashore, where the carpenter from

Rio Grande made another rudder from a tree trunk. Because they used jungle vines to fasten it, they had to replace the vines every three days, but they worked very well. They made their way until a certain stopping point where Nicolau, the man from Flanders they brought from Maranhão, said they were near a Dutch fort. The Dutch did not wait for us to arrive but rather sent more than seven hundred of their allied natives to attack our forces in the river. They did this at midnight and engaged our men in a battle that lasted two hours. God was pleased to grant victory to our forces with the death of two hundred of the enemy natives, not counting the thirty our side captured in two canoes. They learned from among these captives that there were six or seven who were friends with the Dutch, receiving gifts from men on the ships coming from Holland. However, at that moment, there were no ships in port. In the fort, there were no more than thirty soldiers and some slaves from Guinea who were growing tobacco.

When the captain heard this, he ordered they row until they were east to west with the fort. At daybreak, he sent a soldier there in a small canoe with four rowers and a white flag, saying they had to surrender within an hour or they would put them all to the sword. This was ordered by his king, the king of Spain, whose lands and conquests these were.

To this, they responded that the fort was commanded by Count Maurício and they could not surrender it without his orders. They were given little time to do that, but they were aware that this was not the intention of the Portuguese. They knew the Portuguese wanted to wait for assistance to arrive from another fort some ten leagues away. It clarified matters when Luís Aranha answered that he already had orders to proceed and did not need more when he had such a numerical advantage in soldiers. For them to believe this, he ordered that the natives put on little coats, hats, or caps and sit among the white soldiers on the sloops as well as in the canoes. From a distance, they would all appear to be whites. This ploy and some others were sufficient to make the Dutch surrender all their artillery, muskets, harquebuses, supplies, slaves, and goods held in the fort. Our forces then burned and leveled it.

The next day, wanting to attack another fort, the captain ordered a canoe to move forward with forty rowers, all native archers, along with three very courageous white men: Pero da Costa, Jerónimo Correia de Sequeira, and António Teixeira. They went to forge a path but met twelve hostile canoes filled with enemy natives known as *Harauns*. They attacked in the middle of our forces, rejecting our peace and friendship. They showered our forces with arrows, and our people had given up any hope of saving their lives since the others were too distant. They asked God to defend them and then fought so courageously that when their companions did arrive, they had already killed many, slaying many more after the reinforcements arrived. Our forces captured four canoes of natives, and only seven of our people were killed; twenty-five were wounded. Jerónimo Correia de Sequeira had two wounds from arrows, one in his chest and the other in his leg, which badly injured him. He and his two companions were in the first canoe, and their hands were so blistered from the heat of the harquebus barrels that they could not touch anything for more than twenty days. Each of them fired more than forty shots.

After tending to the wounded and resting from the warfare that night, the next morning the captain ordered a company of men to take a message to the Dutch. It told them to surrender because those Dutchmen at the fort in Muturu (this was the name of the first site) had already done so. He had these Dutchmen with him, and the captain sent one of them with his messenger to prove this. The thirty-five men surrendered and turned over the entire contents of the fort, its artillery, and slaves.

The Dutch captain then asked if there was a fortress or estate run by his people along the river, and our captain assured him that there was not. There were two run by Englishmen, but these were downriver. So they returned to our fortress of Pará, but they did not find Captain Bento Maciel there. He had left in his caravel to offer his assistance and sailed on the north side of the river, moving upriver until he encountered them after a month of sailing among a labyrinth of islands.

The next day after they were united, a Dutch nau appeared and anchored a league from them. Bento Maciel went up to it with four canoes, but they were hidden behind the caravel in which Luís de Aranha was attacking. They went under it to destroy it, but this cannot be done quickly without first hitting it with an eight-pound cannon shot and attacking it with a canoe. We did this, killed seven white men, and wounded twenty negros; however, the other men ducked under the waterline of the ship. Seeing how they did not want to fight, our men chopped a hole in their ship next to the water with axes, which caused it to sink. The Dutch even set fire to the gunpowder so that nothing would be saved. In spite of that, some pipes of wine and beer, barrels of cheese, butter, and a large crate of medicines did survive; our forces used these. However, the 125 Dutchmen were all killed by fire or gunshots.

After these great victories, Luís Aranha de Vasconcelos left for Lisbon in his caravel to inform the king of this news. He also had useful information about the Amazon River, since the pilot António Vicente had been recording soundings. He took four of the Dutchmen with him as witnesses as well as a native leader who had guided them and some slaves to sell in the West Indies along the way. He joined the returning silver fleet there but left it near Bermuda. Fifteen days later, he was captured by Dutch pirates. These pirates were very ill with gum disease, which is called "Luanda sickness."[2] They put the captain in a small boat with four Portuguese sailors at Iliceira to find some lemons and return with a large boat capable of carrying the other Portuguese.[3] However, they failed to return (this is very common when one is set free), so they took the other captives to Salé, where they were ransomed.[4] The native and four Dutchmen they took to Holland as free men.

CHAPTER 21

The Fortifications and Other Good Works Completed in Bahia by Governor Diogo de Mendonça Furtado and the Questions Existing among the Governor, the Bishop, and Others

Governor Diogo Mendonça de Furtado was very generous and donated much to charity. He enlarged the church of São Bento at a cost of 2,000 cruzados and gave as much as he could to all the other monasteries. He fortified the city by building an earthen moat along the side of the city facing the land. Because a warehouse next to the customs building had collapsed, he ordered another one built next to his own house. On the second floor, there was a gallery, and the warehouse was on the ground floor. This was very nicely finished, but some did not think it wise to store gunpowder so close to other buildings.

He also began to build a fort in the harbor on a reef that is a little separated from the beach. This was on His Majesty's orders and was financed by a tax on wine, not just here in Bahia but also in Pernambuco and Rio de Janeiro. This came from the owners not on cargoes but on another tax called the *avaria*. This is normally two *patacas* per crate. Of this, four *vinténs* went toward the construction of the fort. This was challenged by some, but actually the fort was very necessary to defend the port and the ships anchored in its shadow. We should not forget to praise the work of the architect, Francisco de Frias, who designed it.

One of those who spoke against constructing the fort was the Bishop D. Marcos Teixeira. He was asked to bless the cornerstone of the fort, but he did not want to. He said that if he appeared, it would be to curse the fort because its construction thwarted the building of the cathedral with the tax revenue. But this was not the reason the governor withheld 6,000 cruzados for the cathedral. The day the bishop arrived in this city, December 8, 1622, these two locked horns. The governor did not want to participate in the formal entrance and reception of the bishop unless he was allowed under the bishop's ornamental canopy to converse with him. The bishop refused to do this, saying he had to proceed wearing his special cape, miter, and pastoral staff, blessing the people as is mandated in the ceremony of the Church. It was not appropriate to do this while engaged in discussion. Because of this, the governor did not attend the ceremony but sent the chancellor and the High Court justices. The governor later visited him at home and since then has personally visited him, many times bringing presents.

Another issue arose regarding their seating in church. The governor wanted them to sit next to each other so they could converse, and the bishop said that was not possible. The ceremonies of the church required him to be quiet and solemn during Mass. Even this was not sufficient for the governor, nor was a royal order that the bishop showed him. It said that in order to avoid any doubts (which had existed between the governor and bishop of Cape Verde), in Brazil and elsewhere, the governor must sit away from the clergy. The bishop would be blessed with incense first and then the governor. Not even this was sufficient, since the governor said that if he were in a church with the bishop, he would fulfill the king's orders. He made a point of never going to a church where the bishop was, so he obeyed the orders in that manner.

The justices of the High Court could not dispute with the bishop over matters relating to the Church, but they did quarrel over the spiritual jurisdiction of correcting vice. The outstanding case of this occurred when the bishop had two married men removed from their ship and ordered them to reside with their wives in Portugal. They had been living in sin for a long time here with other women. The men had not appealed their case but only requested to be allowed to leave, since they had been on board a departing ship. For this, the bishop excommunicated the crown official who was responsible, and there were many debates regarding this action. These were the civil wars between the two men, and there were no fewer among the townspeople. This was a sure sign of the end of the city, since the truth comes from Christ Our Lord, who says that a divided house will be laid to waste and destroyed.[1]

Another sign of the future was that the royal residence of the governor collapsed. If the supports had not been there, it would have fallen down to the ground, even though it was made of stone and mortar and was a strong old building that had never needed repair.

CHAPTER 22
How the Dutch Captured Bahia

On December 21, 1623, a fleet of twenty-six large naus left Holland. Thirteen of these were owned by the Dutch state and the other thirteen were merchant ships. His Majesty advised Governor Diogo de Mendonça of this, since they could appear in Bahia. He asked the governor to inform the other captains as well because they said the ships were headed for Brazil. Right away, the governor informed Martim de Sá, the captain-general of Rio de Janeiro, who then dug a trench around the city and repaired the fort at the entrance to the port. He also ordered the men in the area to organize themselves on their estates into companies and squads. Many did not appear because they lacked shoes and were not ready to fight. In response, the governor organized a company of barefoot men, which he wanted to lead. He went before them barefoot when they were mustered, wearing some linen drawers. They followed him with such confidence that the other companies, which had fine clothes and shoes, had no advantage over them.

There were many other wartime preparations that Martim de Sá made at that time. He did the same for all the captaincies (advising all of them as far as the Rio de la Plata). I mention Rio de Janeiro because I was still there and saw this.

The governor of Bahia did the same with the people living around the bay. Since some of them did not appear right away because they were poor and had nothing to eat in the city, the governor paid a merchant who was a personal friend to give each of these people three vinténs daily. However, since there is no coin worth three vinténs, he said to give them a tostão and that would be eight vinténs. If the poor took the tostão, he would tell them to spend it first, and then he would give them three vinténs. The governor ordered this only for the poor who had nothing. They did not respond to the gift of the tostões, which were not theirs, nor did they provide any reason for refusing them.

Not too many days had passed when news reached the governor from Boipeba that a large ship was nearby and it had captured a slave ship coming from Angola. The governor wanted to send out a party or capture it. However, he needed to ensure it was not part of the Dutch fleet since it had been four months since the ships left Holland. The word was the fleet had been in other ports. This was the *Holanda*, carrying the colonel who would govern the land, Jan Van Dorth. He did not remain on the island of São Vicente in Cape Verde where the other ships remained for ten weeks to take on water and meat and to assemble eight sloops, which they brought in pieces. Because of this, his ship arrived first off the coast of Ilhéus near Morro Hill, waiting for the others to enter the harbor of Salvador. They had already arrived by May 9, 1624, but those on that ship had not seen them.

Once governor Diogo de Mendonça was aware of their arrival, he sent the troops that were still in the city to the various estates. He left his son's company, which was staffed by soldiers paid by the royal treasury, so that he could be wherever he was needed. He sent another company of soldiers to the port of the old city led by Captain Gonçalo Bezerra. This was half a league from the city. He also sent the town secretary, Rui Carvalho, with more than one hundred men with harquebuses as well as sixty native archers with Afonso Rodrigues da Cachoeira as their captain. Lourenço de Brito was made the captain of the attack forces, and Vasco Carneiro was assigned to the new fort. Even though this fort was not finished, it already had some artillery pieces. I will not mention the other estates because the Dutch forces only landed in these two areas that afternoon.

Those troops in the fort in the old city had positioned themselves in the bush so they could fire at the Dutch when they left their lifeboats. However, when they saw that the enemy outnumbered them greatly, they did not want to remain. Francisco de Barros wanted to stop those troops that were in the old city, encouraging them, even though he was old and lame. However, they were so determined to flee that his admonishment had no effect nor did that from Father Jerónimo Peixoto, the Jesuit preacher. The father was on horseback waiting for them, asking why they fled. They could hide in the bush on both sides of the road and fire at the Dutch without revealing their location.

Not even this was sufficient to rid our men of their fear, which they carried like a contagious disease infecting those in the city. Perhaps the first messengers already had that effect, since the men felt that no matter how many people were in the city, their only salvation was to leave. One preacher tried to speak to them, but he was talking to an empty desert. Still, it would have been a good defense if they had organized two flanks of troops in the bush along the road and had attacked the Dutch at the crossroads along the way. Had they done this, even though there were twelve hundred Dutchmen, the Dutch would not have been able to inflict many casualties on our forces.

Those in the new fort did better. Admiral Petre Petrijans or, as the Portuguese called him, "Pero Pires," and his remaining forces all fought bravely. So did Vasco Carneiro and António de Mendonça, who assisted with a handful of soldiers, the rest having fled. Lourenço de Brito, the captain of the attack forces, bravely helped as well. However, there were many Dutchmen, and the construction and repairs of the fort had not been completed, so they were forced to abandon it. Lourenço de Brito was wounded, and thirteen men had died. One of the last to leave was Brother Gaspar do Salvador who had been urging the troops to fight and hearing their confessions. When he bent down to hear what a Spaniard was saying after his leg had been blown off by cannon shot, God was served by another shot removing his other leg and casting it over his head. Another shot had already blown away a piece of the brother's garment.

Because night had arrived, the Dutch feared an attack from the land, so they disabled the artillery and left it, returning to their ships. They did not stop their bombardment of the city and all of the beach during the day and night, killing Pero Garcia and his servants on their balcony. When the governor arrived to ask how he was doing (because he was moving around during that terrible time), Pero Garcia responded, "Sir, I am well because right now the sick are cured and weakness flees." This was a brave sentiment that even our enemies should respect, and after they hear it, show they understand it by placing the blame on the diabolical force of arms. It kills the bravest first, forming a ray that finds the strongest to then inflict the most harm. Pero Garcia was hit in the jaw with gunshot, but the wound left him time to confess and to forgive some of his enemies, who were present. One of these was Henrique Álvares, who was killed by gunshot a little later.

Those Dutch in the old town who had left their ships spent the night in São Bento in order to fight the next day in the city, which the governor was determined to defend. If he had not ridden around the city on horseback urging people to remain, everyone would have left. This could not have happened unless those in charge of the gates and other exits had been the first to leave. That day the bishop and the governor were friends. The bishop went to him with a delegation of clergy and their servants to offer the governor lodging where he lived. The governor was very grateful for the offer and thanked him but said that no place would be better than in the cathedral, but it too was abandoned as were the hosts, the silver ornaments, and everything else. The other priests did the same thing; they were concerned only with getting free and keeping a couple of practical items. They abandoned everything else in their homes, all the goods acquired over the years. This is what the fear of losing one's life will do. One will lose it sooner or later, and often times it is with less honor.

CHAPTER 23
How Governor Diogo de Mendonça Was Captured by the Dutch and Their Colonel Jan Van Dorth Governed the City

Once the governor realized that everyone in town had fled, and there was no shortage of those who suggested he should do the same, he said it would never be right to say that he was one to flee. He would rather be burned by fire. He spotted two Franciscan brothers walking past the square and called them over, and one of them heard his confession. He then took shelter inside his home with only his son, António de Mendonça, Lourenço de Brito, Master Sergeant Francisco de Almeida de Brito, and Pero Casqueiro da Rocha.

In the morning, the Dutch were at the gates of the city and all the entrances from the side of São Bento where they had spent the night.

When they did not encounter any resistance, they entered the city peacefully and took control. Some went to the governor's palace, and at that time they wanted to set fire to the barrels of gunpowder to burn it down. However, Pero Casqueiro took the torch from their hands. Seeing that they had entered, he took his sword and fought them, but the Dutchmen captured him and those with him and took them to their ships.

Two days later, Colonel Jan Van Dorth arrived. As we said in the last chapter, he did not arrive with the other ships. He began at once to govern the affairs on land because the Dutch general, who was an old man named Jacob Willekens, never or very rarely left his ship. The colonel was a man of peace and regretful for the damages caused to the Portuguese. He wanted our peace and friendship. For those who wanted to leave, he gave passports and ordered they be provided with whatever they needed. His own people thought this strange because according to their customs, they captured everything. If the Portuguese had not been so steadfast in their beliefs in the Roman Catholic faith and so loyal to their kings, which they are, these gifts would have softened their resolve to fight against the Dutch. They would have swayed the feelings of those who received them, rather than being convinced by other Dutchmen who fought them with firearms. The Dutch aggressively took whatever they wanted from the fields around the city, as if they owned everything.

Three or four Dutchmen dared to go to the Jesuit reservoir, which is a third of a league from the city. While there, one of them spoke to the Jesuit fathers in Latin, saying, "Quid existimabatis quando vidistis classem nostram?"[1] With that, they used their shoes as bags and filled them with silver and other things they found in the church. They put those on their shoulders and were very happy. However, four negros who belonged to the fathers did not have as much patience and were awaiting them on the path with their bows and arrows. They killed the one who spoke Latin, and the others all fled; they recovered the silver they carried.

Several Dutchmen dared to go to the field of Tapuípe, which is half a league from here, and kill a cow. While they were butchering it, Francisco de Castro, Jorge de Aguiar, five other white men, and twelve natives killed five Dutchmen. Manuel Gonçalves arrived and followed the other Dutchmen who had fled. He killed four of them and injured the two carrying this news. They left the butchered cow for the natives to eat, and the firearms they took for our soldiers.

It was not just the Dutch who were so insolent in this manner, but the negros who joined them were even more so. There was one slave owned by a locksmith who found his master taking shelter in the fields belonging to Pero Garcia. After slapping his master around, he said the locksmith was no longer his master but his slave. Not being content with that, he cut off his master's head with assistance from other negros and four Dutchmen. He took the head to the colonel who gave him two *pataca* coins and then ordered him [the negro slave] hung.[2] The colonel said that if he would kill his master, he would kill him if he could.

Another negro did better, one named Bastião who worked for us in the garden. He also joined the Dutch, but they wanted to take away the large knife on his belt. They threatened to hang him, and he left the city with two or three other negros. At the new fountain, which is just at the exit from the city, they encountered six Dutchmen who began to search their pockets. Since Bastião still carried his knife, he feared they would see it and once again want to hang him, so he plunged it into one of the men's chests, killing him. He then fled on the road that leads to the Vermelho River where he met some servants of António Cardoso de Barros. They were told of what had happened, and they, too, acted as if they fled with Bastião. They all hid in the bush. After the Dutchmen had passed, they came out and followed them. They went as far as a muddy pond and swamp where they killed four Dutchmen and captured one. For the glory of the brave, it would be good to know who one of these dead men was, a brave older man. He was in the swamp up to his waist in mud fighting the arrows shot at him with his sword, hitting them in the air. Bastião saw this and went into the mud striking his arms with a pole so that he could not swing his sword.

CHAPTER 24
How the Bishop Was Elected by the People to Be the Captain-Major and Matias de Albuquerque in Pernambuco Was Made Governor-General

While the city was captured and the governor was a prisoner, some of the town officials from Salvador met in the village of Espírito Santo. This is a village of natives who were converted to Christianity by the Jesuit fathers. It was there that they opened the letter from His Majesty stipulating who would rule in the event of Governor Diogo de Mendonça's death or absence. Mathias de Albuquerque was appointed, and at the time he was governing Pernambuco for his brother, Duarte de Albuquerque Coelho, the lord of that land. They sent word to inform him of this news.

The distances involved are great; the round trip is more than two hundred leagues, and the Dutch were not content to just rule the city but also wanted to rule beyond it, as we have seen in the last chapter. As a result, the people selected Bishop D. Marcos Teixeira as their captain-general to govern them. His first objective was to recover the city, if he could; in order to accomplish this, he appointed Lourenço Cavalcanti de Albuquerque and Melchior Brandão as his colonels. He wrote to many men who were already on their estates. Once he had gathered them, he decided to storm the city on the morning of the Day of Holy Saint Anthony.

The Monastery of Carmo is at the edge of the city, and two Portuguese men were staying there with their wives and families. There were rumors that they were Dutch spies and that they communicated with them using the church bells. In order to prevent them from doing this, Francisco Dias de Ávila and some native archers and men with harquebuses went to apprehend them, but the natives were so disorganized that the two sent the signal before being captured. When the natives arrived at the monastery, they would not allow them to enter so they had to force their way inside. They let out such a great war cry that when the Dutch heard it, they realized what it meant. It was already sunrise, and they saw the natives coming down the stairs of the Carmo, and some were entering the city through a gate near the fort. The Dutch were shooting so many cannon and gunshots at them that they were forced to turn around and return the way they came. The Dutch even followed them for a while. Since there were more Portuguese than Dutchmen, if the Portuguese had formed several flanks and simultaneously entered other undefended parts of the city, they might have been able to retake it.

At that time, some Portuguese were able to enter and leave the city since they had the written permission of the colonel. Lourenço de Brito was able to visit Diogo de Mendonça on the ship. He planned to send a raft for him and a second one for his son along with two native rowers. They would come at night and secretly carry them to shore. He did all this, but once the rafts arrived and they were just about to get on them, they heard the war cry from the Carmo, which we have mentioned. The men on board the ship woke up and prevented them from leaving. Those on the rafts returned to the shore very slowly and were spotted by the Dutchmen. From that point forward, the Dutch were very vigilant, and those who could freely come and go were fearful that the Dutch would change this as a result. They left the city and did not return. There were only two or three married merchants who remained to guard their wares, a number of tradesmen, and some of the elderly poor and infirm who were unable to leave.

CHAPTER 25

How the Dutch Colonel Jan Van Dorth Was Killed and Was Succeeded by Albert Schouten and the Bishop Planned an Assault from His Encampment

Because of this disorganized attack on the city, our forces were discouraged from attempting to do more. The bishop ordered that they patrol in the bush just beyond the edges of the city. The Dutch or the negros who had joined them normally went out to find fruit and other food in the orchards and fields, and they could then capture them. It happened that the colonel was the first to leave the city. He was riding on horseback to the fort of São Filipe, which is one league from the city. On his return, he was riding ahead of the other Dutchmen and negros who guarded him. He had with him only the trumpeter riding another horse. That was when Francisco de Padilha and Francisco Ribeiro, his cousin, met them. They both had harquebuses and were better shots than the colonel, who was using a pistol. They killed the Dutchmen's horses, and once the horses collapsed the men's legs were pinned in their stirrups. Padilha killed the Dutch colonel and Ribeiro killed the trumpeter. The savage natives of Afonso Rodrigues da Cachoeira were nearby, and they arrived right away. They cut off the men's feet, hands, and heads, as is their heathen custom, and left. The Dutch then took the body of their leader.

The next day they buried him in the cathedral with the pomp according to their customs, which are very different from our own. They did not have any crosses, music, or holy water. They just had the body of the deceased in a coffin covered with a woolen mourning cloth. The captains carried the deceased on their shoulders along with the deceased man's son and a horse on the right, who also went in the procession. They beat their drums in an irregular manner, and everything was covered in mourning cloth, in front of the companies of soldiers who had their guns under their arms and their pitchforks pointing toward the ground. Once the deceased entered the church, these people stayed outside. When the body was buried, they all fired their weapons three times. After each of these volleys, there was a long pause while they reloaded.

After they hung the deceased man's firearms from a pillar near his grave, they returned to his house. Before entering it, they read the instructions for succession of the leader, which was Albert Schouten. He had served in that capacity for two days during the initial invasion of the city while Colonel Van Dorth was delayed. After they read the letter, Schouten asked the captains and soldiers if they acknowledged him as their colonel and governor. Furthermore, he asked if they would obey him in everything he would ask of them, and they answered that they would. He then said the usual courtesies, dismissed them, and met with those on his council as well as some others. The Portuguese gave up hope of recovering the city after he ordered men posted all around the city and fortified it everywhere, building a dam on the stream on the land side. This increased the water supply for the fields, since there were many palm trees there. On this side of the city and on the side facing the sea, they built many ramparts and forts with artillery.

The bishop had made his camp one league from the city on a flat mountain top that could only be reached by three paths. He ordered three earthen trenches dug on each path along with two cannons and two additional cannons loaded with stones. The path on the side of the city he assigned to Colonel Melchior Brandão and the troops from Paraguaçu. Another path toward Tapuípe he assigned to Captain Pero Coelho, and the third path, which led to the bush, was guarded by Captain Diogo Moniz de Teles. The main body of soldiers was stationed near the stall or straw house with the captain-major, the soldiers from the presidio, and some others who totaled two hundred.

Meat, fish, fruit, wheat, and everything else available from the bay was brought to this encampment as well as some wine and olive oil brought on ships from Pernambuco to Francisco Dias de Ávila's tower and from there by land to the camp. The captains brought additional supplies from their estates. These captains and their companies were as follows: in Tapegipe in front of the fort of São Filipe, which was occupied by the Dutch, there was a trench and two bronze artillery pieces directed by Captains Vasco Carneiro and Gabriel da Costa and a company of forty soldiers from the

presidio. Not far away on another road was another company with five
falconets and two rock-firing cannons directed by the Captains Manuel
Gonçalves, Luís Pereira de Aguiar, and Jorge de Aguiar. By the port and
the sea was another company led by Captain Jordão de Salazar. Between
the Hermitage of São Pedro and Vigia, the two Captains Francisco de
Castro and Agostinho de Paredes directed sixty men; from Vigia to the
Vermelho River there were forty men on the fields of Gaspar de Almeida,
led by Captains Francisco de Padilha and Luís de Sequeira.

In addition to these leaders, Pero de Campo, Diogo Mendes Barradas,
António Freire, and others led some assaults. Manuel Gonçalves led the
assault from the north side of the city, where the Monastery of Nossa Senhora do Carmo is located. Francisco de Padilha led those from the south
side near the Monastery of São Bento. Of course, they always helped each
other when required, and Lourenço de Brito, at the head of the assault
troops, assisted everyone.

CHAPTER 26
The Assaults Undertaken When the Bishop Governed

Once everything was organized by the bishop in the manner I have
described, Captains Francisco de Padilha and Jorge de Aguiar were aware
that the Dutch had occupied the house of Cristóvão Vieira Ravasco,
the secretary of the appeals court.[1] His house is just a little more than a
stone's throw from the outside of the wall and gate of the city. They went
there one night with ten other men and killed four Dutchmen with their
swords. Afterward, the Dutch then pulled down the house and set it on
fire as well as other nearby homes. The Dutch cleared the fields so there
would be nothing to block their way and nowhere for the Portuguese to
hide. However, there were several skirmishes while this was taking place.
On one occasion, Captains Lourenço de Brito and António Machado and
their troops killed four people; on another occasion, they killed many
others. It was here that Captain Lourenço de Brito said that the negro
Bastião, whom we mentioned previously, went ahead of everyone saying
that his arrows did not reach as far as the gunshot from the harquebuses.
As a result, it was necessary for him to get closer to the enemy, which
he did on other occasions as well. One time when he was walking with
our troops and carrying a sword and our negros told him to withdraw,

he said, "No, do not withdraw, *sipanta, sipanta*."[2] By this he meant that this was not the time to withdraw when they were about to use swords. He had experience fighting the Dutch with swords and felt they were not as skilled using them as they were with firearms; by using swords, our side had already won the battle.

Some other Dutchmen went to Jorge de Magalhães's house, which is more than a league from the city. They burned those houses along the way and robbed those they encountered. The residents fled for the bush in the interior. They wanted to box the ears of one woman who could not flee if she did not give them her gold jewelry. They would have done much worse if Francisco de Padilha and his men had not appeared, killing four of the Dutch and chasing the others as far as the Vermelho River. On another occasion, many Dutchmen went to Diogo Sodré's orchard, in a place called *Vigia*, because from here ships appear on the coast and they send notice to the city before they enter the port. These men brought many negros with them to carry the oranges, sweet limes, lemons, and other citrus that grows there in abundance. However, Captains António Machado and António de Morais attacked them with an additional fifty men each. After a heated battle, they killed nine Dutchmen and then withdrew with only two Portuguese fatalities and several wounded. At that moment, Captain Padilha came to assist with twenty of his soldiers. Pursuing the Dutch on their way back to the city, he made them turn around and fight again, and the two Portuguese captains who had withdrawn joined the fight. They were winning up to the point when the Dutch reinforcements arrived, and then the Portuguese left, since they were out of gunshot and powder. However, in this second battle, they killed many more Dutchmen and captured one alive. His name was Rodrigo Mateus, and they took him to the bishop.

Manuel Gonçalves and the other captains were equally energetic and resilient guarding the side of the Carmo. They were constantly watching to see if any Dutchmen left the city on that side. Next to the Monastery of Carmo, they once killed six Dutchmen; on another occasion, they killed three. When a party of Dutchmen left the fortress of São Filipe to fish in some small nearby shallow lakes, our men fell upon them and caught them before they captured any fish, killing one and taking three captives to the bishop. One of these was the captain of the fort. Another time they killed a negro who was a spy for the expeditions. The Dutch saw that on one occasion our forces were aided in an assault by those in some nearby homes, where in peacetime the captain of the fort lived with his family. One morning they sent five men with pickaxes to destroy these homes, but Manuel Gonçalves, Jorge de Aguiar, and Pero de Campo were waiting for them hidden in the bush. Even though they came out quickly to destroy the homes, our men emerged, killed two of them, and chased the others to the gate of the fort. Without fail, our men would have entered the fort that time if the Dutch had not placed an artillery piece at the gate. It fired a lot of buckshot, forcing our men to retreat.

Another time, a negro belonging to Captain Pero de Campo took a rowboat tied next to the fort and brought it to our forces. This was in spite of all the shots aimed at him, none of which hit him. Captain Manuel Gonçalves then figured that since the Dutch did not have their rowboat, they would travel by land to inform the others what had happened. He waited for them on the road. When he saw two of them on a raft, he swam after them but did not reach them because another pinnace from the city came to their aid.

CHAPTER 27
Other Attacks against the Dutch along the Coast

Since the Dutch were not able to gain very much by land and were not able to reach the plantations, they decided to travel by water to reach them. They were looking to purchase food with their money or in trade for merchandise, what they called *sucapa*. In order to do this, they sometimes took with them some Portuguese who were living among them. This was to demonstrate to the other Portuguese they came in peace, and if they did not want peace, they then fought. The bishop also planned for this, ordering that those who had estates along the waterfront should fortify them, and he gathered troops to help defend them. Each parish had to send twenty men to the bishop's camp for this purpose. By doing this, they were able to defend themselves against the Dutch in some places, while in others they were able to go on the offensive. Bartolomeu Pires, who lives near the mouth of the Matuim River, did this. He noticed that a pinnace carrying some Dutchmen sometimes landed nearby at the estate of Simão Nunes de Matos, which is next to Maré Island. They went there to eat with the overseer because the owner was absent. He went there and invited them for a meal the next day. He also asked António Cardoso de Barros to come assist him and hid them in another part of his estate, awaiting to ambush the Dutch. The chickens had been killed and were roasting as a distraction, and as soon as the Dutch were there, he gave the signal to those hiding. They came out and killed several, among them a Dutch merchant. Our forces captured three while the others fled for the rowboat. Six months later, these three escaped from António Cardoso de Barros's house and joined their own people.

Other Dutchmen went in a nau to Cruz Point on the island of Itaparica. They loaded whale oil there since that is where it is processed. They went to the mill owned by Gaspar de Azevedo, which is along the beach one league from that point. They did not take any sugar, nor did they damage anything but rather they had written him saying they would come to his mill to press sugarcane. In order to do this, they would provide the negros and labor necessary. They only damaged a high wooden cross on his estate, giving it a couple of cuts. Miraculously the cross pivoted and turned another direction. The Dutch walked in that direction and encountered some island residents with Afonso Rodrigues da Cachoeira and his natives. They killed eight Dutchmen with their arrows and fire from harquebuses. Our forces captured a pinnace with three rock cannons and forced the other Dutchmen to leave by swimming; many were badly wounded. As a result, that cross was venerated and esteemed by Catholics to such an extent that pieces of it were distributed; they cured many of malaria and other sicknesses.

The Dutch Captain Francisco went in another nau to Boipeba Island, which is outside the harbor. He went upriver to the town of Cairu, which has twenty residents, using two pinnaces and taking with him men with guns. He and the Portuguese man he brought with him left the boat for the home of António de Couros, the owner of a sugar mill. He and the Dutch captain had become friends while the captain was a prisoner in the city, as we have mentioned in chapter 9. After António de Couros greeted him with the usual words and obligatory ceremonies, he turned to the Portuguese middleman, calling him a traitor to the king and someone who favored the Dutch. António then told the Dutch captain that he did not want peace with him, but rather war. He would find it on the mainland. The Dutchman was so honorable that, either because of the initial promise of peace or because of their previous friendship or some other reason, he did not respond with hostility in word or deed. He simply left for his nau, which he had anchored at São Paulo Hill, the entrance to that river, and from there he returned to the city. He later returned to Camamu with another nau, more pinnaces, soldiers, and another Portuguese man who had been his jailer when he was a prisoner. They brought with them many negros from the ships from Angola to see whether the planters wanted to exchange them for cows, pigs, and chickens. When the planters did not respond to their proposal, they took twelve oxen they found on the lands belonging to the Jesuit fathers, and even these cost them the lives of eight Dutchmen, who the natives killed with their arrows. Because the smaller boats they brought were sailboats, they missed the chance to capture a ship from Viana. It came via Madeira and was carrying wine and was all decked out with flags. When this ship was next to the Dutch ships getting ready to take in the sails and cast anchor, one of the Dutch ships fired on it twice. When those on the Portuguese ship saw the cannonballs, they realized these were Dutch warships. They then hoisted all their sails, which were large, and fled into the bay. One of the Dutch ships, the *Tigre*, went after it. However, because the *Tigre* had to untie its ropes and hoist sails, the other ship had an advantage. This was enough time to save it after it entered the mouth of the Matuim River. Because the Dutch ship was so large at 350 tons and had no pinnaces, it could not damage the Portuguese ship there.

The next day, the pinnaces arrived from Camamu; the Dutch brought them right away to that river, but they did not find the ship because it had sailed a league away to Petinga. So the Dutch attacked the estate of Manuel Mendes Mesas, a farmer, and they took several sheep from the field and returned to their ship.

The bishop then right away sent Captain Francisco de Castro and others to the Petinga River to defend the ship, if the Dutch appeared, as it was unloading. From this ship, they brought six pieces of artillery to the bishop's camp. Knowing that a nau was located between Frades and Maré Islands, sending out its pinnaces to capture ships sailing in those waterways, the bishop sent Captain Agostinho de Paredes to sail there and stop those seizures. He was also ordered to capture the pinnace. However, the Dutch were cautious and had been there for twenty days. The captain, named Cornélio Corneles, had ventured out almost daily with twenty-five soldiers. When he did not go out, his pilot did; they attacked every ship that passed. If the ship put up on land or entered the waterways, the Dutch left it and returned to their ship. I know this firsthand since I was a prisoner on that nau at that time. One day they said they could not make any speed whatsoever. I said it was because they were next to a fort and pointed out the Church of Our Lady of Socorro. One of her many miracles is that she protects that entire area. When I said that, many laughed; however, at the end of the day, they returned to port in the city without capturing any ships.

CHAPTER 28

The Ships and People the Dutch Captured in the Harbor of Salvador

When the Dutch captured Bahia, they found thirty ships anchored in the bay. Some of these were filled with the goods they brought from Portugal, others were carrying sugar and ready to depart, and still others were loaded with cassava flour and other goods for trade in Angola. They captured all of these and unloaded these goods onto their ships and stores. They selected the best ships to arm and serve them and sunk the others. In addition, there were another twenty ships that fell into their hands. There is so much commerce here and ships come from the most remote corners of the earth that four months is not sufficient time for them to know that commerce here has stopped. They came and anchored their ships among the enemy, bringing wheat flour, hardtack, olive oil, wine, silk, and other rich merchandise. At the end, a loaded ship arrived from the Rio de la Plata, carrying D. Francisco Sarmento, who had been the justice in Potosí along, with his wife, children, a son-in-law, and a grandson. The Dutch colonel hosted all of them in his house after they were robbed, providing them with food and clothes.

Among the captured ships, one of the first belonged to the Jesuit fathers, who normally visit their colleges and houses along the coast. On this occasion, their leader, Father Domingos Coelho, was on board coming from Rio de Janeiro and was completing his term. His replacement, Father António de Mattos, was also on board with ten other Jesuit fathers. Four clerics of the Benedictine order as well as my companion and I, from the Franciscans, were also on board.

We saw the morning of May 28, 1624, at Saint Paul's Hill. This is at the opening of the entrance of the bay where we saw two pinnaces and a nau, and they spied us. They quickly captured our ships and their cargoes because we were defenseless. The ships carried crates of sugar, jams, money, and other freight as well as other passengers. They brought us to the port and transferred us to other ships two by two or four by four. That was where we remained until the end of July. Then their general departed with eleven naus for the salt flats, and the admiral's ship left with five naus and two pinnaces for Angola. At the same time, four naus left loaded with sugar for Holland. On this last group, they sent Governor Diogo de Mendonça Furtado and his son, the Superior Court magistrate Pero de Casqueiro da Rocha, the master sergeant, the Jesuit fathers, and the Benedictines. They kept us to exchange for their own who had been captured in the assaults. A local Portuguese man was in charge of these captives; he spoke Dutch, but later they decided he was a traitor and was deceiving them. They held him captive with his brother and a mulatto servant. We desired our freedom so much that my companion thought it best to try to escape by swimming. Even though I wanted to do this, I could not because one who does not know how to swim will sink to the bottom.

I was held prisoner at sea in this manner for four months, and once these months had passed, Manuel Fernandes de Azevedo asked for me. He is one of the residents who remained in the city. The Dutch allowed me to go to his house and walk around town with him as long as I did not approach the walls or fortifications. I was busy hearing confessions from the Portuguese, and no one died without giving confession. Some had died before I arrived, but not many since those who wanted to leave were allowed to do so. Three ships departed, one to Pernambuco and two to Rio de Janeiro, carrying three hundred people. These were mostly sailors and passengers from the ships captured in the harbor. Many also fled to our camp, but the Dutch did not want to allow this. From our camp, a married woman left her husband and fled with her beautiful daughter to the Dutch. The Dutch colonel married the daughter to a Dutch merchant, and they held a large party with music, dancing, and banquets that lasted for three days.

We Portuguese who remained in the city were given the same weekly rations as the Dutch: bread, wine, olive oil, meat, and fish. These people worked as tailors and cobblers; the women were well paid for the shirts they made for them.

CHAPTER 29

After He Received the Appointment as Governor, Matias de Albuquerque
Turned to Assisting Bahia and Fortifying Pernambuco; Francisco Coelho de
Carvalho, the Governor of Maranhão, Remained in Pernambuco

Once Matias de Albuquerque received notice in Pernambuco of Diogo
de Mendonça Furtado's departure and of his appointment as governor-
general, he immediately called a council of the town officials, captains,
religious figures, and other knowledgeable people. He asked if he should
go in person to assist the people of Bahia, and all were opposed to this.
They felt that any help he could bring from Pernambuco would not be
sufficient to recapture the city and that he needed to focus on the defense
and fortification of Pernambuco since danger was nearby. With that in
mind, he immediately ordered António de Morais to return by land with
soldiers and their weapons and supplies to provide assistance. Morais had
left here and found a large piece of ambergris on his way to Pernambuco.
They were joined by others they encountered, and they all arrived in the
bishop's camp and formed a good company of soldiers.

The governor carefully fortified the town of Olinda, creating a wall
along the beach and placing soldiers along it at the critical spots. He did the
same along the Tapado River, which is a third of a league from the town,
and at the village of Pau-Amarelo, which is three leagues away. It is a port
where sloops and pinnaces can enter. Recife is the main port where our
ships are docked and where there are two forts; it is the key to all of Pernambuco. As a result, the governor asked Francisco Coelho de Carvalho,
who had recently arrived from Portugal, to assume the governorship of
Maranhão, to delay his departure, and placed him in charge of the port,
people, and government of Recife. Both of them then wrote to inform the
king this was to better serve crown interests. Francisco Coelho de Carvalho and three companies of soldiers who had accompanied him from
Portugal remained in Pernambuco. They were joined by his son Feliciano
Coelho de Carvalho, his sergeant-major Manuel Soares, Jácome de Reimonde, the head of the treasury of Maranhão, and Manuel de Sousa Deça,
the captain-major of Pará. They only sent one ship to Maranhão with
some women and older men. They were joined by our brother Cristóvão
Severim, who was in charge of fifteen monks from various monasteries

in Portugal and five more monks from Brazil. The administrator of the religious order in Pernambuco, who at that time was Dr. Bartolomeu Ferreira, also gave Father Severim the authority to act as general curate and magistrate, as is done with the Holy Office of the Inquisition to review and censure books, which was very much needed in those parts.

They left Recife on July 12, 1624, and anchored in the Bay of Mocoripe on the eighteenth of the month. That is three leagues from Ceará, where they went to find Captain-Major Martim Soares Moreno in the fort. They remained there for fifteen days, offering sacraments to the whites and conducting missionary work with the natives in two of their nearby villages. The order left two friars with the natives at the request of the captain, who wanted to pacify them. This has worked until the present day.

The others all reached Maranhão on August 6, and they started to build a house and church made of *taipa.*[1] This is where they offered the first Mass the next year on the Day of Our Lady of Candeias. God assisted in its construction, making it his, with several wonders and notable miracles.

One of these was with the stonemasons. They said that in order to plaster the walls they would need sixty *pipas* of lime, but there were only twenty-five. In spite of this, they were able to complete the work and have seventeen *pipas* left over. This was noted by the officials, and they affirmed it was a miracle.

Another miracle occurred when they were carrying a large heavy beam in a cart and the driver fell down. The wheel of the cart ran over him with all its weight, but it did not hurt him at all. The driver got up and continued on his way with the indentation of the wheel pressed into his chest as proof of the miracle.

The father in charge did not work any less than the others in strengthening the spiritual side of those souls, which in appearance seemed corrupted. He also attended to the conversion of the natives. He did the same in Pará, bringing the native Tocantins to live in peace with the Portuguese. They had been provoked by attacks and were nearly in a state of rebellion. He took the sons of the main native figures with him to teach them the catechism and learn our ways, and, on the pain of excommunication, prohibited selling freed natives as they were doing by claiming they were only selling their labor.

He burned many of the heretical books left by the French as well as playing cards and the superstitious prayers many of them recited. He ended the concubines' lives of sin and performed many other services for Our Lord and the good of these souls. This demanded a lot of work, and he was persecuted for this and suffered. He knew that those who suffer for justice are blessed.

CHAPTER 30

In Pernambuco, How Governor-General Matias de Albuquerque
Appointed Francisco Nunes Marinho as Captain General of Bahia
and the Death of the Bishop

Governor-General Matias de Albuquerque became aware of the questions and differences existing between the bishop and the superior crown magistrate Antão de Mesquita de Oliveira about governing the camp and the others in Bahia. The magistrate had been appointed before the bishop was selected, and to end these differences, the governor-general appointed Francisco Nunes Marinho as captain-major. He had held that post in Paraíba and had served the king with distinction in India and elsewhere. In order to make this possible, he sent two large caravels. Marinho was the captain of one of these, while António Carneiro Falcato was the captain of the other. They carried thirty soldiers, gunpowder, supplies, *pipas* of wine, olive oil, and other things they could offer those in Bahia during their time of need.

There was a great storm at sea that forced the two ships to enter the Sergipe del Rei River with their yards and masts broken.[1] After they paused, they continued their journey on land with some soldiers and arrived at the camp at a critical moment because only a few days later, the bishop became ill and then died on October 8 of that year. His departure from this life left everyone sad and feeling ill at ease. He was someone whose nature appealed to everyone, in addition to the wonderful traits with which God adorned him. He was very charitable and giving, devoted to the Holy Sacrament, which led him to attend to the sick. His faith made him easily accessible when he went out during the day or night.

He celebrated Mass daily, contributing his many tears of devotion, and he preached without being a theologian. However, he was a great student of the scriptures, better than many theologians and zealous to save souls. In the end, it is possible to repeat what is written by the learned Sapientiae, that God took him from this world, at such a young age, not having reached fifty, because the world was not worthy of so much virtue.[2] If this is how he served God, he served the king equally well. This can be seen in how he acted as captain-major and governor when Bahia was captured. It was he who went among the men scattered in the bush, dying of hunger and in danger. He brought everyone together in an encampment, as we have stated, and from there gave orders to collect supplies and sustain the people. He supported the poor at his own cost when they could not afford what they required.

It was from this camp that he directed captains and their companies to attack, countering the insolence of the Dutch. If this had not happened, all the estates around the city would have been destroyed. When these troops went forth on these attacks, he gave them strength and encouragement so that even the wild natives eagerly volunteered to join these companies. Then he prayed, asking God for victory; when they returned in triumph, he gave thanks, embracing the soldiers and thanking them not just with words but with gifts. This made them compete to be the most valiant in combat. Although the enemy was not under siege, our forces prevented them from walking fifty paces beyond the city gates to pick a lemon. They could only do this with many people and planning and even that was not sufficient. All of this can be attributed to the bishop's prayers. He not only directed this warfare with diligence, wisdom, and determination like Joshua and other famous leaders but with the tears and prayers of Moses. He understood that the Dutch capture of the city was a punishment from heaven for its vices and sins; he later punished himself. He was so severely penitent that he never shaved his beard, nor did he again wear a shirt but rather wore a cassock of dark heavy cloth.[3] He slept very little and fasted frequently. He prayed and urged all to compensate for their sins, which caused God's wrath to descend upon us. Then God took him from these labors to a saintly rest as one can depend upon His divine compassion.

CHAPTER 31
The Encounters with the Dutch While Captain-Major Francisco Nunes Marinho Governed Our Camp

Even though Captain-Major Francisco Nunes Marinho was elderly and became very ill on his journey to Bahia, this did not weaken his resolve nor impact one iota of his duties. Before his party arrived, he told João

Barbosa, who served him and accompanied him from Paraíba, that no matter how ill he might become, he was not to say anything to the soldiers. He was to take any message and say he would convey it to the captain-major. He was then to return with the answer that he thought best and to do so in the captain-major's name. João Barbosa did this so carefully and with such politeness that all were content.

After he recovered, he used another deception. Since they had very little gunpowder, he showed the men great earthen vessels filled with sand, making them believe they were filled with gunpowder. When they complained because he gave them so little and they asked for more, saying that many times they were unable to follow the enemy because they lacked it, he said they had enough. He preferred to be known as tightfisted or something else rather than have them discover the shortage, which would have made the men fainthearted and abandon the war effort.

They continued the assaults as the bishop had organized, and that was the best they could accomplish. They dug two more trenches, one in Tapuípe and another along the side of São Bento for our men who were there.

He also ordered two ships to patrol the approaches to the harbor. One was at Itapõa and the other at Morro Hill. This was to warn ships coming from Portugal, and they saved three or four this way. Without moving the camp, he shortened the path to the city by one-third of a league so they could respond faster to the fighting. During his rule, Captain Manuel Gonçalves learned from spies that there were some Dutchmen living in the Monastery of Carmo. He attacked them with other captains who served him, and they all fought very honorably. Two Dutchmen were killed as were two of our people. On another occasion, this same captain encountered a few Dutchmen who had left the fortress of São Filipe, and he killed two, forcing the others to retreat. He burned one of their lifeboats and had them cornered. They feared to set foot outside the fortress except to travel by sea.

The Dutch also conducted some raids by sea, such as when they attacked Manuel Rodrigues Sanches's mill, taking fifty crates of sugar and burning the houses and church with no one able to stop them. This was in spite of Manuel Gonçalves and André de Padilha, the father of Captain Francisco de Padilha, who tried to stop them. They were later joined by Colonel Lourenço Cavalcanti and forty men. They forced the Dutch to set sail, killing some and injuring others. The Dutch attacked another mill owned by Estevão de Brito Freire. When they left their ship, they were met by the captain of the parish, Agostinho de Paredes, and some men with harquebuses. Because our forces were few and there were many of the enemy, our men were forced to withdraw above a worker's house, beyond the fields owned by the estate. The Dutch killed several oxen and reached the men with harquebuses and even called our men names. However, at night they departed quickly, leaving behind two dead oxen, and they only took twenty crates of sugar, which they found on the estate. They had already taken twelve crates of molasses from another mill and some pigs from a pigsty. Had they not left when they did, they would not have been able to take as much as they did. The next day, Captain Francisco de Padilha and Melchior Brandão, the captain of Paraguaçu, arrived with many troops. One of the Dutch naus had been stuck at low tide, and it took three or four days for the tide to free it and for them to remove the artillery in their sloops. These captains left with Paredes, making certain the Dutch did not try to move by land, which they did not. Once the nau was free, they sailed for the port in the city.

In addition, Captain-Major Francisco Nunes had planned an attack and constructed seventy ladders with which to assault the fortress of São Filipe in Tapuípe. He wanted to seize it, along with the enemy's gunpowder. However, he did not need to do this because his replacement arrived with gunpowder and all the other needed supplies.

CHAPTER 32
How D. Francisco de Moura Was Ordered by His Majesty to Come Aid Bahia and Govern the Camp

When our Catholic Majesty King Filipe III heard the news of the loss of Bahia, he was keenly aware of its impact. This was not just about the loss but damage to his reputation. By doing this, the Dutch hoped to distract him from the wars currently underway in Holland and their continued assaults along the Spanish coastline. They hoped the Spanish would be unable to attend to Brazil, as they claimed they would. To show them they were mistaken, the king quickly ordered his fleets to make ready. In the meantime, he ordered all the available assistance to leave at once from Lisbon, not just for Bahia but for all of Brazil. This was to keep the rebels from establishing themselves in the colony and from setting foot outside the city they had captured. If they did this, they could endanger the sugar mills around the bay, which pay so much in taxes to the royal treasury.

When this was reviewed by those governing Portugal, D. Diogo de Castro, the Count of Basto, and Count D. Diogo da Silva, the lord steward of the royal household, on August 8, 1624, they immediately sent two caravels to Pernambuco for Governor Matias de Albuquerque to use in aiding Bahia. Their captains were Francisco Gomes de Melo and Pero Cadena, both very familiar with the Brazilian coastline.

They brought as much help as these few ships could carry: 120 soldiers, fifty *quintais* of gunpowder, 1,100 iron bullets of all types, twenty quintais of bars of lead, 1,300 harquebuses from Biscay, all ready to use, fourteen quintais of lead bullets, two hundred lances, and four *arrobas* of wicks.

Francisco Gomes de Melo arrived in Pernambuco at the end of September, where he was received with great joy and the sound of bells. He brought the news that help for Brazil was gathering force in Portugal and Castile. Captain Cadena arrived later, since he had come by way of Madeira to inform them of events.

On August 19, the governors in Lisbon also sent Salvador Correia de Sá e Benevides in the ship *Nossa Senhora da Penha da França* with eighty men from Biscay armed with harquebuses, fourteen quintais of gunpowder, eight quintais of lead, and two quintais of wicks.[1] He went to Rio de Janeiro, where his father, Martim de Sá, was currently governor. For Bahia, they sent as captain-major D. Francisco de Moura, who had been governor of the Cape Verde Islands, with 150 soldiers bringing three hundred harquebuses all ready to use, fifty quintais of gunpowder, ten of wicks, twenty-nine of lead bullion, and 150 molds for making bullets.

With this assistance, D. Francisco de Moura arrived in his native Pernambuco with three caravels. He was the captain of one, while the other two were led by Jerónimo Serrão and Francisco Pereira de Vargas. In Pernambuco, they were joined by Manuel de Sousa de Sá, the captain-major of Pará, and Feliciano Coelho de Carvalho, the son of the governor of Maranhão, who both offered to accompany them. Governor Matias de Albuquerque gave them six large caravels and 80,000 cruzados in additional supplies. They filled the ships with everything and everyone who came on the other caravels, which took them eight days. At the end of that, they departed from Recife and disembarked at Francisco Dias de Ávila's tower. From there, they made their way on land to the encampment.

Once he arrived at the camp on December 3, 1624, they fired six pieces of artillery, which the Dutch heard in the city. Until that point the Dutch had only heard their own artillery so they wanted to know what was happening and capture someone who could tell them. To that end, they made a foray from São Bento and encountered Captain Lourenço de Brito in an ambush. The Dutch killed his sergeant and captured a badly injured man from whom they came to learn that D. Francisco de Moura was the captain-major, that he had succeeded Francisco Nunes Marinho, and that Marinho had followed the bishop, who had died. At that point, none of them were aware of these events except from what the negros were telling them, and they did not believe them.

The Dutch made another raid from the Carmo, which did not end to their liking. That was when D. Francisco had ordered the architect Francisco de Farias to survey that site for constructing additional fortifications. The rear guard was led by Captain Manuel Gonçalves; Gabriel da Costa and the others from there were the troops. They fought with such force in this encounter, killing and injuring many, while only one of our men was killed. The architect told D. Francisco that such brave and energetic soldiers do not require forts, walls, or artificial trenches, since without them they pounce on the enemy like lions.

The Dutch were also lacking meat and fish, and they heard there were many pastures filled with cattle and good fishing spots on Itaparica Island, three leagues from the city. They decided to take possession of the island. For that reason, they left in two naus, some sloops, and four hundred soldiers, led by Captain Hans Kyff and Captain Francisco. Using the lifeboats, they landed on the island at the mill owned by Sebastião Pacheco, and they faced Paulo Coelho, the captain of the island. He and some men with harquebuses were behind a pen holding the pressed cane, and the men were able to wound some of the Dutchmen and prevent them from leaving in their boats. In other mills, they met the same resistance. D. Francisco de Moura ordered Manuel de Sousa de Sá to inspect their fortifications and build more where they were lacking. He did this very carefully. He also placed João de Salazar in charge of ten sailing ships to defend those transporting people or supplies to the camp. After this and after a ship arrived from Holland for the Christmas festival, the raids at sea stopped. It had captured one of our own ships bringing news from Lisbon to Pernambuco in royal letters of the impending arrival of our fleet.

CHAPTER 33

The Death of Colonel Albert Schouten and the Succession of His Brother,
Willem Schouten, and the Continuation of the Raids

After he heard the news of our attacks, Colonel Albert Schouten was very diligent, going around the city and port attending to the fortifications. He knew that in one place or another he would have to defend the city. His main focus was on completing the fort on the beach, which Diogo de Mendonça had started but not completed. However, these duties did not stop him from attending parties and banquets both on land and on the naus, where D. Francisco de Sarmiento and his family were being held prisoners. It so happened that at this time the colonel caught an illness and died in a couple of days.

On the day that he died, which was January 24, 1625, his brother Colonel Willem Schouten, who had been the captain-major or field commander, was promoted to colonel. Captain Hans Kyff was promoted to captain-major. The next day, the funeral was held at the cathedral with the same ceremonies that they followed with the first colonel, which we discussed in chapter 25. However, this time they fired two more volleys from their harquebuses than previously. Perhaps this was because it was the colonel's brother or maybe because that very day sixty soldiers had arrived on a nau from Holland.

On March 13, a second nau arrived, and since it was not windy and those in charge of the ship doubted whether the port were still controlled by their forces, they spent two days at the entrance to the harbor without entering it. Those in the city were no less suspicious, thinking the ship might be part of the fleet sent from Spain, waiting for the others to join it. The colonel took all the necessary precautions; however, everyone calmed down once they realized the ship was one of their own and it carried bricks, which were very much needed. They were for a tower they had started building at the gate in the wall running to the Carmo. They had taken some stones from the new chapel in the cathedral for this. Since they lacked lime, they went in the early morning of the seventeenth of that same month to a house where there was some. The house was beyond the Carmo next to the hermitage of Santo António, and they went there with many negros and sacks to transport the lime as well as 120 armed soldiers. The soldiers were inside the house and nearby homes because it was raining; few were on guard outside. Captain Jordão de Salazar and eighteen men attacked those standing guard. They had been inside the hermitage and understood that few men were outside and that most were inside the homes. The Dutch came forth and fired their weapons, forcing our forces to withdraw. When our men heard these sounds, Francisco de Padilha, Jorge de Aguiar, and the other captains were nearby, so a battle developed. Since it was raining, they could not use their firearms, and they drew their swords. Their forces killed two men and injured twelve while our side killed nine Dutchmen, one of whom was the lieutenant colonel, and they injured many. They also captured eighteen firearms, two spears with battle axes, a drum, and some swords from the dead as well as from those who fled. However, seeing that more Dutchmen were coming from the city, our forces withdrew, giving them the space to collect their dead and wounded but, of course, not the lime they sought.

I have not mentioned the assaults made on the negros allied with the Dutch. Sometimes they came forth to the fields as they knew the paths very well. They came to search for fruit to sell, and several were captured. Captain Padilha took one of these men and cut off both his hands, returning him to the city with a note hanging around his neck challenging Captain Francisco. He was the best known since, as I have said, he was captured by Martim de Sá in Rio de Janeiro. Captain-Major Constantino de Menelau sent him from there to this city, where he was held prisoner for a long time. Captain Francisco responded to this challenge with two hundred armed men and some negro archers. However, when he saw how confidently our men were guarding the area beyond São Bento, next to the hermitage of São Pedro, and he heard rustling in the bush, he thought it was a flank of natives. He believed it was a trap to attack him from the rear. However, it was some negros carrying boards from the hermitage of Santo António in the old town to our camp. This was sufficient to make him refrain from warfare and return to the city.

Captain Francisco de Padilha and his cousin António Ribeiro played another cunning trick on the Dutch. One night they boarded a Dutch brig next to the new fort; it was one of the ships they kept under constant watch. They took the brig from there, in sight of the ship guarding the harbor entrance, to the Vermelho River. On board the brig were two small bronze artillery pieces and four cannons that fire stones. Captain Francisco de Castro and his company joined them on land and Padilha and his men took up the rear so that if the Dutch came after the brig, they would be able to beach the ship and defend it. The Dutch did not attempt this since they could not be convinced (so they say) that the Portuguese took the ship but rather believed that it became untied and the winds and tides carried it away.

CHAPTER 34

The Fleet Sent by His Majesty to Recover Bahia and the
Portuguese Nobles Who Joined It

His Majesty ordered the fleet made ready in no time, sailing from Portugal, Castile, and Biscay to retake Bahia from the Dutch. He said that if it were possible, he would go himself, which was why all of his vassals eagerly volunteered to go. More than one hundred nobles took part on just the Portuguese part of the fleet, led by D. Afonso de Noronha, an elderly nobleman who had been viceroy of India and who was the first to enlist. Then, all the others joined to cross this great ocean like the children of Israel who followed Amminadab to cross the Red Sea.[1]

This fleet left Lisbon on November 22, 1624, the Day of Saint Cecília, led by General D. Manuel de Menezes in the galleon *São João,* which had his son, D. João Teles de Menezes, as its captain as well as a company of soldiers. Also on the ship were D. Álvaro de Abranches, the grandson of the Count of Vila Franca, and Gonçalo de Sousa, the eldest son of Fernão de Sousa, the governor of Angola. These two led two other companies totaling six hundred soldiers.

The admiral, D. Francisco de Almeida, was on the galleon *Santa Ana;* he was also a field commander of a regiment. With him was his captain of the infantry Simão de Mascarenhas of the Order of São João.

The galleon *Conceição* had António Moniz Barreto as its captain and field commander of another regiment while the captain of infantry was D. António de Menezes, the only son of D. Carlos de Noronha.

On the galleon *São Joseph,* D. Rodrigo Lobo was captain, and the infantry was commanded by D. Sancho Faro, the son of the Count of Vimieiro.

The nau *Caridade* had as its captain Lancerote da Franca, who also commanded the infantry. Constantino de Melo held the same positions on the small ship *Santa Cruz.* The nau *Sol Dourado* was captained by Manuel Dias de Andrade. Diogo Vaião was the captain of the nau *Penha da*

França. The nau *Nossa Senhora do Rosário* had as its captain-major Tristão de Mendonça Furtado, and he was in charge of the squadron of ships from Porto and Viana. Its infantry was commanded by Captain António Álvares. The admiralty ship was called the *São Bartolomeu* with Admiral Domingos da Câmara and Infantry Captain D. Manuel de Morais. Gregório Soares was the captain of the nau *Nossa Senhora da Ajuda,* as well as of the infantry. The captain of the nau *Nossa Senhora do Rosário Maior* and of its soldiers with harquebuses was Rui Barreto de Moura; Captain Cristóvão Cabral of the Order of São João led the *Nossa Senhora do Rosário Menor.* On the nau *Nossa Senhora das Neves Maior,* Domingos Gil da Fonseca was captain. On the *Nossa Senhora das Neves Menor,* a nau, its captain was Gonçalo Lobo Barreto. Captain Diogo Ferreira commanded the nau *São João Evangelista.* The *Nossa Senhora da Boa Viagem,* a nau, had Bento de Rego Barbosa as its captain; and Captain João Casado Jácome led the nau *S. Bom Homem.*

The other ships were pinnaces and caravels totaling twenty-six, ten from Porto and Viana and the rest from Lisbon.

The nobility who had departed on these ships as soldiers in alphabetical order were:

A. The already-mentioned D. Afonso de Noronha of His Majesty's Council of State; D. Afonso de Portugal, the Count of Vimioso; D. Afonso de Menezes, the eldest son of D. Fradique; D. Álvaro Coutinho, the Lord of Almourol; Álvaro Pires de Távora, the eldest son of Rui Lourenço da Távora, the former governor of the Algarve and viceroy of India; Álvaro de Sousa, eldest son of Gaspar de Sousa of His Majesty's Council of State and former governor of Brazil; Álvaro de Sousa, the son of Simão; D. António de Castelo Branco, the Lord of Pombeiro; António de Correia, the Lord of Belas; António Luís de Távora, the eldest son of the Count of São João; António Teles da Silva, of the Order of São João, the son of Luís da Silva of His Majesty's council and inspector of His Majesty's goods; António da Silva, the son of Pedro da Silva; António Carneiro de Aragão; António de São Pião, the son of Manuel de São Pião, the Lord of Vila Flor; António Pinto Coelho, the Lord of Figueiras; António Taveira de Avelar; D. António de Melo; António Freitas da Silveira, the son of João Rodrigues de Freitas from the island of Madeira.

B. Brás Soares de Sousa.

D. D. Duarte de Menezes, the Count of Tarouca; Duarte de Albuquerque, the Lord of Pernambuco; D. Diogo da Silveira, the eldest son of D. Álvaro da Silveira and grandson of the Count of Sortelha; D. Diogo Lobo, the son of D. Pedro Lobo; D. Diogo de Noronha; D. Diogo de Vasconcelos e Menezes and D. Sebastião, sons of D. Afonso de Vasconcelos of the House of Penela; Duarte de Melo Pereira; and Duarte Peixoto da Silva.

E. Estêvão Soares de Melo, Lord of the House of Melo; Estêvão de Brito Freire.

F. D. Francisco de Portugal, commander of the frontier; Francisco de Melo de Castro, the son of António de Melo de Castro; D. Francisco de Faro, the son of Count D. Estêvão of Faro and a member of His Majesty's Council of State and the inspector of royal goods; Francisco Moniz; D. Francisco de Toledo and António de Abreu, his brother; D. Francisco de Sá, son of Jorge de Sá; Francisco de Mendonça Furtado and his brother, Cristóvão de Mendonça Furtado.

G. Gracia Veles de Castelo Branco; Gaspar de Paiva de Magalhães; George de Melo, son of Manuel de Melo, the chief huntsman; George Mexia; Gonçalo de Sousa, eldest son of Fernão de Sousa, the governor of Angola; Gonçalo Tavares de Sousa, son of Bernardim de Távora, from the Algarve.

H. D. Henrique de Menezes, Lord of Louriçal; Jerónimo de Melo de Castro; D. Henrique Henriques, Lord of Alcaçovas; Henrique Correia da Silva; Henrique Henriques.

J. D. João de Sousa, governor of the fort in Tomar; João da Silva Teles de Menezes, colonel of Lisbon; João de Melo; D. João de Lima, the second son of the Viscount of Vila Nova de Cerveira; D. João de Portugal, son of D. Nuno Álvares de Portugal, the former governor of Portugal; D. João de Menezes, eldest son of D. Diogo de Menezes; João Mendes de Vasconcelos, son of Luís Mendes de Vasconcelos, former governor of Angola; João Machado de Brito; José de Sousa de São Paio.

L. Luís Álvares de Távora, Count of São João and Lord of the House of Mogadouro; D. Lopo da Cunha, Lord of Sentar; Luís César de Menezes, son of Vasco Fernandes César, the inspector of the royal warehouses; Lourenço Pires Carvalho, eldest son of Gonçalo Pires

Carvalho, inspector of royal works; D. Lourenço de Almada, son of
D. Antão de Almada; Lopo de Sousa, son of Aires de Sousa.

M. Martim Afonso de Oliveira de Miranda, heir to Oliveira; Martim
Afonso da Távora, son of Rui Pires de Távora, the head treasurer of
His Majesty; Manuel de Sousa Coutinho, first inspector of the ships
from India, Lord of the House of Baião; D. Manuel Lobo, son of
D. Francisco Lobo; Manuel de Sousa Mascarenhas; Martim Afonso de
Melo and Joseph de Melo, his brother; D. Manuel Coutinho and two
sons of Marshal D. Fernando Coutinho

N. Nuno da Cunha, eldest son of João Nunes da Cunha; D. Nuno Marcarenhas da Costa, son of D. João Marcarenhas; Nuno Gonçalves de
Faria, son of Nicolau de Faria, the head market inspector.

P. Pedro da Silva, the former governor of Mina; Pedro César de Eça, son
of Luís César; Pero da Silva da Cunha, son of Duarte da Cunha; Pero
Lopes Lobo, son of Luís Lopes Lobo; Pero Cardoso Coutinho; Pero
Correia da Silva; Paulo Soares; Pero da Costa Travassos, son of João
Travassos da Costa, secretary of the high court.

R. Rui de Moura Teles, Lord of Póvoa; D. Rodrigo da Costa, son of
Julianes da Costa, former governor of Tangier, president of the Lisbon
Town Council and of the High Court; D. Rodrigo Lobo; Rui Correia
Lucas; Rodrigo de Miranda Henriques; Rui de Figueiredo, heir to the
estate of his father Jorge de Figueiredo, Luís Gomes de Figueiredo and
António Figueiredo, his brothers; D. Rodrigo da Silveira and Fernão
da Silveira, his brother, the sons of D. Luís Lobo da Silveira, Lord of
Sargedas; Rui Dias da Cunha.

S. Sebastião de Sá de Menezes, eldest son of Francisco de Sá de Menezes,
brother of the Count of Matosinhos; Simão de Miranda; Simão Freire
de Andrade.

There were many more nobles, so many that it seemed that none were
left who had not joined this expedition. In Viana, it happened that three
brothers all wanted to enlist but one needed to remain behind to tend
to his family and the others. None of them wanted to stay behind and
miss this undertaking. The Count of Miranda, Diogo Lopes de Sousa, was
made aware of this, and he resolved the matter by rolling the dice.

The same happened with a father and his son; each wanted to enlist as
a soldier. The case was taken to the count-governor, who decided that the

journey was better suited for the son than the father, but this left them both with their honor intact.

CHAPTER 35
The Financial Contributions of the King's Portuguese Vassals for This Fleet

If the Portuguese had shown themselves to be forthcoming in volunteering for this expedition, they were equally generous in making financial gifts to aid and supply it. This was true not only for those who volunteered. Those who had made the most generous offer possible by risking their lives did not benefit by saving their money. They made generous offerings, and those who could not go gave large gifts to assist the fleet.

The president of the Lisbon City Council gave 100,000 cruzados from the council. His Excellency, the Duke of Bragança D. Teodosio Segundo gave 20,000 cruzados from his estate. The Duke of Caminha, D. Miguel de Menezes, gave 16,500 cruzados. The Duke of Vila Hermosa, president of the Council of Portugal, D. Carlos de Borja, donated 2,400 cruzados, which paid for 200 soldiers. The Marquis of Castelo Rodrigo, D. Manuel de Moura Corte Real, gave 3,350 cruzados, which paid for the men and supplies required for the ship *Nossa Senhora do Rosário Maior*. D. Luís de Sousa, the governor of the fort in Beja, Lord of Brigel and former governor of Brazil, donated 3,300 cruzados and thirty *moios* [664 bushels] of wheat to make hardtack biscuits.[1] The Count of Castanheira, D. João de Ataíde offered 2,500 cruzados; D. Pedro Coutinho, the former governor of Hormuz paid 2,000 cruzados. D. Pedro de Alcaçova donated 1,500 cruzados. António Gomes da Mata, the head courier gave 2,000 cruzados. Francisco Soares donated 1,000 cruzados, and the sons of Heitor Mendes offered 4,000 cruzados.

The church officials also contributed. The illustrious and most reverend archbishop of Lisbon, D. Miguel de Castro, contributed 2,000 cruzados. The illustrious archbishop primate of Portugal, D. Afonso Furtado de Mendonça gave 10,000 cruzados.[2] The illustrious archbishop of Évora, D. Joseph de Melo, donated 4,000 cruzados as did the bishop of Coimbra, D. João Manuel. The bishop of Guarda, D. Francisco de Castro, offered 2,000 cruzados. The bishop of Porto, D. Rodrigo da Cunha, gave 1,500 cruzados; and the bishop of the Algarve, D. João Coutinho provided 1,000 cruzados.

The merchants of Lisbon and elsewhere in Portugal gave 34,000 cruzados, while the Italian merchants provided 500 cruzados and the German merchants 2,100 cruzados. In addition, they gave 150 quintais of gunpowder.

This totaled 220,000 cruzados, which was the cost of the expedition. This was done without using any royal funds from His Majesty. It was very well stocked with all the men would require for the voyage. In addition to the personal supplies each man carried from home, they had 7,500 quintais of hardtack biscuit, 854 *pipas* of wine, 1,368 *pipas* of water, 4,190 *arrobas* of meat, 3,739 *arrobas* of fish, 1,782 *arrobas* of rice, 122 *quartos* [30 casks] of olive oil, and ninety-three *pipas* of vinegar. This does not count the supplies of cheeses, raisons, figs, vegetables, almonds, sugar, sweets, spices, and salt. They also had twenty-two sets of pharmaceutical supplies and two medical doctors, and almost all the ships had surgeons. There were 200 beds for the sick, and many stockings, shoes, and shirts. They carried 310 pieces of artillery, round gunshot, and 2,500 pieces of chain, 2,710 muskets and harquebuses, 209 quintais of lead bullets, 1,355 pikes and half pikes, 202 quintais of matches, and 500 quintais of gunpowder. They also stocked many *palanquetas* of iron, small lanterns, crowbars, spoons, gun ladles, leather gun pouches, and all the other military supplies needed for the artillery, fortifications, and sieges.[3] They also stocked many shovels, hoes, mattocks, picks, scythes, axes, saws, straw baskets, and carts. For fixing the ships, they carried a lot of tar, tar water, fishing bait, various nails, oakum, lead powder, rigging, sail cloth, thread, and many other little things.[4] For any necessities, they had 20,000 cruzados in Spanish *reales.*

CHAPTER 36
How the Portuguese Fleet Awaited the Spanish Ships in Cape Verde and Sailed Together to Bahia

On December 19, 1624, our fleet arrived in the Cape Verde Islands. They had orders from His Majesty that they should wait there for the fleet from Castile to join them. On the fourteenth, the galleon *Conceição* had become separated from the rest of the fleet. Its captain was António Moniz Barreto, field master, and on the twentieth it was pushed on shore in a storm in the shoals of Santa Ana on the island of Maio at eleven at night.

Some 150 soldiers died in the ocean since they did not leave with the first lifeboat of nobles. There would have been even more soldiers drowned but for D. António de Menezes. He is an infantry captain, the only son of D. Carlos de Noronha, and a young man twenty-two years old. He saved them by urging the men to be patient, await the return of the lifeboat, and have hope in God's salvation for them all. He said he would not leave them until they were all safely on shore. D. Francisco Deca said the same; he is the son of D. Jorge Deca. The examples set by these two nobles convinced the men to either get into the lifeboats or use some rafts or boards to save themselves. Among those saved were two of our brothers from this province of Santo António, Brother António and Brother Francisco. They had come as chaplains for the galleon. One came to shore in a lifeboat and the other on a cross made from two boards. This figure of a cross is what offers us our salvation and refuge.

When news reached General D. Manuel de Menezes of the unfortunate shipwreck, he immediately informed the governor of the Cape Verde Islands, Francisco de Vasconcelos, and the lord of the island of Maio, João Coelho da Cunha. This was where the shipwreck occurred. He asked them to send assistance for the survivors, which they did so effectively that all were cured and aided. Their slaves and servants were able to remove the artillery, munitions, sails of the galleon, and other royal property as well as personal effects, which they returned to their owners. The fleet was occupied with this for fifty days as it awaited the arrival of the fleet from Castile, some thirty-two naus.

On the royal flagship, the supreme commander of the navy and army was D. Fadrique de Toledo, and the admiralty ship was led by D. João Fajardo, general of the strait. The expedition from Naples was led by its captain, the Marques of Cropani, field commander of the expedition, and its navy was commanded by the Marques of Torrecusso, field commander of the battalion from Naples. The forces from Biscay were commanded by General Valezilha, and his brother led their navy. The squadron from Quatro Vilas was commanded by General D. Francisco de Azevedo and the galleon *Santa Ana*, which was part of that command, had as its captain D. Francisco de Andruca. That ship carried the field commander of the royal battalion D. João de Orelhana while D. Pedro Osório, the infantry commander of the battalion from the strait, came in another vessel. The other ships carried all the squadrons, captains, sergeants, and officials whose names I do not know but whose actions during the journey will be seen. In this and in the following chapters you will read about what they did; their names are a roll call of the true nobility.

These two fleets were united in the Cape Verde Islands, and after they completed their military ceremonies and courtesies, they departed for Bahia on Shrove Tuesday, February 11, 1625.[1] They arrived in Bahia on March 29, on the eve of Easter, which is our salvation. They only lost the nau *Caridade*, commanded by Captain Lancerote de Franca, on the reefs of Paraíba, but his uncle, Afonso de Franca, the captain-general of Paraíba, came to his aid right away with ships, sailors, and four large caravels sent by the governor. Everyone was saved but for two men who rushed to jump into the sea. They were also able to save the shell of the ship with its rigging, guns, artillery, and supplies. Captain Lancerote de Franca left the ship for them to supply new masts because these had been cut, and he went with his soldiers to Pernambuco. From there, they left for Bahia in seven large caravels loaned by the governor and arrived the same day as the fleet.

CHAPTER 37

How Salvador Correia from Rio de Janeiro and Jerónimo Cavalcanti
from Pernambuco Came to the Aid of Bahia and What Occurred
with the Dutch on the Way

In chapter 28 of this book, we have stated how after Bahia was captured by the Dutch, their admiral Pedro Piers left with five armed naus and two pinnaces for Angola. Their intention was to bring back negros for the sugar mills. They said they had made arrangements with the king of the Congo to obtain slaves. At the entrance to Luanda harbor, there were more of their naus, which had had burned some Portuguese vessels and captured others. This occurred while the bishop was governing after João Correia de Sousa had fled. However, because Fernão de Sousa was the next governor and he became aware of their plans, he quickly fortified Bahia in such a manner that when the Dutch returned, they could not achieve what they desired; they were able to do little more than capture a nau from Seville that was entering the harbor as well as two smaller ships.

As a result, the Dutch sailed along the Brazilian coastline and entered the river in Espírito Santo on March 10, 1625. A couple of days earlier,

Salvador de Sá e Benevides had arrived there with 250 white men and natives in four canoes and a caravel that his father, Martim de Sá, the governor of Rio de Janeiro, had sent to aid Bahia. Francisco de Aguiar Coutinho, governor and Lord of Espírito Santo, had helped them by digging trenches around the town, placing four rock-firing cannons that had been on land in the trenches. When the Dutch left their ships, they fired one of these and killed a man. After the Dutch entered the town, our forces came forward from all sides with a great war cry from the natives. Our forces killed thirty-five and captured two. The first to die by his sword was their captain who had been in front. Francisco de Aguiar Coutinho said to him, "If you are a captain, then you should know me, since I am one as well." After saying that, he gave him a powerful stab that made him collapse.

The guardian of the monastery of our order of Saint Francis, Brother Manuel de Espírito Santo, and his companions went among the Portuguese encouraging them. The enemy soldiers were next to the trenches, and he stood above them holding a crucifix saying, "Know you Lutherans that this Lord will defeat you." With that, he was able to avoid a hail of bullets and went to the bell of the main church, which was close by, and rang the bell declaring victory. With this, the people were filled with sufficient energy to achieve it, and the Dutch general had to withdraw to his naus with nearly one hundred wounded men of the three hundred who had left the ships. They also had some deaths, including their admiral Jacob Willekens and the traitor Rodrigo Pedro, who had lived in that same town with his Portuguese wife. He had been taken to Bahia because of his crimes and fled jail for Holland; he returned as a captain of a nau on this expedition. Filled with this rage, the Dutch general sent a nau and four sloops to burn the caravel commanded by Salvador Correia that he had anchored upriver in a marsh. However, Salvador Correia attacked them in his canoes, killing forty men and capturing one of their sloops.

The next day, the Dutch general wrote to Francisco de Aguiar as follows: "Your lordship is undoubtedly pleased with your recent success, as I am grieved by it. This is the way of war. If you wish to send me my men that you hold captive there, I will rescue them. If not, we will remain here until we run out of food."

The Dutch general hoped that there were fewer dead and more captives on land, but the governor would not send these few captives, so the

Dutch set sail and left on March 18. They left with very few people; when they set out, they encountered the ship owned by the Jesuit fathers. We had captured this ship, and the Dutch had given it to António Maio, master of the ship owned by D. Francisco Sarmiento, in trade for his. It was now arriving once again from Rio de Janeiro loaded with sugar bound for the island of Terceira. They took it as far as the entrance to the harbor in Bahia. From there, they sent a pinnace at night to investigate the situation in the port and the ships anchored there. They were told that was the fleet sent from Spain, unloading enemy ships and burning them, so they headed to Olinda in Pernambuco. There they picked up a negro owned by João Guterres who was fishing on a raft, and they asked if Bahia had been recovered. The slave not only told them yes, it had been, but also that General D. Fadrique de Toledo had ordered all the Dutchmen killed. They believed him (even though it was false), saying, "Was D. Fadrique not Spanish and a descendent of the Duke of Alba?" Because of this, they sailed for Fernando de Noronha Island to take on water and salted meat, which they took to Holland along with the negro. They put the other negros and whites they had captured when they took the Jesuit ship on a small pinnace that landed in Paraíba; they related this news. Salvador Correia, who was victorious in Espírito Santo, left with his people in canoes for Bahia to join the fleet there. He was one of the generals and nobles who was so warmly welcomed.

In the same manner, Jerónimo Cavalcanti de Albuquerque in Pernambuco knew from Lancerote de Franca about the arrival of our fleet in Bahia. Franca had survived the loss of the nau *Caridade* in Paraíba. Cavalcanti left for Bahia in a nau at the orders of Governor Matias de Albuquerque along with two of his brothers, some relatives and friends, and 130 soldiers. Cavalcanti paid the expenses for all these men. They encountered a Dutch pinnace at sea, which had been scouting for our fleet. Now that our fleet had arrived, it remained outside the harbor. Cavalcanti attacked it, and after many cannon shots fired by both sides, five of our men were dead, one of whom was Estêvão Ferreira, captain of the lead ship, who while wounded did not want to retreat before the Dutch killed him. This would only happen with many more killed or injured or if he received a mortal injury. The Cavalcantis entered the Bay of Bahia and were warmly welcomed by all, especially the captain-major Francisco de Moura, his cousin, and the Lord of Pernambuco, Duarte de Albuquerque, who had come on the fleet as a soldier. His Majesty felt he had been well served by these acts and stated that in his letter to Jerónimo Cavalcanti.

CHAPTER 38

How Those on the Armada Disembarked and the Dutch Attacked Them at São Bento, Where the First Battery Was Located[1]

The Dutch hoped for a better Easter than what they had. In the early morning, at the time the church normally sings the "Alleluia," they saw the fleet and thought it was theirs, the fleet they had awaited. However, they saw the fleet spread out in a crescent-shaped line that almost stretched from the point of Santo António to Tauípe, which is the entire bay in the city. They also saw the Portuguese ships and canoes mixing among them; they knew it was the Spanish fleet. They began to prepare for the fight with great care. Their ships came up to the shore next to the forts, and they sunk three merchant ships in front of their own ships to block the passage for our fleet. They had seized these. They took the Portuguese sailors who had been on board into the city, telling everyone there to not leave their homes. They brought a couple of pieces of artillery to the college and elsewhere where they thought the Spanish could enter. They cleared out of the fort of São Filipe, which is one league from the city, thinking that the sixty men needed to staff it would be of better use elsewhere.

Our forces at that time were disembarking next to the fort of Santo António, some two thousand men from Castile, fifteen hundred from Portugal, and five hundred from Naples with their field masters, who were two Spaniards, D. Pedro Osório and D. João de Orelhana; two Portuguese, D. Francisco de Almeida and António Moniz Barreto; and from Naples, the Marques of Torrecusso. The general left D. Pedro Osório, D. Francisco de Almeida, and the Marques at the barracks in São Bento with their regiments, some two thousand soldiers. He left for the Carmo with the others. Then he brought artillery for both locations since both are on hills and virtually the only ones that overlook the town from the land.

With the knowledge of what damage the Portuguese could do from these positions, three hundred Dutchmen living in São Bento came forth with their harquebuses at the third eighth of Easter at ten o'clock and a battle started that lasted two hours.[2] We lost eighty men in this fight because they were scattered throughout the town and the Dutch fired so many shells filled with small shot and nails from the gates and other forts; these shots effectively injured and killed many. There were Castilians, Portuguese, and Italians all mixed together, which made the Dutch very happy. As a trophy, the Dutch had captured a leather vest from a Castilian captain. It was laced in gold. Out of greed, they had dragged his body in a miserable fashion to a foot of the hill within easy reach of a gun being shot from the wall and even closer for the muskets they were using.

When our forces came at night to collect his body for burial, the Dutch shot a few rounds of muskets at them. In spite of this, he was buried in holy ground with the others who died fighting with such spirit in this attack, which were D. Pedro Osório, field commander of the infantry from the regiment from the strait; Captain D. Diogo de Espinosa; Captain D. Pedro de Santo-Estêvão, nephew of the Marques de Cropani; João de Orejo, secretary of the field commander of the infantry; D. Fernando Gracian; D. João de Torreblanca; Francisco Manuel de Aguiar; D. Lucas de Segura; and D. Alonso de Agana. Next to D. Alonso during the battle, they found D. Francisco de Faro, the son of the Count of Faro, with his arms around a Dutchman, whom he killed. There were other dead and injured Dutchmen but few when compared with our losses.

Our men were pent up with fury. The next day, which was Wednesday, April 3, they trained the artillery on the area at the edge of town near São Bento. They blasted large holes in the wall, which the Dutch filled at night with sandbags they had loaded for that purpose. However, they were not completely spared since each night two or three were killed and more were injured. The Dutch did not lose faith because they hoped for the prompt arrival of their fleet, as an English folk healer had affirmed. For that reason, they placed a large flag with their shield on it at the top of the cathedral tower, which is the highest point in town. When their fleet came, it could enter the harbor with confidence, knowing that the town was theirs.

In this manner, they defended and we attacked in every way possible. One of their defensive measures occurred one night when they used two fire ships, using the winds and tides to carry them into our own ships and burn them. Our Portuguese flagship was put in jeopardy, and it surely would have burned if the rigging had not burned and the foresail unflurried, which the Lord God ordered to save us from this danger. The other

Dutch ship attacked the ship of the admiral of the straits, melting the pitch and burning several soldiers. It was freed by the diligence and efforts of D. João Fajardo, who was in charge of the fleet. Three Dutchmen who had set fire to the ship tried to make their escape in a canoe, but it was captured by Roque Centeno in a sloop.

In spite of all these activities, every day in the morning and afternoon the Dutch gathered in the cathedral to sing psalms and say prayers asking for God's assistance. One Sunday morning, we shot a cannonball from our battery of São Bento. It went through the wall of São José's chapel and shot off the legs of four men sitting on a bench listening to the sermon, killing two of them.

Serving in the battery where that shot was fired, and many more, was D. Francisco de Almeida, field commander of a regiment of Portuguese infantry and admiral of the royal fleet from Portugal. With him was D. João de Sousa, commander of the fort in Tomar; António Correia, the Lord of the House of Belas; D. António de Castelo Branco, Lord of Pombeiro; Rui de Moura Teles, Lord of Póvoa; D. Francisco Portugal, commander of the frontier; D. Álvaro Coutinho, Lord of Almourol, Pedro Correia Gama, sergeant-major of this regiment; Captain Gonçalo de Sousa; Captain Manuel Dias de Andrade; Captain Salvador Correia de Sá e Benevides; Captain Jerónimo Cavalcanti de Albuquerque and his brothers; and other Portuguese nobles.

Also present was the regiment from Naples commanded by Carlo Caracciolo, the Marques of Torrecusso, when he had not moved to another site. In the regiment from the strait, there were many nobles and captains, all of them eager to crawl in the dirt. They seemed more like ditch diggers or porters carrying bundles of wood to the trenches, but when they fired their cannons and muskets, and especially facing the fire from the enemy, they were valiant soldiers.

CHAPTER 39

About the Second Battery at the Monastery of Carmo with General Dom
Fadrique de Toledo and Two Other Batteries Created from It

Those soldiers in the battery at the Carmo with General D. Fadrique did as much as the others mentioned above. However, since those in São Bento had been stirred up by the Dutch attack, those at the Carmo were

chomping at the bit to engage the Dutch as well. There was a small piece
of the wall at the Monastery of Carmo that helped them with their trench,
but other than that they had to dig the entire length by the city. The gate to
the city is on the north edge, and their trench also faced the enemy ships on
the west; on April 9 our men began to fire on them. They repeatedly pelted
the Dutch ships with cannon shot and sank the largest of these ships, with
Captain Sansão, which had two rows of artillery. The water there is shallow because it is close to the shore and the ship was large, so much of it
remained above the waterline. Nevertheless, the Dutch lost some supplies
and cargo as well as four men who were killed and twelve injured.

This battery did no less damage to the city, punching holes in the wall
and gate and destroying many homes. The Dutch colonel promised his
men two *patacas* each to work at night repairing the walls and trenches,
since they worked for free during the day. In this manner, the work
was never-ending. With all this building and destroying, repairing and
knocking down the wall, the bombardment continued, and some people
were killed on both sides.

Among many shots fired, this battery at the Carmo fired a notable one
at the Dutch in front of the doors of the cathedral. The cannonball hit the
ground under a sergeant's feet and left him unharmed but for making him
leap in the air and kick his feet as if he were dancing. The cannonball continued on its trajectory to the hospital wall, breaking through it, killing
two surgeons attending to the wounded and injuring one of these men a
second time.

In the same manner, some of our men were killed, such as Martim
Afonso, heir to the town of Olivença. He went home to change his shirt,
which was dirty after carrying wood and firing muskets. He sat next to the
window getting a little air and was shot in the leg by the Dutch. He died
three days later with the valor and Christianity that one would expect of
such a noble person. He left for Lisbon while injured, even though his relatives and friends told him not to make the journey. He responded by saying he was anointed with holy oil and had to make the journey.[1] This was
the strength of his desire to serve his king, which he had demonstrated
not just on this occasion but on many others. His Majesty rewarded this
service after Afonso's death with gifts made to his children, as we shall see.

He was one of the members of the Portuguese nobility who served
in this battalion of the Carmo, someone whom we have discussed and

have been discussing with your excellency, the reader. The others were D. Afonso de Noronha; the Count of São João, Luís Álvares de Távora, the brother-in-law of the heir to Olivença; the Count of Vimioso, D. Afonso de Portugal; the Count of Tarouca, D. Duarte de Menezes; Duarte de Albuquerque; Francisco de Melo de Castro; Álvaro Pires de Távora; João da Silva Telo; Lourenço Pires de Carvalho; D. João de Portugal; Martim Afonso de Távora; António Teles da Silva; Captain D. João Teles de Menezes; Captain Cristóvão Cabral; Captain D. Álvaro de Abranches; Captain D. António de Menezes; Captain D. Sancho de Faro; and others.

General D. Fadrique ordered that two more batteries be created in this area. One was to be in Palmeiras, where the field masters D. João de Orelana and António Moniz Barreto were located along with Tristão de Mendonça, captain-general of the squadron from Porto with his two nephews Francisco and Cristóvão de Mendonça. In addition, there was D. Henrique de Menezes, the Lord of Louriçal; Rui Correira Lucas, Nuno da Cunha, and António Taveira de Avelar; Captain Lancerote de Franca; Captain Diogo Ferreira; and others. This location was very important because it was higher than any of the others, and the Dutch had not fortified that side of the city as well as they had fortified other locations. When our forces started firing their artillery from this hilltop, they were able to kill and injury many men, but of course the Dutch killed some of ours as well. Among the dead was Captain Diogo Ferreira, who was one of the three brothers from Viana who came on this expedition after rolling the dice, as we have discussed in chapter 33. João Ferreira had come here as superintendent of the treasury of Brazil on an armed ship that he supplied at his own cost. He died in Lisbon of a high fever. He lost the roll of the dice, gaining his life and goods in his home, but he cried because he had not been one of the brothers to fight.

The other battery that was organized here was with D. Francisco de Moura and the men from Bahia and the assault troops. Some of the servants of Duarte de Albuquerque Coelho, captain, governor, and Lord of Pernambuco, were also there. This battery was in a very dangerous position because it was the distance of one shot of a harquebus from D. Fadrique and his men. It was very close to the city and the Jesuit college, where the Dutch had a battery with six pieces of artillery. Both sides inflicted great harm.

CHAPTER 40

Regarding the Other Trenches Dug near São Bento and How the
French and the Dutch Were Divided

D. Manuel de Menezes and D. João Farajado created their battery next to
São Bento well before the two I have mentioned above. They made a new
one on the hill next to the sea overlooking the riverbank called *Gabriel*
Soares. They did a lot of damage with their five pieces of artillery, not only
to the Dutch ships but to the forts along the beach, which can be seen
from there, and to some forts in the city.

Between this battery and the one in São Bento, the Marques de Torrecusso, the field commander of the Neapolitan squad, made another battery. It was close to the gates of the city, so close that the Neapolitans could
cause damage with the little artillery pieces, not just the larger ones. It
would appear they were very eager to use their hands; with the energy of
Italians, they dug a ditch that allowed them to walk safely to the city wall.

These seven locations mentioned in these three chapters are where
our forces made batteries to challenge the city. There was no letup in
the thunder from the bombardments, small cannons, and gunfire from
one side or the other. It was every fifteen minutes day and night for the

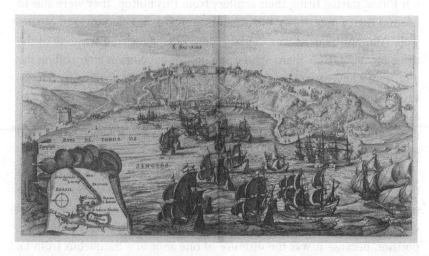

Figure 8. Bird's-eye view of the destruction of São Salvador de Bahia de Todos os Santos,
Brazil, by the Dutch fleet. Includes inset map of the Bay of São Salvador. Includes scene
of naval warfare, fortifications, battalions marching, dwellings, churches, topographical
details, inclines, and ships. Items in the image are numbered for identification in the text.
—Engraving by Johann Ludwig Gottfried 1631. ©John Carter Brown Library.

twenty-three days of the siege. There were so many cannonballs fired that it was a miracle people escaped injury in their homes or on the streets. Someone who was curious counted them and said that the enemy fired 2,510 cannon shots at us and we responded with 4,168.

In order to make this clearer, I have drawn a description of the city and shown the location of the forts, inside and outside the city, as follows: (see above).

Our enemies knew from these beginnings what would happen when our forces entered the city. With this fear in mind, the French began to separate themselves from the Dutch and made the decision to join our side. At that time, a Portuguese soldier from India, whom the Dutch had captured coming from Angola, had enlisted with the Dutch for pay. He came and went on guard duty with the Dutch. When he learned of the French plans, he decided that he and four of them would set fire to the gunpowder and escape. He thought that with this service, which is no small thing, he could then ask for a pardon to save his life. However, someone told the Dutch colonel, and he apprehended the Portuguese man and one of the Frenchmen and hung them. The other two escaped to our side. The colonel then issued an announcement from the streets, accompanied by ten or twelve drums, that anyone who knew of someone who planned to flee and who then denounced them to the Dutch authorities would receive 400 cruzados. From that day forward, the Dutch did not let the Frenchmen out of their sight.

CHAPTER 41

How the Dutch Soldiers Rebelled against Their Colonel Willem Schouten,
Removed Him from Office, and Elected His Replacement

On April 26, which was a Saturday, the day dedicated to Our Lady, the Holy Virgin, a day when she normally shows favors to those devoted to her, she singled out those soldiers in her battery and the trenches at the Carmo. She infused them that day with such energy and courage that some of them, showing no fear of the enemy artillery and gunfire, reached the city gate. A soldier from Aragón named João Vidal from the company of D. Afonso de Alencastre was able to remove the flag over the gate. He then avoided the enemy bullets aimed at him, taking the flag to his captain; the captain took it to the general. The general chided him for acting without his orders but recognized the man's valor by paying him eight *escudos*.[1]

It also happened that a Dutch soldier while on guard duty, by shaking a wick, allowed the sparks to fly into a barrel of gunpowder, and twenty-five soldiers were burned so badly that they could not use their weapons. They say on such occasions that being badly burned is worse than death because the dead are only absent in a fight. The injured and wounded also require surgeons and nurses who are busy attending to them.

The Dutch were so eager for victory that they put it before their lives. Because their colonel was unaware of this turn of events and at other times his troops had noted his lack of attention, they decided to strike together. This was discovered by his female Portuguese friend. Thirty soldiers went to their leader's house to kill him, and they found Estêvão Raquete, captain of the merchant company, who was with him. He escaped but they injured the colonel with a cut on his head and hands. This act was done with the consent of his captains. The proof of this is that none of these soldiers was disciplined. The privy council removed the injured colonel from office and appointed Captain-Major Hans Kyff to be the new colonel and Captain Buste to be the new leader of the infantry.

The insolence of these soldiers is incredible. Not only did the new colonel put Estêvão Raquete into jail to silence him, but two soldiers went there to kill him. They would have done so if the other prisoners and the very colonel who had arrested him had not come to his aid. Other soldiers went to the home of the Portuguese woman and would have killed her too, had she not fled to the home of a married Portuguese man who hid her. Taking their revenge, they stole what they found, as the colonel had given her many things.

The vigilance and care of the new colonel was also incredible; he worked day and night making the rounds of the trenches. He collected all the artillery to use when that beyond the trenches was broken and used all sorts of fire and other wartime inventions to keep our forces at bay until their fleet arrived with assistance. This is what they hoped and on what they based all their confidence.

CHAPTER 42
How the Dutch Agreed to Surrender

Those who place their confidence in human endeavors are duped, and this is what the Dutch experienced here in the city of Bahia. They believed that they could defend the city by removing a captain and replacing him with someone more diligent and industrious. It is certainly true what the Psalms say, that if the Lord does not protect the city, he does not watch over those who do.[1]

Three entire days did not pass before they saw the folly of their intentions. They recognized they were unable to repair the damage inflicted by our batteries. They realized that they needed to negotiate, an idea that the previous colonel had dismissed. They arranged a ploy under the cloak of honor and came forth at the Carmo, beating a drum with a letter for General D. Fadrique. In it, they said that morning they had heard one of our trumpets. They thought that it was an invitation to make peace, which they also wanted, and they had terms to conclude that.

To this D. Fadrique responded that he did not use trumpets to summon those who were besieged but rather called them with the sound of artillery. However, if they wanted peace, and it was something that did not offend the honor of God or the king, he was ready to listen. At that point, they began to negotiate. The Dutch wanted peace so badly that those at the front lines of the Palmeiras battery surrendered when they presented the letter. This battery was under the command of D. João de Orelhana and António Moniz Barreto, while Tristão de Mendonça was captain-major of the squadron from Porto. This same Tristão de Mendonça came forward to speak with them along with Lancerote de Franca, captain of the infantry. They escorted them to the colonel in the Carmo barracks by order of His Excellency João Vicente de Sanfelice and Diogo Ruiz, the lieutenant to the head infantry colonel. There were other notes back and forth until peace was concluded, which was done publicly in a written statement in the presence of the members of the Dutch Privy Council, which included Guilhelmo Stop, Hugo António, and Francisco Duchs. Representing His Majesty was the Marques D. Fadrique, the Marques of Cropani, D. Francisco de Almeida, and António Moniz Barreto, the colonels of the infantry of the two Portuguese squads; D. João de Orelhana, colonel of the infantry of a Castilian squad; D. Jerónimo Quexada, the head auditor of the Castilian fleet; Diogo Ruiz, lieutenant to the head infantry colonel, and João Vicente de São Félix.

After the meetings, these people agreed that the Dutch would return the city to General D. Fadrique de Toledo in the name of His Majesty in the state in which it existed on April 30, 1625, that is, with all its artillery, arms, flags, supplies, military stores, war provisions, ships, money, gold, silver, jewels, merchandise, black slaves, horses, and everything else that had been in the city of Salvador as well as all of the prisoners that had been there. The Dutch also agreed that they would not take up arms against His Majesty until after they reached Holland. In the name of His Majesty, the general declared that all the Dutch could freely leave the city with their street clothes and those for sleeping. Captains and other officials could each take their trunks or boxes, and soldiers could take their knapsacks but nothing more. Their ships would be given written permission from His Majesty to return to Holland unharmed if they were encountered on their route home. They would be given comfortable provisions for a voyage of three and a half months, and they would be given the nautical instruments needed for their navigation. The Dutch would be treated in a peaceful manner and would be given weapons for their defense on the trip. They would depart for the ships without those, except for the captains, who could leave with their swords.

This agreement was signed in the barracks of Carmo on April 30, 1625, by D. Fadrique de Toledo Osório, Guilhelmo Stop, Hugo António, and Francisco Duchs.

CHAPTER 43
How the City Was Reoccupied; the Thanks Given to God for the Victory and the News Sent to Spain

On May 1, 1624, the Day of the Blessed Apostles São Filipe and São Tiago, the gates of the city were opened, and our forces entered in an orderly manner and placed pillories where they would be needed. The Dutch (who still numbered 1,919) were gathered in houses on the beach, under the watchful guard of Spanish soldiers. They were later moved to their ships, which their carpenters and workmen were busy preparing and repairing.

The Portuguese who had voluntarily remained with the Dutch were jailed, and an inventory was made of their belongings; another inventory was made of everything that had fallen into the hands of the Dutch and all they obtained. They found six hundred negros, some of whom had fled from their masters to the enemy out of a love of liberty, while others had come off the slave ships from Angola.

The Dutch also handed over six ships and two sloops, which were all that remained of the twenty-one that had been present when our fleet entered the harbor. The others had been burned or sunk.

The Dutch also surrendered sixteen company flags and standards that had been in the cathedral tower. From the lead ship, they yielded 216 artillery pieces, forty of which were bronze and the others made of iron; thirty-five cannons to fire stones; five hundred quintais of gunpowder in barrels; gunshot, bombs, grenades, and other fire-making weapons in great quantity; 1,578 muskets, 133 pistols and harquebuses; a great deal of raw copper ore; 870 wicks; eighty-four armored breastplates; and many other breastplates and those to protect the back. In the goods collected, they found twenty-one quintais of wicks from the warehouses of merchants as well as in houses and on the ships, many of which they had brought from their land and still more they had stored in the Jesuit college. The merchants lived there when they had buyers. If the college served as their place of residence, the church was a wine cellar until the wine was exhausted. It then became a hospital.

In the same manner, all the other churches in the city had been desecrated. Our own order's mother church was used as a warehouse for gunpowder and guns, and a captain and his soldiers lived in the residence hall. The chapel of Nossa Senhora da Ajuda was another storage site for gunpowder. The church of the Misericórdia was used as a hospital. The cathedral was where they prayed and buried their captains. The others were buried in a cemetery at the Rossio, which is in front of the Jesuit college. As a result, there was no other church where the dead had to removed except for the cathedral. The heretics were affected by this since two of their colonels and some other captains were buried in the cathedral. Several Dutchmen were summoned to indicate their graves, remove the bodies, and rebury them in a field. Then the first Mass could be conducted *in gratiarum actionem* [in thanksgiving]. The vicar-general of the bishopric of Brazil sang it in a very solemn manner with the prebendary Francisco Gonçalves on May 5.[1] The deacon and subdeacon were two Castilian religious figures, the chaplains from the fleet.[2] Father Gaspar of the Holy Order of Prayer gave the sermon. He came as confessor for D. Afonso de Noronha. This Mass united all the generals from all the fleets as well as the captains and members of the nobility in the fleets from Portugal and Castile. They did the same in all the other churches to give thanks for the victory and to say prayers for all the Catholics who died obtaining it.

Here I must confess my inability to relate all the jubilation, gratitude, and happiness we all experienced seeing our pulpits, which had been where the Dutch spread heresy, returned to the truth of our holy Catholic faith. The altars, which had been stripped of our saints' images, we now saw were replaced with great reverence. More than anything else, we saw our God in the holy sacrament of the altar, something we had been denied for a year. Our tears had been like bread day and night just as when David's enemies asked him, "Where is your God?"[3]

This gave us even more pleasure when we saw our tears transformed into happiness, giving us our daily host, which is of course God in a type of bread.[4] We then gave thanks for the gifts from our Catholic king since it was by way of his forces that this happened. Everyone knows that if his kingdom of Castile is represented as a beautiful young lady with a sword in one hand and stalks of wheat in the other, it is not to represent strength and fertility but rather that through arms the divine host of the Catholic faith is enjoyed in all of his conquests.

News of this victory was specially entrusted to D. Henrique de Alagon. In the Dutch assault on São Bento, he was injured by two bullets. He was accompanied by Captain D. Pedro Gomes de Porrez, of the Order of Cala- trava. They went in the pinnace led by Captain Martim de Lano.

The letter from D. Fadrique to His Majesty, which they carried with them, read as follows:

My Lord, I have taken the charge of battle for Your Majesty to this province of Brazil, and Your Lordship has been victorious with it. If I have served Your Majesty in this manner, then I am exceedingly honored. I have completed the tasks entrusted to me of providing shelter for those in the city, returning Your Majesty's churches, and dispensing justice. These were Your Majesty's orders as well as punishing the guilty, supplying a few ships with supplies for their return, and preparing and dispatching those who surrendered to their native land. These and another thousand things I lack the time to relate to Your Majesty, and anything missing in this message I will relate in the next one.

D. João Farajado has served Your Majesty better than I have. He par- ticipated with great care in the capture of those Dutchmen leaving their ships. This was no less important than the battle on land. He also served in the second battery that attacked the Dutch ships, sinking some of them. In all these things, he has wanted to serve Your Majesty and assist me with so many responsibilities.

The same can be said of D. Manuel de Menezes. The Marquis of Cropani has worked (even though he is elderly) as if he were a young man with energy and zeal on many occasions. His actions merit honors and a reward from Your Majesty, and I am obligated to ask Your Majesty for them.

The letter continued in this vein, praising others and all of them in the generous manner used by the Castilian nobility. The letter was dated May 12, and it arrived quickly in Madrid where His Majesty ordered a solemn thanks to God for this mercy. This was in addition to the other great victories he experienced in 1625. Cádiz was freed from a powerful fleet of 130 English ships; the Indies fleet that that year was bringing seventeen million in gold, silver, and goods from these lands escaped harm. The miracle was that after the English left Cádiz harbor, His Majesty sent six caravels, offering them big rewards, to find the Indies fleet and tell them to dock in Lisbon or Galicia to avoid falling prey to the enemy. One of the caravels fell into the hands of the English, and they believed that they could find the fleet at forty degrees north latitude and capture it, so they left Cádiz promptly and sailed for that heading. God was served that none of our caravels met the English fleet, and they sailed directly to Cádiz twenty days after the English had left to look for them. His Majesty was informed of this. The English misfortune and our good luck did not end here. The English fleet was so badly damaged by a storm that only a minor part of it returned home.

In Flanders, the powerful city of Breda was taken from the heretics, and in Brazil (as we have said) Bahia was recaptured from other Dutchmen who had occupied it the year before. It must have been the leap year and the year of the jubilee which the Vicar of Christ in Rome proclaimed.[5] He so generously offered and communicated to the faithful the treasure of the church.[6] Through confession, they would be absolved of all sins and censures; frequently these block divine mercy and benefit and we are burdened by punishments. However, the happiness of this year can be attributed to Spain for celebrating and canonizing Saint Elizabeth, the queen of Portugal, born in Aragón.[7] We believe that her intercession and mercy are why God currently offers and will in the future offer many acts of mercy to these kingdoms.

CHAPTER 44

The War Governor Matias de Albuquerque Ordered against the Natives of the Copaoba Mountains Who Rebelled While the Dutch Were Here

It was not just the natives along the seashore who rebelled against the Portuguese during the Dutch occupation. Those in the interior and mountains of Copaoba did as well, killing eighteen of their neighbors and taking six young ladies and some boys captive. To address this, as soon as Francisco Coelho had departed, the captain-major of Paraíba, Afonso da Franca, ordered Captain António Lopes de Oliveira and, under his command, Captains António de Valadares and João Afonso Pinheiro to lead an expedition. They were accompanied by many white men and Father Gaspar da Cruz with the Tabajares, our friends and the enemies of the Potiguar rebels. They were to wage war on them and punish them as they deserved. These people were no longer in the mountains because they had anticipated the arrival of the Portuguese (very common in those who feel guilty) and burned their own villages and churches. Many of them had received the sacrament of baptism. They had run off to join the Tapuias, more than one hundred leagues distant, to get their help defending them from the Portuguese. They offered as presents the young ladies and the boys they had captured in Paraíba.

When Governor Matias de Albuquerque was informed of this, he offered Captain António Lopes de Oliveira and the other captains support for the expedition leaving from Paraíba. This was pending the arrival of more information and a meeting of his council on the justice of waging this war. He called for a meeting in his house of the important religious figures, theologians, and others trained in canon and civil law. They concluded that this was a *just war* and those captured could be enslaved. In Brazil, these are the spoils of war for the soldiers and even act as their salaries. The natives have no other belongings, and those who fight in these wars do not receive any other payments. The governor immediately ordered Captains Simão Fernandes Jácome and Gomes de Abreu Soares to join the expedition and, as their leader, called upon Gregório Lopes de Abreu and his companies.

When these people arrived in Paraíba and learned from António Lopes de Oliveira where the natives had fled, they sent supplies and some men

by sea to Rio Grande. The others left on land with a company of soldiers.
By order of the governor-general, these were led by Captain Francisco
Gomes de Melo and Pero Vaz Pinto, under the command of Gregório
Lopes de Abreu. They began to march through the bush where they
suffered great thirst and hunger. They marched for three days without
finding drinking water, and, at that point, in desperation and lacking any
human remedy, they put their faith in the mercy and intercession of Holy
Saint António, whose image they carried with them. They prayed to him
one afternoon and dug a hole in dry earth asking him to fill it with water.
It was a miracle that after the shovel only hit the earth a couple of times,
so much water flowed forth that everyone's thirst was quenched by that
evening. The next day they were able to fill their containers for the road
and then the hole went dry.

Three days' journey from there, they captured some natives to act as
guides. Previously one of the natives had run off and warned the others
of their arrival. When our men arrived, the natives were ready to fight.
But this was not sufficient to prevent our forces from energetically killing
many; our Tabajares did not spare women or children because of their
animosity toward the rebels.

After the Tapuias had seen the battle for two days, they asked Gregório
Lopes, our commander, why he had come so far into their lands to wage
war when there had never been whites there before? What had they done
to cause this? He responded by saying they had no quarrel with them
but rather they attacked because they [the Tapuias] were protecting and
defending the Potiguarás. These people had rebelled against their king.
They had sworn to be his vassals yet had aided the Dutch and killed several of their Portuguese neighbors in violation of the peace treaties they
had made. They [the Portuguese] had come to set things right, and they
would not leave until they captured them [the Potiguarás] and took them
to the governor or they would die trying.

In the same straightforward manner, the chief of the Tapuias brought
forth the leaders of the rebellion, one named *Cipoúna* and the other *Tiquaruçu*, to conclude a peace agreement, which they did. The outcome of this
was that our forces wanted to hand them over to the governor with all
those from the Copaoba Mountains so that he could dispense justice as he
saw fit. Our men gave them a month to respond. Captain Gregório Lopes

agreed to these terms because many of his troops needed supplies, and he took with him many of their sons as hostages as well as the white girls and boys who had been captured.

They did not agree to these terms, and our men killed their leader Tiquaruçu with a knife in front of all the others. He was the guiltiest. Not so with Cipoúna, who took a chance and brought all his people for the governor to judge. The governor did not keep any of them for himself but rather asked the High Court justice, João de Sousa Cardines, to assign them to the soldiers and other residents. They would serve them as their punishment for rebelling. The Jesuits gathered many of them, since they were better able to instruct and guide them, better than in private homes, as I have said before.

CHAPTER 45
On the Fleet That Came from Holland to Aid the Dutch and What Else Occurred until Our Fleet Departed

It was not possible to say that the war was over, even though we had regained possession of the city from the Dutch, since we awaited the arrival of their fleet to come to their aid. A ship arrived from Angola that had news of a nau and a pinnace near the Morro Hill that had captured two of our ships. One of these had come from Lisbon with supplies for the fleet from Portugal and the other came from the island of Madeira with wines, also intended for the men on the fleet. These had been sent by the Count of Vimioso from his captaincy of Machico.[1] Tristão de Mendonça and Captain Gregório Soares left at the orders of their general, D. Manuel de Menezes, and they captured the ship carrying supplies. It had the Dutchmen in it, and they were brought in, and later D. Fadrique, who did not tolerate others questioning his authority, had Tristão de Mendonça apprehended. D. João Farajardo also ordered a pinnace to collect the ship with the wines. These Dutch prisoners related that their fleet would be arriving with help. A few days later, on the morning of May 26, it appeared at the entrance to the harbor.

Their fleet consisted of thirty-four naus, fifteen of which were the large ones of state and the rest merchant ships. Thus, there were two captains. At two o'clock in the afternoon, they entered the harbor in a line, one after the other, with so much confidence that they probably believed the city was still in their hands. The advice given by the Marques of Cropani was good: our ships should not shoot because they will be right next to them. He also suggested removing the royal Portuguese flag from the cathedral tower and replacing it with the Dutch flag they had captured. Furthermore, our fleet could fire a few shots into the city; cannons in the city could fire at the fleet. This would confirm what the Dutch believed, and they would fall into our hands. However, D. Fadrique quoted Alexander the Great, saying that there was no honor in victory achieved through deception. Instead, he ordered the smallest ships to sail out but not to engage the enemy until they reached the captains' ships. They set sail so late and should have been the first to arrive with favorable winds and tides. Now, this was the other way around; the day was almost over, and the enemy was withdrawing. So, our men fired a shot to signal their return. This was also necessary since one of our galleons, the *Santa Teresa*, was stuck on the shoals of Itaparica, but when its main mast was cut, it was freed and out of danger.

The Dutch had three ships stuck on the shoals and went out that night to rescue them at high tide. They only lost two lifeboats that broke free or were untied and the Dutch captain's flag that the admiralty ship from Naples shot down. This was where we lost the most glorious undertaking we could have achieved. Along with what we accomplished in the city, our enemies' arms would have been broken so they would have been unable to harm us so quickly. However, it seems that God wanted them to remain in Brazil as punishment for our sins, as he left the Canaanites for the children of Israel.

They went from this bay to the Bay of Traição, and D. Fadrique was informed of this by way of Pernambuco. He ordered that the fleet be readied quickly to see if they could capture them, in case they were still there. In order to do this, he sent João Vincêncio Sanfelice, whose opinion was very valued in these matters, and General Francisco de Vallecilha, who was knowledgeable in maritime affairs. They met in Pernambuco with Governor Matias de Albuquerque and other knowledgeable people to discuss the details and size of the Bay of Traição. They wanted to know if they encountered the Dutch fleet there, could the Spanish fleet enter the bay and dislodge it? In the event that was not possible, what then would be the best course of action? They wanted to make plans now in order to avoid wasting time when they arrived in Pernambuco.

To conduct this meeting, the governor called for all the pilots to join him in his house and express their opinions. They agreed that the mouth of that bay was only fifteen or sixteen spans deep and that it would be impossible for the Spanish fleet to enter it. In addition, the deepest part of the bay was occupied by the Dutch fleet. As a result, it would be better for our fleet to anchor at the sandbar and attack on land to force them to leave. In order to do this, they had prepared one hundred yokes of oxen and carts to transport the artillery as well as one thousand natives from Paraíba and one thousand white men from Pernambuco with those sent by D. Fadrique. This would be sufficient to accomplish this. With this decision, they concluded discussing matters pertaining to Bahia.

He also ordered the hanging of four Portuguese prisoners who had voluntarily remained in the city with the Dutch as well as six of the negros who had joined them. This was after each one was heard and judged by the auditor-general. He distributed the goods the Dutch had taken from the residents and merchants to the soldiers. They brought out a crier who proclaimed, right to the point, from the first chapter of Joel, *residuum erucae comedit locusta.*[2] What was left *residiuum locustae comedit bruchus* was consumed by the one thousand soldiers whom the general left in the presidio of the city.[3] They were commanded by master sergeant Pedro Correia, who had been in one of the regiments from Portugal. He was an old, experienced soldier who had served in the wars in Flanders.

The infantry captains were Francisco de Padilha, Manuel Gonçalves, António de Morais, and Pero Mendes, who had been captain of the assault forces. The captain-major and governor on land was D. Francisco de Moura, who held those titles before. He said his goodbyes to the monasteries, giving each a donation of 200 cruzados. The ships the Dutch had sunk he ordered salvaged so that they could be sold to repair the walls, which had been badly damaged when they were made into bulwarks with defensive trenches.

They set forth on July 25, asking for Our Lord to guide them on that Day of Holy Saint James, the patron saint of Spain. However, because the wind was blowing against them, they could not leave the bay until August 4. By that time, three of the ships had Dutchmen on board, separated from the others, and they departed.

CHAPTER 46

The Return of Our Fleet to Portugal and the Dutch to Their Land

Our fleet departed Bahia in a storm, as I stated at the end of chapter 44. A hole opened in one of the galleons from Spain, allowing the water to pour in, and it was forced to return. Once repaired, it left in the company of another ship, which was unable to leave with the fleet. These survived another storm once they left, one that was so strong that they were unable to reach Pernambuco where they were awaited with high expectations. This was not because they were needed to fight the Dutch, who had departed, but rather to honor the arrival of His Excellency and the others by attending many planned parties. The lord of the region, Duarte de Albuquerque Coelho, was especially saddened because he was unable to see the ships. He suffered the fate of Tantalus, not being able to enjoy what he saw or what was around him, neither their departures from Bahia nor their arrival in Pernambuco.[1]

At this point, each ship went where the storm took it. Much later, some of them survived in the Azores where the admiral's ship was lost off the island of São Jorge. However, Admiral D. Francisco de Almeida and those with him survived by continually working the pump. They had no food since it had spoiled in the water, and many crew members became ill and died on this same island. Among these was D. António de Castelo Branco, Lord of Pombeiro. Our Lord has him in His glory as I trust in His divine mercy. From what I know of the man while he was in Bahia, he gave his confession and took communion weekly and attended Mass daily. He was generous in charity and had other virtues, which like precious stones cast onto the fine gold dust of nobility, made them brightly shimmer.

From the island of São Jorge, the admiral and his men left in a few ships for Terceira and from there for Lisbon. The first night they suffered such a strong wind that it broke the masts on one ship and the ship sank. The others sailed for six days in the storm before they reached Lisbon. They gave thanks to God for freeing them from such dangers. The galleon carrying D. Afonso de Alencastre was taking on a lot of water, and they could not save it. The passengers were transferred to another ship, and they burned the sinking ship. Constantino de Melo and Diogo Varejão encountered six Dutch ships and fought with them, and Varajão's ship surrendered, leaving only de Melo's. They continued fighting with such valor that he would have won except for the three naus of state that survived. In the end, they captured his ship, took him to Holland, and robbed him of all he carried except for his fame as a captain, which was widespread and is a good thing to tell all the world.

D. Manuel de Menezes, general of the Portuguese fleet, arrived in Lisbon on October 14, having fought with two Dutch galleons at the stopover on São Jorge Island. They came loaded from Mina. After attacking one, he left the *Santa Ana das Quatro Vilas* that sailed in its wake with D. João de Orelhana serving as field master. He went after the other ship, which was escaping, and, with luck, he would have captured it since his ship was strong and swift. But he had to turn around and assist the *Santa Ana* because it was burning. It had been boarded and surrendered to the Dutch. Many of the men had moved to our ship, and they removed those remaining who did not want to leave. I do not know whether it was these men or whether it was an accident, but their ship caught fire, and it immediately spread to our ship and engulfed them both. Only 148 men were saved by diving into the water, and when D. Manuel saw the fire, he stopped chasing the fleeing galleon and helped by launching small boats, rafts, boards, and anything else to save the drowning men. The others all died in the fire along with the field master D. João de Orelhana, D. António de Luna de Menezes, and many others.

D. Fadrique de Toledo along with most of the fleet had drifted with time to the mouth of the Bay of Málaga. Some nobles left from there to travel to Portugal, and in Seville they learned in a letter from His Majesty that there was an English fleet of 130 ships anchored in the port of Cádiz. They quickly returned the way they had come, believing this was required of them rather than a long journey that took them home. Those who returned were João da Silva Telo; D. Duarte de Menezes, the Count of Tarouca; D. Lopo da Cunha, the Lord of Santar; his brother-in-law Francisco de Melo e Castro; D. Francisco Luís de Faro, the son of Count D. Estêvão de Faro; António Taveira de Avelar; and D. Nuno Mascarenhas. They took the road from Seville to Jerez, where the Duke of Medina-Sidónia, the nephew of Rui Gomes da Silva, and so related to the Portuguese, offered them an exceptional display of hospitality and courtesy, which such valor merited.

They discussed the reason for their arrival, which was to continue to Cádiz to assist in its defense. They asked the duke for a galley to take them there. The duke told them of the difficulties with this, so they went to defend the bridge at Suasso, where there were four thousand men waiting. However, a notice later arrived from D. Fernando Girão in Cádiz saying that he had been able to assist three hundred men to secretly enter the city. These were the Portuguese nobles who were at the forefront with their pikes. They had walked three leagues in rain and water in many places up to their knees until they entered the city at eleven o'clock at night. D. Fernando Girão went to look for them in their lodgings and assured them the enemy would lose their fleet, since with their aid, they could destroy it. In Cádiz, they undertook all sorts of dangerous military actions until the enemy departed.

No lesser praise should be given to D. Afonso de Noronha, António Moniz Barreto, Henrique Henriques, and D. Afonso de Alencastre. Even though they arrived in Cádiz after the enemy had left, theologians tell us that having an active willingness is equal to the deed, if it cannot be done. His Majesty was grateful, writing to the council saying that he had been informed of the valor of the Portuguese nobility who served him on this occasion. They were prepared to die in his service, not lacking in willingness, and their spirit was boundless. He ordered that each be given what the crown awards to surviving children or heirs of those who died in royal service. He further ordered that they be awarded all the other gifts he had awarded to those who had died in this enterprise with no additional requests necessary.

The substance of his letter was as follows:

Governor friends, I, the King, send you greetings as those that I love.

Having understood the good deeds and the service done by the Portuguese nobles who captured the Bay of All Saints and desiring them to know how well I was served and what satisfaction I have in their persons, it is good that in the first place they, the sons of Martim Afonso de Oliveira, receive the same gifts awarded to those who died in this undertaking. These sons should consult me should there be anything else by which I can show my appreciation and sentiments regarding the death of their father since he was such an honorable nobleman and so zealous in my service. This is not awarded because of any particular trait of his but rather because of my satisfaction in the manner in which he served as well as in the acts themselves. For the other nobles, it is my wish that they be awarded all the gifts given to those who died in my service, since there was nothing more they could have done. It is my deepest wish that those who serve me know my gratitude and willingness to reward them with these same gifts. There is no need for additional requests, negotiations, notes, or trips. This is given for service to me, and for that reason, I make this decision without any opinions from the council, and it will be resolved this way. Written in Madrid on September 18, 1625. The King.

It is not possible to witness a greater demonstration of love from His Majesty for the Kingdom of Portugal since this was done without any opinions from the council of state and only done out of love. The king did this of his own accord, writing a royal decree that was so favorable for this kingdom. He was no less generous to those from the Kingdom of Castile, giving one and the other great gifts, but the greatest gift was from God this year of 1625. That was the general jubilee, which the Vicar of Christ in Rome so generously began, offering the faithful the treasure of the Church.

The Lord freed Cádiz (as we have seen) from the powerful English fleet and miraculously saved the Indies fleet, which that year was carrying seventeen million in gold, silver, and goods from Spanish America. The miracle was such that while the English were anchored in Cádiz Bay, His Majesty sent six caravels with large prizes to reach the Indies fleet, directing them to anchor in Lisbon or Galicia to avoid capture by the enemy. One of the caravels fell into the hands of the English, and they were certain they would be able to capture the fleet if they waited for it at forty degrees north latitude. As a result, they quickly left Cádiz harbor for that heading. God was pleased that none of our caravels reached the Indies fleet, and they came to Cádiz directly twenty days after the English had left, moving to where they thought the fleet would appear. His Majesty was informed of this. When he learned this news, he gave thanks to God for such a huge act of grace, especially so when he learned the English fleet was nearly destroyed by a storm and only a small part of it returned home.

In Flanders, the powerful city of Breda was taken from the heretics. In Brazil, Bahia was recaptured from other heretical Dutchmen who had occupied it the year before. It must have been the canonizing of Saint Elizabeth, the queen of Portugal, from Aragón that made this possible. Through her intercession and mercy, we can believe, God currently offers and will offer many acts of mercy to these kingdoms.

The Dutch also suffered through great storms at sea after they left Bahia, even though their ships were not fully loaded, which is a plus only realized in storms. No less a fate awaited them on land when they reached Holland. They were all immediately arrested by their own people and sentenced to death for surrendering and leaving the city so soon. In addition, they had relinquished all the goods they had gained in Bahia and not awaited the arrival of the fleet to aid them. The women, children, and relatives of these people came to their aid and explained they all would have died had they not handed over the city. They explained the late arrival of the fleet, the great dangers in which our forces had placed them, and other things. In the end, the authorities freed them and allowed them to live; their punishment was to not receive the salaries they were due.

Those on the Dutch fleet who had come to their aid left the Bay of Traição for Puerto Rico, which is in the Spanish Indies. They found the people there with their guard down, and they left their ships and sacked the town. The captain of the fort at the harbor entrance came to help. The entrance to the port is tight, and he closed it so they could not leave where they entered. The Dutch were so hard-pressed that they would have surrendered what they had taken as well as some of their own goods in order to be allowed to leave. The captain did not agree to this because he felt he had won and because he feared the king would disapprove. He was mistaken on both counts. The enemy was very strong in their naus and had all their stolen goods bundled and packed beneath them. They were only awaiting a dark night with winds and a storm to allow them to leave. It came one night, and they escaped and could not be stopped or damaged, except for an old nau that they made into a target. His Majesty ordered the captain's head cut off, not for accepting the agreement offered by the Dutch, but because he thought everything was the captain's fault.

CHAPTER 47
How Governor Matias de Albuquerque Ordered a Party to Locate the Cargo of a Nau from India Shipwrecked on Santa Helena Island

It was Divine Providence that the two galleons mentioned in the last chapter remained in Bahia. One of these was from the squadron from Biscay, called the *Nossa Senhora da Atalaia*, with Captain João Martins de Arteagoa. The other was from the squadron of the straits and was

named the *São Miguel*, with Captain Francisco Cestim. These ships were
very useful and required to collect the cargo from the nau *Conceição*. It
unloaded its cargo on Santa Helena Island because it was taking on water
and sank. It was on its return voyage from India in the company of four
other ships. These were led by Captain-Major D. António Telo. Since
the *Conceição* could not continue its voyage, they removed what they
could from it along with its crew and Captain D. Francisco de Sá and left
António Gonçalves to remain on the island with 120 white men and some
Africans to guard the goods. They wrote a note to the governor of Brazil
and dispatched it in a lifeboat, asking him to send ships.

The little boat arrived in Pernambuco, where Governor Matias de
Albuquerque was, on August 18, 1625. He informed D. Fadrique and
asked D. Fadrique to allow the four *urcas* there awaiting the arrival of the
armada with supplies [to leave for Santa Helena]. These were led by Captain João Luís Camerena. D. Fadrique received this news by sea and sent
these two galleons from Bahia because he needed the four *urcas* and their
supplies for the fleet. When the governor heard this, he sent a caravel
with provisions to Santa Helena Island captained by Mateus Rodovalho.
He also sent two naus to Bahia, one called the *São Bom Homen*, with Captain António Teixeira, and the other, the *Churrião*, with Captain Custódio
Favacho, carrying provisions paid for by His Majesty and supplied by
Jerónimo Domingues. These were to accompany the two galleons, which
they did, as did a third nau called the *Rata*, sent by D. Francisco de Moura
and led by Captain Rodrigo Álvares.

They arrived at Santa Helena Island on December 27, 1625, and found
the men from India in trenches with the goods. They had constructed
three batteries and placed six pieces of artillery on them. They had first
fought a Dutch nau and later four Dutch and English naus. They fought so
bravely that the Dutch and English did not dare land on the island and left
with many dead.

Our ships were almost done loading the cargo when a large Dutch nau
arrived, larger than the naus used on the run to India. It had forty pieces
of artillery, and it slipped between the two galleons. They began to fight
the Dutch ship and boarded it, attacking those on the deck who knew
they had lost. Our forces took command of the deck and cut the rigging
and sails, calling for those under the netting to surrender. They said they
would not because the devil was in their hearts. They then fought like

those possessed by demons, wounding and killing with their pikes sticking through the netting, firing the cannons filled with stones aimed at
many of our men. Among those who died was Captain Arteagoa. Because
they feared the fire the Dutch were using, they separated from it, and the
Dutch nau left with all the riches it brought from Ternate.[1]

Our men completed the loading but left the anchor cables and other
rigging because there was no more room.

They left on February 7, 1626, led by Captain-Major Filipe de Chaver-
ria, who was acting for the captain who had died in the battle. They
arrived in Pernambuco on March 1, and the governor provided them
with all they needed for their voyage. The same merchant supplied them
as did the customs official João de Albuquerque de Melo. They set sail for
Portugal in the company of other merchant ships on the eighteenth of
that month and arrived safely in Lisbon on May 15.

CHAPTER 48
Regarding the Dutch Who Sailed along the Coast of Bahia to
Paraíba in the Year 1626 and the Departure of Governor Francisco Coelho
de Carvalho for Maranhão

On April 19, 1626, three Dutch warships appeared at the entrance to
the Bay of All Saints next to Morro Hill. One of them had heavy artillery
pieces and 140 soldiers. They sank a caravel coming from Angola whose
captain, António Farinha from Sesimbra, refused to strike his sails. They
saved all the white people and some of the 170 negros the ship was carrying. They kept them on their ships for eleven days, and they were well
treated since (as they later said) these were their orders from the Prince
of Orange.[1] This was out of respect for the good treatment offered to the
Dutch by D. Fadrique de Toledo when we recaptured the city. They later
unloaded these people at the Contas River, where they stopped to collect water. They met with another squadron of four ships and a pinnace
coming from Pernambuco. They all anchored there on May 20 except for
the pinnace, which was a swift ship with only ten artillery pieces. It sailed
from one place to another along the coast. This pinnace seized a sloop
at Paripuera, thirty leagues from Pernambuco to Bahia, a boat sent by
the governor to give warning. It also captured a ship from Viana, which
had left Recife loaded with six hundred crates of sugar. Because it was

overloaded and the crates were placed among the artillery pieces, our men could not use them; they failed to capture the Dutch pinnace. This is something His Majesty's ministers should take care to avoid in these parts. This was not the first ship lost because of this, and it will not be the last if there is no oversight to prevent overloading.

These ships also captured one headed for Angola and a caravel coming from Madeira loaded with wine, unloading all the crews on the island of Santo Aleixo.

They chased a caravel coming from the rivers of the Congo that took shelter in Pau-Amarelo's port and another ship from Sesimbra that went into the shallow waters near Cape Saint Agostinho. While it was along the entrance to Recife, it entered the port. Three ships from Lisbon and two from the Canaries did the same because the governor sent a boat to warn them at the cape. This is a stop for those ships headed for Pernambuco in May and other winter months.

Governor-General Matias de Albuquerque sent two local natives and a mulatto, each on his own raft, to start fires on the Dutch ships, which were more than four leagues at sea, beyond the reef. One of these men, named *Salvador*, reached the stern of the captain's ship but was discovered by a dog that alerted the crew, and the crew extinguished the fire. They alerted the others with a warning shot, and, in their anger the next day, the Dutch burned a captured caravel. Its captain had refused to pay them the fifty cruzados they wanted. With that, they hoisted anchor and departed.

Francisco Coelho de Carvalho, the governor of Maranhão, was finally able to leave as well. He had been in Pernambuco for two years and was unable to depart for Maranhão because of the Dutch. In addition, he was awaiting the payment of 20,000 cruzados from the king. As soon as the Dutch were gone and his way was clear, he departed on July 13, 1626, in a fleet of five ships loaned to him by Governor Matias de Albuquerque. As he was leaving the harbor of Recife, Albuquerque ordered the cannons in the fort to fire a salute.

He traveled in one of the ships with his son, Feliciano Coelho de Carvalho, and the master sergeant Manuel Soares de Almeida. The captains of the other ships were Manuel de Sousa Deca, captain-major of Pará; Jácome de Reimonde, the superintendent of the treasury; and João Maciel. It took them fifteen days to reach Ceará because they did not sail at night.

They remained there another fifteen days, and the governor supplied the fort with gunpowder and artillery and paid the salaries for the soldiers. Captain Martim Soares Moreno was awarded the Order of Saint James by the king for his services. It had not been any small thing he had done, not just in the exploration of Maranhão, as I have stated in the first chapter of this book, but also in his actions as captain of Ceará. The pirates feared him so much that even though they anchored there several times, they were afraid to disembark. He was so eager to have them land that he joined the natives and was naked and painted to be their color. He thought that the pirates would think these natives were their friends and not fear them. Thus, they would leave their ships, and he would capture them, but even this did not work. In performing this deception, it appeared he was not performing his job adequately. When His Majesty awarded him this order, it was with a small allowance, which was why God gave him a lot of ambergris on that beach to ensure he was never hungry.[2]

Father Cristóvão Severim was in Ceará for the same reason. He is the father superior of Maranhão and had only been there a few days but spent many on the way there overland. He had suffered terrible thirst and hunger and fought with the native Tapuias, Arechis, and Uruatins. The natives attacked his party twice and killed one of the natives traveling with him, wounding thirteen other natives and three Portuguese. There were so many more of the enemy than the few men with him. There were only six white men with harquebuses accompanying the father to help him. In their encounters, they fought so bravely they were able to escape from the natives. They left some of the enemy dead and wounded and arrived in Ceará, where the father and his companion were welcomed by the Jesuits. They were traveling with Governor Francisco Coelho de Carvalho and from there they all departed for Maranhão. On that section of the trip, after passing the Cove of the Turtles, they lacked pilots familiar with the coast. They struck some shoals in a huge storm, and they thought all was lost. However, Our Lord sent in more water and with that and after casting some cargo overboard, they were able to set sail and continue their voyage to Maranhão. The governor and those with him were sheltered there. This is where we will leave them for other historians in their works because His Majesty has separated that government from Brazil, from where I am writing, and I am about to finish this history as well.[3]

CHAPTER 49

How Diogo Luís de Oliveira Arrived to Govern Brazil and His Predecessor
Matias de Albuquerque Departed for Portugal

On August 25, 1625, Diogo Luís de Oliveira left Lisbon to govern Brazil.
He had been a field master in Flanders. He arrived in Pernambuco on
November 7 and left the *urcas* beyond the entrance bar because he did not
have a lot of time to remain there. He came in a sloop and went to stay
at the Monastery of Saint Anthony, which we have in Recife. He stayed
there until the Day of Bishop Saint Martin, which is November 11.[1] He
then went to the town accompanied by eighty gentlemen.

At the customs building at the town entrance, a triumphal arch was
erected. It was of a pleasant design ornamented with verses, designs, and
epigrams worked into it. From there, two lines of soldiers with harquebuses were along the wall to the gate of the Misericórdia where there was
a second arch, equally beautiful in design. They stopped at this arch, and
André de Albuquerque, the oldest town councilor, gave a speech. From
there, they escorted him under a canopy to the main church. Leading the
way was the field master general of Brazil, D. Vasco Mascarenhas (a new
position created for Brazil) and the captains-major of Pernambuco, André
Dias de Franca, and of Itamaracá, Pero da Mota Leite. They were all new
arrivals from Portugal who came with the governor. The people of Olinda
were there as well and greeted them with a great deal of applause. After
the prayers and usual ceremonies, they went to the house of his anteces-
sor, which had been vacated for the occasion.

The two of them visited each other many times and showed great
friendship while the governor was there, which was until December 20,
1626. A message arrived saying that a Dutch ship with two sloops was at
the entrance of the harbor of Guiena They had captured a ship belonging to Pero Peres loaded with sugar, chased another ship that docked in
Paraíba, and pursued a third vessel from Biscay loaded with wine from
Madeira. The governor left hoping to be able to capture this Dutch ship;
however, the thief fled when he spotted so many ships. The governor and
his party arrived safely in Bahia, and the first thing he did was to arrange a
solemn Mass for his deceased brother, the heir to the estate of Oliveira, in
the Church of Nossa Senhora do Carmo where he was buried.

Two months after his arrival, on March 3, 1627, thirteen Dutch ships entered the harbor and captured twenty-one of our vessels docked in port with cargos of three thousand crates of sugar. The Dutch lost two of their ships including that of their captain. Their general Pero Peres, an Englishman, was on board. He had been an admiral in the conquest of Bahia. They lost this ship because of their brashness in wanting to get so close to the land that they were stuck in shallow water. The artillery from our fort destroyed his ship without the other ship being able to assist him. It caught on fire, and the crew climbed higher until the ship sank and the water extinguished the flames. Only a few were saved by swimming or fleeing in lifeboats. Later on, the governor ordered a salvage operation, which was done by some negro divers owned by Gaspar de Azevedo. They found twenty bronze and forty iron artillery pieces and one hundred barrels of wet gunpowder. They used the nitrate to mix with local powder. All this partially compensated for the damages they caused.

When Matias de Albuquerque saw that the Dutch had taken the *urcas* in which he had planned to return to Lisbon, he chose to travel on a light caravel. He departed on June 18 after three other Dutch ships left. They had been around the entrance to Pernambuco harbor for two months. He took with him Dr. Bartolomeu Ferreira Lagrato, the vicar of Paraíba and administrator before this jurisdiction was united, and a brother of our order.

The entire time Matias de Albuquerque served in Brazil, which was seven years as captain-major of Pernambuco and governor-general of Brazil, he was very honest. He did not accept anything from anyone, nor did he give offices to his underlings. When he waged war or other times in His Majesty's service, he was always diligent and indefatigable, working day and night. He was never carried around in a hammock, as is the custom here in Brazil, but rather went on horse or by boat. When he used these, he did not sit but stood and guided. He had a good memory and remembered people even if he had only seen them once. This was extended to the ships that docked in port only once. When one returned after a long time, before the captain arrived, he knew who composed the crew. Sometimes a ship would come with a new mainmast, and he would spot it with a telescope from a distance and say, "That is such and such a ship, which was here a year ago, but it now has a new mainmast." That would be affirmed by the captain after he arrived and was questioned.

He had good luck with his administration even though there were disasters. On the return voyage, God spared him from the innumerable pirates that infest the sea, taking him to safety in fifty-two days to Caminha. There he met the Duke of Caminha and the Marques of Vila Real, D. Miguel de Menezes, his relative. We will leave him there and conclude this history because I am sixty-three years old, and it is now time to deal with my life and not that of others.

[The following passages from the *Santuário Mariano* must come from a complete copy of this work, but such a copy has not yet been found. It is also not known exactly where these passages would have appeared in the complete text.]

Additional Section 1

In regard to the spiritual well-being of the colony, it should be known that when the bishop of Bahia, D. Constantino Barradas, went to visit Pernambuco and the other churches in the north, such a long journey was tiresome and dangerous for him. In order to address these difficulties, he wrote the king of Castile, D. Filipe III, in 1615, requesting he make Pernambuco and Rio de Janeiro bishoprics, separate from the administration of Bahia since the land was fertile with many taxes. This was in order to lift the burden from the bishop of Bahia of visitations to Pernambuco, Paraíba, and the other lands of the north as well as to Rio de Janeiro and lands in the south. The king was resolved to name ecclesiastical administrators who would be independent of the bishop. In order to do this, he obtained a bull from Pope Paul V separating Pernambuco, Paraíba, and lands in the north from the jurisdiction of the bishop in Bahia, and he did the same with the lands in Rio de Janeiro and the other lands to the south. These bulls conceded the right to the king to name the administrators, and they would be subject to his discipline and authority and their sentencing would be under his review.

Additional Section 2

After this initial discovery, Francisco Caldeira de Castelo Branco left the Maranhão River, which is 130 leagues from Grão-Pará. He was in the company of two religious figures of Saint Anthony, called Brother António da Merciana and Brother Cristóvão de São José, and they sailed upriver thirty leagues, where they disembarked on the south shore and selected a good site. They built a wooden fortress, and they named it

Presépio since they had left Maranhão on Christmas Day to begin this expedition.[2] They did all this with no difficulties from the native people. However, this did not end their fear of them, since there so many who came to assist them and request tools and other things that had been given to the first natives. They did not have anything more to give them nor did they have gunpowder or bullets to defend themselves.

Realizing this impossible and dangerous situation, Captain Francisco Caldeira ordered a messenger to travel overland with letters requesting supplies from the captain-major of Maranhão, Jerónimo de Albuquerque. He selected António da Costa for this expedition, and he left on March 7, 1616, along with Pedro Teixeira, two other white men, and thirty natives. They could row a canoe when it was needed and also find the way on land. There are a number of large, salty rivers there, and they had many days of great hunger and thirst since most of the natives in the region are wild. They had never before seen white men or men who wore clothes. Some of them were hospitable and offered festivities; others ran away in fear. Still others would have killed them but for the defense provided by the natives traveling with them. It was mostly God who defended them and brought them to Maranhão because a great deal of goodwill came to the souls of those natives who live there.

They arrived in Maranhão on May 7, two months after leaving Pará, and were warmly welcomed by Jerónimo de Albuquerque. When he learned why they were there, he quickly sent a sloop captained by Salvador de Melo, his nephew, with thirty men with harquebuses and 2,000 cruzados worth of trading goods and soldiers' salaries. This was a great help for Pará at that time, and António da Costa left for Pernambuco with other letters for the governor-general.

Captain Francisco Caldeira did not have any difficulties from the natives from Pará or the Amazon River in colonizing the region. He faced contention and discord from his own men, who not only refused to obey him but held him captive and selected another as captain. This was why the natives refused to make peace, saying clearly that they did not want peace with people who did not enjoy it themselves.

Because of this, and because of some injuries they received from people trading in their villages and killing them, the natives rebelled and laid siege to this new town in Pará. Captain Manuel Soares de Almeida was able to escape from it and went to Pernambuco to seek help. That was where he found Governor-General D. Luís de Sousa, and, once he was informed of this, he quickly ordered a fleet of four ships. The governor sent Jerónimo Fragoso de Albuquerque to discover who was guilty, to charge them, and send them to Portugal. He remained there as captain until the king was able to issue an order. The king was also aware of this disturbance and uprising and ordered Monsieur Reverdière, a Frenchman, to be held in the Tower of Belém. He was in Lisbon with a petition and would not return there in the middle of this disturbance. It was possible to presume this of him because he seemed so fond of that land. In recognition for his services to the king, having evacuated Maranhão, its fortress, and its artillery, he only asked to send two merchant ships there each year. This seemed to originate from a love of that land rather than from greed because at that time there were not even any mills making sugar nor was there any brazilwood. These are the goods merchants want from Brazil. In that manner, they understood that he had the hunger for gold because he said he could mine it easily from the upper Amazon. He said the Amazon was navigable and sprang from a golden lagoon where the natives had booty in their canoes of gold chains because there was so much of it around them.

When Jerónimo de Albuquerque arrived at the fort in Pará and found our people still surrounded and hungry, after addressing this and his supplies, he sent Francisco Caldeira as a prisoner along with the other guilty parties to Portugal. He pursued the natives nearly two hundred leagues upriver where he died after having accomplished many things. So did Captains Custódio Valente and Pedro Teixeira as well as others who greatly distinguished themselves, but especially Captain Bento Maciel, who had come from Maranhão with eighty Portuguese men and six hundred allied native archers. They caused great devastation for the other natives since many fled from their villages into the bush and fell into the hands of the Tapuias, their enemies, who killed them and ate them. Others were of value to the Portuguese in the fort since they asked for peace and mercy.

Father Manuel Filgueira de Mendonça, the curate of that new village, gathered the natives in a town in Separará, which is at the east entrance to the harbor of Pará. He promised to help and defend them if they remained faithful to the Church. In that way, the region was pacified and the number of residents grew.

Additional Section 3

Cape Frio is a noteworthy stopping point or exquisite site along the southern coast. It is at twenty-three degrees south latitude as is Rio de Janeiro, because at that point the coastline runs east to west and there are many deep bays along it. The French like it a lot for that reason. It also has some islands and good anchorage for all sorts of ships.

Because of this, the French continued to frequent that area. There is a lot of high-quality brazilwood there. When the French cut and gathered it for dye, other ships accompanied them and robbed our ships passing by from Rio de Janeiro, Rio de la Plata, and elsewhere. The king was informed of this. In particular, five French ships were there at that time, loaded with axes, saws, and other tools needed to cut the brazilwood trees; they were loading the wood in total safety. This was in spite of the forces sent by Captain Constantino Menelau, the captain-major of Rio de Janeiro, to defend it. Cape Frio is in his district, but the ships had already been loaded and departed in peace. The king was aware that they easily loaded their ships there because there were no nearby settlements. It was far away from Rio de Janeiro, and they could not send help quickly to stop the French. The king wrote to Governor Gaspar de Sousa strongly urging him to colonize and fortify the area. The governor learned that Estêvão Gomes, a resident of Rio de Janeiro, could accomplish this task since he was a wealthy man and an owner of two sugar mills. In all of the encounters they had with the pirates, he was one of the first to assist energetically with his slaves and canoes and had the support of all the captains-major. He passed a provision asking him to go to Cape Frio and start a settlement and to do as he hoped. He passed a second provision for Constantino Menelau stating that royal funds would pay for soldiers, supplies, and everything else required for the colonization and defense of that region.

Estêvão Gomes accepted the task given to him and spent much of his own money to colonize and fortify the area. The natives from a nearby village were a great help in these tasks. The Jesuit fathers had brought them from Espírito Santo. They went forth with them to confront twenty-odd Dutchmen. They left a large nau there to find water, and they killed eighteen. Only three or four were able to escape in a lifeboat to warn other Dutchmen in a second boat headed for the same place to find water. They were on their way to India and really needed water. Because of that, they were ready to kill fifty Portuguese captives from a ship bound for Mina.[3] They would have done this but for their preacher, who although a heretic, said that it was an injustice for the innocent to pay for the crimes of the guilty. He also said they had not sinned by defending water on their land. Their own men who had escaped complained less about the Portuguese than about the cruel natives, so they sent a longboat with a white flag and a letter addressed to the captain, asking for several *pipas* of water in exchange for their Portuguese prisoners.

The captain informed the governor of Rio de Janeiro, to whom he reported, but the governor was no longer Constantino Menelau but rather Rui Vaz Pinto, who succeeded him. This new governor created an advisory committee of religious figures and town counsellors to address this issue. They agreed that he should give the Dutch the water, which they did, and the Dutch freed all the Portuguese prisoners except for the captain of the ship, whom they took with them.

The negros told a big joke about this trade, saying that a negro was worth more than fifty white men because negros were normally sold for forty *milréis* (that was the price then) and white men cost less than one *pipa* of water.

The captain also made peace with the native Guaitcases who live nearby, who had never been subjugated, even though Miguel de Azeredo, when he was captain of Espírito Santo, and others from Rio de Janeiro had tried in the past. These natives lived in marshy lands more like sailors than those who live on land. Just when our forces would reach them, they would escape into the marsh, and our men could not follow on foot or on horseback.

Because they suffered from a deadly outbreak of the sickness causing pustules, they surrendered to Captain Estêvão Gomes, saying they wanted to be our friends and trade with the whites. By this turn of events, this new region of Cape Frio was pacified in 1615, more or less. This town is of no little importance, but the Portuguese only know how to conquer, not colonize.

In this port, there is a deep section or bay, something unique in nature, as if it were deliberately dug along the edge of a rocky place, which acts like a wall or fort at its entrance. The bay is long and stretched out and able to hold many ships. They can be anchored in safety, as if they were home, protected from injuries from the winds with just this bar separating them from the sea. From January until the end of February, the waters in this bay collect at its edges and in hidden inlets where it is transformed into the purest form of salt and in such quantity that it can fill many large naus.

What we have stated here is regarding the quality and fertility of the land. If it were populated by outsiders, it could become a large city. But now it is so small that it is a city in name only. It is so poor that hardly anyone lives there, just a few fishermen. Even though the town is the oldest in the area, someone viewing it would think it was just established because of the few inhabitants, as I have said.

When Estêvão Gomes founded the town, he also constructed the principal church. It is dedicated to the Assumption of the Mother of God, and she is the town patron and the lady whose compassion blesses its residents. It is the only parish in the city of Cape Frio.

NOTES

BOOK 1

Foreword

1. These details of Frei Vicente's life are drawn from Maria Lêda Oliveira, *A "História do Brazil" de Frei Vicente to Salvador: história e política no Império Português do século XVII* (Rio de Janeiro: Versal/São Paulo: Odebrecht, 2008), 1:15–47.

Tables

1. These lists and dates are from David P. Henige, *Colonial Governors from the Fifteenth Century to the Present* (Madison: University of Wisconsin Press, 1970), 233–319.

The History of Brazil, 1500–1627

2. Father Manuel Severim de Faria lived from 1582 to 1655 and was a Renaissance scholar and author of numerous works on Portuguese history as well as political, economic, and religious themes.

3. Plutarch was a Greek biographer and author of essays who lived from 46 to 120 CE.

4. Also known as Diodorus of Sicily, a Greek historian who lived in the first century BCE and wrote a multivolume universal history.

5. While writing favors the favor itself, and lessens the labor: / While his growing chest glows with work.

6. Luís de Camões is one of the greatest poets of Portugal. He lived from 1524 to 1580 and is most famous for *The Lusiads*. João de Barros was a great historian who lived from 1496 to 1570 and is best known for his *Décadas da Ásia*. Diogo do Couto lived from 1542 to 1616 and was another famous historian of Portuguese Asia, author of *The Veteran Soldier*.

7. A noble's request carries the weight of a command.

8. Bishop and saint who lived from 320 to 401 CE.

9. Bishop Simpliciano, *De diversis quaestionibus ad Simplicianum*. "I fear that these things which I have said may not have met your expectations and may have been tiresome, since out of all of that which you inquired you should wish me to send one little book, I sent two books, and the same of considerable

length, and perhaps I responded by no means promptly but diligently to the questions."

10. Gen. 27:8–10. Isaac and Rebecca had twin sons, Jacob and Esau. Esau was firstborn, but Jacob tricked their blind father into giving him the older son's blessing.

Chapter 1

1. That is, four continents if North and South America are counted as one and Antarctica and Australia (unknown to the Portuguese at the time) are not counted. There is no proof the Portuguese were aware of the existence of Brazil before 1500; nevertheless, there is an old debate in some of the literature regarding this.

2. The host is the consecrated wafer offered to the faithful during Mass. Catholics believe that the host becomes part of the body of Christ as a result of ceremonies conducted during the Mass. The chalice is a cup that holds the wine, which in turn is the blood of Christ. This process is known as *transubstantiation.*

3. The *invitatorium* is the opening or beginning of Mass, inviting the faithful to join the ceremony.

4. Come let us adore Christ the king, who rules over all men [nations], who gives fullness [richness] of spirit to those who consume him.

5. Leaving convicts behind to learn the local languages and customs was part of the process of Portuguese expansion into the south Atlantic.

Chapter 2

1. May 3 was traditionally celebrated as the day of the Discovery of the Holy Cross, until this was changed by Pope John XXIII in 1960. In more recent times, May 3 is the feast day of Saint James the Lesser.

2. The kings of Portugal during the early modern period (1450–1800) used the titles of "King of Portugal and of the Algarves on this side of and beyond the sea in Africa, Lord of Guinea and of the Conquest, Navigation, and Commerce of Ethiopia, Arabia, Persia, and India." Salvador is referring here to the fact that Brazil was not in their titles.

Chapter 3

1. A league is 3.5–4 miles.
2. The Treaty of Tordesillas, signed in 1494.
3. Pedro Nunes (1502–78) was the chief cosmographer of Portugal.
4. Equal to one hundred miles for each degree of latitude.
5. Sometimes called "the Spice Islands," the Moluccas are in eastern Indonesia and are the home of nutmeg and cloves, making them very valuable. While

the Treaty of Tordesillas established the Atlantic boundaries for Spain and Portugal, the corresponding line on the other side of the globe was not determined at the same time. Magellan believed that the Molucca Islands were on the Spanish side of this line. This line was later determined by the Treaty of Zaragoza in 1529. Both the Molucca Islands and the Philippines were on the Portuguese side.

6. Magellan left Spain with five ships and more than two hundred men (exact figures are contradictory). The expedition returned in one ship with only a handful of men.

Chapter 4
1. That is, the sun passes over the tropical zone twice a year as Earth rotates and the sun reaches the Tropics of Cancer and Capricorn.
2. Frei Vicente uses *negro* to mean either native Brazilian or African.

Chapter 5
1. A lapidary is a specialist who works with gemstones.

Chapter 6
1. An *angelim* is a large evergreen tree.
2. A span has a length of approximately 8.5 inches, so ten spans is about seven feet.
3. *Timbos* and *cipós* are long-stemmed woody vines.
4. Nails were made of iron and were expensive in colonial Brazil.
5. A plant in the pineapple family.
6. *Tatajuba* is also known as dyer's mulberry or fustic, *Maclura tinctoria*; *araribá* is *Centrolobium robustum*, also called zebrawood.
7. *Copaiba* is a tree from the genus *Copaifera*. "Cold humor" refers to the Galen's theory of medicine, according to which there were four humors, the imbalance of which caused illnesses.
8. The two ceremonies here are unction or extreme unction, the anointing of the sick with oil, and chrism, a ceremony when an individual joins the faithful.
9. Pipes or *pipas* held two hogsheads of liquid. The amount varied but was around 126 gallons.
10. *Genipa americana* is a large tree native to South America and the West Indies that produces fruit that natives use to dye their skin black.
11. The five wounds of Christ on the cross: one was in each hand, two were on the crossed feet (the three nails already mentioned), and the fifth was caused by a lance in his side.
12. A cedrate is a type of lemon.

13. Abrantes is a town in central Portugal.
14. Savory and borage are herbs used in cooking.

Chapter 7

1. Fedegoso (*Cassia occidentalis*) has traditionally been used for a wide variety of diseases, including internal parasites and skin infestations.
2. The figueira do inferno is *Datura stramonium.*
3. Called the "sensitive plant" (*Mimosa pudica*), whose leaves close at a touch.

Chapter 8

1. Cassava, also called manioc, is a fibrous starchy root vegetable or tuber.

Chapter 9

1. A capybara is a large rodent related to the guinea pig.
2. This is the Brazilian tapir, a large four-legged mammal.
3. Bezoars are stones from the intestines of large animals.
4. Agoutis and pacas are similar rodents, larger than guinea pigs.
5. Anteater.
6. Brown howler monkey.
7. A jaritacaca or maritcaca is a Brazilian skunk.
8. *Preguiça* means lazy or idle. This is the sloth.
9. Possum.
10. Rattlesnakes.
11. Termites.
12. A small round berry.

Chapter 10

1. Scarlet ibis.
2. Blue and yellow macaw.
3. Frei Vicente is mistaken here; ambergris is a natural substance produced in the intestines of a whale. It is often used to make perfume.
4. Swordfish.
5. Known as the blue land crab.

Chapter 11

1. Tucum is a tropical palm tree.
2. Glass herb or erva de vidro is *Peperomia rotundifolia.*
3. The psalm continues with "and blesses your people within you."
4. That is, sacramental wine and flour for the host.

Chapter 12

1. Diogo de Avalos y Figueroa (1554? to 1610?), author of *Miscelanea Austral y Defensa de damas*, published in Lima in 1602.
2. *Tapuia* was a term used in this period for non-Tupí-speaking natives.
3. Father José Anchieta (1534–97) was a Jesuit priest who arrived in Brazil in 1553. He wrote the *Arte de Gramática da lingua mais usada na costa do Brasil*, which was published in 1595.

Chapter 14

1. Christian tradition forbids the marriage of a man with his niece or sister-in-law, but this impediment can be removed under some circumstances.
2. There are several works with this (or a very similar) title. Frei Salvador might be referring to Johannes Nider's work of 1468 or Johannes Gerson's *Tractatus de contractibus*, published in 1473–74.

Chapter 15

1. The catechism is a summary of the beliefs of a religion.

BOOK 2

Chapter 1

1. These were stone pillars, which were erected along the coastline of Africa as well.
2. Also called *donataries*, these men had virtually complete control over their lands.

Chapter 2

1. One of the greatest Roman generals, who lived from 236 to 183 BCE. He defeated Hannibal in the Second Punic War.
2. Governor of Portuguese India, 1542–45.
3. The Company of Jesus or Jesuits and the Order of the Brothers of the Blessed Virgin Mary of Mount Carmel or Carmelites are two orders within the Catholic Church.

Chapter 3

1. This passage is problematic since in the original Frei Vicente says "deadly and poisonous," yet if they were poisonous, the dead game would not be edible. Also, if they had little contact with these people, how would they know what game they hunted or how they caught sharks?

Chapter 4

1. D. Jorge de Meneses served in Portuguese Asia from 1520 to 1530 and was governor of the Molucca Islands from 1527 to 1530.

Chapter 5

1. Viana do Castelo is an important port city in northern Portugal.

Chapter 7

1. This is a possible reference to the *graviola*, a tropical fruit with spines, or to dragon fruit.

Chapter 8

1. Rafael Bluteau, Dicionário da Lingua Portuguesa (Lisboa: Simão Thaddeo Ferreira, 1789), 2:438: "Pernambuco" comes from the Tupí words "pára-ña (wide river) and mbuka (hollow or broken)."
2. *To careen* means to remove a ship from water to clean the hull or make repairs.
3. Galicia is the province of Iberia directly north of Portugal.
4. Meaning "how beautiful!" in Portuguese.
5. Today this is the oldest functioning church in Brazil, a national historical monument.

Chapter 9

1. A *dízimo* is a tax of one-tenth normally paid to the church, in this case to the king.

Chapter 10

1. Twenty-five *braças* would be 150–175 feet.

Chapter 13

1. The Casa da Índia was the major trading hub of commerce in Asian goods; located in Lisbon.
2. *Décadas da Ásia.*

Chapter 14

1. Francisco de Orellana (1490–1546) was a Spanish explorer and the first European to sail the length of the Amazon River in 1541–42.

BOOK 3

Chapter 1

1. Elvas is an important town in the middle of the eastern border with Spain.
2. This appears to be an error, since she was known as Catarina Paraguaçu.

3. In the original, it is not clear who cut the anchor line, but it was probably the natives.

Chapter 2

1. These were known as "the Queen's Orphan Girls." Periodically, small groups of such young ladies would leave Lisbon for Brazil or India, and each would have a dowry awarded by the king. In this case, the city of Salvador also awarded dowries.
2. From *The Lusiadas of Luiz de Camões,* trans. Leonard Bacon (New York: Hispanic Society of America, 1950), book 9, verse 58, p. 329.

Chapter 3

1. Saint José de Anchieta (1534–97) was a Spanish Jesuit, one of the founders of São Paulo and Rio de Janeiro. He wrote the *Arte de Gramática* of the Tupí language. He was canonized in 2014. Saint Francis Xavier (1506–52) was a similar Jesuit missionary in Portuguese Asia, one of the first Christian missionaries to reach Japan, and he was canonized in 1622.
2. Members of the council of a cathedral or bishop's council.

Chapter 4

1. His nickname was "the *cataraz*" because there were several men with this name. The meaning of this term is unknown. Diu was a critical fortified city held by the Portuguese in northwest India.
2. Cochin is a city in southwest India and was historically a friendly outpost for the Portuguese.
3. Goa, located in the middle of India's western coast, was the capital and largest city in Portuguese Asia.
4. D. Luís (1506–55) was the son of King D. Manuel I and Queen Maria of Aragón.
5. Nestor in both *The Iliad* and *The Odyssey* gives wise advice. Achilles was the hero of the Trojan War.

Chapter 5

1. The Alfama is the oldest part of Lisbon, located at the edge of the Tejo River. Saint Pedro Gonçalves (González) (1190–1246), also known as Saint Elmo, was a Spanish Dominican priest and is one of the patron saints of sailors.
2. At the time this work was written, Xabregas was an open area at the edge of Lisbon, the site of the Monastery of Madre de Deus, founded in 1509.
3. Bassein was an important city in Portuguese Asia, located north of the island of Bombay.

4. D. Filipe or King Philip II of Spain and I of Portugal (1527–98); Fernando I (1503–14), younger brother of Carlos V.

Chapter 6

1. The term "just war" refers to a definition of when and how a war can be legitimate in terms of the Church.
2. "Honor regis judicium diligit" from the Clementine Vulgate Bible, Ps. 98:4–6

Chapter 9

1. Quilon, on the western coast of India in Malabar, was an important trading partner for the Portuguese to acquire pepper.
2. This does not agree with the number of men (700) Frei Vicente previously stated. If the three boats each held 170 men, that would leave 190 men to walk on land. On the other hand, it is hard to imagine 170 men on one lifeboat or a homemade pontoon. I suspect a more accurate statement would be "there were many men," rather than 700.
3. Patani was at the center of a trading nexus and small kingdom on the Malay peninsula.

Chapter 10

1. Father Manuel da Nóbrega, SJ (1517–70), was the first leader of the Jesuits in Brazil. He was instrumental in founding many cities, including Recife, Salvador, Rio de Janeiro, and São Paulo. He established the Jesuit College in Salvador and wrote the *Diálogo sobre a conversão do gentio*.
2. A boatswain is an officer on a ship in charge of the rigging and the anchors.
3. Saint Sebastian's Day is traditionally celebrated on January 20. Significant for this story, he is also the traditional patron of warriors.

Chapter 11

1. Frei Vicente is in error here. May 16, 1566, was a Monday.
2. This was a Monday.
3. Agua de flor is a tea-like beverage made with rum and gin.
4. Sintra is a small town outside Lisbon and near the coast. The Berlinga Islands are very close to the coast of Portugal north of Lisbon.
5. Pederneira was small coastal village located in the present town of Nazaré, Portugal.
6. Atouguia is a parish located in the modern town of Peniche. Cascais is a coastal city near Lisbon.

Chapter 12

1. A *canada* is four *quartilhos,* so what he has done is to drastically increase the size.

2. This is Salvador Correia de Sá (1540–1631), who was known as "the elder" to distinguish him from his famous grandson, Salvador Correia de Sá e Benevides.

Chapter 13
1. He ruled Portuguese India as governor-general from 1573 to 1576. Monomatapa was a wealthy and powerful gold-producing kingdom in southern Africa.
2. This was an additional torture, bringing the prisoner to the edge of death repeatedly.

Chapter 15
1. A presidio is a fortified military camp.
2. King Sebastião, against the advice of many people at the time, launched an ill-fated campaign to conquer northern Morocco. He and his army died there at the Battle of Alcácer Quibir in 1578.

Chapter 16
1. São Lourenço was the Portuguese name for Madagascar.

Chapter 17
1. Ali Adil Shah was the ruler of Bijapur. Nizam Shahi, the ruler of Ahmednagar, attacked Chaul, a fertile Portuguese farming and trading town south of modern Mumbai, India.
2. This is a reference to the famous Battle of Lepanto, fought in 1571. The Holy League, led by John of Austria, defeated the Ottoman navy in "the largest naval battle in western history since antiquity."

Chapter 18
1. *Barbasco* is the Portuguese term for Tephrosia vogelii, also known as *fish bean* or *fish poison bean,* an herb or small tree.

Chapter 21
1. Minor orders are positions in the Catholic Church lower than a priest.
2. Limoeiro was the main jail in Lisbon. Normally prisoners were held there until sentencing and then banished. It would have been unusual to sentence a prisoner to time in the jail.
3. He is referring to the papal bull or edict "Pontifex Romanis Pacis," issued by Pope Julius II in 1509.

Chapter 22
1. Ash was used in the final cleansing process of making sugar.

Chapter 23

1. Brazil was divided into two administrative parts, as stated here, from 1574 to 1578 and again from 1608 to 1612.

Chapter 25

1. A palisade is a fortified enclosure.
2. In the original, it says "sell" the village, but I believe "trade" is closer to the meaning.

Chapter 26

1. The first count of Portugal was D. Henrique, and Cardinal Henrique was the last king of the House of Avis.
2. The *Cortes* is a formal meeting of the three estates, i.e., the clergy, the nobility, and the peasantry. The meeting in Almeirim was called by King-Cardinal D. Henrique on January 11, 1580, to determine his successor.

BOOK 4

Chapter 1

1. Governor-general of India from 1573 to 1576.
2. D. António was one of many claimants to the throne of Portugal, as noted previously.

Chapter 4

1. May 3 in the current Catholic calendar.

Chapter 6

1. Three squads of thirty horses each equals ninety horsemen. Frei Vicente does not explain what happened to the other 105 horsemen.

Chapter 7

1. Te-Deum laudamus.

Chapter 8

1. Hardtack is hard biscuit made to last for a long time, such as on a voyage.

Chapter 10

1. August 5 is the feast day of Our Lady of the Snows.
2. Lower parts of the cannons.

Chapter 13

1. Saint Thomas's Day was traditionally celebrated on December 21, but in recent times was moved to July 3.

Chapter 15
1. Ponte de Lima is a small town in the extreme north of Portugal.

Chapter 19
1. Itapuã is a neighborhood in the city of Salvador.
2. The Misericórdia was the largest charity in the Portuguese world, with chapters in virtually every city throughout the empire.
3. The pillory was a tall stone pillar in a central public square. The guilty could be punished for minor offenses by being tied to it for public ridicule.

Chapter 23
1. The first Sunday after Pentecost, which is the fiftieth day after Easter.
2. An auto-da-fé was the public enforcing the rulings of the Inquisition.
3. In the original, "Only a thief asked him for a cape because at the same time they got the shoulders." That is, he was very generous.

Chapter 25
1. Original text stops here. Chapters 26–29 are missing from the text.

Chapter 32
1. June 24.
2. A firepot is an earthen container used to carry fire from one place to another; it can be used as a weapon.
3. A gentleman's habit is one of the honorific military orders and is awarded with a stipend. Examples of this are the Order of Saint James or the Knights of Christ.

Chapter 33
1. Leiria is a small town north of Lisbon.

Chapter 34
1. The Universidade de São Paulo edition notes that Frei Vicente has confused this attack with another from the Dutch in 1604.
2. An amount equal to 896,000 to 1,024,000 pounds.

Chapter 39
1. This section of text is missing in the original.

Chapter 40
1. This passage is not clear in the original. However, since Frei Vicente tells us the negros were fond of the meat, they might be more likely to be packing it. He does make a clear distinction between the two groups, telling us that those who process the oil do not pack the meat. One group was composed of both

whites and negros. Presumably the other group was not mixed. Since the oil was more valuable and harder to extract, it was probably done by fishermen or other experienced people.

2. Balsam oil is oil from a tree that grows in Central and South America and is a natural remedy for healing wounds.

Chapter 41

1. Évora is an important city in the interior of Portugal, due east of Lisbon.

Chapter 44

1. Father Francisco Pinto is buried in the main church of Messajana, Ceará. His death is remembered there every March 8.

Chapter 45

1. *Mixti fori* means under the jurisdiction of both the church and state courts.

Chapter 47

1. *Mel* is one stage of the cooked liquid extracted from sugarcane.
2. Arguin is a small island off the coast of West Africa where the Portuguese built and maintained a small fort and trading outpost.
3. It is not clear here what the author means.

BOOK 5

Chapter 2

1. A prelate is a higher member of the clergy.

Chapter 5

1. June 24.
2. Bonfires are a traditional aspect of Saint John's Day in many places in Iberia and Latin America.
3. Traditionally celebrated on July 2.

Chapter 6

1. His woodwinds or, in this case, shawms or early types of reed instruments.

Chapter 20

1. Potosí is a city in modern Bolivia. During colonial times, it had a very large and productive silver mine, producing tons of silver for the Spanish crown. Transporting the royal fifth of the production to Spain was a difficult and demanding task since it had to be carried to the port of Callao in Peru and shipped to Panama, where it crossed the isthmus by donkey and then was collected in Portobello in the Caribbean and shipped to Spain.

2. Luanda sickness is scurvy.
3. Iliceira here may mean the Portuguese coastal town of Ericeira.
4. Salé is a coastal city in modern Morocco. Ransoming captives was a lucrative and common business practice.

Chapter 21

1. "And Jesus knew their thoughts, and said unto them, every kingdom divided against itself is brought to desolation; and every city or house divided against itself shall not stand." Matt. 12:25.

Chapter 23

1. What were you all thinking when you saw our fleet?
2. A Christian and pre-Christian tradition is to place a coin over each eye of the deceased for him/her to pay Charon, the ferryman, to cross the River Styx to enter the afterlife.

Chapter 26

1. Ravasco was the father of one of the most famous literary and missionary figures in colonial Brazil: Father António Vieira.
2. *Sipanta* is not a Portuguese word and its meaning is unknown.

Chapter 29

1. *Taipa* is a mixture of mud and lime.

Chapter 30

1. Yards are horizontal supports holding the sails of a ship.
2. *Sapientiae* is a book of wisdom.
3. A cassock is a one-piece full-length garment, such as that worn by a priest.

Chapter 32

1. Salvador Correia de Sá e Benevides was a remarkable figure in colonial Brazilian history. Not only did he participate in this struggle with the Dutch in 1625, but he later recaptured São Tomé and Angola in 1647 for the Portuguese during the restoration of Portuguese independence. He is the subject of an excellent biography by C. R. Boxer, *Salvador de Sá and the Struggle for Brazil and Angola, 1602–1686* (London: Athlone Press, 1952).

Chapter 34

1. Leader of the 112 descendants of Uzziel, the Levite. 1 Chron. 15:10 and 15:11.

Chapter 35

1. One *moio* is approximately twenty bushels.
2. The archbishop primate of Portugal is the archbishop of Braga.

3. A palanqueta is a short iron bar with a ball at each end that is fired from a cannon.
4. Oakum is tarred rope used to repair ships.

Chapter 36

1. Shrove Tuesday ("Mardi Gras") is the last day of carnival, before the forty days of Lent that end with Easter.

Chapter 38

1. A battery is a location where heavy guns are placed, normally on a protective wall or fort.
2. "The third eighth" refers of the eight divisions of the day, the third being *tierce*, starting around nine o'clock.

Chapter 39

1. Here holy oil refers to his receiving last rites, a ceremony to prepare those about to die.

Chapter 41

1. Probably an eight *escudo* gold coin, used by the Spanish.

Chapter 42

1. "Unless the Lord builds the house, the builders labor in vain. Unless the Lord watches over the city, the guards stand watch in vain." Ps. 127.

Chapter 43

1. A prebendary is a senior member of the clergy.
2. A deacon is a clergyman below the order of priest.
3. My tears have been my food day and night, while people say to me all day long, "Where is your God?" Ps. 42:3.
4. The host is used in communion.
5. The Vicar of Christ is another title for the Pope; 1624 was a leap year.
6. In 1625, Pope Urban VIII declared a jubilee year forgiving the faithful of their sins.
7. Saint Elizabeth of Portugal, known as Saint Isabel in Portuguese. She lived from 1282 to 1325 and was the wife of King D. Dinis. She was canonized in 1625.

Chapter 45

1. One of the captaincies on Madeira.
2. What enemies have left behind, friends take and will help and aid them.
3. The swarming locust has eaten.

Chapter 46

1. Tantalus is a figure from Greek mythology. He was punished for his crimes by being tied in water that he was unable to drink below a tree hanging with fruit that he could never reach.

Chapter 47

1. The island of Ternate in the Spice Islands of (modern-day) eastern Indonesia was the source of cloves.

Chapter 48

1. The Prince of Orange is one of the titles of the ruler of the Netherlands. In this case, he is referring to Prince William of Nassau.
2. Ambergris is a substance produced by whales. It was valuable and was used in perfumes and mixed with tobacco.
3. The north and south of coastal Brazil were separated in their administration from 1572 to 1578 and again from 1607 to 1613. Maranhão, Pará, and the north were then separated from the reunified colony, known as "Brazil," from 1621 to 1652.

Chapter 49

1. Saint Martin of Tours.
2. *Presépio* or *Manger* was the first name of the modern city of Belém (Bethlehem) in Pará.
3. São Jorge da Mina was a trading outpost in West Africa where slaves and gold were traded for firearms, cloth, salt, and other goods.

INDEX

Abreu, Gregório Lopes de, 132, 151, 153, 296, 297
Abreu, Rui Mendes de, 214, 223, 236
Adorno, António Dias, 11, 110
Adorno, Francisco, 87
Adorno, Paulo Dias, 81, 82, 88
Aguiar, Jorge de, 251, 256, 258, 272
Aguierre, Arias, Diogo, xli
Aimorés, 30, 49, 50, 221; war with, 163, 164, 192, 193, 203, 205
Aitacases, 46
Albuquerque, Afonso de, 58, 95, 210, 216, 238
Albuquerque, André de, 175, 310
Albuquerque, António de, xxxix, xl, 225, 228
Albuquerque, Gregório Fragoso, 225, 229, 231
Albuquerque, D. Inés, 54
Albuquerque, Jerónimo Cavalcanti de, 282, 283, 285
Albuquerque, Jerónimo de, 54, 57–61, 90, 100–103, 181, 182, 185, 187, 188, 223–29, 231–33, 241, 313, 314
Albuquerque, Jerónimo Fragoso de, 237, 241, 314
Albuquerque, Lourenço Cavalcanti de, 253, 267
Almeida, Bernardo Pimentel de, 82, 191
Almeida, Luís de Brito de, 108, 111, 117, 118
alpins, 19
Álvares, Diogo (Caramuru), xxi, 52, 72, 81
Álvares, Manuel, 178
Álvares, Sebastião, 111

Alzega, D. Diogo de, 130
Amaral, Francisco de, 234
Amaupiras, 29, 52
Amazon River, 4, 5, 29, 241, 245, 313, 314; exploration of, 241, 245; region, 4, 5, 29, 313, 314
ambaíbas, 18
ambergris, 24, 205, 263, 309, 322, 333
Anchieta, José de, SJ, 29, 75, 87, 96, 323, 325
andaz, 17
Andrade, Álvaro Nunes de, 63
Andrade, António Rodrigues de, 171–72
Andrade, Pedro da Cunha de, 178
Andrade, Simão da Gama d', 74, 276
angelins, 11
Angola, xxii, 49, 180, 217, 248, 260–62, 273, 275, 280, 289, 292, 298, 307, 308, 331
animals: domesticated, xix, 20, 193; wild, xix, 21, 46, 207
antas, 20
António, D., 73, 77, 78, 106, 123–25, 127, 128, 131, 202, 328
António, Brother (Frei), OFM, 279
Apeba, António, 177–78
Aperipé, 109
Apuabete, 28
Arabé, 200
Araconda, 122
Araçuagi Point, 68
Aragão, Baltasar de, 223, 233–35
Arambepé River, 114
arará-canindés, 23
araribá, 12, 321

Araribóia (Martin Afonso de Sousa), 98, 99, 117

Araripe, 62, 134

Aratibá, 206

Araújo, Francisco de, 166, 192

Arechis, 309

Arguin, 219, 330

Arte de Gramática (Anchieta), 29, 323, 325

artillery, types of, 92, 105, 150, 193, 221, 243, 255, 258, 260, 270, 272, 278, 293, 307, 311

Arvelos, Sebastião Gonçalves, 63

Assento de Pássaro, 112, 143, 157, 162, 174, 182, 184

Atalaia, Count of, 196

Augustinian order, 196

Aveiro, Duke of, 49

Ávila, Garcia d', 109

Ávila, Francisco Dias de, 253, 255, 269

Azeredo, Marcos de, 11

Azevedo, Melchior de, 88

Azeredo, Inácio de, SJ, 103

Azores Islands, xxxii, 73, 91, 103, 125, 301

Bacelar, Afonso Rodrigues, 115

Baepeba, 168, 169

Bahia, region, xvii, xxii, xxiii, xxiv, xxxii, xxxviii, 49–52, 69, 71, 72, 74–84, 105, 111, 115, 117–19, 127, 134, 163, 165, 166–73, 177, 188, 193, 195, 196, 199, 200, 203, 212–15, 217–20, 239, 261, 266, 268, 290, 295, 300, 304–7, 310–12; Bay of All Saints, xvii, xviii, xx, xxv, xxvi, 41, 49, 131, 303, 307; captaincy of, 52; cathedral of, 49; feeding people in, 108–9, 265; golden time of, 114; governors of, 81, 84, 94, 97, 98, 109, 117, 190, 193, 202, 223, 237, 240, 245, 247, 263, 265–66, 269; location of, 51; people from, 11, 76, 83, 133, 171–73; relations with native peoples in, 29, 80, 109, 192; ships arriving in or departing from, 77–79, 84, 97, 104, 133, 166, 213, 218, 233–68, 273, 278, 280–82, 287, 301, 305; sugar mills in, 169, 217; taxes and, 42, 245; why so named, 50. *See also* Dutch; Salvador (city)

Barbosa, Francisco, 185

Barbosa, Frutuoso, 131–37, 144, 145, 148, 173, 175, 197

Barbosa, João, 267

Barradas, D. Constantino de, 215, 312

Barreiros, D. António (bishop), 113, 131, 133, 165

Barreiros, António Moniz, 241, 242

Barreto, António Moniz, 127, 273, 278, 283, 287, 291, 303

Barreto, Diogo Moniz, 71

Barreto, Francisco, 97, 139–45, 177

Barreto, João Pais, 181

Barreto, Manuel Teles, xxxviii, 127, 131, 133, 163, 173, 175

Barros, António Cardoso de, 71, 76, 107, 252, 259

Barros, Cristóvão de, xl, xlii, 107, 108, 117, 163, 165–70

Barros, Francisco de, 181, 248

Barros, João de, xlix, 66–68, 319

Barroso, Cristóvão, 8

Bastião, 252, 256

Batatam, 197

beans, types of, 14

beijus, 19

Benedictine order, 261

Benevides, Salvador Correia de Sá e, 269, 285, 327, 331

Bicar, Lourenço, 194

birds, 23, 24, 207

Biscay, 203, 269, 273, 279, 305, 310

boasting and bragging, as a war strategy of the natives, 37, 99, 101, 102, 183. *See also* native peoples; war

Boipeba Island, 50, 248, 259

Borges, Pedro, 71, 81

Borges, Sebastião, 223, 236

Botelho, Diogo (European), xxxviii, 195–97, 200–204, 208, 212, 239

Botelho, Diogo (native), 206

Braço de Peixe (Piragiba), 112, 138, 141, 142, 145, 148, 149, 158, 159, 174, 182, 184, 188, 205

Branco, D. Simão de Castelo, 47

Branco, Francisco Caldeira de Castelo, xli, 231, 233, 235, 312

Braga, Francisco de, 64

Brandão, Ambrósio Fernandes, 139, 143

Brandão, Melchior, 253, 255, 268

Brazil: climate of, 9–10; early names for, 2–4, 67; as refuge for those in Portugal, 73; size of, 4, 73; shaped like a harp, 5

Brito, Lourenço de, 248–50, 253, 256, 270

Brito, Sebastião Paruí de, 216

Buenos Aires, 130
Búzios, 182, 183, 185

Caapara, António Álvares, 167
Cabedelo, 133, 180
caboreíbas, 13
Cabral, Pedro Álvares, xviii, 1, 2, 41, 48
Cachoeira, 178, 191, 193
Cádiz, 129, 295, 302–4
caiçara, 37
Cairu, 259
Caldas, Francisco de, 112, 141
Calheiros, Manuel da Costa, 181, 187
Camamu River, 50, 164, 167, 260
Camarão, 186
camarinhas, 23
Camelo, Francisco, 181
Camelo, Pero Lopes, 181
Caminha, Duke of, 277, 312
Camoci, 198
canafístula, 17
Cananéia, 45, 89, 195
Canavazes, Jerónimo de, OC, 177
cannibalism, xx, xxi, xxiii, 39, 52. *See also*
    captives
canoes, 12, 43, 52, 87–90, 95, 98, 99, 108,
    194, 208, 209, 227, 238, 242–44, 281, 282,
    285, 313–15
Cão, Diogo Martims, 193
Cape Branco, 5, 150
Cape Frio, 98, 99, 117, 208, 209, 238, 315–17
Cape Santo Agostinho, 4, 60
Cape Verde Islands, 4, 5, 8, 18, 28, 203,
    246, 248, 269, 278–80
Capiguaribe, 60, 100
captives: taken by Dutch, 243, 245, 296;
    taken by natives, 38, 46, 313, 316; taken
    by the French, xxiii, 63
capybara, 20, 322
caraíbas (something divine), 1
caraguatá, 12, 26
Caragatim, 197
caravel, xxxvi, 3, 8, 41, 52, 58, 61, 62, 63,
    68, 81, 87, 88, 94, 114, 119, 120, 132, 148,
    150, 156, 157, 162, 171, 176, 181, 182, 190,
    191, 196, 210, 216, 218, 225, 231, 236, 242,
    245, 265, 269, 274, 280, 281, 295, 304,
    306–8, 311
Carcome, D. Diogo de, 241
Cardim, Fernão, SJ, 212
Cardoso, Simão Rodrigues, 132, 134

Caridade (nau), 273, 280, 282
Carijós, 28
carimã, 19
Carioca River, 88, 194
Carlos V, D. (king of Spain), 5, 77–79, 123,
    326
caroba, 18
Carvalho, Álvaro de, 190–93, 202
Carvalho, Feliciano Coelho de, 179, 181,
    189, 218, 263, 269, 308
Carvalho, Francisco Coelho de, 263,
    308–9
Carvalho, Martim, 133, 136, 138, 146, 147
Carvalho, Paio Coelho de, 237
Cascais, Pero de, 235
cascavéis (rattlesnakes), 22
cashews, xx, 14, 15, 27, 152
cassava, 19, 39, 51, 93, 152, 174, 217, 261, 322
Castejon, Francisco, 134–36, 146, 147, 155,
    173
Castile, 4, 5, 8, 62, 123, 127, 269, 273, 278,
    279, 283, 293, 294, 304, 312
Castro, Diogo de, 111, 119–21, 172, 269
Catarina, D. (queen of Portugal), 8, 74, 83,
    84, 87, 90
Cavalcanti, Filipe, 100, 101, 134, 135, 139, 156
Ceará, xxxviii, 198, 200, 210, 223, 231, 264,
    308, 309, 330
churches: in Bahia as used by the Dutch,
    251–53, 283, 293, 294; cathedral in
    Bahia, 49, 73, 74, 235, 236, 240, 254, 271,
    293; the French and 219; , in Igaraçu,
    54; in Itamaracá, 61, 134; and justice,
    215; ; in Lisbon, 220; in Maranhão,
    264; and native peoples, 188, 201, 205,
    206, 296; Our Lady of Penha, 48; in
    Pena (Portugal), 94; in Rio de Janeiro,
    95; sanctuary in 113; in São Paulo, 44;
    seating in, 246
Churrião (nau), 306
Cide, João, 197
Cipoúna, 297, 298
Cirinhaen River, 101
clothes: for Europeans, 1, 86, 195, 197, 247,
    261, 292, 313; for native peoples, 31, 110,
    111, 148, 149, 203
coconuts, xix, 12, 14, 27, 34, 93
Coelho, D. Beatriz de Albuquerque, 54, 58
Coelho, Domingos, SJ, 261
Coelho, Duarte de Albuquerque, 52, 54,
    61, 99–103, 239, 253, 287, 301

Coelho, Gonçalo, 41
Coelho, Jorge de Albuquerque, xl, 54, 61,
    90–93, 134, 166
Coelho, Julião, 178
Coelho, Matias de Albuquerque, xxxviii,
    xxxix, xl, 103, 240–42, 263, 265, 269,
    282, 296, 299, 306, 308, 311
Colaço, João Rodrigues, xli, 189, 196
Conceição, (a galleon), 273, 278, 306
Congatan, Pedro, 197
Contas River, 111, 307
conversion: to Christianity, xx, xxii, 75,
    200, 212, 264; importance of, 200;
    methods used, 201, 223
convicts (degredados), xx, 2, 72, 74, 236, 320
copaiba, 13, 321
Copaoba, 157, 158, 296
copis (termites), 22
corimã (fataça), a type of fish, 108
Correia, Diogo Nunes, 173, 174
Correia, Jorge de Figueiredo, 49, 50, 276
Corso, Antão Paulo, 128, 129
Cosmas and Damian, Saints, 54, 60, 65,
    100, 134, 139, 140, 196, 225
Costa, D. Duarte da, 75, 76, 79, 80, 84
Costa, Julião da, 178
Couros, António de, 259
Coutinho, Francisco de Aguiar, xxxix,
    48, 281
Coutinho, Francisco Pereira, 52, 53, 71
Coutinho, Vasco Fernandes, xxxviii, 45,
    46, 47, 49, 81
cows, 73, 109, 300, 376, 386; island of 135
Crato, priory, 77
Cricaré River, 82
Cropani, Marques de, 279, 284, 291, 295,
    299
cruzados, 11, 46, 47, 58, 73, 102, 131, 146,
    177, 178, 189, 194, 204, 205, 214, 215, 234,
    241, 242, 245, 246, 269, 277, 278, 289,
    300, 308, 313
Cueva, Pedro de la, 173, 175
cuia, 31
Cumá Point, 68
Cunha, Aires da, 66–68
Cunha, João Coelho da, 279
Cururuipe River, 76
Cururupiba, 191

debt, 3, 67, 80, 81, 104, 177
Devil, xix, xxi, 2, 32, 51, 57, 76, 146, 306

Diablo, Afonso Martins, 84
Diabo-Grande, 199, 200, 232
Dias, Boaventura, 118
Dias, Diogo, 115, 116, 118
Dorth, Jan van, 248, 251, 254
dowries, 74, 105, 107, 189, 197, 325
Drake, Sir Francis, xxiv, 128
Duarte, Henrique, 187
Duchs, Francisco, 238, 291, 292
Dutch: funerals conducted by, 254, 255,
    293; method of fighting, 190, 191, 243,
    244, 251, 256, 257, 261, 267, 268, 272, 281,
    283, 284, 290, 299, 302, 306; prisoners
    taken by, xviii, xxxii, 245, 251, 262, 282,
    283, 289, 307, 316; relations with locals,
    196, 251–53, 296, 297; ships, 190, 247,
    248, 260; trade conducted by, 258, 280,
    311, 316

Elvas, 68, 71, 324
Espinha, Bartolomeu Luís de, 50
Espinha, Luís Álvares de, 112
Espirito Santo, captaincy, 11, 46–48, 81, 82,
    193, 208, 216, 252, 280–82, 315, 316
Espirito Santo, Manuel de, OFM, 281
Equino, André, 130
estates: of the deceased, 176, 276; of sugar
    planters, 170, 178, 268
Évora, xviii, 207, 277, 330
executioners and hangmen, 38, 39, 96

Fajardo, D. João, 279, 285
Falcão, Rui de Aveiro, 187
Falcão, Simão, 135, 139, 148
Faria, António de, 165
Faria, Sebastião de, 131, 167, 168, 220
Fedegoso, 18, 322
Fernandes, Jerónimo, 187
Ferraz, Baltasar, 234, 235
Ferreira, Baltasar, 24
Ferreira, Diogo, 274, 287
Ferreira, Jorge, xli, 89
Ferreira, Martim, 46
figueira do inferno, 18, 322
Figueiredo, Custódio de, 190
fish, 3, 24, 31, 32, 42, 46, 47, 50, 52, 58, 68,
    78, 108–10, 130, 164, 172, 190, 203, 204,
    220, 255, 262, 270, 278
fishing (piraiqué), 108
Flanders, 137, 225, 242, 243, 295, 300, 304,
    310

flour, war, 19, 36, 37, 93, 141, 151, 152
Formoso River, 119
fortifications: in Olinda, 263; in Rio de
    Janeiro, 83, 86, 89, 245, 247, 281, 315
Frades, Island of the, 191, 260
Fragoso, Brás, 81, 88
Franca, Afonso da, xl, 280, 296
Franca, André Dias de, xl, 310
França, Lancerote de, 273, 280, 282, 287,
    291
Franciscan order, xvii, xxxii, 131, 187
Francisco, Brother (Frei), OFM, 279
Freire, Estêvão de Brito, 190, 191, 268, 275
French: fighting with, xxii, xxv, 43, 56,
    62–64, 84, 88, 89, 92, 93, 99, 116, 118, 132,
    137, 152, 157, 161, 185, 198–200, 219, 221,
    222, 227–29, 234; men cutting wood,
    114, 116, 117, 132, 157, 315; native allies of,
    xxv, 83, 87, 98, 132; naus, 42, 64, 72, 83,
    88, 91–93, 98, 99, 114, 116, 117, 119, 127,
    132, 136, 151, 155, 156, 162, 182, 219, 221,
    226, 234; peace with, xxiii, 199, 229–33,
    289; settlements made by, 62, 63, 83, 95,
    185, 223, 225, 315
Frias, Francisco de, 227, 246
Furtado, Diogo de Mendonça, 239–41 245,
    262, 263

Galego, João Peres, 178
Gama, Pedro Correia, 285
Garaguinguira, 197
Garcia, Pero, 249, 250, 252
gemstones, in Brazil, 321; emeralds, 11, 48,
    111, 193
genipapo, 67, 92, 95, 96, 98
giitis, 14
Giraldes, Francisco, 175, 190
Giraldes, Lucas, 50, 175
Góis, Pedro de, 45, 46
Gold, Priest of, 102, 103
Gonçalo, 210
Gonçalves, Afonso, 54, 55
Gonçalves, Francisco, 293
Gonçalves, João, 62, 63, 65
Gonçalves, Manuel, 251, 256–58, 267, 270,
    300
governor and bishop, relations between,
    246, 247. *See also* churches, seating in
Grã, Luís da, SJ, 75
Grande, Cardo (native leader), 182
Grande, Ilhe, 188

Grande region (Rio Grande do Norte),
    154, 182, 187, 189, 190, 192, 196, 212, 242,
    243
Grande River (Rio Grande), xxiv, xxv, xli,
    26, 49, 154, 181, 182, 185, 187, 189, 190,
    192, 196, 212, 224, 226, 234, 242, 243, 297
Grão-Pará, 241, 312
Grifo Dourado (urca), 177
guaiamus, 26
Guaitcases, 316
Guaraci, 179
Guararapes, 60
guarás, 23
guaribas, 21
Gueena River, 62

hammocks, 31, 33–37, 39, 137, 193, 205, 212,
    213, 311
Harauns, 244
harquebus, 83, 89, 92, 134, 135, 151, 152, 158,
    160, 164, 167, 174, 180, 184–86, 198, 199,
    221, 225–28, 232, 243, 244, 248, 253, 254,
    256, 259, 268–71, 274, 278, 283, 287, 293,
    309, 310, 313; definition of, xxxvi
healers, native, 34, 188; methods used, 18
Henrique, D. (king of Portugal), xxiv, 87,
    94, 97, 123, 124, 131, 134, 187, 196, 328
Homem, Gaspar de Figueiredo, 194
Homem, João, 178
Homem, Manuel Mascarenhas, 181, 189
horses, 20, 45, 135, 136, 139, 149, 158, 159,
    171, 217, 254, 292, 328

Ibiapava (Boapaba) Mountains, 197, 198,
    212
Ibura-guaçu-mirim, 95
Igaraçu River, 53, 54, 61
Ilhéus, captaincy, xxiv, 49, 50, 52, 88, 111,
    112, 164, 175, 192, 221, 248
illness, 13, 18, 35, 104, 108, 124, 125, 148, 182,
    216, 271, 321
Iniaoba, 202
Iniguaçu (Great Net), 115, 116
Inquisition, visitations of, 175, 264, 329
interpreters, xxiv, 59, 101, 135, 141, 142, 149
Itapoã, 267
Itapucuru, 68, 202, 203
Itamaracá, 43, 53, 54, 61, 62, 64, 65, 66,
    100, 115, 116, 118, 134, 137, 138, 139, 146,
    156, 164, 173–75, 179, 196, 207, 217, 237,
    310

Jaguaribe, 197, 210
Jaguaripe: River, 150, 192; shore, 164, 178
Jaques, Cristóvão, 41
Jardim de Holanda (nau), 190, 248
jaritacaca, 21, 322
javelins, 20
jirau, 32
João I, D. (king of Portugal), 4
João III, D. (king of Portugal), 3, 8, 41, 49, 52, 53, 62, 66–68, 190
José, Cristóvão de São, OFM, 242, 312
jurubeba, 18
justice, 8, 60, 71, 81, 95, 97, 113, 122, 124, 160, 162, 175, 190, 215, 218, 234, 236, 239, 246, 261, 265, 296–98, 316; governing with, 80, 117, 214, 224, 294; king's, 8; and Portuguese relations with natives, 60; and war captives, 38; 122. *See also* justices
justices, 96, 135, 160, 190, 213–16, 234–36, 239–41, 246, 276, 312; building for, 95; ecclesiastical, 124, 215; High Court, 71, 135, 162, 175, 190, 218, 234, 239, 298

Kyff, Hans, 270, 271, 290

Lagoa, 119, 179
Lagrato, Bartolomeu Ferreira, 311
La Reverdière, Lord of (Monsieur), 227–30, 233, 314
Leão, Diogo Martins, 120, 136
Leitão, Gonçalo Mendes, 100
Leitão, D. Pedro de, 94, 96, 100, 113
Leitão, Martim, 133, 134, 138–41, 144–46, 148–50, 153, 156, 157, 160, 161, 163
Leite, Pero da Mota, 310
Lemos, Duarte de, 47
Lemos, Gaspar de, 2
lime, 17, 26, 150, 176, 193, 257, 264, 271, 272, 331
Linhares, Countess of, 97, 105
Lins, Conrado, 225
Lins, Cristóvão, 100, 151, 154
Lisbon (city), xxii, 100, 106–8, 124–25, 212, 216, 232, 275–78, 287, 295, 304, 314, 324–27, 329, 330; ships departing from, 62, 66, 68, 72, 75, 103, 177, 207, 216, 232, 239, 241, 268–70, 273–74, 298, 308, 310; ships destined for, 91, 97, 104, 113, 196, 231, 245, 286, 301–2, 307, 311
live herb, 18

Lobo, Martim Lopes, 180
Lobo, Miguel Álvares, 182, 184, 186, 187
Lobo, Pero Lopes, 100, 156, 175, 185, 276
Lucena, Álvaro de, 93
Lucena, Vasco Fernandes de, 56, 59, 60
Luís, D., 77, 78, 103, 104, 123, 216, 240, 241, 325

Machado, Jerónimo, SJ, 143
Maçurandubas, 13
Madeira Island, 103, 260, 269, 274, 298, 308, 332; wine from, 260, 298, 308, 310
Magalhães, Jorge de, 257
Magé River, 107, 108
Magellan, Strait of, xxiv, 128, 136, 194, 238
majacus, 24
malaria, 259
Malvirado, 219, 220
Mamanguape River, 151
Mamelucos: defined, xxiii, 110; role of, xxiii, 110, 115, 139, 140
Mandiopuba, 197
Mangue, 182
Manja-Leguas (patacho), 240
Manuel I, D. (king of Portugal), 1, 2, 5, 8, 41, 123, 325
Maracu, 68
Marambaia River, 238
Maranhão, xvii, xxxix, 66–69, 115, 200, 212, 223, 224, 226, 228–37, 241–43, 263, 264, 269, 307–9, 312, 313, 314, 333; Bay of, 226
Marciana, António da, SJ, 242
Marcos, 54, 63, 64
Maré, 258, 260
Margarida, 193
Marim, António Leitão, 181
Marinho, Francisco Nunes, xxxix, 265, 266, 270
Mattos, António de, SJ, 261
Matuim River, 2, 258, 260
Mayor, D. Alonso de Souto (governor of Chile), 130
Mearim, 68
mechuacão, 18
Meira, Brás Pires, 173
Mel-Redondo, 199, 200
Melo, António de, 196, 274, 275
Melo, Francisco Gomes de, xli, 269, 297
Mendonça, António de, 249, 250
Mendonça, Francisco de, xl, 193, 275

Mendonça, Heitor Furtado de, 175, 277
Menelau, Constantino de, xl, 238, 272, 315, 316
Meneses, D. Aleixo de, 197
Menezes, D. Beatriz de, 189
Menezes, D. Diogo de, 213, 216–18, 223, 239, 275
Menezes, D. Jorge de, 47
Menezes, D. Manuel de, 273, 279, 288, 295, 298, 302
Mequiguaçu, 206
metals, precious found in Brazil, 128, 190, 193. *See also* silver
Milho Verde, 206
miracles, 22, 44, 48, 49, 54, 56, 57, 75, 94, 150, 198, 220, 237, 261, 264, 289, 295, 297, 304
Miranda, Diogo de, 164, 187
Miranda, Manuel de, 197–99
Misericórdia, institution of, xxxvii, 61, 74, 97, 105, 108, 166, 293, 310, 329
Monim, 68
Monge, João, 82
Morais, António de, 257, 263, 300
Morais, Gaspar Dias de, 137, 139
Morales, Francisco de, 155, 156, 173
Moreno, Diogo de Campos, 214, 225, 229
Moreno, Martim Soares, xxxviii, 197, 224–25, 264, 309
Morgalho, André Fernandes, 167, 191
Morim, Diogo, 81, 82
Moura, Alexandre de, xl, 189, 207, 236, 237
Moura, D. Francisco de, 268–70, 282, 287, 300, 306
Moura, D. Filipe de, xl, 100, 134, 164, 173
Mourão, Duarte Martins, 88, 98
Mucuripe, 231
Muturu, 244

nails: cost of, 278, 321; use of, 12, 34, 85, 93, 209, 218, 278, 284, 321
native peoples: burial practices, 35, 36; children, 33; curses, 50, 160, 246; festivals of, 30, 34, 36; gender roles of, 31, 33; inability to pronounce *l, f*, or *r*, 30; leadership within, 30, 31; love of hearing someone speaking, 29; marriage customs, 31–33, 37; nature of their language, 29; origins, 28; visitation ceremony, 31. *See also* cannibalism; captives; war

negros, xxiii, 9, 59, 113, 115, 116, 121, 252, 282, 292, 311, 316, 321, 329, 330; from Angola, 49, 260, 280, 307; from Guinea, 201, 242; labor of, 66, 199, 203, 205; and runaway communities, 203; as soldiers, 61, 100, 123, 171, 174, 179, 180, 225, 244, 251; working with the Dutch, 254–57, 272, 292, 300. *See also* native peoples; slaves
Neves, Bernardino das, OFM, 182, 189, 225
Niobi River, 205
Nóbrega, Manoel da, SJ, 87, 326
Noronha, D. Afonso de, 273, 274, 287, 293, 303
Nossa Senhora da Ajuda (nau), 274
Nossa Senhora da Atalaia (galleon), 305
Nossa Senhora da Boa Viagem (nau), 274
Nossa Senhora das Neves Maior (nau), 274
Nossa Senhora das Neves Menor (nau), 274
Nossa Senhora da Penha da França (nau), 269
Nossa Senhora do Rósario Maior (nau), 274, 277
Nossa Senhora do Rósario Menor (nau), 274
Nunes, João, 146, 153, 276
Nunes, Pedro, 4, 320
Nunes, Simão, SJ, 197, 200, 210, 258

ocean winds and currents, 9, 10, 41, 52, 66, 68, 85, 91, 93, 111, 114, 128, 129, 130, 134, 137, 157, 162, 177, 209, 214, 218, 220, 232, 234, 237, 242, 271, 273, 284, 299–301, 305, 317
oil: fish, 203; olive, 3, 13, 27, 85, 203, 255, 261, 262, 265, 278
Olinda, xxiii, 53, 54, 56, 57, 100, 102, 112, 132, 145, 156, 157, 196, 263, 282, 310
Oliveira, Antão de Mesquita de, 265
Oliveira, António Lopes de, 152, 296
Oliveira, Diogo Luís de, xxxviii, 223, 310
Ofrecha, Pedro de, 203
Orelhana, D. João de, 279, 283, 291, 302
Osório, D. Pedro, 279, 283, 284
Osquer, Duarte, 166
Ouro, Padre do. *See* Gold, Priest of

Padilha, André de, 267
Padilha, Francisco de, 254, 256, 257, 267, 268, 272, 300
Padilha, João de, 186

Padrão Point, 51
Pais, João, 100, 101, 139, 144, 145, 216
Paiva, Pero de, 177
Palácios, Pedro de (Brother Pedro), OFM, 48
Palha, Vicente Rodrigues, xvii, xxxii. _See also_ Salvador, Vicente do, OFM
Palhares, Francisco de, 226, 232
palm trees, xix, 12, 14, 27, 255
Pamplona, José Afonso, 185
Pão de Açúcar, 89
Pão de Milho, 219–21
papas, 19
paquevira, 36
Pará, xxxix, 242, 244, 263, 264, 269, 308, 313, 314, 333
Paraguaçu River, 42, 72, 178, 192, 193, 255, 268
Paraíba: conquest of, 117, 118, 131; fort built in, xxiv, 45, 137, 138, 141, 144–52, 154–56; River, 45, 67, 114, 117, 118, 132, 134, 144, 148; royal contract concerning, 131
Paratibe, 100
Paredes, Agostinho de, 235, 256, 260, 268
Parente, Bento Maciel, xxxix, 241
Paripuera, 307
Pássaro, Assento de, 112, 143, 157, 162, 182, 184
passion fruit, 14
Pau-Amarelo, 263, 308
Pau-Seco, 188, 206
Pedra Verde, 182
Peixe, Braço de (Piragibe), 112, 138, 141, 142, 145, 148, 149, 159, 174, 182, 184, 188, 205
Peixoto, Jerónimo, 249
Penacama, 157
Pereá (Apereá), 68, 232
Pereira, Bartolomeu Simões, 127
Pereira, Pedro Álvares, 202
Peres, Pero, 310, 311
perguiça (sloth), 22
Pernambuco, captaincy, 53, 58, 59, 61, 99, 170; arrival of the governors-general from Lisbon via, 216, 239, 270, 308, 311
peró (term used to for the Portuguese), 67
Petinga, 260
Philip II, D. (king of Spain and Portugal), xxxiv, 326
Piedade, Manuel de, OFM, 225, 233
Pinaré, 68

pineapple, xli, 14, 321
Pinheiro, D. António, xlii, 178
Pinheiro, Gregório, 178
Pinto, Francisco, SJ, 212, 213, 330
Pinto, Luís, 178
Pirajá, 113
pirates, xxiv, xxxiii, 48, 51, 63, 91, 103, 104, 108, 128, 129, 177, 194, 216, 218, 221, 245, 309, 312, 315
Plata, Rio de la, xxii, 4, 5, 28, 44, 45, 129, 130, 165, 166, 236, 237, 247, 261, 315
Poço, António do, 185
Ponte, Sebastião de, 113
popes, 4, 13, 96, 106, 165, 312, 320, 327, 332
Porquinho, 111, 120, 121, 122, 171, 172, 173
Porto Seguro, 1, 48, 49, 81, 117, 192
Potiguarás, xxv, xxxiii, 29, 112, 114, 116–19, 131–33, 136–38, 141–43, 145, 148, 151, 153–57, 160, 161, 173, 175, 179, 181–89, 192, 201–3, 205, 225, 297
Presépio, 313, 333
Punaré, 200

Quadros, Diogo de, xlii, 220
Queirós, Jácome de, 178, 234

Rata (nau), 306
Ravasco, Cristóvão Vieira, 256, 331
Real River, 52, 108, 109, 163, 203, 220
Recife: port of, 53, 91, 100, 114, 137, 148, 156, 231, 237, 240, 263, 264, 269, 307, 308, 310, 326; why so named, 53
Regente (nau), 226
Ribeira, Diogo da, 130, 131, 136
Ribeiro, António, 272
Ribeiro, Bernardo, 179
Riberio, Francisco, 254
rice, 18, 19, 278
Rifot, Monsieur, 180, 181
Rio de la Plata, xxii, 4, 5, 28, 44, 45, 129, 130, 165, 166, 236, 237, 247, 261, 315
Rio de Janeiro: bay of, xxxii, 29, 42, 46, 86–90, 94–98, 107, 117, 118, 129, 131, 192, 193, 209, 216, 217, 312, 325, 326; French in, xxii, 82, 83, 96, 98, 315; soldiers defending the city, xxii, 127, 136, 208, 238, 247, 261, 262, 269, 272, 280, 281, 282, 315, 316
Rocha, Bento da, 183, 186, 187
Rocha, Cristóvão da, 171, 172

Rocha, Tomé da, xlii, 156, 171, 177
Romeiro, Francisco, 50

Sá, Estácio de, xl, 84, 87–89, 95
Sá, Fernão de, 81, 82
Sá, Martim de, xl, 208–10, 238, 247, 269, 272, 281
Sá, Mem de, xxii, xxxiii, 80, 81, 83, 86, 87, 94, 95, 97, 98, 104, 105
Sá, Salvador Correia de, xl, 97, 98, 127, 129, 269, 285, 327, 331
sagüins, 21
Salazar, Jordão de, 256, 272
Salema, António de, xl, 115, 116, 118, 216
salt, xxvi, 9, 19, 26, 27, 108, 109, 114, 190, 191, 204, 210, 211, 221, 262, 278, 282, 313, 317, 333
Salvador (city), xvii, xviii, xxv, xxvi, xxxi, xxxii, xlii, 74, 195, 234, 248, 252, 261, 292, 325, 329; establishment of, xx, 72, 326. *See also* Bahia
Salvador, Gaspar do, OFM, 249
Salvador, Vicente do, OFM, xvii, xviii, xix–xxvii, xxxi–xxxiii, 219, 319, 321–23, 326, 328, 329
Samperes, Gaspar de, 182, 187
Sanfelice, João Vicente de, 291, 299
Santa Ana, 209, 278
Santa Ana (galleon), 273, 279, 302, 309
Santa Catarina, island, 130
Santa Catarina, Melchior de, OFM, 165
Santa Clara (nau), 114
Santa Cruz, 49, 67, 125
Santa Cruz (naveta), 273
Santa Helena Island, 305, 306
Santa Maria a Nova (nau), 87, 88
Santa Maria da Barca (nau), 78
Santa Teresa (galleon), 299
Santo Aleixo, 157, 308
Santo Amaro, 43, 49
Santo António, 176, 221, 271, 272, 279, 283
Santo António (nau), 91
Santo António (point), 283
Santos, town, 43
São Barnabé, 118
São Bartolomeu (nau), 274
São Bento, 179, 196, 245, 250, 256, 267, 270, 272, 283–85, 288, 294
São Bom Homen (nau), 306
São Domingos, 106, 114
São Filipe, 176, 254, 255, 257, 267, 268, 283

São Filipe and Saõ Tiago, 135, 292
São Francisco (nau), 69, 177
São Francisco River, 29, 51, 53, 57, 76, 90, 91, 102, 107, 111, 112, 119, 120, 170, 171, 172, 179
São João (galleon), 87, 273
São José, Cristóvão, OFM, 242, 312
São João Evangelista (nau), 274
São José, 233, 285
São Joseph (a galleon), 273
São Lourenço, 104, 118, 327
São Luís, 67, 68, 227, 223
São Miguel (galleon), 306
São Miguel River, 119
São Miguel, João de, OFM, 182
São Paulo (nau), 76, 84
São Paulo: Hill, 49–51, 234, 260; town of, 28, 44, 89, 194, 195, 216, 325, 326
São Sebastião, 129, 162. *See also* Rio de Janeiro
São Simão (galley), 81
São Vicente: captaincy of, xli, 24, 64, 82, 86–89, 95, 96, 98, 127, 128, 130, 190, 194, 215; River, 43, 44; town of, 10, 18, 27, 28, 43–45, 61, 248
Sardinha, D. Francisca, 85, 86
Sardinha, D. Pedro Fernandes, 74
Sarmiento, D. Francisco, 271, 282
Sarmiento, Pedro de, 128, 129, 136
sasapocais, 13
sassafras, 17
Schouten, Albert, 254, 255, 271
Schouten, William, 271, 289
scurvy, 245, 331
Sebastião, D. (king of Portugal), 44, 83, 103, 106, 107, 117, 123, 214, 275
Sequeira, Diogo de, 187
Sergipe: captaincy, xxiii, xlii, 52, 84, 105, 169, 171, 177, 221, 265; natives of, 163, 164, 167, 170, 172, 220
Seta, 120
sharecroppers, 50, 57, 205
ships: building, 11; cargoes, 162, 190, 194, 208, 224, 234, 245, 262, 286, 305, 306, 309, 311; repair, 79, 91, 99, 103, 129, 130, 218, 224, 236, 292, 300, 301, 324, 332; types of, xxxvi. *See also* Bahia; caravels; Lisbon; *individual names of naus*
shipwreck, xxi, xxii, 67, 68, 104, 114, 169, 195, 197, 235, 237, 279, 305
Silva, Fernão da, 97, 118

Silva, Francisco Barbosa da, 119, 170, 185
Silva, Henrique Correia da, 239
Silva, Luís de Melo da, 67, 68, 79
Silveira, Duarte Gomes da, 149, 157
silver, 47, 68, 177, 178, 193, 234, 242, 245, 250, 251, 292, 295, 304, 330
slavery, xxii, 89
slaves: African, 201, 203, 205, 252, 279, 292, 333; aiding the Dutch, 243; native, xxii, xxiii, 3, 24, 49, 54, 55, 57, 59, 60, 66, 80, 90, 116, 135, 164, 168, 196, 203, 234, 243–45, 252, 282, 316; sale of, xviii, xxii, 58, 81, 248, 280, 292, 333. *See also* negros
smallpox, 182, 185
Soares, Francisco, 196, 277
Sol Dourado (nau), 273
Sora, Baltasar Rodrigues, 170
Sorobi, 109
Sousa, D. António de, 216
Sousa, D. Francisco de, xxxviii, 45, 175, 178, 181, 188, 190, 194, 195, 215, 219, 223
Sousa, D. Inês de, 128
Sousa, D. Luís de, xxxviii, 239, 240, 277, 314
Sousa, Francisco Pereira de, 196, 269
Sousa, Gabriel Soares de, 177–79
Sousa, Gaspar de, xxxviii, 127, 223, 231, 233, 235, 274, 315
Sousa, Martim Afonso de, 43, 45, 64, 190
Sousa, Pero Coelho de, 197–99, 210, 212
Sousa, Pero Lopes de, 43, 45, 54, 61–67
Sousa, Rui Boto de, 178
Sousa, Tomé de, xxi, xxxviii, 71–75
Sousa, Vasco de, 237
Spanish, naus come to aid Brazil, 128
sugar, mills, xxxv, xxxii, 12, 13, 27, 42, 46, 47, 49, 50, 52, 60, 62, 84, 99, 101, 107, 118, 134, 166, 167, 170, 173, 189, 191, 196, 203, 205, 216, 217, 234, 238, 241, 259, 269, 280, 315
Surupiba, 183

Tabajaras, xxv, 60, 141, 145, 186, 188, 189, 197, 201
taiaobas, 17
taibu (possum), 22
Taipé River, 50
tamandua (anteater), 21
tamaracá, 35
Tamoios, 29, 84, 86, 89, 98, 107, 118
Tapado River, 263

Tapegipe, 255
tapeis, 23
Tapirema River, 62, 140, 157
Tapuias, 28, 30, 192, 211, 296, 297, 309, 314
taquaras, 33
tataiúba, 12
Tataperica, João Vaz, 197
Tatuapará River, 109
tatus (armadillos), 20
Tavares, João, xxxix, 148, 149, 151, 153–55, 158–60, 173, 182, 225
Tavares, Simão, SJ, 145, 158
Tavira (person), 186
tax, 3, 42, 58, 73, 154, 176, 194, 203, 214, 216, 245, 269; avaria, 245; dízimos, xxxvii, 58, 176, 324; used to pay for fort, 246
Teixeira, D. Marcos, 246, 253
Teles, Henrique Moniz, 196
Tibiri River, 141, 143, 151, 162
Tigre (nau), 260
timbós and cipós, 12, 321
Timudo, André Pereira, 242
Tinharé Island, 50, 164
Tiquaruçu, 297, 298
tisanas, 19
Toledo, D. Fadrique de, 279, 282, 285, 291, 292, 302, 307
Toledo, D. Fernando Álvares de, Duke of Alba, 129
Toledo, D. Francisco de, Viceroy of Peru, 128, 275
Tomasia, D., 211
tostão, xxxvii, 5, 248
Tourinho, Leonor do Campo, 49
Tourinho, Pero Campo, 48, 49
trade, items used in with natives, xxiii, 34, 49, 52, 58, 62, 66, 83–85, 90, 110, 115, 120, 122, 138, 185, 188, 316, 328
trees, types of in Brazil, 2, 11, 12–18, 26, 182, 321, 322, 327, 330
Tucum, 26, 322
Tujucupapo: native leader, 153, 160; river, 62
Tuim-Mirim, 197, 199
Tumã, 171
Tupinamba, 29, 193
Tupinaquim, 50

Ubaúna, 200
Ulhoa, Diogo Lopes, 178
Uruatins, 309

Valadares, António de, 184, 296
Valdez, Diogo Flores de, 128–30, 133
Valente, António da Costa, 181
Van Dorth, João, 248, 250, 251, 254, 255
Varela, Lourenço, 178
Vasconcelos, D. Luís Fernandes de, 78, 103, 104, 108
Vasconcelos, Francisco de, 279
Vasconcelos, Luís Aranha de, 241, 245
Vaz, Lopo, 166, 167
Vazabarris, 169, 177
Veiga, Lourenço da, ix, xxxviii, 111, 119, 123–25, 127, 131
Veiga, Tristão Vaz da, 124, 125
Velho, Jorge, 111
Vermelho River, 252, 256, 257, 272
Viana do Castelo, 48, 54, 134, 203, 207, 235, 240, 324
Vidal, João, 289
Vieira, Francisco, 177
villages: defense of, 32, 36, 37, 60, 101, 119, 122–24, 138, 142, 158, 160, 168, 174, 296, 297, 313, 314; how new site is selected for, 32; native, design of, 30, 31
Villegaignon, Nicolas, 82, 83, 96
Vitória, 47
viracoches (sea foam), 1

war: flour, 19, 36, 37, 93, 141, 151; just, xxiii, 80, 101, 168, 206, 296, 326; method of conducting, 36–38, 43, 46, 47, 52, 56, 57, 59, 81, 83, 100, 109, 112, 137, 141–43, 153, 157, 158, 168, 173–75, 187, 192, 200, 228, 244, 247, 260, 281, 296, 308; recruiting Europeans to fight in, 83, 225; recruiting natives to fight in, 60, 83, 88, 100, 154, 168, 224; traps used in, 32, 56, 59, 89, 90, 116, 119, 121, 135, 142, 153, 158, 159, 164, 183, 185, 191, 194, 221, 222, 272
water, drinking, for ships, 4, 76, 85, 88, 122, 130, 133, 134, 138, 145, 150, 158, 167, 169, 178, 184, 191, 194, 196, 198, 209, 210–12, 219, 220, 238, 278, 297, 307, 315, 316
West Indies, xxxii, 5, 18, 64, 65, 103, 132, 146, 175, 224, 231, 245, 321
whales, xxvi, 24, 95, 203–5, 259, 322, 333
wheat, 18, 19, 27, 28, 45, 52, 195, 219, 255, 261, 277, 294
Willekens, Jacob, 251, 281
women: European, 14, 45, 47, 262; European, on ships, 76, 86, 192, 263, European, and warfare 55, 65, 127, 305; native, captives and, 39; 111; native, gender roles of, 33, 115, 206–7, 224; native, language used by, 29, 30; native, marriage customs of, 31–33, 164, 207; native, older women and greetings used, 31, 38–39, 164; native, and warfare, 164, 188, 198. *See also* dowries

Zorobabé, 188, 192, 202, 203, 205–7
Zorrilha, Francisco, 178